Who Matters at the World Bank?

Who Matters at the World Bank?

Bureaucrats, Policy Change, and Public Sector Governance

KIM MOLONEY

OXFORD
UNIVERSITY PRESS

OXFORD
UNIVERSITY PRESS

Great Clarendon Street, Oxford, OX2 6DP,
United Kingdom

Oxford University Press is a department of the University of Oxford.
It furthers the University's objective of excellence in research, scholarship,
and education by publishing worldwide. Oxford is a registered trade mark of
Oxford University Press in the UK and in certain other countries

Published in the United States of America by Oxford University Press
198 Madison Avenue, New York, NY 10016, United States of America

British Library Cataloguing in Publication Data

Data available

Library of Congress Control Number: 2021951808

ISBN 978–0–19–285772–9

DOI: 10.1093/oso/9780192857729.001.0001

Printed and bound by
CPI Group (UK) Ltd, Croydon, CR0 4YY

Contents

Acknowledgments

The story of mothers and academia is rarely a straight line. This is especially true for single mothers where such a status can be preemptively coded as "non-productive academic" or where it is whispered that "academia is not for single mothers". To both I say, "hogwash".

This book was my dissertation before it disappeared into a "publish or perish" world of prioritizing journal articles. It re-emerges as a book eleven years after Ph.D. graduation. Its disappearance had less to do with my status and more with its task: linking the public administration discipline with the international relations / international organizations discipline to explain 32 years of policy change at the World Bank.

Both my Ph.D. and my book focus upon the World Bank's public sector management and public sector governance. The dissertation covered 25 years (1983-2007) with one theory and two approaches. This book covers 32 years (1980-2012), uses one theory and one approach, required additional interviews, new research, new grant, an update to 2020, a reordering or deletion of many sub-sections, and a rewrite of every sub-section that remained. Each citation with a date after mid-2010 is new along with many pre-2010 citations which were discovered as I wrote this book. Many of the new citations dramatically altered the book. My dissertation is "there" in this book but its fingerprints are faint. No book is written alone. I am grateful to the following.

In 2003, I began a dual MA-MPA with the School of Advanced International Studies (SAIS) at Johns Hopkins University and the Maxwell School at Syracuse University. A frequent faculty question was "why"? No one believed that international relations (SAIS) and public administration (Maxwell) could jointly explain anything. My gut said they could interact but I did not have the words. Chapter 2 shares the words that I could not articulate then. Three faculty were influential. The first is the now retired Riordan Roett of SAIS. Our spring 2005 independent study on the Washington Consensus and the World Bank was one backbone for the dissertation and book. At Maxwell, Jeremy Shiffman and Rosemary O'Leary gave guidance.

This book is impossible without David Rosenbloom. His Ph.D. class on the intellectual history of public administration changed my academic life. His supervision during the dissertation, his ongoing advice, and our co-authorship of an article have influenced my outlook. William LeoGrande's "half steps" guidances moved me from uncertainty to motion. His own books are stories of nuance and actor interplay. His footnotes are a joy. It may appear odd to compliment someone for their footnotes, but my point is sincere: He taught me to exhaust angles and to not forget "the forest". Scholars with fascinating footnotes are my favorite authors to read. For this book, see footnote 2 in Chapter 3, footnote 11 in Chapter 4, and footnotes 8 and 9 in the Appendix. I met Deborah Braütigam before enrolling at American University. It is a testament to her goodwill, collegiality, and international organization knowledge that she agreed to join my committee in its last six months and to guide me toward graduation. Her comments refocused what are now Chapters 2 and 3 plus the Conclusion.

This book benefitted from nearly sixty not-for-attribution interviews. Interviewee candor about the Bank, its bureaucratic politics, and its histories helped piece together policy change. None were more important than the late Dr. Ben Fisher, a 30+ year Bank veteran. My meeting with Ben in spring 2008 set into motion all that came afterward, including my attendance at the May 2008 Bank Operations course. He said that I was the first non-banker permitted to attend this course. To understand the Bank, we must understand its operational life. Ben provided the crucial link.

Kate Weaver and her 2008 book (which she kindly provided to me nine months before publication) shaped my dissertation. Our meeting more than a decade ago at Washington DC's Union Station gave me confidence to speak with Bank staff.

The Cosmos Club Foundation honored me as a 2008 Cosmos Scholar. The School of Public Affairs at American University had faith in my abilities via a three-year tuition scholarship, graduate assistantship, Dean's scholarship, and a fourth-year scholarship. After Ph.D. graduation, the American Political Science Association awarded me a Centennial Center scholarship. This last scholarship helped with new interviews, timeline expansion, new archival research, and a book proposal draft.

The late Ronald Johnson of the Research Triangle Institute was my first "metronome". His humor and deadline impositions helped me meet Ph.D. deadlines. This "metronome" role became a heavier burden after my Ph.D. graduation. Four persons served as a collective "metronome" for this book. Kanishka Jayasuriya and Garry Rodan read the first and last chapters of my second book draft. Their initial backing gave me faith that I must finish. I am particularly grateful for Kanishka's persistent encouragement. Clay Wescott of the World Bank was an interviewee who became a friend. Clay is my third "metronome". His offer to read this book's final draft and his comments on that draft provided reassurance. His emails every two or three months asking about book progress were appreciated. I met Diane Stone at a workshop for Ph.D. students writing on the Bank in 2010. In 2015, she asked me to co-edit our 40-chapter Oxford Handbook on Global Policy and Transnational Administration (2019) with Oxford University Press. As my fourth "metronome", she encouraged me, suggested the title (Who Matters), and kindly told me to "get on with it already".

We all need people who believe in us and who encourage us. I have been blessed to know so many.

In the eleven years since Ph.D. graduation, the sub-fields of international public administration (IPA) / international organization bureaucracy studies as well as global policy and transnational administration have exploded. Dozens of post-2010 influences are in this book. The work of Michael W. Bauer, Christoph Knill, and their IPA "academic progeny" are a highlight. In Australia, I found Xu Yi-Chong and Patrick Weller's 2009 book after Ph.D. defense. Their articulation of constructivist limits for studying international organizations influenced Chapter 2. When I last saw Xu and Weller in 2019, their refrain of "just get it done" mirrored the encouragement of others.

During the interview period, Sonja Wälti and Laurie-Ann Agama provided a place to stay and much needed cheer. Sigrid and Thomas provided laughter and housing more times than I can count. David Rushton created algorithms to make the Bank's Projects Database manageable. Amy and Scott Brown were my "New Hampshire office"; They kept dissertation versions for worst case e-scenarios. For the book, Bobby Chen was my "Jamaica office" and kept book drafts. His humor and life advice lighten my load.

The writings of Jennifer Brinkerhoff, Jean-Claude Garcia-Zamor, Krishna Tummala, M. Shamsul Haque, and Ali Farazmand have showed me how to write non-traditional public administration scholarship. Early on, Matt Andrews gave crucial advice on the Bank, public administration, and how to write. Jennifer Diascro was a professor and later, a friend. Tamar Gutner at American University, Anthony Harriot at the University of the West Indies, and the late Jonathan West at the University of Miami gave support at key moments. Leslie Pal provided support as I finished the book at Hamad Bin Khalifa University in Doha.

At Oxford University Press, Olivia Wells steered the proposal through its early stages. Dominic Byatt led full manuscript review and the pitching of my book to the Board. Vicki Sunter and Vigneshwer Thirunavukkarasu ably led this book to publication. I am grateful to Dominic for publishing a book in which international relations / international organization studies *and* public administration have a starring role. The main reason this book was not written after Ph.D. graduation was that nearly twenty academics during the intervening years told me that I cannot do both, that I must choose, and no Press will publish a book that engages international relations / international organizations and public administration. I am grateful to Dominic, the Board, and the three blind reviewers who ignored the naysayers. This book's argument, its Tables, and its conclusion are stronger because of the reviewers, their attention to detail, and their helpful comments.

Growing up, answers were rarely fixed. Books were everywhere. My late mother's intellect far exceeded her high school education. She became an adult just after WWII and broke late-1940s gender barriers by joining the U.S. Army. My late father had a similar education. He became an adult during the Depression. For those with parents of that generation, our worlds as children were richer because of their life experiences. My parents' passion for *60 Minutes*, James Michener, big bands, and jazz made me who I am today.

Like my dissertation, this book is dedicated to Maya and Luke. Maya's arrival two days after the end of my first Ph.D. semester changed everything for the better. Her Maya-imposed "typing breaks" or her sleepy breathing as I worked late at night are memories close to my heart. She is now 16 years old with a love of physics, math, and astrobiology, a quick wit, and a passion for anime. Luke arrived in the midst of writing chapter 4 of my dissertation. He was a happy baby with a big smile and peaceful demeanor. At 13 years old, the softness of his heart is matched by his passion for Marvel, anime, and a love of stocks, statistics, and math. They inspire me daily.

List of Tables

1

The World Bank as an Organization

Peering Inside the Black Box

Powerful. Ideological. Neoliberal. Technocratic. Insensitive. Each word is among the innumerable and often negative adjectives used to describe the World Bank. But are such descriptors accurate? Can the World Bank, its thousands of civil servants (and its tens of thousands over time) and its 18,000+ projects since 1947 be conclusively summarized by such descriptors? If the Bank's detractors are critical of its apparent one-size-fits-all project and policy approaches, then we might also be critical of those who paint the Bank with similar broad strokes.

This book suggests that scholarship has often discounted the depth and breadth of sector policy contestation among and between Bank staff (as internal stakeholders or bureaucrats) and the Bank's external stakeholders. This scholarship has frequently overlooked the human beings, as employees of the Bank, who vigorously debate, shape, and reconsider policies. The Bank's "voice" is rarely as singular and unified as its critics may suggest. This book anchors itself with the key bureaucrats and external stakeholders who influence Bank policies and projects. Its goal is to explain policy change across 32 years of public sector management and public sector governance work at the Bank. This is a unique and important endeavor.

The World Bank, as an organization, has an internal terrain demarcated by constant ideological battles and strategic politicking—each of which influence Bank sector policy outputs. The World Bank's international civil servants, as human beings, as employees, as individuals or members of unit, department, or network, remain understudied. Their influence, as internal stakeholders, on the Bank's policy outputs are traceable and as argued throughout this book, crucial to understanding policy change. Similarly understudied are how international civil servants, in concert with or even in opposition to the Bank's key external stakeholders, battle over intellectual direction. Battle "winners" shape subsequent Bank sector policies and projects.

Each policy debate defines and redefines the Bank as an organization. By focusing on the Bank's most prescribed policy sector, public sector management and public sector governance, the volume highlights how internal contestation and bureaucratic politics shapes the Bank's sector policy outputs, where and why key

Who Matters at the World Bank?. Kim Moloney, Oxford University Press.
© Kim Moloney (2022). DOI: 10.1093/oso/9780192857729.003.0001

member-states and other external stakeholders exercised influence, and why Bank staff (and not external stakeholders) led this sector agenda after 1991. Interspersed are discussions about relations between the Bank's internal reforms and its lending incentives, why the Bank's evaluative mechanisms insufficiently altered sector policy incentives, and why any analysis of the Bank's decision in the mid-1990s to engage civil society must depend on the civil society stakeholder. Questions answered include why and how did public sector management and governance evolve into a key sector within the Bank? What were the key internal sector debates? How did sector debates shift over time? Who "won" or "lost" and why? How do debate "winners" and "losers" shape sector debates?

In an illustration of just one of dozens of bureaucratic battles and policy changes traced throughout the book, I will briefly note how the "governance" term was chosen. Fuller articulations are in Chapter 5. The battle's output was a Bank newly focused on the development phrase *du jour*: good governance. Before 1991, neither the Bank nor other bilateral or multilateral development actors had good governance on their development agenda.

In the months before publication of the key 1991 report (*Managing Development: The Governance Dimension*), staff fought intense internal battles over whether this new sector addition would be called "development management" or "good governance." This battle was about more than semantics. As noted in Chapter 5, this battle involved multiple internal stakeholder groups. This included long-term staff who had engaged in a decade-long internal dissent (see Chapter 3) against the Bank's so-called "neoliberal" turn after 1980. It included leaders such as former Senior Vice President Ernie Stern who preferred a technocratic, economist-oriented "development management" term and others who worried "governance" was a theoretically underdeveloped notion with non-measurable outcomes. It included staff who wanted the Bank to learn lessons from the United Nations' *Adjustment with a Human Face* (Cornia et al. 1987), a Bank General Counsel who feared that "good governance" violated the Bank's Articles of Agreement, and others who hoped that with the Cold War's end, an amorphous "governance" emphasis might cement post-Soviet economic growth. One interviewee, a person involved in drafting the 1991 Report, recalled that since the Report was a Bank document

> [that] meant drafts circulated to senior people. They would read/mark what they did not like and then traditionally, you take out what the senior people say. But Sarwar [who headed the Report-writing team] would selectively disregard them—he thought they'd forget it and so, he'd rephrase it. It went through seventeen drafts. Stern was still there—and Ernie changes governance to "development management" ... but then in the end, Geoffrey Lamb [another coauthor] changed it back, the published version emerges as governance.
>
> (WB30)

Seventeen drafts and high-profile internal disputes were *not* minor internal bat-tles. They were a display of bureaucratic willpower to shape a sector's future. The implications were enormous for the Bank's policy direction, that is, which per-sons entered the Bank's key sector policy circles, but also how Bank projects would be refocused and which conditionalities (later renamed "benchmarks") would be encouraged amongst borrowing member states.

The battles did not end there. The Bank's Executive Directors expressed reser-vations about this policy shift. Emblematic of their disagreement was a peculiar preface to the 1991 report. Its peculiarity was emphasized by the fact that only the most contentious reports (excluding *World Development Reports*) are pref-aced by a memo from a Bank President. The 1991 report contained such a memo. The memo underlined a fractious internal battle over the governance term. The Bank President, Barber Conable, described Board conversations about the report as "lively and thoughtful" and that "governance is an emotive word, and more im-portantly, a potentially contentious issue internationally and within many of our member countries. It is not surprising that there were divergent views expressed by Executive Directors on the subject" (World Bank 1991b, President's Memo).

As noted in this "teaser" example and as repeatedly observed in the stories, de-bates, and sector policy shifts detailed in this book, the Bank is not a black box. Policy debates rage within the Bank. It is expected. The presence of bureaucratic small "p" politics, as understood by the public administration discipline, is normal. *The normality of bureaucratic politics has implications for constructivist as well as principal-agent scholarship on international organizations (IOs).* As noted through-out this book, internal debate outcomes frame subsequent Bank policy outputs. Bank policy outputs reorient internal and external "winners" and "losers." In a book about the Bank's most prescribed sector, debate "wins" or "losses" were not merely a short-term output. They influenced policy battles and subsequent sector policy shifts years later.

The World Bank is a complex, bureaucratic, and expertise-driven multilateral development organization. Its employees are highly educated (often with PhDs from top universities) human beings who cannot be simplified into labels like agent, principal, or a Weberian technocrat who awaits direction from the Bank's most powerful member-states. Nor, perhaps controversially for international re-lations' constructivist scholars or principal-agent theorists (see Chapter 2), should they be. The Bank's civil servants are a cohort of thinking, breathing, and adept individuals committed to the Bank's mission. In a leaked 2013 internal staff sur-vey, 90 percent of respondents stated that they were "proud to work" at the World Bank. This is a one-point increase from the 89 percent who felt the same in 2009 (World Bank 2013, 4). Neither is an aberration.

We cannot ignore a bureaucrat's "inside power" to shape Bank sector policy outputs; or the bureaucratic and policy power of the world's hundreds of thou-sands international civil servants working within 803 international government organizations (UIA 2013). If we understand international civil servant debates, bureaucratic maneuverings, and resulting sector policy shifts, such debates may be linked to externally-driven pressures upon international organizations. Whether such pressures come from member states, non-governmental actors, or externally-influenced policy learning, internal and external interactions help predict stakeholder influence over the sector policy outputs that shape member-states.

Of the nearly 60 interviews conducted for this book, only one interviewee asked that I turn off my tape recorder, mid-interview. Upon doing so, this key author of the Bank's first-ever Public Sector Strategy in 2000 opined on its controversial update, the Bank's 2007 Governance and Anti-Corruption (GAC) Strategy. The interviewee noted that GAC staff and "technical public administration" staff (the latter staff category, which included my interviewee, is the interviewee's label of persons aligned with the soon-to-be-displaced 2000 Strategy) were different groups within the Bank (WB31). GAC supporters used political economy and stakeholder analysis and included more economists than political scientists. The latter focused on public sector management and were dominated by former UK government officials working at the Bank. Between the late 1990s to 2010 or so, such ideological differences divided Bank staff. Another interviewee believed that despite GAC approval by the Bank's Board, the GAC "does not go very deep within the Bank" and that GAC was simply a public-relations idea (WB23). This opinion about GAC's depth turned out to be wrong. By 2012, public sector governance (and public sector management) had become the Bank's "DNA" but also its first-ever (and still only, in 2020) policy sector "to have a Bank-wide remit" (World Bank 2012, 53, 62).

One interviewee viewed the GAC as a "revenge of the economists" upset that some "blue-collar types announced that they knew how to do projects" (WB31). Bank economists, the drivers of the 2007 GAC Strategy, were worried they would have to "rummage around this blue-collar business about how the public sector works" (WB31). In this sense, the blue-collar term is shorthand for technocratic public sector management staffs. This debate illustrates just one of the many internal debates about which intellectual perspectives, which disciplinary traditions, and which staff groups should capture the sector policy limelight.

Such internal battles are not new. They are constant. *Most importantly, they are normal and they are to be expected. Bank civil servants are human beings who do debate (and should debate) sector policy change.* This book is a mesohistorical study in which internal policy debates and their influence over policy change become its show-stopping star. Each were uncovered via interviews and extensive archival work before clarification via process-tracing, stakeholder analysis, and an interaction with the public administration discipline (see Chapter 2) to understand how Bank staff shaped its internal structure and its policy outputs. In doing so, we learn where bureaucrats chose to follow external stakeholder leads (US, UK, G7, International Monetary Fund (IMF), and civil society are considered) and at other times, acted independently of not only member-states who "own" the Bank but also, civil society.

As discussed in Chapter 3, the 1980s version pitted the Bank's neoliberal economists against a smaller "institutional development" group. This was preceded by a 1979 to 1982 period in which the Bank's Keynesian poverty-focused economists were replaced by neoclassical economists loyal to the US President Ronald Reagan and UK Prime Minister Margaret Thatcher. The Bank's 1980s preference for neoliberal public sector policies was not accidental. Policy shifts reflect external-internal stakeholder prioritization and how Bank is legitimized as an institution, in whose interest the Bank serves, and whether Bank objectives are achieved.

Other book chapters challenge a frequently-held wisdom about US influence over the Bank. If one analyzes the Bank's voting shares, it is hard to against argue with this numerical "truth." Yet it is more accurate to argue that (a) the Bank is dominated not just by the United States[1] but also the UK and to a lesser extent, the other five G7 members (Canada, France, Germany, Italy, Japan). Since 2008 or so, this list of influential actors might also include China and their Executive Director; and (b) contrary to international relations' realist theory, a numerical "truth" need not always be an actualized "truth." Certainly, the 1980s period of Bank public sector management policies were shaped and led by the US (and UK) whereas the post-1991 period of policy change within public sector management and governance was not led by external actors but *by Bank staff.*

In one explanation of how the Bank staff are expert at Board-level "divide and conquer" strategies. Here is how the US can be outmaneuvered:

> We might have a loan that we oppose, and we are unsuccessful in either having it put on the shelf for restructuring or whatever else. Eventually, it ends up going to the Board and we may be active ourselves in trying to get other people to join us in our position. If it's a loan, there are very few exceptions to the rule that borrowing countries will not vote against a loan. Management can usually count on China and India—the two biggest borrowers—to say how wonderful a loan it is to start off the Board discussion. If it's a loan in Asia very likely they are able to peel off Japan to speak in favor of the loan. If it's a loan to West Africa, they can peel off the French. If it's a loan to East Africa or India, they can peel off the British. They can make and create divisions within the donor community, and

---

[1] Former Bank General Counsel Ibrahim Shihata noted the US had a prominent Board role for five reasons: "First, [the U.S. Government] is the originator of the idea of the establishment. Second, it is the largest shareholder. Although its share in the capital is still less than 17 percent, but its role is much more than that. Third, it can sometimes easily get the majority of the votes backing its position because with Europe, Canada, and Japan, you have the majority basically. Four, the Bank is here, next door to the U.S. Treasury, so there is an intimate relationship. Fifth, and most important, the President is American and is *de facto* chosen by the American Government" (Shihata 2000c).

they have the unanimity of the borrowing community. *It doesn't take much to end up being isolated.*

(Coady 1993, emphasis added)

In other words, power mathematics do not fully define when the Board uses their power. US vote shares do not automatically translate into US-preferred sector policy outputs at the Bank.

To understand policy change, we must also understand the Bank's internal incentives. Internal incentives interact with bureaucratic politics and stakeholder influence to alter policy change. This analysis leads to another Bank reality: the challenge of holding one banker or a group of bankers responsible for policy and project failures. As one interviewee noted, "the fundamental problem in the Bank—and it continues today—is that staff, and by implication, managers, bear none of the risk of project failures ... Essentially, if a project fails, it's too bad for the borrower but very little consequence for the Bank staff because they have either moved on or it just does not happen" (WB8). One's Bank career does not end if you are associated with bad projects. Since multiple staff create, implement, and monitor one project, blame appropriation is difficult. Staff also suggest the best-planned project will not work if clients are half-interested or unwilling to prevent corruptive influences. An outcome of project design by committee is that blame determination becomes clouded.

Who Matters, Policy Change, and the World Bank

The outcomes of World Bank policies and projects matter. *It is because Bank outcomes matter that we must understand the influences behind policy change outputs at the Bank.* In contrast, purely outcome-focused research asks whether Bank policies improve a country's development. Outcome-focused analyses are only an indirect way to trace Bank policy shifts. Instead, this book draws upon stakeholder theory and the bureaucratic politics approach to ask when, where, and why external and internal actors influence Bank *sector policy outputs.* It assumes that bureaucratic politics is expected, normal, and should be viewed as uncontroversial for the discipline of international relations. If we understand how policy *outputs* are created, debated, and implemented, only then may we alter *outcomes.* As explained in Chapter 2, this book shows how concepts and theories from the discipline of public administration may explain policy change within international organizations (Moloney and Rosenbloom 2020; Bauer et al. 2017; Fleischer and Reiners 2021). In doing so, this book pivots from two typical explanations from international relations for IO behaviors: the organizational sociology influences upon international relations' constructivist approaches and rational institutionalist influences upon principal-agent scholarship.

This book also pivots, in part, from a burst of new "international public admin-istration" (IPA) (or international organization bureaucracies) scholarship largely published after 2010. Much IPA scholarship often starts with a limited critique of its organizational sociology and/or constructivist choice. In contrast, this book uses the public administration discipline as its start- and end-point, employs links to actor-focused components of public administration to critically engage prior approaches, and highlights how constructivist misunderstandings of Max Weber's work on bureaucracy amplified disconnects between constructivism and principal-agent theory with the broader public administration discipline. Two, un-like most IPA scholarship, this book focuses on one sector of an IO's outputs, it is not ahistorical, and it pays attention to internal and external actor influences upon policy change. But this book also sets itself firmly within the IPA literature. This book, like much of the IPA scholarship, dispenses with typical principal-agent theory since this book and much of the IPA scholarship understands that international civil servants are more than principals or agents.

This book highlights how a nuanced understanding of why bureaucrats mat-ter, when and where external and/or internal actors alter the sector policies of an organization, and why it is inherently non-problematic to an IO's member-states that internal actors may drive policy change. Each are standard assumptions of traditional public administration literature. If scholars desire a mid-range theory capable of explaining international organization influence in international rela-tions (Checkel 1998), then this book showcases how the public administration discipline may provide an avenue for achieving that objective.

The book discovers that while key member-states like the US and the UK have vote-share and budget-share power, their influence over sector policy change within public sector management and public sector governance largely dissipated by the early 1990s (see Chapters 3 and 5). In contrast, the Bank's public sector management (not yet, public sector governance) staff did not have no influence but instead, limited influence in the early-to-mid 1980s (see Chapter 3) before an internal organizational reform in 1987 gave public sector management a signif-icant boost (see Chapter 4). Staff in public sector management (since 1980) and public sector governance (since 1991) experienced a dramatic expansion in sector influence after August 1991 (see Chapters 5 to 8) that continued until the end of this book's timeline in 2012. Between August 1991 and 2012, internal civil servant power over sector policy change would soon dominate external actor power and interest in this sector of the Bank's work. However, and unlike other sectors of World Bank work (e.g., environment, health, gender), civil society influence over policy change in this book's sector of inquiry was either non-existent or short-lived and topic-specific (see Chapter 9). The Appendix explains how the World Bank operates for students, scholars, and practitioners unfamiliar with its opera-tion. A Postscript updates this book's 32-year history from 2012 to 2020 and finds that the sector remains dominant, retained the GAC Council, and its sector topics intact even as organizational and international pressures shifted in the 2013–2020 period.

By choosing the World Bank's most prescribed sector (public sector management and public sector governance) and employing a mesohistorical study (1980 to 2012) across 32 years of the Bank's 75+ year history, this book differentiates itself from prior Bank and other IO scholarship via its engagement of two parts of the public administration discipline, its tracing of organizational and sector-specific policy changes, and its ability to explore the interaction between external and internal stakeholders with influence over this sector at the Bank. There is no better sector at the World Bank for this analysis. In 1980, this sector was infrequently a policy and project output of the Bank. By 2012, this sector had become the Bank's "DNA" but also its first-ever (and still only) sector "to have a Bank-wide remit" (World Bank 2012, 53, 62). In answering the question posed in this book's title: who matters at the Bank, this book also answers how this one sector of the Bank could rise to prominence against all odds and with different forces pulling it up and down at various points in time. The output is a book that explains who mattered, why they mattered, and how sector policy changed in the most prolific sector of Bank work in the last four decades.

2

The World Bank as an Organization

Public Administration in International Organization Studies

By tracing sector policy shifts, stakeholder influence, and its accompanying bureaucratic politics, we learn how power, ideology, and incentives influence an international organization's (IO) sector policy outputs. This book's sector of interest is public sector management (the sole sector term until August 1991, abbreviated to PSM) and public sector governance (a new term created in August 1991 or PSG). The IO is the World Bank and the period reviewed is 1980–2012. The year 1980 is the start of a global recession; it is the year of Ronald Reagan's election as President of the United States; and it is three years before the Bank created its first-ever Public Sector Management Unit. The year 2012 is the end of Robert Zoellick's term as World Bank President as well as the Bank's publication of an updated Governance and Anti-Corruption (GAC) Strategy in which this sector had not only become the Bank's "DNA" but also the first-ever (and still only) sector "to have a Bank-wide remit" (World Bank 2012b, 53, 62).

The transformation of one sector's policies from near non-existence to becoming the Bank's "DNA" requires study. This book engages 32 years of sector-specific policy change within the Bank's PSM/PSG agenda. Two research questions guide this book: (1) Why did the World Bank's PSM/PSG increase (in project approvals per year) between 1980 and 2012? (2) Why, and how, did public sector governance policy objectives vary between 1980 and 2012?

This book explains thirty-two years (1980 to 2012) of policy change within one World Bank policy sector. Internal Bank staff debates about policy direction interacted with external stakeholders to originate, drive, and modify sector policy outputs. The dependent variable is policy change within the Bank's PSM/PSG work. Table 1 in the Appendix[1] showcases sector policy change via project approvals from 1968 to 2012. Table 1 also shares data back to 1968 (first PSM project) and forward to 2020 (for book postscript). The independent variables are external stakeholders, a boundary stakeholder, and internal stakeholders. The bureaucratic politics of actor interaction and debate shape policy outputs and, ultimately, policy

---

[1] All tables referenced in this book may be found in the Appendix.

Who Matters at the World Bank?. Kim Moloney, Oxford University Press.
© Kim Moloney (2022). DOI: 10.1093/oso/9780192857729.003.0002

change within this sector over time. The three independent variables and their components are summarized in Tables 7–16. Tables 17 links the independent variables with thirteen propositions for future research.

The historical timelines, stories, debates, and policy shifts discussed throughout this book showcase how internal debate along with external and internal stakeholder interactions shape organizational reform, international civil servants, and how organizational incentives explain sector policy changes. When we open the Bank's organizational "black box", we find international civil servants with policy and project power. This power is capable of shaping sector policy outputs and the lives of those impacted by Bank policies.

Sector policy change and its concurrent institutionalization must be explained. As such, this book is less about rehashing debates between so-called "neoliberal" perspectives at the Bank and institutional, managerial, or administrative perspectives but, rather, the book explains how, when, where, and why within this important development sector, policies shifted. In doing so, the question that is repeatedly asked is *who* matters, *when* do they matter, and *why* they matter. The implications are not only relevant to a newly burgeoning area of international public administration and IO bureaucracy studies, but also to broader IO studies as well as the international relations theories which often overlook the "organization" as analytically inconvenient and thus, "black box" its internal debates.

The World Bank Project Database details the 14,011 projects approved by the Bank between its 1947 incorporation and 2012. Of these projects, 46.2 percent had a PSM/PSG component. This rises to 17,989 projects and 53.3 percent having a PSM/PSG component when the timeline is extended to 2020 for this book's postscript. But these numbers are not the whole story. In fact, PSM/PSG-related projects approvals never rose above 2.6 percent of the Bank's annual projects approved between the first approved PSM-related project (Indonesia, 1968) and the year (1979) before this book's timeline begins.

As per Table 1, after 1980 this sector's projects began to slowly rise as a percentage of the Bank's project portfolio from 2–5 percent (1980 to 1985) to between 47 percent (in 1989) and 82 percent (in 2000). In 1983, when the Bank published its first PSM-focused *World Development Report*, the Bank had paid little attention to improving a client's administrative or managerial capabilities. Just eight of the Bank's 256 approved projects in 1983 (3.1 percent) had a PSM focus. By 2012, PSM shaped 351 of the 532 approved projects (66 percent). Viewed alternatively, between 1990 and 2012, PSM/PSG was part of no less than 71.4 percent of Bank approved projects *per year*. In addition, between 1980 and 2007, nearly 1119 of the 6476 approved projects with a PSM/PSG component placed the majority of project attention on the PSM/PSG sector (World Bank 2008d, 2015, 2021a).[2]

---

[2] Primary = 51% or more of project monies targeted PSM and/or PSG. Due to differences in how the Bank shared its project database with the public, the percentage of project monies devoted to a sector after 2007 are no longer available.

By 2012, the Bank's updated Strategy required PSM/PSG sector specialists to work in all "existing Bank networks" (IEG 2011b, xxiii). The PSM/PSG sector would become the first sector (and still the only) in the Bank's nearly 80-year history to have "a Bank-wide remit" (World Bank, 2012, 5). As noted in Table 1 and in this book's Postscript, this trend did not dissipate after 2012. Instead, the creation of a GAC Council and the Bank's new requirement that PSM/PSG must be considered in each aspect of Bank work further increased this sector's policy influence. Between 2013 and 2020, PSM/PSG involvement in Bank projects varied from 67 percent (2014 and 2015) to 85 and 86 percent (2018, 2019, and 2020).

This book explains when external, boundary, and internal actors mattered (and why) in what is a remarkable transformation of one sector of international development work at the World Bank from 1980 to 2012. This includes which actors most influenced the identification of this new policy sector for the Bank, which actors swayed its multiple reconfigurations, and which actors encouraged this sector's expansion across 32 years. The World Bank is an organization with policymaking power. The "who matters" within this sector at the Bank determines who influences not just sector policy and project approval but also sector policy interaction with the Bank's client states and the lives of tens of millions around the world.

The next sections briefly highlight scholarship on the World Bank and identify the literature and knowledge gaps before using Xu and Weller's excellent 2009 book as an introduction into why and how the discipline of public administration might provide insights for IO policy change studies. In doing so, this chapter engages constructivist scholarship on IO behavior, suggests where constructivist understandings of bureaucrats and bureaucracy may be unnecessarily narrow, and the limits that arise from such a choice. This is followed by the placement of this book within a quickly evolving international public administration and transnational administration scholarship anchored not in international relations but instead, portions of the public administration discipline. The purpose, motivation, components, and operationalization of the book's analytical framework via bureaucratic politics and stakeholder theory is discussed. Before concluding the chapter, alternative approaches not used in this book are briefly noted.

Literature and Knowledge Gap

There are hundreds of articles and books on the World Bank. While Table 1 provides Bank basics for this sector, this short section can only highlight the broadest categories of scholarship. This overview is not intended to be fully comprehensive or to slight those not included. In the sections which follow, the scholarship which most significantly influenced this book's approach, its analytical framework, and its contributions are discussed at length. In addition, discussions about alternative approaches to understanding policy change at the Bank are temporarily put to one side so they may be considered in the second-to-last section of this chapter.

There is no single best way to organize scholarship on the Bank. Given a risk of replicating scholarship which will also be used in later chapters, the next paragraphs sort scholarship on the Bank by actors and ideas with scholarship about events incorporated into later chapters. This is followed by a discussion of the gap this book seeks to fill and the scholarship which substantially influenced this book's analytical framework and its subsequent considerations.

Multiple external actors engage the Bank. This includes scholarship written on IMF–Bank relations (Birdsall 2003; Hammond and McGowan 1992; IEO 2020; Güven 2012; Kranke 2020; Vestergaard and Wade 2015; Biersteker 1990; Wade 2011), the role of Bank Executive Directors (in general) or the US (in particular) (Ascher 2003; Gwin 1994; Braaten 2014, Braaten et al. 2018; Fleck and Kilby 2006; McKeown 2009; Morrison 2013), and NGOs (Paul and Israel 1990; Fox and Brown 1998; Kerler 2007; Anderl et al. 2021; Edwards 2009; Ebrahim and Herz 2007; Dellmuth and Bloodgood 2019; Philipps 2009). In contrast, scholarship exclusive to a study of Bank Presidents is infrequent (Balkvis 2005; Bazbauers 2014; Salmon 2005; Edwards 2009) even if Bank Presidents are often mentioned in scholarship on the Bank. Of the internal PSM units and later, networks and boards mentioned in this book, very few have received sustained scholarly attention. In contrast, several former Bank Chief Economists have written about the Bank (Krueger 1983, 1986, 1990; Stiglitz 2000; Summers 1993) an observation that also holds true for a long-serving Bank General Counsel (Shihata 1995, 2000a, 2001).

Key ideas in this book's timeline have also received scholarly attention. This includes, but is not limited to, structural adjustment and neoclassical economics (among the many, see Sharma 2013; Hammond et al. 1992; Harrigan and Mosley 1991), the Washington Consensus (Naím 2000; Broad and Cavanagh 1999; Soederberg 2001; Broad 2004; Williamson 1990, 2000a), new institutional economics (Clague 1997; North 1995; Nabli and Nugent 1989; Theobald 1999), good governance (Grindle 2004, 2007; Hout 2007; Best 2014; Dubois et al. 2019; Theobald 1999; Santiso 2001; Kiely 1998; Erkkilä and Piironen 2014; Mkandawire 2007; Doornbos 2001; Nanda 2006), anticorruption (Larmour 2011; Berkman 2008; Chen 2016; Dubois et al. 2019; Marquette 2004, 2007), among others.

More specific to this book's purpose, scholars have considered how the Bank's external actors influence policy shifts even if far fewer have asked how the Bank's internal environment affects Bank actions (for exceptions, see Weaver 2008; Stein 2008; Xu and Weller 2009; Vetterlein 2007; Williams 2008; Allan 2019; Chwieroth 2015). A specific focus on the Bank's internal bureaucratic environment and how it influences the PSM/PSG sector is rare (Weaver 2008; Stein 2008; Brinkerhoff 1994; Yanguas and Hulme 2015; Moloney 2009) even if scholarship on the Bank's good governance agenda (in general) is extensive (among the many, see Crawford 2006; Grindle 2004; Santiso 2001; Kiely 1998; Erkkilä and Piironen

2014; Mkandawire 2007; Williams 2008; Thomas 2007; Guhan 1998; Doornbos 2001; DeFrancesco and Guashino 2020; Nanda 2006; Rose-Ackerman 2017). In addition, despite sector research on how the Bank's indigenous policy norms (Sarfaty 2005), social development (Vetterlein 2007), gender (Gerard 2019), education (Enns 2015; Heynemann 2003) and the environment (Gutner 2005; Nielson et al. 2005; Park 2005) impact *organizational* change, very few have asked how stakeholders *and* bureaucratic politics interact for *policy* change.

There are several partial exceptions to the above generalization. Each may be considered as potentially complementary to this book's analytical framework. My italicized comments about each partial exception are hints about where this chapter is going, how it will lead to this book's analytical framework, and how this book desires to contribute to both the IO studies and public administration disciplines. Despite the next paragraphs being written with a "how I differ" styling, each contribution influenced this book's analytical framework and the possibilities unearthed via mesohistorical timelines.

The first partial exception is books and articles on the Bank with similar mesohistorical timelines (Thurow 1997; Shihata 2001; McKeown 2009; Kraske et al. 1996; Williams 2008; Graham 2014; Vetterlein 2007; Fioretos and Heldt 2019; Allan 2019). Each helped with cross-checking my reviewed Bank documents and interviewee recollections even if each book or article was not about PSM/PSG nor did they employ this book's analytical framework. Cross-checking is an exercise that is thankfully relatively free of inter- and intra-disciplinary debates.

The second partial exception to the above generalization is an article on the fifteen years before the Bank's approval of its structural adjustment lending instrument in 1980. The author shares my interest in organizational history and understands that bureaucratic imperatives may outweigh external actor influences (Sharma 2013). He argued that contrary to most studies of Bank structural adjustment lending, instrument creation reflected internal operational issues more than external actor motivations. This argument has significant merit. *This book is not focused on lending instrument development (even if briefly mentioned in Chapter 3) but rather, policy change within one sector of Bank work. The observation about internal factors as more important and significant than external actors is repeatedly noted in this book.*

The third is an article not on the Bank but a comparison of the European Commission plus two Secretariats: Organisation for Economic Cooperation and Development (OECD) and the World Trade Organization (WTO). The author noted that a bureaucracy's structural arrangements, organizational capacities, and bureaucratic specializations alter IO administrative behaviors (Trondal 2011). Although the article is ahistorical, its observation that structure influences internal administrative behavior is important. *In my book's sector policy history of PSM/PSG change over 32 years, opportunities exist to uncover where structures interact with sector-specific policy shifts (a narrower focus than the "administrative behavior" of Trondal (2011)) and how external and internal actors shape sector policy change within one IO.*

The fourth is a book that explains the rise of the good governance agenda at the World Bank. At first glance this book shares a purpose with my book: it is mesohistorical and it is interested in one half of this book's public sector management and public sector governance agenda. However, and unlike my emphasis on stakeholders and bureaucratic politics, Williams' book is interested in ideas. That is, how the Bank "thinks about and conceives of the problems facing developing countries, and how it thinks about and conceives of solutions to these problems" (Williams 2008, 16). If my book is focused on the actors and their politicking, Williams' book focused on how ideas (in particular, liberalism) shaped good governance. At the Bank, ideas arising from *en vogue* economic theories do matter. Neoclassical economics, new institutional economics, and political economy each appear in my book's history of sector policy change over 32 years. *But in my book, ideas are understood as arising specifically from actors who may or may not have the power to alter policy. The ideas reflect structural and policy rearrangements of who matters, how they matter, and where their influence is or is not felt.*

The fifth is a mesohistorical study on social development policy shifts (Vetterlein 2007). Like my book, the author is interested in how internal and external actors explain policy change even if the area of interest (social development) differs. She also describes change across relevant eras and relies on similar methods to my book. In addition, her conclusion that external and internal actors may interact to create policy change is carried forward into my book. Vetterlein (2007) seeks to combine constructivist and principal–agent theories to understand IO behaviors. In contrast, my book is less interested in marrying constructivism with principal–agent theory. Neither are commonly used within the public administration discipline for reasons that are explained later in this chapter. *Instead, I desire to introduce the concepts of a discipline (public administration) infrequently consulted in IO studies. In doing so, this book pivots away from constructivism and principal–agent understandings of IO policy change and suggests other concepts and a bureaucrat-focused disciplinary language for understanding policy change.*

The sixth is an article that discusses the intersection of neoclassical economics with fifty-two years of Bank history (Allan 2019). Like Vetterlein (2007) and like my book, Allan (2019) seeks to understand the complex interactions within and outside the Bank. His concept is the policy nexus which appears to be derived, in my understanding, from political science with an unacknowledged link to what my discipline of public administration identifies as policy network studies. By analyzing network evolution over time, moments of change (or nexus) are found. I disagree with Allan's (2019) self-diagnosis that his study is simply a "special case" (185) of constructivist literature. Instead, Allan (2019) and Vetterlein (2007) help scholars go beyond a constructivist fascination with organizational culture. Each are more than special cases. *Just as my book adds to Vetterlein (2007) by articulating an actor-centered approach but from a discipline infrequently engaged in IO studies, this too becomes another difference between my book and Allan (2019).*

The seventh is a book which asks why employees of IOs suggest they are apolitical when their policies and analyses may lack that characteristic (Maertens and Louis 2021). One of the book's intellectual anchors is Barnett and Finnemore's use of "Weberian sociology" (Maertens and Louis 2021, 11), which is used to question international civil servant neutrality. The authors make a significant contribution to international relations' recent interest in depoliticization, its creation, and how it is operationalized. But, as noted in this chapter, the public administration discipline discovered nearly 75 years ago that "apolitical" and "civil servant" are words which infrequently belong together. The resulting concept—politics–administration dichotomy—has been articulated since the late 1940s, via passive and active representative bureaucracy studies (starting shortly thereafter) and more recently via downsizing, political interference, at will employment, contracting out, and any number of assaults on domestic bureaucracies. As such, the authors' understanding of depoliticization cannot be an output of my book. Instead, one output of my book is the sharing of public administration's disciplinary knowledge that there are small "p" politics is everywhere. This also reflects (especially in the US) a public administration discipline which does not give "Weberian bureaucracy" much credence. This reasoning about Weber is shared in this chapter's section on constructivism.

In perhaps an initially clumsy attempt to speak across disciplinary divides before being far less clumsy (I hope) in my later sharing this book's analytical framework, the reader may wish to understand that there are at least four levels of "p" politics. There is (a) big "p" politics or political system choice, (b) middle "p" politics such as legislatures and their political parties, (c) the small "p" politics of (international) civil servants and their bureaucratic politics, and (d) the smallest of the "p" politics (daily minutiae of implementation) (Moloney 2014). The small "p" politics of policy change is a focus of this book with an occasional reference throughout the book to the smallest of the "p" politics.

As such, this book is not about depoliticization, in general, as a theoretical or normative goal. Like the discipline of public administration (as understood in most US and some non-US circles), *this book views an (international) civil servant's small "p" politics as expected and as an empirical observation which is both unremarkable and normal.* This book's referent within the public administration discipline is the politics–administration dichotomy. This dichotomy did not arise out of nowhere. Intellectual debates preceded its articulation. These debates mirrored the times (1880s to early 1940s in the US) but also shared similarities with modern international relations' "discovery" in the early 2000s of politics within

IO bureaucracies. For IO scholars, their "discovery" created a hole in how IR understood IOs and more broadly, realist theory and liberal-institutionalist theory. In tracing the articles and books of international relations which appear to approach the public administration discipline and this book's framework, my goal is to understand international relations' intellectual positionality and a "how they [international relations] know what they know". Thus, the next sections of this chapter will briefly go back in time (within the public administration discipline) to discuss alternative ways of "knowing" IO bureaucracies and thus, question international relations "discovery". In doing so, IO studies may also help the public administration discipline too. IO studies may assist my domestically focused bureaucracy buddies to consider the global and to reflect on how supranational acts shape domestic realities.

As such, the eighth partial exception is one which, more than the prior seven, comes closest to how public administration could study an IO bureaucracy even if the author is not from the discipline. In the article, the author compares two policy agendas within the Bank (social protection, fragile states) and asks how each agenda obtained space among competing sectoral and topic agendas (Makinder 2020). Anchored by ideas, their discourse, and their exchange at macro-, meso-, and micro-levels, Makinder (2020) inserts ideas and their ideational power into questions of institutional power and its outputs. Her analysis finds that individuals, heads of department, key Bank documents (e.g., *World Development Reports,* among others) may matter but that on their own, each is not enough to explain the rise in a topic's importance. It is by linking topic evolution with the Bank's lending imperative and other internal incentives that one can explain influence. *In doing so, her analysis parallels my own: international civil servants matter, incentives matter, and internal power dynamics may change over time.*

Makinder (2020) goes where Vetterlein (2007) and Allan (2019) do not. She focuses upon actors, organizational incentives, and IO documents to trace policy evolution. My book has a similar purpose but from an arguably harder-to-ignore disciplinary footprint. That is, it uses just a few of the insights from a discipline known for its work on domestic bureaucracies to study IO bureaucracies and policy change. In so doing, my book cannot overlook external actor power to shape IO bureaucracies and their policy outputs. By engaging external actors with potential influence as deeply as internal actors, questions about who matters (and how) are answered.

The ninth and tenth contributions, when combined with the prior partial exceptions, are the originating intellectual basis for this book. The ninth is the work of Xu and Weller (2009, 2018) and the tenth is by constructivist scholars whose work restarted international relations' exploration of IO bureaucracies (Weaver 2008; Barnett and Finnemore 2004). If this book intends to reasonably suggest that the public administration discipline may have a pivotal role in understanding IO policy change and in contributing to midrange theory development (Checkel 1998), then the book must engage constructivism and discuss how its assumptions differ (often dramatically) from a century-plus of public administration scholarship. Such differences are the stage upon which the book's analytical framework and analyses of PSM/PSG sector policy change appear.

But first, Xu Yi-Chong and Patrick Weller's work creates a doorway into an introduction of the public administration discipline to studies of IO bureaucracies and policy change. The following sections will use Xu and Weller's work (2009, 2018) to help establish international civil servant influence. This is necessary step before the chapter can discuss how international relations' constructivist scholars misread Max Weber, the implications of that misreading, and how the public administration discipline offers insights into understanding policy change and IO behavior. This is followed by a discussion of this book's analytical framework via bureaucratic politics and stakeholder theory. After placing this book firmly within evolving international public administration and transnational administration scholarship, my method and its considerations are discussed. A note on theories, approaches, and concepts not utilized by this book (and why) is briefly mentioned before concluding this chapter.

Using Public Administration to Study "Who Matters"

In 2009, Xu Yi-Chong and Patrick Weller published a book that explored Bank decision-making processes and staff arrangements. Their scholarship is a direct descendant of a 1973 book by Robert W. Cox and Harold K. Jacobsen in which the two authors brought together the decision sciences with international organization studies (Cox and Jacobson 1973). Unlike Xu and Weller's book, however, Cox and Jacobsen's book did not create as much intellectual momentum. This may be due to a concurrent inward turn within public administration, a turn within economics away from the decision sciences made famous by Herbert Simon (future recipient of the Nobel Prize in Economics) and as this chapter soon illustrates, the lack of interest by international relations in expanding Graham Allison's bureaucrat-focused analyses of the Cuban Missile Crisis to IOs (Allison 1971; Allison and Halperin 1972; Simon 1946, 1947, 1956).

Into this void arose international relations' constructivism in the mid-to-late-1990s with its organizational culture focus and, as the next sections suggests, a misreading of Max Weber's insights on bureaucracy. In a rebuttal to international relations' constructivist approach, Xu and Weller dismiss constructivist views that its "inevitable" that international civil servants have "dysfunctional behavior". Xu and Weller (2009, 9) wrote, "any single outcome is the drawing together of multiple actions from a number of staffs with different perspectives." They are similarly critical of principal–agent approaches. Bank principals cannot "fulfill some of the heroic roles nominally allocated to them" (7) and suggest that researchers which identify an entire organization as an "agent" of a principal such as a Board or state is simplistic. Principal–agent studies treat agents "as though they *should* be the passive recipients of the decisions of principals. *Cases where they diverge from the wishes of principals are interpreted as misuse of power, preferring their own interests to those of their superiors*" (Xu and Weller 2009, 7, emphasis added).

For Xu and Weller, "… control over decision-making may be tantamount to control over the outcome" (Xu and Weller 2009, 4). Labeling international relations' constructivist and principal–agent theorizing as "unrealistic," they sought to "relax the strict assumptions about unitary actors to develop a conceptually and empirically more diverse idea of [international organizations]" (Xu and Weller 2009, 9–10). Their book provides the key jump-off point for my book. Whereas my book asks how sector policy outputs were created and debated within the Bank's most prescribed sector from 1980 to 2012, Xu and Weller (2009, 5) focused on process but with an emphasis on "how the Bank works, what drives its staff, and what their expectations are" without consideration of one sector or of specific time periods.[3]

In his critique of constructivism, Checkel (1998) reminded scholars of international relations to "avoid the charge that they are reducing one unit of analysis—agents (states, decision makers)—to the other—structures (norms). In doing so, scholars have overlooked how norms arise in the first place (and the role of agency and power in the process), and how, through interactions with particular agents, norms change over time" (Checkel 1998, 340). Checkel desired a middle-range theory capable of connecting the dots. *This book modestly attempts to help connect the dots and to further contribute to creating a potential mid-range theory of policy change within IOs.*

Whereas Xu and Weller (2009) focused on organizational tensions, this book uses stakeholder theory and bureaucratic politics to understand relationships among and between external and internal stakeholders in shaping Bank policy; or, as noted by others, "international bureaucrats matter" (Eckhard and Ege 2016, 969; Kennard and Stanescu 2019; Johnson 2014; Bauer and Ege 2016; Weller and Xu 2010). Just as international bureaucrats matter, so too do external actors. Internal and external stakeholder power, legitimacy, urgency, and issue criticality influence policy outputs. The internal and external stakeholders may work together, apart, at cross purposes, at different moments in time, or even not at all. As such, scholars must "explain how the interests and identities of particular agents, in the presence

---

[3] Xu & Weller (2009) might concur with Moises Naím, former Venezuelan minister, and *Foreign Policy* editor: "No doubt, ambiguity of mission, goal congestion, and strategic volatility in the Bretton Woods institutions are largely the consequence of their external environment. But they are also undoubtedly the consequences of how decision making at the top of these institutions is organized. In general, once an objective is incorporated as part of the agenda, it becomes almost impossible to remove it. Political factors, organizational inertia, and the governance of these institutions make it very difficult to shed goals, at least formally" (Naím 1995, 87).

of norms, change—or, equally important, do not change over time" (Checkel 1998, 344). *This book uses public administration as an actor-, process-, and organization-focused discipline to suggest ways to approach Checkel's (1998) objective: provide a mid-range theory of change to link micro- and macro-observations.*

One focus of this discussion is the steps which follow: a brief exposure to the public administration discipline via questions raised about the dominant approach to IO policy and organizational change scholarship: constructivism. This includes asking whether constructivist use of Max Weber is appropriate. The answer has less with constructivist anchors within so-called Weberian administration than with a narrow constructivist understanding of Weber and more broadly, of the public administration discipline, the bureaucrats (and organizations) studied by public administration scholars, and the influence of international civil servants as policy change actors.

Constructivism, Weber, and the Foundations of Public Administration

The intellectual referent for constructivist scholarship on international organizations arises out of organizational sociology and, in particular, Talcott Parsons' translation of Max Weber. As noted in this section, this referent led to an unnecessarily narrow application of Max Weber's contributions to the study of bureaucracy. As importantly for this study of IO policy change, this led to (mis)characterizations that bureaucracies will "misbehave" if their internal actors agitate against, or proactively influence, an IO's key member states (on the UN, see Trettin and Junk 2014).[4] This is an unrealistic straitjacket for understanding international civil servant influence. For constructivists, Weber's ideal type and its associated rationalities are not just a way to describe an ideal bureaucracy but a *normative* ideal. For such scholars, bureaucratic irrationality forbids the Bank from fully obeying its key member states. This apparent disobedience leads to an "organized hypocrisy" whereby the Bank is expected to reduce poverty and encourage economic growth but, instead, is found to be unable to control its irrational (e.g., bureaucratic, cultural) tendencies and thus, struggles to achieve its mission (Weaver, 2008).[5]

For some, the impact of Weber's writings on "rationality and rationalization" led to "unbridgeable contradictions for sociology" (Shenav 2003, 192). It was not that rational or sociological approaches must be supreme but that sociology's "strength ... lies in maintaining this ambivalence" (Shenav 2003, 193). This

---

[4] For an opposite view, scholars have argued how powerful states may "benefit from the rational-legal, delegated, moral, and expert authority of secretariats" (Dijkstra 2017, 53).
[5] In a study of UN peacekeeping, two scholars labeled such behavior as "bureaucratic spoiling" (Trettin and Junk 2014).

ambivalence is underemphasized by constructivist scholars and, as noted in the last section of this chapter, it is also underemphasized by several of the other common approaches to understanding policy change within IOs. Drawing heavily upon Talcott Parsons' interpretations of Weber, organizational sociologists desire outcomes where rationality is possible (Shenav 2003; Parsons 1947). Thus, it is no surprise that by reading the theoretical underpinnings (and crucially, the footnotes) of key constructivist texts on international organizations (e.g., Weaver, 2008, Barnett and Finnemore, 2004), the influence of organizational sociology on constructivist approaches to IO behavior becomes clear.

The result is that rationality had become an "*a priori* construct in sociological analysis, and an instrument for social management" rather than an idea useful in "social critique" given that the "deceiving role of rationality" was left out of most discussions (Shenav 2003, 197, 198). In Weber's own words, his ideal types were simply a "methodological device" and thus "it does not involve a belief in the actual predominance of rational elements in human life" (Weber 1947, 92). Moreover, rationality is but one (unachievable) goal of human interaction. We must be careful to not confuse "ideal" with "practical" or "rational" (see also Xu and Weller 2015, 2–3).[6] It may actually be irrational to strive for rationality and/or to normatively judge our inability to be "rational". If, as Nobel Prize winning economist Herbert Simon noted, we are "bounded" in our rationality, then civil servant analyses require new assumptions (Simon 1947, 1956; see also Haas 1991, 28–49).

When two prominent constructivist scholars wrote, "impersonal rules are the building blocks of a bureaucracy," they cited Weber's "modern bureaucracy" as their building block. This allowed an extrapolation that bureaucratic rules must "shape the activities, understandings, identify, and practice of the bureaucracy and consequently help to define the bureaucratic culture" (Barnett and Finnemore 2004, 17–19). In short, they put Weber in a box that Weber himself tried to avoid. Or, as noted by international organizations theorist Ernst Haas in 1991, Weber's ideas lead to "sparsely populated cells" and thus, a "less economical procedure that forgoes the search for clusters or straight paths" is required (Haas 1991, 10, 11). My book speaks to this Haas objective.

In their seminal book, Barnett and Finnemore (2004) studied the rules available to bureaucrats and the self-actualizing powers that bureaucrats ascribe to those rules. Given their normative concern about IO "misbehaviors", a straw-man risk arises. Their observation of international civil servant disobedience to Weber's ideal types creates space for a subsequent (normative) critique. This is a narrow view of civil servant behavior. The constructivist perspectives neglect to emphasize that bureaucrats might retain other characteristics. Or that they might have

---

[6] Although Johnson (2014) uses principal–agent theory to study IO bureaucrat influence (an approach whose limits are discussed later in this chapter), she mirrors the observations of Xu and Weller (2008) by correctly observing that scholars should not expect international bureaucrats to be "automatons of states" (Johnson 2014, 28).

other responsibilities outside their rule-making function. Or even that reinterpreting rules need not be a deviant behavior.[7] For the authors, the bureaucrat's desire to uphold the rules became why the United Nations did not intervene in the 1994 Rwandan genocide. In their view, the United Nations bureaucrats, subsumed by their rules, kept the United Nations' political leadership from stopping the genocide (Barnett and Finnemore 2004, 148–155).

Although Weber worried that bureaucracies may tend toward "plutocracy" and impersonality (Weber 1947, 340) and that impersonal relationships may lead bureaucracies to actively resist change, such trends need not develop. In her 2008 book, Catherine Weaver sought to understand international civil servants and their "deviance" through an understanding of organizational change at the Bank. A key problem from a public administration perspective is that this "deviance" assumption is left unchallenged. Although Barnett and Finnemore (2004) realized that "neutrality is often, probably always, impossible … there is often no neutral stance one could take in many of the situations [international organizations] confront", they still argued that "[international organizations] *need to find one* in order to maintain the claim that they are impartial and are acting in a depoliticized manner" (Barnett and Finnemore 2004, 21, emphasis added).

For a public administration scholar, this neutrality or expectation of a depoliticized cadre of international civil servants is an observation that runs contrary to a century-plus of intellectual history within the public administration discipline— as very briefly discussed in the next section. *The output is constructivist scholarship that gives international civil servants an impossible task: be neutral despite the difficulty of doing so and if they do not succeed, be criticized for not being neutral. By anchoring their work on a narrow conception of bureaucracy and bureaucrat legitimacy, constructivists have left little space for contextualized understandings of IO behavior and policy change.*

Introducing the Public Administration Discipline

One contribution of this volume is to tease out the interaction of international relations theory with an infrequent disciplinary partner: the public administration discipline. Public administration engages both the civil servants and public organizations of government life. It is argued in this book that public administration's

---

[7] One note is needed. Critical constructivism argues that "interests emerge out of the representations that define for actors the situations and events they face" (Weldes 1998, 218) whereas contingency theory considers the structural constraints placed upon an organization from its external environment. In both, the organization or interests are isolated actors separate from their internal descriptive statistics (critical constructivism) or their external environment (contingency theory). Their units of analysis also differ from each other as well as the public administration discipline. Contingency theory is more explicit about its agent (the organization) than critical constructivism (focused on actor groups) whereas the public administration discipline will consider both groups plus the individual civil servant.

frequently domestic focus on context, civil servant behavior, and the power of bureaucracy has application to IOs and its international civil servants (e.g., Moloney and Rosenbloom 2020; Bauer et al. 2017; Fleischer and Reiners 2021).

Since the late 1940s, public administration scholars have articulated a simple observation about civil servant behavior: modern public administration theory and its practice observes no dichotomy between (policy and bureaucrat) politics and administration (Waldo 1984 [1948]). In his 1948 book, Dwight Waldo noted that the prevailing view of administration, a politics-administration dichotomy with origins in the late 1800s (e.g. Wilson 1887), was inherently flawed. Policy politics and administration could not (and potentially *should not*, especially in a democracy) be separable. Individual bureaucrats are small "p" political creatures who cannot fully shed themselves of their personal traits (education, gender, religion, social class, geographic origin, sexuality, ethnicity, and so on) upon entering civil servant life. That politics infuses administration and that administration itself is a product of the political environment effectively overturned a prior five decades of research within the public administration discipline that administrators (and their organizations) can or should be neutral. Moreover, Waldo argued that the state cannot be homogeneous as it relied upon political will. Since political will was not homogeneous, administrative structures and policy objectives also reflect this non-homogeneity (Waldo 1984 [1948]).

Waldo dismissed the "orthodox" project of America's late nineteenth and early twentieth centuries which encouraged American civil servants to separate politics from administration via scientific management techniques (e.g., Taylor 1911). Waldo feared that scientific management and its rationality principles might become a "religion of humanity" (Waldo 1984 [1948], 48). Using America's bureau movements of the 1910s and 1920s as his example, he noted that the bureaus did more than input expert knowledge to create efficient outcomes. They also inputted moral values to "fix" public life. Since values may vary by culture, organization, and location, administrators must acknowledge the political nature of their work and of themselves and to disavow attempts to force rationality—as defined by scientific management—into solutions lacking context for the circumstances served by the administrator (Waldo 1984 [1948]).

It is hard to overstate Waldo's influence on the public administration research that followed. It was not that Waldo did away with Max Weber—it is unknown if at the time of Waldo's 1946 Ph.D. dissertation or his subsequent 1948 book whether he knew of Weber's work (Parsons' English translation of Weber was published in 1947)—but that Waldo reframed already-present debates within public administration studies. Ideal types could remain as ideals but not to the extent that modern bureaucracy and its civil servants would be admonished for failing to achieve what is practically impossible and also, normatively undesirable.

Of course, the aforementioned cannot discount that bureaucracies can become self-serving entities. Instead, the line (or really, the gulf) between rational and self-serving is far wider than imagined by constructivism. International civil servants cannot leave their small "p" politics, personal characteristics, or intellectual training at the Bank's door. They are not, and should not, be simply neutral actors who "do as they are told" by Bank member states. Their individual, group, and organizational attributes inform policy outputs and policy change. Since civil servants are small "p" political creatures, so too is the World Bank and its international civil servants. Their small "p" political nature, as international civil servants, requires we study their influence over policy creation, and to learn how their interactions with external stakeholders influence policy change.

Other public administration research has considered whether civil servants lose their religious, gender, ethnic, or other identities upon entering civil servant life. In 1944, J. Donald Kingsley observed that Britain was an increasingly middle-class society. Kingsley asked whether such class changes were "represented" within a civil service traditionally drawn from Britain's elite social circles (Kingsley 1944). The subsequent representative bureaucracy literature asks whether a civil servant's passive characteristics (e.g., gender, religion, sexual orientation) are actively represented within public policy making and implementation (e.g., Dolan and Rosenbloom 2003). Similarly, we may question whether a Bank civil servants' Anglo-American or disciplinary background influences Bank policy output. In fact, Bank scholars do ask such questions but unfortunately, they do so without using the established representative bureaucracy literature (Stein 2008; Ascher 1983; Novosad and Werker 2014). The contribution of public administration studies to such questions is overlooked.

The non-homogeneous and apolitical nature of Bank staff becomes a central pivot in explaining the depth and intensity of internal debates on PSM and PSG. The Bank's staff *are* small "p" political in their interaction with member states, the G7, the IMF, and non-state actors. They are also political amongst themselves as they vociferously debate sector policy shifts. Whether it is a pitting of the Bank's neoclassical economists against its microeconomists (Chapter 3), those who desired "good governance" versus "development management" (Chapter 5), staff who pushed for the Bank's first-ever Public Sector Strategy (Chapter 6) and then later, debated the rise of political economists within the Bank (Chapter 7) or argued that the Wolfowitz presidency harmed the sector (Chapter 8), staff are political. Over time, or at least during the 32 years covered in this book, staff battles change sector policy and as a result, change the Bank.

If we acknowledge such intellectual history within public administration, then we must modify Barnett and Finnemore's (2004) label of IO behavior as "deviant" when it disobeys member state directives. We can also reframe Weaver's (2008) desire to bridge the rationalist-constructivist divide. Forcing civil servant actions into an ideal type overlooks an opportunity to understand policy change. *It is not about simply switching the causal arrow of blame from the bureaucracy to the actors who influence or created the organization; rather, it is an opportunity to gain detailed understandings of bureaucratic behavior within an IO.* In doing so, researchers may find that during one period within one sector, an external actor such as an NGO or member state was the predominant influence over a particular policy shift. At other times, a longer series of internal reforms may influence policy change. An actor whose role was prominent in one year may not be as influential in the next. This perspective may also suggest why certain NGO actors were more likely than others to have their voices heard within the Bank.

By acknowledging dichotomy implications, an output is a nuanced understanding of policy change capable of explaining organizational behavior. The outcome is a fuller understanding of IO behavior in an increasingly transnationally administered global arena (Stone and Moloney 2019b). For this book and its sector of interest, this analysis leads to the conclusion that, after August 1991, its international civil servants were far more responsible than external actors for driving the Bank's ever-expanding understanding of PSM reform and as of 1991, PSG. Until that point, external actors such as the US, the IMF, and the G7 drove sector policy change. How this happened and who mattered most are questions answered in this book.

International Public Administration and Transnational Administration

This section firmly places my book within an evolving international public administration (IPA) and transnational administration literature. With origins in the 1950s and 1960s, IPA was reborn as a sub-discipline in the late 2000s. This section discusses how IPA studies (or IO bureaucracy studies) differ from international relations as well as how this book differs from typical IPA studies. This is crucial since the last ten years have witnessed an explosion in IPA scholarship focused upon the administrative and policy life within IOs. IPA literature harkens less to the foundation IO bureaucracies work of Robert Cox or Ernst Haas but instead, frequently uses Barnett and Finnemore's (2004) constructivism as its intellectual predecessor. Early IPA efforts also pivoted from a proliferating literature on the European Union and its multilevel governance and asked about administrative behaviours and how to reform IOs (Balint et al. 2000; Bauer 2002; Bauer and Knill 2007).[8] EU studies became a key tributary to today's IPA and transnational administration scholarship (Ladi 2019).

---

[8] IPA's anchoring within public administration may also reflect less of an American understanding of public administration and its intellectual history than a European tendency to see political science and public administration as linked disciplines. In the US, and after the early 1970s, political science and public administration split into two distinct disciplines. This split reflected a federal desire to professionalize training with hands-on skills and specific administrative considerations for those destined for civil servant careers.

Specific to IPA and starting with a book on management reforms in international organizations (Bauer and Knill 2007), there has been an explosion in non-EU IPA scholarship even if many IPA scholars are largely situated at German and Norwegian universities. In an attempt to marry their discussions with international relations' use of constructivism and principal–agent theory, IPA scholars have explored how to deepen multidisciplinary discussions among scholars of public administration, global policy, international organizations, and international relations (Fleischer and Reiners 2021; Bauer et al. 2017, 2018, 2019; Ege et al. 2019; Trondal 2016; Volkmer 2019). Although most IPA literature anchors itself as an offshoot of international relations' constructivism, David H. Rosenbloom and I recently observed that the IPA sub-discipline and its broader public administration discipline must critically assess constructivist limits for explaining IO behaviour (Moloney and Rosenbloom 2020; see also Cox and Jacobson 1973; Haas 1991; Xu and Weller 2009, 2018; Weller and Xu 2015).

IPA literatures are embedded within broader discussions of transnational administration and global policy (Stone and Moloney 2019a; Stone and Ladi 2015; Moloney and Stone 2020). Both IPA and transnational administration scholarship agree with certain international relations theories that the state may no longer be the most important global governance actor (Johnson 2014; Risse-Kappen 1995; Kramarz 2016). This observation continues into this book. Yes, the states that "own" the World Bank matter. This is especially true in the first decade of PSM at the Bank. But after August 1991 and through to 2012 in the Bank's most prescribed sector (PSM/PSG), key Bank member states did not drive the sector agenda. The Bank's international civil servants drove sector policy change.

Despite a suggestion from the global policy and transnational administration literature that other actors may also matter such as NGOs, think tanks, transnational public-private partnerships, scientific networks, global citizen activists, and transgovernmental networks (e.g., Stone 2001, 2008; Legrand 2019; Green 2018; Westerwinter 2018; Jönsson et al. 2010; Schäferhoff et al. 2009; Tallberg et al. 2013; Demortain 2017), the World Bank, for this sector, may be an exception. Not only is the Bank the most important development-focused IO but the Bank influences non-state actors' understanding of what is or is not PSM/PSG. As others have noted, "nobody even comes close" to the Bank when it comes to its global influence (George and Sabelli 1994). This is as true today as it was in 1994 or even 1980, this book's start point.

Within studies of global policy and transnational administration, IPA scholars ask how the administrative and policy arrangements of IOs impact its work. This includes but is not limited to IO legitimacy, accountability, policy impact, public sector reform agenda, its budgetary arena, its personnel management, and so on (among the many, see Balint et al. 2000; Knill and Bauer 2016; Knill et al. 2016, 2017, 2019; Ege 2017a; Ege and Bauer 2017b; Ege et al. 2019; Bauer 2012; Bauer and Ege 2016; Patz and Goetz 2017; Moloney and Stoycheva 2018; Moloney et al. 2019;

Bayerlein et al. 2020; Eckhard and Ege 2016; Tallberg et al. 2013). This literature engages formal IOs like the World Bank (e.g., Xu and Weller 2009) and/or UN agencies. More recently, scholarship *on informal* IOs has entered our discussions (Vabulas 2019; Roger 2020; Becker 2019).

There are parallels between IPA scholarship and the scholarship of international relations and to some extent, international political economy. Each discipline concerns themselves with IO legitimacy, accountability, and in some cases, transparency. Each suggests IOs shape global governance. However, there are at least four interrelated differences between IO studies driven by scholars of international relations and international political economy versus IPA scholarship. Each are found within this book of policy change within the PSM/PSG sector at the World Bank.

The first is that IPA's unit of analysis is rarely the institution but, instead, the organization (e.g., March and Olsen 1989). This is not an unimportant distinction. Institutional scholars are rarely scholars of public personnel, administrative law, bureaucratic representativeness, and the "messier" administrative life (Olsen 1991, 2006). At the risk of a hasty generalization given limited space, institutional scholars tend not to consider the power or influence of individual international civil servants (beyond apolitical assumption of their principal or agent nature) and his or her office or department to alter policy agendas. Nonetheless, and unlike realist scholars of international relations (Mearsheimer 1995), institutional scholars implicitly understand that institutions matter. However, and unlike scholars of organizations, of bureaucracies, and of individuals or groups of civil servants, institutional scholars tend to black box the organization or at best, suggest that an entire institution can be explained via principals and agents and/or that a singular culture animates the institution (Vaubel 2006; Elsig 2011; Delreux and Adriaensen 2017; Bradford et al. 2018; Chwieroth 2015).

If scholars of international relations and international political economy characterize IO's as self-directed actors in which member states, the IO's Board, or the President are the "principal" in archetypical principal–agent relationships (Oestreich 2012; Johnson 2014; Lyne et al. 2006), then the discipline of public administration suggests that such observations are neither unique to IOs nor, as argued by public administration, the only explanation for organizational behaviour. That is—harkening also back to Xu and Weller (2009), the theory is often "not a generalizable explanation for the myriad relationships that actually exist between principals and agents in the bureaucratic world" (Waterman and Meier 1998, 197).

Second, IPA scholars are willing to explore an IO's organizational nuances and to suggest different actors within an IO's organizational structure influence policy outputs. This scholarship may engage an IO's organizational routines and administrative styles (Enkler et al. 2017; Knill et al. 2019; Bayerlein et al. 2020; Fleischer 2021) or attempt to formulate an international civil servant's preferences (Ege 2020). While such studies may share a view with international relations that an appropriate unit of analysis is the entire IO, IPA scholars tend to dig deeper into the IO to explain behavior and, increasingly, to undertake cross-IO comparisons (Bayerlein et al. 2020; Knill et al. 2016; Tallberg et al. 2013; Trondal 2011).

Third, and as highlighted in this book, IPA studies assume international civil servants are actors with bounded rationality, as small "p" political actors who may work contrary to an IO's member state "owners", and as experts who engage internal and external actors in policy debates about which policy directions and projects should be an IO's focus (Xu 2018; Weller and Xu 2010a, 2015; Xu and Weller 2008, 2009). This observation, just like the observations within this book, is accepted as normal, as expected, and without normative concerns attached.

This actor-centred view believes "international bureaucrats matter" (Graham and Jordan 1980; Eckhard and Ege 2016, 969) and for this book, in particular, acknowledges how analytical sociology's analyses (e.g., Hedström and Bearman 2009) create spaces for public administration to enter IO studies. By viewing international civil servants, the processes they create, and the offices and departments in which they work as worthy units of study, their bureaucratic politics and their stakeholder interactions help us understand the actors who encouraged policy change. This policy change is not separable from expertise, knowledge, and their networks (e.g., Littoz-Monnet 2017; Busch and |Liese 2017; Sending 2017; Haas 1991; Park 2009; Marcussen 2006; DeFrancesco and Guashino 2020; Sindzingre 2004) but instead, is an expansion of how change is made.

However, and where this book differs from IPA scholarship, is my book's agreement with Xu and Weller (2009) that public administration's contribution to IO and IPA studies requires articulation. This is both a fourth point about IPA versus international relations as well as a lead-in into how this book distinguishes itself from the first ten years of a rejuvenated IPA scholarship. Unlike much IPA scholarship which uses constructivism as its foundation for why their work matters, my book does the opposite: it suggests why constructivism is an inappropriate start point before highlighting how the public administration discipline may further inform IPA studies.

In addition, and unique to IPA scholarship, this is a mesohistorical study that allows us to understand individual bureaucratic influences upon policy shifts but also to trace shifts over one third of a century. The reason for a frequently ahistorical IPA scholarship is less a reflection on IPA capacity to engage lengthier IO studies but instead, an IPA tendency to prefer analyses at discrete moments in time. In addition, IPA scholarship infrequently focuses upon just one sector of an IO's work over such time periods. This book is exclusive to the Bank's most prescribed policy and project sector: PSM and PSG (see Table 1). That this sector also happens to be public sector management and public sector governance and this book is anchored within the public administration discipline is coincidence.

The next sections discuss how bureaucratic politics and stakeholder theory are joined to create this book's analytical framework. This framework moves away from IPA's fascination with constructivism and organizational sociology to em-phasize how individual and group actors within an IO and external to an IO influence policy change.

Introducing Bureaucratic Politics

Between 1980 and 2012, the Bank moved from nearly zero public sector manage-ment and public sector governance projects to sector incorporation into nearly three-quarters of the Bank's projects (see Table 1). This book draws on one ap-proach (bureaucratic politics) and one theory (stakeholder theory) to explain the dynamics of such significant project and policy change. When combined, they explain not only the growth in PSM/PSG between 1980 and 2012 but *who mat-tered* in evolving sector policy debates. The cumulative output is a contribution to a nascent theory of policy change within one sector of World Bank work with potential applicability to other sectors and other IOs.

International civil servants, as bureaucratic actors and internal stakeholders, are important links to understanding of *who matters* in policy change within IOs. This who matters question is about more than expertise, knowledge, and its networks (e.g., Littoz-Monnet 2017; Busch and Liese 2017; Sending 2017; Haas 1991; Park 2009; Marcussen 2006; DeFrancesco 2020; Sindzingre 2004; Maertens and Louis 2021). Knowledge and expertise are created by and carried via actors. Actors op-erate in an organizational forum. Individuals and units (as actors) interact, set processes into motion, change policies, and alter organizations across time. To ar-ticulate this idea, two steps are required. The first is to consider organizational size and when bureaucratic environments matter (Betton and Dess 1985). The sec-ond step requires us to understand the bureaucratic politics model (Allison and Halperin 1972; Freedman 1976).

With 10,000+ staff and 100+ country offices, the World Bank is a large orga-nization. Scholars have posited that the larger the organization, the more that the organization's internal or bureaucratic environment influences output (Betton and Dess 1985). Betton and Dess (1985) reference Hannan and Freeman's (1977) work, which observed that internal factors may outweigh external influence via the "sunk cost of firms, communication structures, internal politics, and the dominance of institutional norms" (Betton and Dess 1985, 751).

Betton and Dess's (1985) proposition may help scholars explain when, where, and why certain internal actors not only discussed PSM/PSG policy change but would also, by August 1991, dominate external actors in the ongoing evolution and institutionalization of this sector of Bank work. This includes identifying when internal actors mattered (see Tables 8, 10, 12, 14, and 15) and when internal ac-tors outweigh external influences "sunk cost of firms, communication structures, internal politics, and the dominance of institutional norms" (Betton and Dess 1985, 751) (variables I7–I10 in Tables 8, 10, 12, 14, and 15).

The addition of a new corollary (variable I6 in Tables 8, 10, 12, 14, and 15) to Betton and Dess (1985) allows an additional inside-the-organization analysis to determine when one part of an organization (e.g., PSM Unit in Chapter 3) reflects different internal influences than another (e.g., Chief Economist/DEC in Chapter 3). This book's key internal actors are the international civil servants and their various units, departments, and sectors as well as the evaluative and internal accountability actors within the Bank. The interplay of each internal actor and policy change is articulated via Tables 8, 10, 12, 14, and 15.

To deepen policy change understanding, the second step is required. The bureaucratic politics approach asks scholars to consider less what the bureaucrat *ought to do* and instead, to focus on what bureaucrats *actually do*. This includes determining how decisions are made and who makes decisions. Bureaucratic politics explains "actions as the product of bargaining and compromise among the various organizational elements" (Frederickson and Smith 2003, 49). It is a "middle-range approach to the policy-making process" (T Hart 1998, 236) originally formulated in three models. The level of analysis changes with each model.

Model 1 considers government, or in our case, international organizations, as an entity acting with rational interests. Model 2 considers the organizations within government as having their own particularities and impacts. Model 3 considers the bureaucratic politics behind a particular decision output from government, a process Allison called "pulling and hauling" (Allison 1971; Caldwell 1977). Of the three models posited by Allison, Welch (1992) argued that Model 1 (unlike Models 2 and 3) was more likely to encourage "cumulation of theoretical interpretation" and the promotion of "analysis rather than concrete description" (Welch 1992, 115–116). That is, Model 1 is less about bureaucratic politics in the particular than about the bureaucratic politics of the organization.

Similarities between Model 2 and 3 led Allison and Halperin to combine them into one model of bureaucratic politics (Allison and Halperin 1972; Freedman 1976). Their combined model *captures policy shifts arising from internal bargaining and learning*. It highlights where power is held, which actor holds power, and how actors influence policy outputs (Bendor and Hammond 1992; Allison and Halpern 1972). It articulates how policies are altered through internal politicking, why bureaucratic politics explains policy change and organizational learning, whether policies resist external pressures, and when bureaucratic politics are a more potent explanation than others. This combined model is used in this book as a complement to stakeholder theory (see next section). This allows us to tease out when, where, and why internal stakeholders influenced the PSM/PSG agenda when compared to actors external to the Bank (see variables I11 and I12 in Tables 8, 10, 12, 14, and 15). A bureaucratic politics approach helps answer *who matters* at the Bank.

Given the difficulty of fully tracing each individual PSM staff member's influence and summarizing the careers of dozens if not hundreds of staff into Tables, internal actor Tables 8, 10, 12, 14, 15 are focused on the key policy-making entities within the Bank for this sector across 32 years even if, as each chapter illustrates, the importance of key individuals within each era may change. Both Models II and II along with Betton and Dess's (1985) contributions are evaluated in chapter-specific tables before being drawn together in Table 17 to consider testable propositions for future research. The propositions are a focus of the Conclusion.

Operationalization of the Bureaucratic Politics Approach

The public administration discipline suggests civil servants cannot (and perhaps, should not) separate policy and bureaucratic politics from administration (Waldo 1984 [1948]). Civil servants are political creatures. If our goal is to understand policy change, then we must understand the civil servants who shape policy. The difficulty of that task with suggesting causality is not new. Bureaucratic politics has been critiqued for its difficult operationalization (Michaud 2002).

This operationalization problem is partially resolvable by evaluating and tracing decision-making within a specific policy sector. Of course, by narrowing the topic to a sector instance (PSM and PSG) and a specific time period (1980 to 2012), a new criticism may arise: improved operationalization may still limit generalizability. Others might assert that the bureaucratic politics approach may become too event-centric. And yet, bureaucratic politics scholars must focus on particular events because "they are the occasions for choices that produce the decisions and actions that are to be explained. This choice-centrism, in turn, brings with it the assumption of rationality" (Weldes 1998, 222). One by-product of choice-centrism is that scholars may underestimate "an evolving stream of interactions" (Kuperman 2006, 537).

To overcome this concern, the book traces a "patterned and linked" mesohistory that avoids the "random clashes of fragmented, selfishly motivated actors" (Freedman 1976, 449) typical of single-focus event-centric bureaucratic politics research. If done well, we can understand a sector's policy history, follow its debates, and increase our understanding of sector policy change. In addition, this book's consideration of bureaucratic politics within a defined sector of Bank outputs and over a significant historical period lessens the "small-n" problem (Nielson and Tierney 2005). The 32-year sector history covered within this book increases the number of policy debate and policy change observations. By lengthening the historical period, reviewing related external and internal influences, reading key documents, interviewing forty-three Bank staff and another fourteen members of the NGO, think-tank, and IMF communities this book sheds light on how actors and events interacted to shift the Bank's PSM/PSG policies over time.

To operationalize bureaucratic politics approaches, scholars need variables. Unfortunately, data for such variables are frequently unavailable. We know that "reliance upon memoirs or interviews with participants of a historical event can be 'notoriously unreliable'" (Caldwell 1977, 100) and scholars "run the danger of imposing their theory on the data, rather than testing their theory on the basis of their data" (Caldwell 1977, 100). Although memoirs on their own need not be unreliable, case study validity increases when scholars triangulate interviewee comments with documents from inside and outside their studied organization. This book corroborates interviewee commentary via hundreds of reviewed Bank research papers, newspaper, and magazine articles along with scholar and NGO activist interpretations of Bank history. By letting interviewees and documents "speak", we can process which ideas were known when, who most influenced sector developments, and trace policy change.

Chains of evidence and pattern-matching link external actors with subsequent organizational change and learning. Even so, there is no simple way to measure this relationship or as Robert Yin wrote, "there are no fixed recipes for building or comparing explanations" (Yin 1981, 61). A potential solution is to create evidence chains that tentatively suggest research implications (O'Leary 1993, xii). Rosemary O'Leary (1993) borrowed Yin's (1981) concept of pattern-matching, which in its simplest form matches actions across organizational documents and time. For example, if the US wanted PSM projects to focus on privatization and if the US government has influence, then the Bank's response should be to increase the number of privatization projects. Chapters 3, 5–8 pay particular attention to the links between archival documents and within-sector topic diversification.

Introducing Stakeholder Theory

In 1978, Pfeffer and Salancik published a theory of external control of organizations. Critical of Katz and Kahn's (1966) open systems concept, Pfeffer and Salancik argued that "the coalition of interests participating in an organization at a point in time defines the activities of the organization" (Pfeffer and Salancik 1978, 26). Influence may be manifested in multiple ways. For example, the US may influence the World Bank through money (via financial contributions or guarantees), votes (whether it approves or disapproves a project), its encouragement of a particular candidate for World Bank President (an appointment traditionally influenced by the US), and policy rhetoric (statements from key US officials). Nonetheless, this external theory of organizations tells us little more than that external actors' matter. The *who matters* and why they matter is helped by specifications within stakeholder theory.

For this book, stakeholder theory is paired with the bureaucratic politics approach to become its analytical framework for analyzing sector policy change and answering the "who matters" questions. Stakeholder theory suggests that actors tend to "have in common a willingness and competency to act with an intent to influence the organization. In turn, the organization is aware of these groups and recognizes the need to deal with them" (Jonker and Foster 2002, 188). If we assume public administrators are not, and cannot be, apolitical creatures (e.g., Waldo (1984 [1948]), then we know that civil servants (as individuals or groups) are internal stakeholders with power to influence policy change. This book's use of bureaucratic politics to explain stakeholder power is neither accidental nor an exercise in semantics. If we desire an actor-centered theory of policy change, we need actors. The inevitability of social interaction (whether via politicking or not) makes both the actors and their acts worthy of study. As designed, the "bureaucratic politics" incompletely separates actors from the action. Actors, their acts, and the "politics" around those acts frame policy change.

Organizations are embedded within social systems (Stern and Barley 1996; Stinchcombe 1968; Berger and Luckmann1966). The World Bank is no different. The application of this organizational understanding (an understanding shared between public administration and analytical sociology in contrast to the constructivists' use of organizational sociology) the World Bank is more than a singular culture. It is a diverse social system of internal and external actors with differing opinions. Each may influence Bank policy outputs.

Stakeholder theory helps scholars to identify an organization's key actors by their possession or attributed possession of one or more attributes: "(1) the stakeholder's *power* to influence the firm (organization), (2) the *legitimacy* of the stakeholder's relationship with the firm (organization), and/or (3) the *urgency* of the stakeholder's claim on the firm" (Mitchell et al. 1997, 854, emphasis in the original). Others add criticality or "sense of being a significant, momentous, serious issue or even a 'defining moment'" as important (Jonker and Foster 2002, 5). Each is relayed via variables E1–E4 and variables I1–I4 in Tables 7–16 for each historical era. In this book, stakeholders help determine the effect of stakeholder interaction upon Bank policy shifts.

Identifying stakeholders is difficult as there can be "no single attribute" for their identification (Mitchell et al. 1997a). Stakeholders are identifiable by the "common sense" which is defined by an analytical construction and our institutions (Stinchcombe 1968, 41). Since one's "common sense" may not be another's, Bank and non-Bank interviewees narrowed my original stakeholder list[9] to the eight external

---

[9] Potential stakeholders were divided into three groups: boundary, external, and internal. *Interviewee comments and subsequent analysis retained <u>only</u> the italicized stakeholders for PSM/PSG*

actors, one boundary actor, and multiple internal actors specified in the following paragraphs.

Once identified, how are stakeholder influences discovered and understood? With specific reference to external actors, Pfeffer and Salancik (1978) noted that influence occurs when there is dependency between organizations and external actors. They identified three factors in resource dependency: "First, there is the importance of the resource, the extent to which the organization requires it for continued operation and survival. The second is the extent to which the interest group has discretion over the resource allocation and use. And, third, the extent to which there are few alternatives, or the extent of control over the resource by the interest group, is an important factor determining the dependence of the organization" (Pfeffer and Salancik 1978, 46–47). For example, if the World Bank is the "organization" and the US Government (as represented by the US Executive Director) is an "interest group", then we can analyze influence.

To increase specificity, Pfeffer and Salancik (1978) delineate ten conditions under which organizations comply with external actors. The more conditions that are met, the more likely an organization is controlled by an external actor. The ten conditions include:

(1) The focal organization is aware of the demands; (2) The focal organization obtains some resources from the social actor making the demands; (3) The resources is critical or important part of the focal organization's operation; (4) The social actor controls the allocation, access, or use of the resources; alternative sources for the resource are not available to the focal organization; (5) The focal organization does not control the allocation, access, or use of other resources critical to the social actor's operation and survival; (6) The actions or outputs of the focal organization are visible and can be assessed by the social actor to judge whether the actions comply with its demands; (7) The focal organization's satisfaction of the social actor's requests are not in conflict with the satisfaction of demands from other components of the environment with which it is interdepen-

---

sector policy change in this book. Other sectors and IOs may value different stakeholders. The only **boundary actor** with significant impact is the *Bank's President.* **External actors** had four groups. Group 1 (Bank): Board of Governors, Development Committee, *Executive Directors.* Group 2 (NGOs/Think-Tanks): American Enterprise Institute, *Bank Information Center,* Bretton Woods Project, Brookings Institution, Center for Global Development, Development GAP, *Fifty Years is Enough,* Government Accountability Project, Heritage Foundation, Institute for International Economics, *International Budget Partnership, Public Services International, Transparency International.* Group 3 (Associations/Other Organizations): Bretton Woods Committee, Corporations, Credit Rating Agencies, Institute for International Finance, *International Monetary Fund.* Group 4 (States/Coalitions): European Union, *G7 Group of Nations,* G20 Group of Nations, G77 Group of Nations, Low-Income Countries, Middle-Income Countries, *US Government,* United Nations; **Internal actors**: *Chief Economist, Country Directors (HQ),* Country Directors (in country), *Development Economics (DEC), Independent Evaluation Group (IEG), Inspection Panel, Institutional Integrity (INT),* NGO-World Bank Committee, *Quality Assurance Group (QAG), Results Secretariat, Sector Directors (HQ),* Sector Directors (in country), World Bank Institute.

dent; (8) The focal organization does not control the determination, formulation, or expression of the social actor's demands; (9) The focal organization is capable of developing actions or outcomes that will satisfy the external demands; and (10) The organization desires to survive.

(Pfeffer and Salancik 1978, 44)

In this case, the "focal organization" is the World Bank. The "social actor" could be the US or even an NGO. Each of the ten conditions for stakeholder control and influence is evaluated in concert with identified actors across time via variables E5–E14 within Tables 7, 9, 11, 13, and 16. Each actor can force the Bank into a partial dependency either politically or monetarily (US government or Executive Directors, G7/8, broadly considered), organizationally (IMF, World Bank President) or via social networks and public opinion (NGOs).

Identified External, Boundary, and Internal Actors

This section explains the external actors, boundary actor, and internal actors that were considered across 32 years of Bank PSM/PSG history.

External Actors—IMF, G7, NGOs, US Executive Director

The Bank has external actors with potential influence over the PSM/PSG agenda including the IMF, the G7/8 Group of Nations, NGOs, and the US Executive Director. The IMF is a partner Bretton Woods Institution to the World Bank but is not a member of the World Bank Group. The IMF has its own managing director (traditionally a European appointed by European governments) whereas the IBRD and IDA are two of the IOs within the World Bank Group (WBG) who share a President that by tradition is an American citizen with an appointment influenced by the US President (see also Appendix: How the World Bank Operates).

It is difficult to study the World Bank without understanding the IMF. Countries cannot become World Bank members without holding IMF membership. The IMF focuses on macroeconomic issues and the World Bank focuses on "softer" development issues such as health, environment, education, infrastructure, agriculture, among others. But this is not a hard rule. The two institutions share responsibility for several PSM/PSG subtopics including tax policies, customs policies, and statistical capacity development. Financial management and public expenditure management work are also undertaken in close cooperation. Complications arising from their shared PSM/PSG relationships are discussed in subsequent chapters.

The leaders of the G7 Group of Nations[10] representing Canada, France, Germany, Italy, Japan, Russia, United Kingdom, and the United States meet on annual basis. Event communiqués summarizing key discussions and decisions are released at the end of meetings. IMF and Bank representatives often attend. The G7 is an external actor because although the US is a powerful member of the Bank's Executive Directors as well as a G7 member, the G7's policies, approaches, and analyses are not exclusively driven by the United States.

Despite the 1981 creation of a long-defunct NGO–World Bank Committee, NGO influence on World Bank policies and projects did not gain momentum until the late 1980s (WB43, see also Chapter 9). NGO influence on the World Bank coincided with a late 1980s rise in NGO activism worldwide (Williams 1990; Salamon 1994; Matthews 1997). Early anti-Bank activism was frequently confined to environmental movements and was implicitly coordinated by NGOs such as the Bank Information Center. Many NGOs worried that structural adjustment was inherently discriminatory against the world's poor. As NGO activism increased, a plethora of smaller NGOs spread anti-Bank messages. Annual Bank/Fund meetings in the 1990s and early 2000s were often accompanied by thousands of protestors.

This book considers the NGO community in general and specifically to certain organizations. Focus is placed upon five NGOs: the Bank Information Center (BIC), the International Budget Partnership of the Center for Budget and Policy Priorities (IBP), Public Sector International (PSI), Transparency International (TI), and Fifty Years is Enough. In concert with interviewees, the NGO list was chosen based upon known advocacy vis-à-vis the Bank within PSM/PSG. Of the five, the BIC and Fifty Years focus exclusively upon Bretton Woods Institutions.

The US interactions with the World Bank are transmitted via the US Treasury Department to the US Executive Director who sits on the Bank's Board. There has been much written about US influence (in general) at the Bank (Fleck and Kilby 2006; Braaten 2014; Braaten et al. 2018; Morrison 2013; McKeown 2009; Ascher 2003) with most suggesting that the US has significant influence over Bank policies and projects. In contrast, there is limited research on specific Executive Director interactions with Bank policies (Nielson and Tierney 2003). This lack of research extends to scholarship on the UK Executive Director. While interviewees mentioned that the US and UK were powerful arbiters within the Bank's Board during the first years of this policy sector's emergence, this book suggests that specific to the PSM/PSG sector, US and UK influence was largely non-existent after 1991.

Although Executive Directors may represent one or more countries, their offices, salaries and budgets are provided by the Bank (George and Sabelli 1994). The US Executive Director is an exception whose salary is paid by the US Treasury

---

[10] Between 1997 and 2014, the G7 was the G8 with the addition of Russia.

(Irwin 1994). Interviewees frequently mentioned instances where non-G7 Executive Directors play important PSM/PSG roles but without access to detailed Board meeting minutes (beyond a sharing of meeting agendas after 2004), conclusions remain tentative.

Former Bank General Counsel, Ibrahim Shihata, observed a psychological impact ascribed to Executive Directors. If the Director tells the Bank "'You are great,' you [the Executive Director] will be not considered successful. That's the inevitable part, criticizing proposals, because that's the Executive Director's job. At least that's what they often see as their job. This tendency becomes more pronounced when you have big title, big office, and you are deprived of the day-to-day power to influence what's happening. As a result, the Executive Directors tend to be more aggressive in their intervention" (Shihata 1994). In contrast, one former Executive Director who represented Canada and twelve other nations found that other than Canada and Ireland, none of the other countries cared much about the Bank nor did they read what he sent them. Often his only contact was in the weeks before Annual Meetings to brief each country on issues to be discussed (Potter 1993).

This reality is not delinked from strategic reflections. Excluding perhaps the power and influence of the US Executive Director, most "rich country directors, mostly upper-middle ranking civil servants, know they have little to gain from confronting a Bank President who can get through on the telephone to their bosses, the finance ministers, at any time of the day or night. And poor-country directors hesitate to confront top management if they think it might jeopardize capital flows to their countries or compromise their comfortable compatriots inside the Bank" (George and Sabelli 1994, 217–218 citing *The Economist*).

Boundary Actor—The Bank's President

It has been suggested that the more control an external actor has over an organization, the less independence a boundary actor (e.g. World Bank President) has from external influence (Provan 1982). Although the President is the *de facto* appointee of the US and the US Executive Director retains the largest Board share, it is not always true that the Bank President is an American puppet. Despite having "considerable agenda-setting power" (Weaver and Leiteritz 2005, 375), the World Bank President can "referee" between external and internal forces (Gros and Prokopovych 2005, 51). Unfortunately, most Bank-focused scholarship has not exclusively focused upon Bank Presidents. Where the Bank President is discussed, the tendency is to describe rather than explain the President's behavior. Since 1980, President-level involvement within PSM/PSG has varied. There can be mixed reviews (1987 Reforms, Chapter 4), benefits (Wolfensohn, Chapters 6 and 7), and drawbacks (Wolfowitz, Chapter 8).

The Internal Actors: Units, Counsel, Evaluation

The units responsible for the Bank's PSM/PSG policies have shifted over time. From the early 1980s to the mid-1990s, PSM specialists worked in a short-lived Public Sector Management Unit (PSMU) in development economics, or where a regional Vice President had added a PSMU. After the 1996–1997 "matrix" organizational reform, a newly created "Public Sector Board" sat in another newly created Public Sector Anchor within a newly created Poverty Reduction and Economic Management (PREM) network. The mid-2000s also saw the construction of a "GAC Council" led by a Bank Managing Director with membership from each Bank Vice President to coordinate PSM/PSG across the Bank. The story of location is also a story of PSG/PSM sector importance from a limited locational space in the 1980s to being the only sector with a Bank-wide Council in 2012. The Units also include PSM/PSG country or regional specialists who work from in-country offices or from the headquarters.

In the first twenty years covered by this book, the Bank's General Counsel (Ibrahim Shihata) occupied an important intermediary role among evolving PSM and PSG debates and the Bank's Articles of Agreement. The General Counsel's involvement in this sector is not accidental. This is because PSM (and later, PSG) had the possibility of becoming too "political" and thus potentially violating Article 4, Section 10 of the Bank's Articles of Agreement.

Another group of internal actors are the Bank's Internal Evaluation Group (IEG), the Integrity Vice Presidency (INT), the Inspection Panel, and a now-defunct Quality Assurance Group (QAG) and Results Secretariat. Although evaluation activities interact with each decade of PSM/PSG history, this book will engage each actor in Chapter 9. Building upon Chapter 3 along with Chapters 5–8's historically driven storytelling, placing evaluative histories into a separate chapter allows the reader to use the Bank's established PSM/PSG history to reflect upon the (insufficient) efficacy of the Bank's evaluative mechanisms to encourage policy change within this sector.

Internal Actors: DEC and Bank Economists

The Development Economics (DEC) Vice Presidency strives to be the Bank's internal "think-tank". The Bank's Chief Economist is typically the Bank's intellectual leader. The importance of DEC and the Chief Economist to PSM/PSG policy has shifted over time. Just as in the past, DEC remains primarily staffed by economists. To the best of interviewee knowledge, no DEC staff had terminal disciplinary degrees in public administration, public management, or public policy. Nor does it appear that DEC retains much disciplinary input from political scientists (excluding political economists), anthropologists, or sociologists (WB11). In the late

1980s and early 1990s, DEC was home to the Bank's six or seven PSM staff, most held doctoral degrees in economics. Since the late 1990s, PSM/PSG staff were more likely to work within non-DEC units created post-mid-1990s or to retain their sector focus within a Bank region.

The economists' ascendancy to the top of the Bank's policy hierarchy began under World Bank President George Woods (1963–1968). In 1964, Woods hired Milton Freidman (future 1976 Nobel Laureate in Economics) as his Economic Advisor. Friedman encouraged the Bank to hire economists and worked to change Bank preferences from infrastructure projects (and its engineering personnel) toward policy-based economic development. He provided the "technical veneer" required to expand Bank projects beyond infrastructure development (Stein 2008, 13).

During McNamara's early years (1968 to 1981), the Bank continued to seek non-infrastructure development. He viewed economic growth as insufficient (on its own) to lift countries out of poverty. An operational result were requirements that project evaluations consider policy impacts on income distribution (Kaletsky 1982a). According to one former Bank regional vice president, McNamara's strategy divided staff. One group

> subscribed to the view that a development institution such as the World Bank had to explicitly promote the production of an access to at least five basic needs. The other group believed that such needs would be met more or less automatically with growth in gross domestic product that exceeded the rate of increase in population by a comfortable margin. Those of us who held the first position were supported by President McNamara and by some, though not all, operational vice presidents. Those who promoted the second view looked to Ernie Stern, who was at that time vice president of South Asia Region, for leadership. McNamara's departure in the summer of 1981, followed soon after by that of Mahbub al Haq [a prominent poverty-first advocate within the Bank], brought the basic needs project to an end.
>
> (Burki 2005, 126)

Often overlooked by critics of structural adjustment, the Bank internally debated this agenda throughout the 1980s despite economist ascendancy being secured in the last years of McNamara's presidency. By the early 1980s, the Bank only employed "10 or 15" non-economist social scientists on its staff and many Bank senior staff were former academic economists (Chenery 1983). Yet even among the economists, there were battles between the neoclassical economists and those such as Mahbub ul Haq and Hollis Chenery who held Keynesian perspectives. This debate is detailed in Chapter 3.

By the mid-2000s, eighty of eighty-three DEC researchers were economists (Rao and Woolcock 2007). By favoring the economics discipline, the Bank explicitly demotes other disciplines. Economist domination of the Bank's intellectual agenda after the early 1980s meant that "development policy at the Bank reflected the fads, fashions, controversies, and debates of one discipline" (Rao and Woolcock 2007, 480). Such knowledge networks may "absorb and potentially deflate critique" (Stone 2013, 258). Due to multigenerational recruitments of like-minded economists, there remain "high entry costs for other disciplines as competing disciplinary perspectives cannot enter without translation into economics which dilutes their clarity and effectiveness; this, in turn, reinforces the (often disdainful) economists views regarding the rigor and relevance of other disciplines, thereby creating a vicious circle" (Rao and Woolcock 2007, 480).

But Bank policies do change. Although critics allege the Bank retains a neoliberal bias, today's Bank PSM/PSG policies are substantially different from the early 1980s. That sector's policies are no longer dominated by privatization or cutting one's civil service even if a country's public sector wage bill remains a top Bank (and Fund) concern. This does not mean that the older prescriptions cannot be found—they can be—but as noted in subsequent chapters, sector policy advice variation and diversity increased over time.

Methodological Approach

This is a qualitative case study of 32 years of policy change within one sector of World Bank work. Process-tracing highlights the when, where, and why behind the Bank's evolving public sector governance policies. The process-tracing method explores "the processes that may have led to an outcome" and in doing so "helps narrow the list of potential causes" (George and Bennett 2005, 207). Process tracing is essential for a study covering three+ decades of sector history within the World Bank. This allows the placement of dozens of policy shifts, sector expansions, organizational structures, evaluative efforts, and internal organizational reforms into one analysis of when and why an actor mattered and from where policy power arose. Chapter-specific tables summarize this process by tracing output for boundary and external actors (see Tables 7, 9, 11, 13, and 16) and internal actors (see Tables 8, 10, 12, 14, and 15). Table components arise from stakeholder theory and the bureaucratic politics approach.

Process-tracing advantages for theory-building include an ability to create "numerous observations within a case". Each must

> be linked in particular ways to constitute an explanation of the case. It is the very lack of independence among these observations that makes them a powerful tool for inference. The fact that the intervening variables, if truly part of a causal process, should be connected in particular ways is what allows process-tracing to reduce the problem of indeterminacy (the problem often misidentified in case studies as the degrees of freedom problem).
>
> (George and Bennett 2005, 207)

The book's methodological heart is a detailed historical narrative with "an analytical causal explanation couched in explicit theoretical forms" (George and Bennett 2005, 211). Causal processes are not assumed to be linear. They may be path dependent or have interactive effects. Stakeholder power, legitimacy, urgency, and criticality as noted in Tables 7–16 vary over time.

Single case studies that use process-tracing create multiple observations within one subject. This allows the discovery of historical nuances, the identification of interrelationships among actors and the resulting theoretical implications. Theory development is hampered when there is "more than one hypothesized causal mechanism consistent with any given set of process-tracing evidence" (George and Bennett 2005, 222). Given author inability to be present during thirty-two years of policy debates, case study validity is increased through triangulation and a "rich, thick description" of available evidence (Creswell 2009, 191). Tables 7–16 are the "big picture" output from each chapter's "rich, thick description" in which key actors are found in the table columns and the theory or analytical constructs are the table rows. Table content is derived from triangulation. Triangulation helps scholars consider "different data sources of information by examining evidence from the sources and using it to build a coherent justification for themes" (Creswell 2009, 191).

Archival research was also utilized. But it has its critics. Scholars must not "attach particular significance to an item that supports their pre-existing or favored interpretation and, conversely, to downplay the significance of an item that challenges it" (George and Bennett 2005, 99). Researcher bias may create misleading or inaccurate interpretations of historical events. Researchers must consider when and why an archived report was released and to "consider *who* is speaking to *whom, for what purpose* and *under what circumstances*" (George and Bennett 2005, 99–100, emphasis in the original). To lessen any unintentional bias, triangulation was emphasized.

Prior scholarship on the Bank and the Bank's own publications helped create an initial list of questions for the 57 semi-structured interviews. Publications were read for content, for who within the Bank authored publications, and placement within evolving PSM/PSG topics across time. Table 2 lists the reviewed document categories and their available years. While Executive Director meeting minutes were made available after 2004, they had limited analytical values as they were little more than a meeting agenda. Popular press articles, think tank analyses, and scholarly research were also read to deepen analysis.

Bank organizational directories (no longer public after September 11th, 2001) provided important clues to staff movements and unit/office names in the first two decades of this sector's history. Also reviewed were transcripts of former Bank staff conducted by the Bank Historian. Although the Bank Archives list 160 Historian-conducted interviews, interviewees decide if their transcript should be public. Of sixty-five publicly available transcripts, twenty-six were relevant to this book.

Hundreds of Bank PSM/PSG publications were reviewed. The ability to publish research is an important, and perhaps more important task, than project work for staff careers (see Chapters 4 and 9). This research is used as another proxy for understanding policy change at the Bank. A selection of relevant Bank-published PSM/PSG research articles are discussed in Chapters 3, 6, 7, and 8 to highlight important PSM/PSG questions and to showcase how sector sub-topics changed over time. For example, in the 1980s, the Bank's earliest PSM policies had a structural adjustment focus. By the mid-1980s, sector topics included public enterprise reform and privatization. By the late 1980s, public expenditure management, financial management, and civil service reform were added. In the early 1990s, good governance, decentralization, tax reform, property rights, rule of law, and judicial reform became important components of PSM with PSG. From the mid-1990s and to 2012, anticorruption, accountability, pension reform, participatory objectives, and service delivery were added (see Table 5).

Case study limitations include selection bias, misidentification of scope conditions and necessity, insufficient degrees of freedom, lack of representativeness, single case research designs, and insufficient independence among cases (George and Bennett 2005, 22–34). Selection bias may occur when cases are self-selected or when the case is a "truncated sample along the dependent variable of the relevant population of cases" (George and Bennett 2005, 23). From among the listed sectors within the Bank's Project Database, PSM/PSG is the book's chosen sector. Importantly, and unlike others (Weaver 2007, 2008; Weaver and Leiteritz 2005, Weaver and Park 2007; Nielson and Tierney 2003, 2005; Nielson et al. 2006; Gutner 2005), my dependent variable was *not* truncated with a 1980 start-date.

To address degrees of freedom, George and Bennett (2005) noted that process-tracing creates multiple observations over time. The dependent variable (policy change within the Bank's PSM/PSG agenda) has significant variance and the historical period (32 years) avoids single observation issues. Since the lack of representativeness of one IO to other IOs or even other Bank sectors cannot be overcome in one book, any policy change conclusions remain tentative and contingent.

Fifty-seven interviews were conducted for this book (see Table 3).[11] Fourteen interviews were conducted with external actors like the IMF, NGOs, and think tanks. The remaining interviews were conducted with current or former Bank staff. Twenty-nine of the forty-three World Bank interviews had Bank-specific PSM/PSG experience gained in one or more of the following units: the original Public Sector Management Unit, Development Economics, World Bank Institute or its previous incarnation as the Economic Development Institute, Operations Evaluation Department or its successor, the Independent Evaluation Group, region-specific PSM/PSG positions, the Public Sector Board, the Public Sector Anchor, or the GAC Council.

---

[11] Interviews were not for attribution. Specific interviewee names are on file with the author and the publisher.

Several staff were interviewed specifically for their lead authorship or key involvement in the 1983 and 1997 *World Development Reports*. Others were selected given their involvement in key sector documents including *Managing Development: The Governance Dimension* (1991), *Beyond the Washington Consensus: Institutions Matter* (1998), the 2000/3 Public Sector Strategy, and/or the 2007/12 GAC Strategies. Only eleven Bank interviewees had no particular PSM/PSG experience. They were interviewed for their experience with Institutional Integrity, the Inspection Panel, the Results Secretariat, or other relevant units. Five were chosen for their long-term service to the Bank. Four of those five had served at the Bank for 30+ years and a fifth had 20+ years. Such interviewees helped answer questions about Bank operations, internal reform efforts, and the roles of the President and Executive Directors over time.

Interview profile diversity reflected the Bank's worldwide focus. Interviewees came from at least a dozen countries including but not limited to Australia, Canada, China, Colombia, Egypt, Finland, Germany, India, Israel, the Netherlands, Nigeria, Pakistan, United Kingdom, and United States. The majority of interviewees held a PhD and had an average length of Bank service of greater than twelve years. This diversity did not extend to gender: three of fourteen non-Bank interviewees and eight of forty-three Bank interviewees were women. Table 3 lists the interviewee number, organization, and category. Interviews were not for attribution. The list of interviewee names has been passed to the publisher.

Outside an initial set of structured questions, most questions were contextualized to the specific NGO or think tank, Bank Unit, or Bank publication under discussion. Although it has been argued that closed-ended questionnaires are best for improving reliability in case study formats (Yin and Heald 1975), the number of external and internal actors and the historical coverage prohibited such a choice. Questions aimed to understand interviewee involvements along with their impressions of other actor roles and influence. If policy conflicts were raised, interviewees were asked to name interested actors, state the problem, identify the sides, discuss the solution, and explain long-term consequences.

I also benefited from a one-week course titled, "Introduction to Bank Operations". Course leaders indicated that I was the first non-banker allowed to enroll. My fellow students were new Bank staff. The course shaped my early understanding of the Bank's structures and operations via Bank leadership, hierarchy, project cycle, and history. The course also taught "*Bankease*" or "*Bankspeak*" a Bank-specific "language" relevant to its operations and policies (Moretti and Pestre 2015).[12] Mastering the lingo was crucial to increasing credibility with interviewees and to navigating information relevancy.

The result is five chapters (Chapters 3, 5–8) that detail PSM/PSG policy change across 32 years of Bank history with a chapter (Chapter 4) discussing its largest

---

[12] See also the Bank's "Historical Dictionary" (Tenney and Salda 2013).

organizational reform across the 32 years (1987 reforms) and its PSM/PSG impact as well as a non-public report (1992 Wapenhans Report) on organizational incentives. Both provide context to the historical chapters but are too important to simply slot into a historically driven chapter. Chapter 9 engages other actors with potential influence including NGOs as well as the Bank's evaluative, integrity, and results-focused efforts.

Policy Change: My Model versus Other Theories

This book employs an actor-driven lens to explore PSM/PSG policy change across 32 years of Bank history. It determines who matters within this policy sector and how policy changed (see Table 4). By using stakeholder theory and the bureaucratic politics approach, we can showcase when and where identified actors had influence over policy change. Yet, and in a 2009 Special Issue on Policy Change within the *Journal of Comparative Policy Analysis*, contributors reflected on policy change scholarship and its challenges. Challenges included questions about whether the organizational structures or its agents influence policy change, the influence of endogenous or exogenous variable choices, if change is revolutionary or evolutionary, if dependent variables should be outputs or processes, and benefits of policy change studies that are not ahistorical (Capano and Howlett 2009). This book's approach answers many of those challenges:

> *Agents versus Structure*: This book's emphasis on agents (stakeholders, both internal and external) as policy change leaders does not imply that structure is undiscussed. Chapter 4's discussion of the Bank's 1987 structural reform and still-unresolved debates posited within the 1992 Wapenhans Report address structural concerns. Burying Chapter 4's observations within strict historical timelines would limit the "pause" required to consider any impact on subsequent policy changes. As noted in the chapters, multiple mini-shifts in organizational structure would become intervening variables within chapter timelines.
>
> *History and Exogenous/Endogenous Choices*: This book's 32-year history of PSM/PSG change provides encouragement for the historical approaches needed within policy change studies. This study's mesohistorical time period allows readers to observe when and where each variable had influence (Raynor 2009). By engaging archive- and interview-driven methodological approaches, predictions of endogenous- or exogenous-driven variables are not imposed within research designs (e.g. Howlett and Cashore 2009) but instead, articulate themselves across the historical period. This allows one of this book's most important observations to arise: the power of external stakeholders over the Bank's earliest years of PSM/PSG (1980 to 1991) is

significant. In contrast, after 1991 and until our 2012 end-date, international civil servants drove this sector policy agenda.

Dependent Variable as Outputs or Processes: The dependent variable in this book is policy change within one sector of the Bank's work (PSM/PSG) from agenda start (1980) to agenda amplification as the first-ever Bank sector to be labelled as crucial for *all* Bank sectors (2012). This dependent variable choice limits typical dependent variable biases within policy change scholarship while encouraging an output-focused agenda. This addition is not unimportant. The timeline of many international relations scholars' studies of the Bank's PSG history (it is infrequently PSM and PSG) does not begin until the mid-1990s (Weaver 2007, 2008; Weaver and Leiteritz 2005; Weaver and Park 2007; Nielson and Tierney 2003, 2005; Nielson et al. 2006; Gutner 2005). This is fifteen years after the sector agenda had begun.

By the mid-1990s, the Bank's internal structure (see Chapter 5) had already modified itself to respond to the Bank's new perspective that the state mattered. *By limiting the dependent variable, the deviance identified by constructivist scholars may not be deviance at all.* The chosen stakeholder theory and bureaucratic politics approach further emphasizes that output. That is, at points in this book, the reader will observe the march of sector policy change via increased Bank interest in this sector but also via stakeholder interactions, new debates, and world events. Process-specific change is also observed at multiple points whether it is lack of attention paid to of non-headquarter offices (see Chapter 3), how Bank Strategy documents and *World Development Reports* are created (see Chapters 3, 5–8), or how evaluations (insufficiently) influence policy change (see Chapter 9).

This book's theory and approach are not the only options available to explain more than three decades of Bank sector policy change. While limited space prevents full conversations, this section briefly explains seven other options which were considered. The discussion starts with the most frequently asked "why did you not use" questions about the advocacy coalition framework and principal–agent theory. Each is discussed before briefly commenting on five other potential alternatives to this book's analytical framework.

The advocacy coalition framework (ACF) is a system-focused model that incorporates identified sub-systems inside and outside the analyzed organization to understand policy change (Sabatier 1988; Sabatier and Jenkins-Smith 1999). ACF assumes individuals have Herbert Simon's understanding of bounded rationality (Simon 1956). A frequent ACF research desire seeks to explain policy change across a significant period (Sabatier 1988) and as such, appears to match this book's research questions. Crucially however, ACF "identifies beliefs as the casual driver for political behaviour" (Weible et al. 2009, 122) and thus, views four paths to policy change: external events; policy learning; internal events; and negotiated agreements. Again, and at first glance, each ACF path appears relevant to this book. However, there are two challenges to ACF utilization in this book. Each challenge led to its exclusion.

The first is that measuring "beliefs" across time is relatively difficult in meso-historical studies. This is compounded by the challenge of each ACF scholar using a "slightly different set of indicators to measure" beliefs (Ripberger et al. 2014, 510). In contrast, it is relatively straightforward to methodologically defend this book's choice of stakeholders. It is also not difficult to counteract any concern about actor-centred bureaucratic politics approaches through sector foci by employing sufficiently long timelines to create enough "n" observations necessary for analytical insights. If ACF's mechanism to understand policy change is difficult-to-measure beliefs, this book's mechanism is the easier-to-measure bureaucratic politics of identified stakeholders.

The second challenge is that most ACF studies focus on states. This reflects its original intention (e.g. Sabatier 1987). Even where IO-related ACF studies are published, they differ from this book's purpose. For example, ACF has been used to explain change within the Common Agricultural Policy (Nedergaard 2008). However, this use of ACF drew less from Simon's bounded rationality considerations than its opposite: rational choice theory. This is not unimportant. Such a choice runs counter to this book's bureaucratic politics approach as well as relations between bureaucratic politics and Simon's view of bounded civil servants. Others have used ACF to explain shifting coalitions among states and IOs in the internationalization of anti-smoking and alcohol policies (Princen 2007). While this ACF use is appropriate, it cannot undertake the contextual inside-the-IO explanations for policy change that this book accomplishes. It is the unboxing of the IO's black box via actor-driven approaches to explain policy change across 32 years of sector policy that differentiates this book.

Principal–agent theory is often used by international relations scholars to explain IO behavior. The number of scholars who have used this theory to explain IO behavior is too many to list here (e.g., Delreux and Adriaensen 2017; Vaubel 2006; Vaubel et al. 2007; Graham 2014; Hanreider 2014; Johnson 2014; Lyne et al. 2006; Nielson and Tierney 2003). Principal–agent theory suggests that the interaction between principals and agents is not only clearly identifiable but the influence of such bilateral interactions can be articulated. From a public administration perspective, two problems arise. Each led to its exclusion from this book.

The first is that principal–agent theory like its rational choice institutionalism cousin, overlooks Simon's argument about rationality's limits. The theory's unit of analysis deemphasizes the individuality and nuance of daily interaction within bureaucracies. This hampers its ability to conceptualize multiple actors and their interactions as well as to capture interactions across mesohistorical timelines. The second risk is principal–agency theorists' acknowledgment that "unilateral influence" in IOs is a likely a simplification (Hanreider 2014). This book's chapters repeatedly highlight that risk. While principal–agent scholarship could emphasize reform coalitions as actors encouraging IO change, this suggestion also leaves the theory open to the ACF challenges articulated above.

A potential exception is a recent study of the World Health Organization (Graham 2014). The author acknowledges that fragmentation by internal WHO agents poses challenges for the WHO's member states or principals. This is an explicit statement that pluralities of actions within IOs are worthy of study. Like this book, the author's timeline is long (twenty-five years) but her study also differs from this book. While she does not focus on just one sector of WHO's work (such as this book's focus on PSM/PSG), she does marry many characteristics of principal–agent theory with additional insights common to the public administration discipline but without acknowledging that such insights are found within decades of research within the public administration discipline. It is hard to conclusively know why the discipline is overlooked. Based on anecdotal conversations, reasons may include international relations' belief that principal–agent theory *is* what public administration scholars use (nearly all within public administration do not use it), that public administration studies only matter for domestic bureaucracies (IPA scholarship disproves that point), and that Weber's writings are a touchstone (for many within public administration, they are not).

Another five approaches with potential merit include policy entrepreneurship, incrementalism, punctuated-equilibrium theory, path dependency, and institutional isomorphism. Policy entrepreneurs encourage policy change in ways that may challenge the status quo (Mintrom and Norman 2009; Jones et al. 2016). Entrepreneurs are identified as individuals although groups of individuals may qualify. Throughout this book, readers will find instances of policy entrepreneurship even if that concept, as noted below, was purposefully not used as a book anchor. The discovery of policy entrepreneurs within the Bank (in general, see Park and Vetterlein 2010; Chwieroth 2008) and its PSM/PSG agenda (this book) replicates other IO studies employing policy entrepreneurship. This includes studies on the failure to create the International Trade Organization (Trofimov 2012), the UN's response to HIV-AIDS (Nay 2012), the influence of the Global Commission on Drug Policy (Alimi 2015) or even World Bank pension privatization reforms over twenty-five years (Béland and Orenstein 2013).

Using just one chapter of this book as an example, readers will discover that Chapter 3 notes at least four moments of potential policy entrepreneurialism: the arrival of President Reagan's preferred Bank Chief Economist, the 1985 Indonesia Report on institutional development, related efforts by staff such as Arturo Israel, and efforts by Kim Jaycox to raise the sector profile. Given an IO's "expert-dominated environment ... policy entrepreneurs have the ability to have a strong impact" (Béland and Orenstein 2013, 134), such Chapter 3 findings are not surprising. Similar examples are peppered throughout the book. This includes Chapter 7's discussion of which civil servants sat on which side of the debate about supply side versus demand side governance (for a partial discussion of the demand side debate, see Yanguas and Hulme 2015).

However, and as argued by two policy entrepreneur scholars, "we should not assume that policy change is always and everywhere driven by entrepreneurship" (Mintrom and Norman 2009, 650). Finding potential policy entrepreneurship does not mean that thirty-two years of sector policy change was exclusively led by entrepreneurial actors. Actors need not be "entrepreneurs" to encourage policy change. This concern is particularly relevant in mesohistorical timelines where individuals or small groups do not continually upset the status quo and/or are wholly responsible for significant policy change across such timelines (Bakir 2009).

In contrast to policy entrepreneurs, incrementalism is an output of indecision, posturing, or risk avoidance (Mintrom and Norman 2009). Scholars employ incrementalism to study precise moments of policy change (DeFrancesco and Guashino 2020). At many points throughout this book, readers will observe incremental policy change. At other points, policy change is fast and dramatic. Notable examples of the latter include the 1987 internal reform (Chapter 4) and President Wolfowitz's interaction with the Board on the Governance and Anti-Corruption Strategy (Chapter 8). Even if a reader quibbles with this book's positing that each event suggests antecedents and thus, shorter timelines conducive to incremental approaches, questions about dependent variable bias re-emerge. This bias is carefully countered with this book's purposefully mesohistorical timeline, its non-limitation of the dependent variable, and its detailing of incremental and not-so-incremental policy change within the Bank's PSG/PSM agenda.

Crisis moments create space for another approach: punctuated-equilibrium theory. This theory observes the power of crises (threats to Bank staff and the Board via Wolfowitz' actions in Chapter 8 or the 1987 reforms in Chapter 4) to create momentum for policy and institutional change. One part of this theory explores how ideas influence institutional change (Bakir 2009). This may be articulated via sovereign-level shifts (e.g. Kingdon 2003) or the mesohistorical analyses within this book. However, this book's framework allows scholars to view the Bank not just as moments of one or more crises (Bakir 2009) but, instead, also allows for explanations of when non-crisis events may also encourage policy change. This creates space to view the far more frequent and often quieter non-crisis moments of deliberation and politicking among involved policy actors.

In his seminal 1990 book on *organizational* change within IOs, Ernst Haas labelled change as occurring via incremental growth or turbulent non-growth (Haas 1991). Like my book on *policy* change, Haas (1991) observed that regardless of the speed of change, IOs do adapt and learn. This observation creates space to drill into the Bank, to open its black box, and to learn how stakeholders encouraged sector policy change, sometimes pushed back against change, and throughout the 32 years under study, adapted and modified the Bank's PSM/PSG agenda.

With Haas (1991) in mind, it is arguable that a sixth option, path dependency theory, is relevant to placing crisis within its historical context and also for explaining how an organization's quiet moments may institutionalize paths of dependency. This theory's use in explaining policy change within an IO has to-date been limited (e.g. Hanreider 2015) but its interaction with historical-institutionalism has similarities to this book. If this book were situated within comparative politics discipline instead of (international) public administration or if a book goal were not to converse about bureaucratic actors vis-a-vis international relations' constructivism, path dependency, and historical institutionalism (for a partial historical institutionalism focus, see Weaver and Moschella 2017), this theory may lead to other interesting work.

Bearing similarities to path dependency and historical institutionalism is institutional isomorphism. Path dependency and institutional isomorphism acknowledge "structural resilience" (Hanreider 2015, 216) and how structures influence policy outputs years later (Frumkin and Galaskiewiez 2004; Andrews 2014; Tao 2019; Guler et al. 2002; Larmour 2011). Related isomorphism approaches question why institutional change may appear slowly (coercive isomorphism), explore network cohesion or viewpoint similarities among actors (cohesive isomorphism), and how staff training (or normative isomorphism) teaches an organization's values but cements the difficulty of change. If an isomorphism study were undertaken, authors might not focus on local shifts but broader socio-cultural and institutional shifts (Dacin 1997). However, a discussion of the Bank's historical evolution and its placement vis-à-vis other IOs, may be best left to others (e.g. Woods 2003; Stone and Moloney 2019c; Joshi and O'Dell 2013; Volkmer 2019; Tallberg et al. 2013). Explaining which actors matter across thirty-two years of Bank PSM/PSG history using stakeholder theory and bureaucratic politics is more than enough for one book.

Conclusion and Next Steps

The Bank is a complex organization. Explaining how its PSM/PSG policies changed over time is as multifaceted as the Bank's organization. The following chapters focus on key debates, how debates shaped PSM/PSG policies, and where external and internal actors fit within each debate. How debates were resolved, who matters and why, and the implications for subsequent periods are discussed. One generation's "answer" to PSM/PSG was modified by the next. Table 4 summarizes the "who matters most" by actor and by era while Table 5 summarizes the evolution and expansion of sector-specific PSM/PSG topics across the surveyed 32 years. Five of the next eight chapters are ordered by time period and with key policy turning points:

- January 1980 to October 1989 (Chapter 3): Creation of the World Bank's first Public Sector Management Unit in 1983 and publication of the 1983 World Development Report (WDR): *Management in Development*

- November 1989 to September 1996 (Chapter 5): Cold War end with new Bank involvement in Russia along with Central and Eastern Europe, publication of the Washington Consensus, and a Bank inkling that public sector institutions mattered more than the Bank had previously considered even if privatization and neoliberalism still mattered more
- October 1996 to December 1999 (Chapter 6) and January 2000 to December 2003 (Chapter 7): The Bank confirmed that corruption cannot be ignored and the state mattered to development. This about-face from earlier 1980s thinking was further institutionalized via its 1997 *World Development Report* and the Bank's first Public Sector Strategy in 2000 and
- January 2004 to June 2012 (Chapter 8): President Paul Wolfowitz's PSG re-considerations (and by extension, PSM) were published as the Bank's 2007 Governance and Anticorruption (GAC) Strategy. The decision in 2007 and 2008 to further elevate this sector into the Bank's first-ever GAC Council and a concurrent decision that GAC would be incorporated into every sector, country, and operational unit meant that unlike the early 1980s where this sector for attention, by 2012 the opposite was in place: PSG (and PSM) had become the Bank's "DNA" (World Bank 2012a 53, 62).

In contrast, Chapters 4 and 9 step back from historical shifts to review *the* key organizational reform across the 32 years (1987 Reform) and a subsequent report (Wapenhans Report) on the Bank's internal incentives (Chapter 4) as well as relative non-influence of external NGOs and internal evaluative actors on sector policy change (Chapter 9). The decision to separate from the historical chapters may be unusual but each are defended. In short, the 1987 organizational reform set up the next 25 years of PSM/PSG sector growth, its deepening, and its institutionalization. It cannot be treated as an add-on to the chapter which precedes or follows it. Similarly, burying the 1992 Wapenhans Report in another chapter might have diminished the lessons that it seeks to impart. Each lesson helps understand the historical chapters that follow. The decision to separate NGOs and the internal evaluative actors (Chapter 9) from the historical chapters was done to highlight their relative non-importance for the PSM/PSG sector. With the exclusion of Transparency International, all profiled NGOs and internal evaluative actors had limited influence over policy change in this sector.

The Conclusion reviews the book's analytical framework, makes several overarching observations about the 32 years of PSM/PSG history, and uses the book's analytical framework (Tables 7–16) to link to thirteen propositions of IO policy change (Table 17). Each proposition is drawn from this book's mesohistorical study of policy change within the Bank's PSM/PSG sector. Each proposition is an opportunity for future sector, IO, or comparative IO research.

3

Minimize the State, Free the Market
(January 1980 to October 1989)

By 1980, many developing countries were increasingly unable to debt finance their budgets and/or pay accumulating arrears to the international financial community. This chapter details how the international economic environment when combined with external actor pressures, forced the Bank to modify its lending and sector-specific responses. The Bank's lending response (in conjunction with the IMF) was structural adjustment (Wright 1980). Structural adjustment was a policy-based lending instrument informed by neoclassical economics (popularly termed "neoliberalism") in which state influence over the market was to be minimized, the state itself is to be small, and an export-oriented approach was encouraged. Bank prescriptions included reducing public sector wage bills, balancing budgets, repaying debts, and beginning in the mid-1980s, privatizing state-owned enterprises. The expected outcome was economic growth and, by extension, poverty reduction: the rising tide of growth was expected to lift all boats.

There are innumerable articles and books on the 1980s Bank (from among the many, see Bradshaw and Huang 1991; Hammond and McGowan 1992; Fischer 1995; Easterly 2003; Abouharb and Cingranelli 2008; Rodrik 1990; Biersteker 1990; Murray 1983). However, if the story of the 1980s Bank was that simple, then this chapter would end here. *But it was not that simple.* Nor, as importantly, do analyses of the 1980s discuss how bureaucratic battles *within the Bank* not only determined who mattered in this sector's agenda from 1980 to 1991 but also who mattered in the years after 1991. *While external actors like the US, the UK, the IMF, and the G7 may have mattered most prior to 1991, their influence over subsequent PSM/PSG policy shifts and topic expansions was largely minimal after 1991 (see Table 4[1]).*

In the 1980s Bank, there was not yet any discussion of public sector governance (PSG). The term "good governance" was not introduced until August 1991. As such, this chapter focuses on the two major PSM policy battles in the 1980s Bank. As noted in Chapter 2, the battles, events, markers of change, and the actors who mattered were obtained via interviewees, document analysis, and process-tracing.

---

[1] All tables referenced in this book may be found in the Appendix.

Who Matters at the World Bank? Kim Moloney, Oxford University Press.
© Kim Moloney (2022). DOI: 10.1093/oso/9780192857729.003.0003

For the 1980s era, the two PSM-specific policy battles were over ideology and approach.

The first was ideological. Should client states retain their state-owned enterprises (and just manage them better) or were smaller state sectors more appropriate? The latter perspective won that battle. Its proponents included the Bank's US and UK Executive Directors, the other G7 nations, the IMF, and top Bank leaders. Its rise was assisted in 1982 by the retirement of two senior Bank staff economists (Mahbub ul Haq and Hollis Chenery) and the hiring of a neo-classical economist (Anne Krueger) as Bank Chief Economist. The second debate was over approach: should client states focus on macroeconomic and "structural adjustment" or on institutional development reforms? The Chapter 3 "winner" was the former but, as noted in Chapter 5, the non-disappearance of the latter re-emerged in a new form after 1989. The non-disappearance of institutional de-velopment as a PSM policy option was assisted by key individuals and key internal events that laid the groundwork for PSM to add PSG in the early 1990s.

This chapter, along with the November 1989 to August 1991 portion of Chapter 5, are the only moments across 32 years of Bank PSM/PSG sector policy history in which the Bank's key external actors (in particular, the US and UK) drove this sector's policy agenda. As noted in Chapter 9, NGOs in the 1980s did not interact with this sector's policies and it would only be in the very late 1980s that their voice against the Bank in general (not specific to PSM) was mobilized. With the publication of *Managing Development: Governance Dimension* in August 1991, it would be the Bank's international civil servants (and not the US/UK/G7 or IMF or NGOs) who led future PSM and PSG sector policy shifts. This chapter ends its analysis just weeks before the fall of the Berlin Wall in November 1989. As noted in Chapter 5, this external event along with ongoing internal sector pol-icy debates among Bank staff, necessitated a chapter break. The implications for sector-specific policy change within IOs are revisited in the concluding chapter.

Before the Bank was "Neoliberal": Poverty and the ul Haq Memo

In the late 1940s and 1950s, Bank loans focused on post-WWII reconstruction, a mission fitting to the Bank's first name: International Bank for Reconstruction and Development (IBRD). From the 1950s to the mid-1970s, Bank staff were largely engineers who focused on the hardware of development: bridges, roads, dams, and electricity generation (WB25, WB38). Later, as countries successfully achieved independence, the development part of the IBRD name was institu-tionalized by creating the International Development Association (IDA) within the World Bank Group in 1960. IDA focuses on low-income countries; IBRD prioritizes middle-income countries (see Appendix).

When Robert McNamara became Bank President in 1968, he wanted the Bank to think beyond development and economic growth. In other words, poverty reduction also mattered. In his 1971 speech before the IMF/Bank Annual Meetings, McNamara argued that "adequate nutrition, the availability of employment, a more equitable distribution of income, and an improvement in the quality of life are the goals the more than two billion people of the developing world are seeking … unless we deal with these fundamental issues, development will fail" (World Bank 2009d).

McNamara viewed economic growth as insufficient (on its own) to lift countries out of poverty. An operational result was a requirement that project evaluations consider policy impacts on income distribution (Kaletsky 1982a). According to a former Bank regional vice president, McNamara's strategy divided staff. One group

> subscribed to the view that a development institution such as the World Bank had to explicitly promote the production of an access to at least five basic needs. The other group believed that such needs would be met more or less automatically with growth in gross domestic product that exceeded the rate of increase in population by a comfortable margin. Those of us who held the first position were supported by President McNamara and by some, though not all, operational vice presidents. Those who promoted the second view looked to Ernie Stern, who was at that time vice president of South Asia Region, for leadership. McNamara's departure in the summer of 1981, followed soon after by that of Mahbub ul Haq [a prominent poverty-first advocate within the Bank], brought the basic needs project to an end.
>
> (Burki 2005, 126)

This division is reflected in the Bank's approved projects between 1947 and 1979 (see Table 6). In the 1940s and 1950s Bank (before IDA creation), the IBRD largely lent to countries which are considered high-income today. Projects largely focused on infrastructure investment. This choice reflected not only the staff complement at the Bank but also a prevailing perspective that modernization simply required a rapid investment in the infrastructure that fuels economic progress. This was notable in the work of W.W. Rostow (Rostow 1959, 1960) as well as after-the-fact Bank-written analyses such as *Patterns of Development, 1950 –1983* (Syrquin and Chenery 1989).

Between 1955 and 1969, the top three prescribed sectors of Bank projects were infrastructure-related. This includes transportation, railways, highways, electric, hydro, irrigation/drainage, and telecommunications (see Table 6). However, and within two years of McNamara's arrival, agricultural adjustment would become the third-most prescribed sector of projects after highways and financial sector development. Between 1975 and 1979, nearly 10 percent of Bank projects involved an agricultural component. Absent throughout the first thirty-two years of Bank history (1947–1979) is discussion of what would become PSM in 1983 and later, PSM and PSG in 1991. As noted later in this chapter, the Bank's first PSM project was not until 1968 with PSM projects never encompassing more than 2.6 percent of approved projects in any one year between 1968 and 1979 (see Table 1).

At a 1981 UN conference, McNamara observed economic growth alone may not ensure poverty alleviation (McNamara 1981). Assisting McNamara was the Bank's Vice President for Development Policy, Hollis Chenery, who had authored *Redistribution with Growth* in 1974 (Chenery 1974, 1980). Chenery argued that reducing poverty and not just economic growth mattered for socioeconomic development. By 1977, the Bank added "what governments are doing on income distribution" as an important loan consideration (Pace 1994).

Often overlooked by structural adjustment critics is that the Bank internally debated this agenda throughout the 1980s despite economist ascendancy in the last years of McNamara's presidency. By the early 1980s, the Bank only employed "10 or 15" non-economist social scientists on its staff and many Bank senior staff were former academic economists (Chenery 1983). Yet even among the economists, there were debates between the neoclassical economists and those such as al Haq and Chenery who held Keynesian perspectives. It is to this debate which this chapter now turns.

The earliest publicly available PSM publication is a 1980 internal Development Economics Vice Presidency (DEC) memorandum. DEC is the intellectual heart of the World Bank. It is headed by the Bank's Chief Economist and since the early 1980s, most of its staff have held PhD's in Economics. The memo wished to "establish the case for a differentiated approach," whereby public enterprises are considered individually rather than "*en masse*" (ul Haq 1980, ii). The memo's author was Mahbub ul Haq. Like Chenery, he advocated a poverty-first Bank mission (Burki and Haq 1981; Haq 1980a, 1980b).

Ul Haq observed that prior to 1980 the Bank produced two types of public enterprise reports. The first focused on market solutions along with "pricing and investment behavior" and the second on "the distribution of authority within the organizational structure" (ul Haq 1980, 2). He worried that the Bank was biased toward reporting the "more pathological cases" (ul Haq 1980, 4). In twenty Bank post-project appraisals, just three considered a context-dependent government–public enterprise relationship (ul Haq 1980, 25). The majority "glossed over" or "neglected" "industry-specific solutions … [and] the problems of organization and decision-making *within* public manufacturing enterprises" (ul Haq 1980, 28, emphasis in the original). Ul Haq worried that Bank methods prohibited appropriate understandings of state-owned enterprises (SOE). This concern was one seed of the intellectual debate within the Bank against structural adjustment approaches. Questions included whether the Bank should subscribe to theoretically attractive and short-term policy shifts under structural adjustment lending or longer-term, messier, harder-to-measure case-by-case SOE analyses and later, the institutional development of the state. (WB6)

In a prescient manner and echoing a criticism that plagued the Bank during the 32 years covered by this book, ul Haq wrote that the Bank confused "allocative efficiency" (pricing and investment policies) with "managerial efficiency" (incentives within enterprises to improve performance) and failed to consider an enterprise's "social objectives." For many bankers, allocative and managerial efficiency were the same. Moreover, the Bank argued that SOE social objectives are "inappropriate" considerations since social objectives were de facto political. Political objectives were not the Bank's concern. Political objectives were client government responsibilities (ul Haq 1980, 6–8).

This concern about "politics" had a legal backing and like discussions over efficiency's (non-) importance to sector lending, debates continue today. Article 4, Section 10 of the Bank's Articles of Agreement prohibits its political interference in member states. As this sector's agenda ultimately deepened and expanded between 1980 and 2012, internal critics, developing country states, and the Bank's General Counsel would frequently use Bank Articles to explain why the Bank cannot modify this sector's policy direction. PSM and later, PSG were viewed as interfering in member-state political affairs. However, and whether the decision was to allow structural adjustment lending in 1980, strengthen privatization emphases in the mid-1980s, add "good governance" to the agenda in 1991, include anticorruption emphases in 1996, and/or utilize "political economy" in the 2000s, critics initially claimed that new PSM/PSG sector policy shift violated the Bank's Articles. In each case, and only after significant internal debate (see also Chapters 5–8), did sector policies shift, expand, and deepen not via Articles modification but through reinterpretations of the Articles' intent.

Shortly after Bank President, Alden W. Clausen, arrived in 1981, he convened an in-house task force on poverty. The task force was led by Hollis Chenery and assisted by ul Haq. Report writers worried that the Bank's "current concern with energy and structural adjustment, combined with the transition to a new chief executive, make many staff members question the Bank's commitment to this [poverty] objective" (Kraske et al. 1996, 225; quoting the Task Force Report). Even though Clausen noted in his 1982 Annual Address that a "key and central aim of the World Bank is the alleviation of poverty" (Kraske et al. 1996, 225; quoting Clausen's speech), the task force concluded that poverty was not a top concern and even under McNamara, poverty reduction "was never the policy of the Bank" (ul Haq 1982).

Moreover, and despite a 1975 Bank report encouraging redistributive mechanisms in agriculture, "Bank projects lacked the institutional capacity to assist the poorest, even if they had wanted to do so" (Williams 1983, 194). This observation about institutional development along with questions about what is or is not political interference were more seeds from which internal dissent over "neoliberal"

PSM agendas would grow. With Chenery and ul Haq's departure in 1982, intellectual momentum behind a nascent poverty-first focus was lost. It is possible that the timing of their departure was coincidental or perhaps, it reflected a new momentum toward neoclassical economic perspectives. Also ongoing were international economic and political crises whose unraveling would force the Bank's hand and ultimately, its 1980s PSM policy outputs. It is to these events that our chapter now turns.

International Economic Crises Shape US and UK Reaction

The 1970s were roller-coaster years for the international economy. The Organization of the Petroleum Exporting Countries (OPEC) used its near monopoly on oil production to raise prices, lower production, and transform member-state poverty into a different future.[2] This decision had numerous impacts. Higher oil prices meant that countries had to pay more for oil. Developing countries were least able to afford (and to pass on) price increases. To make ends meet, they turned to international commercial banks for loans. Commercial banks lent "petrodollars" to clients, including developing nations. Many poor nations agreed to loans with variable interest rates tied to the US Federal Reserve rate. A 1986 article in *Washington Quarterly* magazine nicely summarized this history:

> Not for a century or more had private banks financed the external requirements of sovereign nations to such a degree as that which occurred during the 1970s. Despite misgivings, nonetheless, lending continued and debts mounted … The fact that the non-OPEC high borrowers were willing and able to go into debt at commercial rather than concessional rates of interest [i.e., countries chose to borrow from commercial banks rather than the World Bank or IMF] in order to maintain high growth was equally important … Between 1975 and 1979 while LDC [less-developed country] debt was expanding by 25 percent a year, exports were just about keeping pace, rising at a rate of 22 percent.
>
> (Hartland-Thunberg 1986)

---

[2] In a 1993 interview with the Bank's Historian, Willi Wapenhans recalled his attendance at a party in Riyadh in Spring 1973 where he ran into Prince Saud Al-Faisal (future Saudi Foreign Minister from 1975 to 2015) who told Wapenhans that he (Al-Faisal) recently returned from a visit to New York City. Here is Wapenhans recollection of that meeting: "Wapenhans: He [Al-Faisal] said before he left New York he had a scotch at the bar in the Waldorf Astoria and, he asked, what I thought he paid for it. I thought the question strange and did not quite know what to make of it. And he [Al-Faisal] said, 'Well, I'll tell you what I paid, I paid one barrel of oil' and he said, 'Do you think that can last?' I was dumbfounded, because I had not thought about the problem in those terms. Bank Interviewer: Two and a half dollars? Wapenhans: Two dollars and 35 cents for a barrel of oil and a scotch and soda in the Waldorf Astoria was two fifty" (Wapenhans 1993). Six months later, the first oil crisis began.

However, the second oil shock (in 1978) led to a "totally avoidable" world recession from 1980 to 1982. This recession forced the Bank and its staff to respond even if its recessionary origins had been avoidable:

> The second oil price increase ... was the result of panic among oil buyers in countries highly dependent on oil imports ... *The main reason why the second oil price shock produced a more severe recession than did the first was a different policy reaction on the part of the United States.* By 1979, the United States was no longer in a position to choose between fighting unemployment or inflation ... Macroeconomic policy, especially monetary, was tightened, interest rates started to rise, GNP declined, and unemployment mounted ... *The world settled into recession. The impact on the LDCs was devastating. They were hit by a triple blow.* Between 1979 and 1982, their oil import bill approximately doubled. At the same time, sharply rising interest rates caused the interest payments on their foreign debt also to double. Meanwhile, their export income was hit by the effects of recession in the industrial countries ... The markets for their exports of manufactured goods sank as the recession deepened ... Between 1979 and mid-1982, their aggregate indebtedness doubled from $350 billion to $700 billion. Their export income, meanwhile, remained about the same. The consequences for the large debtors were acute balance-of-payment pressures.
>
> (Hartland-Thunberg 1986, emphasis added)

The OPEC crises, the US response, and unsustainable debt levels with variable interest rates created an untenable situation for many developing countries. However, it also mattered that many newly independent countries were unable and/or politically unwilling post-independence (where consolidating domestic political legitimacy mattered) to control government spending. Decades, if not centuries, of inequality were to be seemingly ameliorated by an oft-paternalistic and newly independent state attempting to reorient state expenditures for citizen uplift but also, in many cases, to retain power.

Between 1970 and 1982, developing country interest payments rose from US$2.7 billion (in 1982 dollars) to US$49.5 billion. By 1982, interest payments were 50 percent higher than 1980 (World Bank 1983; Clausen 1988 [1983]). Interest rate increases were financial shocks many countries could not afford.[3] Although the 1980–1982 world recession led to oil price decreases, the recession hurt the labor-intensive agriculture of developing countries. Commodity prices "were lower in 1982 than at any time since World War II" (World Bank 1983, 11). Many debtor economies relied on oil-consuming industries and had government policies that slowed responsiveness to changing world environments. To

---

[3] Bundesbank's former President viewed the US Federal Reserve's action as "The Elephant in the Boat" of the world economy (Solomon 1981, 573).

service debt, debtors needed foreign exchange. Worsening economic outlooks led developing countries to reflexively increase protectionist tendencies.

No matter where one sits on an ideological pendulum between large states with state-led markets and small states with lightly regulated markets, many developing countries entered the 1980s crippled by commercial debts. The fear that countries might renege and/or defer repayments pushed key external actors (US/UK, G7) and ultimately the Bank and the Fund into action. Their actions included a new lending instrument (structural adjustment) that conditioned economic reforms (e.g., Sharma 2013) in exchange for low-interest, long-term loans that countries were otherwise unable to competitively source on open markets. It was not in the strategic interest of the US or UK Executive Directors to encourage fiscal and monetary inefficiencies. Even if a client-state's goal was not socialism, political instability resulting from a poorly performing state might, it was reasoned, turn developing countries away from the economically liberal model of the West and toward the Soviet Union. *In a Cold War environment, this fear troubled the G7 nations whose votes largely controlled the Bank and Fund.*

The Bank's structural adjustment loan quickly became its lending vehicle of choice (Wright 1980; Rodrik 1990). Bank Vice President Ernie Stern (who was integral to PSG emergence and the 1987 reforms, see Chapters 4 and 5) helped lead Bank economists toward structural adjustment. Yet, despite a Board being largely controlled by G7 nations, some were initially skeptical about adding policy-based lending to its prior investment lending practices. The Board needed convincing.

As one senior Bank staffer recalled, the Board "only reluctantly agreed to the notion of structural adjustment lending. The Board was unhappy to begin with that a major departure in policy of this nature of the Bank had been foisted upon them by a very brief document—as I recall, it was a document of four or five pages—and that left them very unhappy" (Please 1986, n.p.).[4] Please (1986, n.p.) continued his recollection:

> [A] major change in policy was in effect being forced down their throats on the basis of a very slim document. I think it was this document that really started the

[4] As Please explained, "I think there was a real concern with the people I spoke to at that time on the Board, the Alternates, the assistants, etcetera, that the Bank has always said that it could do a lot through policy dialogue. When we had submitted projects to the Board in the 1960s and the 1970s in the early part of a President's report we said all the good things we were doing in the policy area of the sector and at the macro level, before going on to [sic] present the project. Somehow I think there was a sense by the Board members of having been 'let down' that when it came to saying we had to have structural adjustment lending, we were saying that in fact we hadn't achieved all those good policy changes. It was so urgent in 1980-plus that policy reform be introduced because the international environment in which developing countries were operating had turned so negative for them. The Board felt that the Bank was being just a little two-faced because it had said it had been able to effect all these policy changes in the 1970s, now it turned out they couldn't; therefore policy reform was urgent and they needed structural adjustment lending. There was therefore a certain lack of credibility of what the Bank staff had been saying previously, and there was some unhappiness about this" (Please 1986, n.p.).

whole thing off on the wrong foot, caused a certain amount of, let's be honest, a certain amount of antagonism toward Ernie Stern himself who was seen as the author of that paper ... even though there was high regard for him of course in terms of his knowledge and ability.

Nonetheless, the Board approved the addition of structural adjustment lending to its lending instrument portfolio in April 1980 (Wright 1980). Despite structural adjustment simply being just the name of a lending instrument, "structural adjustment" soon become shorthand for "neoliberalism" or more formally, neoclassical economics' view of development and the state, specifically.

Largely under-analyzed, even today, were countering perspectives within the Bank. That is, the importance of internal debates for explaining subsequent Bank PSM/PSG policies and the fact that while the G7 may "control" the Bank, the naturalness of civil servant activism, civil servant small "p" politics, and civil servant challenges to assumed authority cannot be overlooked. Human beings, and yes, civil servants included, cannot have their influence understood without understanding the environment in which they interact and drive agendas. One key effort was a 1985 Indonesia report arguing that "institutional development" was a more appropriate, context-driven approach to PSM. Its emphasized reforming state institutions, improving civil servant capacity, and streamlining managerial processes. Involved interviewees noted how the Indonesia report used the seeds of a pre-1982 poverty-first and case-by-case contextual agenda to push back against neoclassical economics and structural adjustment lending. It is yet another indicator highlighting the Bank was not a monolithic "black box" in which civil servants merely obeyed Board or senior manager dictates.

Setting the Stage: The Berg Report

In late 1979, the Bank's African Governors asked it to report on the region's development problems. Nicknamed the "Berg Report" after its author Elliot Berg, the report called for improved public sector resource efficiencies and greater private sector involvement. As per one review of the Report, Berg was "one of the Bank's principal ideologues" (Loxley 1983, 197) and thus, it is unsurprising that the Reagan administration approved of the Berg perspective that "a reduction in some Third World governments could serve as a blueprint for a new international aid strategy" (Atkinson 1981). Referencing the Bank's newly-created tool (policy-based lending), the article continued, "Reagan officials want to discourage loans to countries where markets and prices are controlled and to attach policy conditions on many more loans than now carry them. A Treasury source said yesterday that this is 'entirely consistent' with the Berg report, which he called an indication that the Bank is beginning to follow the aid policies Reagan supports" (Atkinson

1981). To restate for this book's purpose, lending instrument choice was an early instance of the Bank being encouraged to do what a powerful external stakeholder wanted it to do.

The Berg Report used the world's poorest region to provide an empirical basis for why economies faltered. The report analyzed the continent's agricultural sector, but it was Berg's conclusions about *an inefficient state sector overly involved in the market* which captured attention (Sender and Smith 1985; Loxley 1983; Hoogvelt et al. 1992; Williams 2008). Combined with balance of payment issues and an apparent African unwillingness to integrate agricultural production into world markets (Guyer 1983), its recommendations were clear. That is, the Berg Report coincided with emergent Reagan–Thatcher perspectives (Margaret Thatcher, then-Prime Minister of the UK) on the state's role in an economy, a new structural adjustment instrument capable of parlaying money and conditionalities necessary to ensure US/UK concerns were addressed.

Creating a PSM Agenda: 1983 *World Development Report*

The 1983 *WDR* was the first time the Bank formally considered public sector and institutional issues as important to development. As the Bank prepared its first PSM-focused *WDR*, not everyone followed the Berg Report lead and disregarded poverty-first views. Research for the 1983 *WDR* research began under poverty-first economist Hollis Cheney who retired midway through the process. Research was concluded under a neoclassical economist: Anne Krueger (for her views, see Krueger 1983, 1986, 1990). The 1983 *WDR* reflected differences between Chenery and Krueger.

As the 1983 *WDR*'s Team Leader, Pierre Landell-Mills observed in a *Bank's World* staff newsletter, "We looked at it this way: Management issues are at the core of development problems. The Bank has more than 30 years' experience in a wide spectrum of countries. We deal with management problems every day in our operational work. What have we learned about what works? What approaches to development management have been most successful? ... Our concern was to pinpoint the management approaches experience has shown to be cost-effective" (Tillier 1983, 9). Under Chenery, the Bank assumed SOEs were an unpleasant fact of life even if the Bank observed SOEs to be inefficient users of state resources. The Bank's solution (or at least the solution of the 1983 *WDR* writers) was not to cut or to privatize but to figure out how SOE's could work better. With Krueger's arrival as the Bank's Chief Economist, her view was less charitable.

To prepare for the 1983 *WDR*, the Bank commissioned thirteen preparatory papers of which eight are locatable. Of the two published non-Bank reviews of the 1983 *WDR* (Murray 1983; Felix 1983), neither mentioned the preparatory papers. In one such paper, the lead *WDR* author, Pierre Landell-Mills noted the "central concern underlying these papers is the search for *greater efficiency* in setting and pursuing development goals. The papers focus on the role of the state, emphasize appropriate incentives, and assess alternative institutional arrangements. They offer no general prescriptions, as the developing countries are too diverse ... to allow the definition of a single strategy" (Shinohara 1981, iii, emphasis added). None of the available *WDR* papers could be strictly described as "neoliberal." Instead, the papers show Bank staff struggling with the "how" of PSM reform.

One paper on Japan and Korea emphasized their state role in encouraging private enterprise through export-led growth (Shinohara 1981). Another compared state- and privately owned development finance companies (Gordon 1983). Others discussed governmental planning (Agarwala 1983), managing the public service (Ozgediz 1983), managing SOEs (Shirley 1983), the role of decentralization (Rondinelli et al. 1983), and the national strategic capabilities of developing countries (Kubr and Wallace 1983). The papers debated whether the politicization of centralized administration was reasonable (Rondinelli et al. 1983) or whether technical rationality and incentives could overcome politics in government planning (Agarwala 1983). The latter debate echoes in a 2000–2007 debate over "supply side" PSM reforms versus "demand side" PSG (see Chapters 7–8).

The decentralization–centralization debate was not just about economic arguments. The debate had political ramifications for those who supported state involvement in the economy and those who questioned state roles. To illustrate the divide, here is an extensive quote from one paper's introduction:

A widely held suspicion in the Third World is that the principal mechanism of economic decentralization—the market—is immoral and anarchic, and that its impersonal operation rewards the few at the expense of the many. Many neoclassical economists would agree that markets in developing countries work imperfectly. But most would conclude that the proper solution to this problem is to find ways of removing obstacles in order to allow the market to operate more freely. Many Third World intellectuals and policymakers have a different interpretation: they believe market imperfections justify continuing central control and intervention. *This is not simply an economic debate; there are powerful political reasons for maintaining central control and intervention.* Many political leaders emphasize the primacy of the public sector, which provides positions in the civil service and parastatal institutions with which to reward loyal political followers ... Clearly, policies promoting centralization usually pay off, at least in the short run, in material and political returns for the dominant elites. As long as economic centralization reinforces centralized political control, it will have strong supporters—who usually appeal to the need for national unity—despite the most persuasive rationalistic economic criticisms. *Thus, throughout ... discussion of administrative reorganization ... it should be remembered that attempts*

to counter centralization are intensely political activities; they inevitably produce
political consequences."

(Rondinelli et al. 1983, 5–6, emphasis added)

In other words, country contexts matter and structural adjustment may have
political ramifications—the Bank should not be surprised if client states push back.

Another preparatory paper discussed four methods for improved SOE performance (or "operating efficiency") including "setting clear and attainable objectives
linked to performance criteria, achieving control while reducing undue interference, holding managers accountable for results, designing managerial incentives
and developing a cadre of managers with appropriate skills" (Shirley 1983, 1–2).
Only at the paper's end were liquidation and divestiture discussed along with
difficulties in pursuing such approaches. Word-space was also dedicated to SOE
alternatives such as price-stabilization funds, subsidies, price controls, income
support, producer cooperatives, and regulation of the private sector (Shirley 1983,
61–69).

Others discussed how technical assistance for non-engineering activities could
be improved through increased commitment from donors and clients, improved
technical assistance design, and moving away from non-negotiable blueprint approaches to project design (Lethem and Cooper 1983, abstract). Not only did
this paper use context matters language of the 1970s but also non-engineering
was a word with historical importance. It reflected post-1970s interests in public
policy and economic reform. They worried that technical assistance was "thrown
at problems" without understanding how so-called "behavioral problems" of client
governments impacted on project success (Lethem and Cooper 1983, 17–21).[5]

Landell-Mills' ambivalence was soon overwhelmed by Anne Krueger's arrival
in late 1982. One banker recalled that Krueger "didn't like anything that Hollis
[Chenery] ever did" and that what "Krueger has done is to cut off anybody who
ever had any relationships with Hollis Chenery, *per se*, irrespective of the person's
merit" (King 1986; see also Williams 2008). Shortly thereafter, *WDR* writers were
told that "[the authors of the 1983 *WDR*] were just trying to commit murder efficiently and we really had to think about changing our attitudes on this subject"
(WB12). By "commit murder efficiently," Krueger implied that any tinkering with
SOEs was a wasted activity. Efficiency-first was the new motto. More pointedly, an
involved member of staff recollected Krueger's view as "why make the state more

---

[5] In reference to the Bank's prior social pricing debates of the 1970s, one scholar found Bank staff
using their technical and disciplinary-specific expertise to "consciously or unconsciously, convert personal disagreement with policy into technical caveats about the applicability of the policy in specific
cases" (Ascher 1983, 425). In the representative bureaucracy literature of the public administration discipline (for a start, see Dolan and Rosenbloom 2003), such action equates to turning one's intellectual
characteristic (perhaps a disbelief in Keynesianism) into "active representation," where discussions over
technicalities become covers for personal ideological differences. The potential active representation
of ideological or disciplinary perspective is repeatedly noted in this book.

efficient? I want to kill the state" (WB39) or as another banker wondered, "why should the Peruvian government run movie theaters?" (WB12). As a neoclassical economist, Krueger backed the "getting your price right" theory where market prices determined a greater portion of government activities (WB12).

The mixed policy messages arising from the initial *WDR* preparatory papers became less mixed by the time the 1983 *WDR* was published. Its introduction acknowledged, "Good economic management depends, first and foremost, on the adoption of policies that stimulate enterprise and efficiency, but it depends also on the quality of the public sector institutions responsible for executing these policies and for providing public services" (World Bank 1983, iii). To the untrained reader, this may not seem like much of a statement. But it was a breakthrough statement for a Bank who had long considered infrastructure and agriculture to be "development." The *WDR*'s focus on economic management *and* institutional quality were new. The report's introduction indicated the world's economic situation had forced the Bank's hand: "The underlying concern is the search for greater efficiency in the pursuit of governments' social and economic objectives. The current economic slowdown makes the task more urgent, as well as more difficult" (World Bank 1983, 4).

The report wanted to maximize efficient resource allocation ("prices, markets, and administrative interventions") and operational efficiency ("maximize the use of labor and capital through the sound management of enterprises, projects and programs in both the public and private sectors") (World Bank 1983, 42). Minimizing costs and formulaic ways to measure output were the solution. Discussion of whether achieving efficiency comes at the cost of effectiveness or equity were ignored. The underlying assumption was that economic growth, on its own, cures all. Economic growth benefits from state efficiency and free markets. For these authors, growth would trickle-down if countries got their economic fundamentals right.

In addition, and perhaps as a surprise to Bank scholars who often conflate neoliberalism with an early Bank interest in privatization, the Bank listed divestiture (privatization) as just one of several options available to governments. The Bank stopped short of a full privatization recommendation as it might be "hard to implement," was "politically sensitive and prompt[ed] charges of corruption" or may lead governments to sell their least-attractive SOEs (World Bank 1983, 86). The *WDR* also side-stepped whether efficiency is a privatization output: "It is misleading to discuss efficiency in terms of ownership. What matters more is creating the conditions that encourage efficiency in both private and public sector activities … Both developed and developing countries are keen to find ways to make state enterprises more efficient" (World Bank 1983, 4).

Despite Krueger's neoliberal push and the *WDR*'s ambivalence about appropriate solutions, the *WDR* was only published after "considerable criticism" from the Board (WB12). Criticism focused upon its privatization discussions. Even though there was no specific privatization chapter, a highly controversial page (85) was devoted to liquidation and divestiture. This page was enough for certain Board members to argue that the Bank would violate its Articles of Agreement if it encouraged privatization. Privatization was tantamount, in this view, to interfering in a country's political affairs. As former Bank Senior Vice President Willi Wapenhans later noted: "The Bank's attempts to contain nepotism [in client countries] were highly criticized as external interferences and its concern regarding state enterprises was opposed as ideologically inspired" (Wapenhans 1993). Since several Board members, or those they represented, were from socialist-leaning countries, it is easy to understand why they would oppose any Bank suggestion that privatization is an apolitical act.

So, what happened next? The next two sections indicate that yes, based on the chapter's story so far, external actors matter most. But as noted in the last half of this chapter, a fuller re-telling of the 1980s policy debates lies ahead. This fuller discussion will be one lead into not only the Bank's addition of governance (PSG) to its agenda but also to Bank civil servant domination of sector policy shifts in this agenda until this book's 2012 end-date.

External Actors Dominate the Bank's Public Sector Agenda

Between 1983 and 1989—and more than any other subsequent historical period in this sector—the US (in concert with the UK), the G7, and the IMF largely shaped this new sector's agenda (see Table 1). Their position reflected strategic motivations. The IMF's position reflected an organizational mandate to pursue short-term macroeconomic policy reforms to which neoclassical economics offered many options. For the Bank, structural adjustment was a short- to medium-term lending policy instrument. The Cold War, the OPEC oil crises, developing country over-borrowing, and subsequent fiscal crises helped strategically reframe the Bank's 1980s agenda. The economic growth of developing countries was tied into Western support for neoclassical economics' "small state, free the market" ideas, international development, and the Cold War. Senior bankers who might have argued for a poverty-first development perspective (or at least, a Keynesian outlook) such as Mahbub ul Haq and Hollis Chenery had left the Bank by 1982. The emerging theoretical perspective converged with Western desires for economic growth and predictable political alignments in developing countries.

Recalling Chapter 2, a stakeholder's importance is identified by their "*power to influence the firm*," "the *legitimacy* of the stakeholder's relationship with the firm*," and the "*urgency* of the stakeholder's claim on the firm" (Mitchell et al. 1997, 854, emphasis added) (see E1–E4 variables in Table 7). Between January 1983 and October 1989 and among external actors, the US, via its Executive Director, held the greatest power, legitimacy, and urgency over the Bank. The criticality of developing countries' economic growth was linked to the US's (and thus, the Bank's) strategic perspectives. This perspective was bolstered by a long-held purpose of the Bretton Woods institutions. In 1946, the Bank was created not just to enhance international economic stability but also to bolster a US-led model after WWII.

As the Bank's largest shareholder and the primary oppositional force to the Soviet Union, the US used its power to influence the Bank. This includes early opposition to the Bank and then, in the mid-190s, changing its tune. The Americans preferred a neoclassical PSM policy as the state, in this view, was an inefficient arbiter of market prices and growth. SOEs and other bloated bureaucracies required reform. Its ability to influence or control the Bank is also found in variables E5–E14 of Table 7. The US's ability to assert its agenda and to override other Executive Directors' concerns revealed US power (and *active use* of its power) within the institution. The next sections illustrate the external actor role during this era. The relevant actors, stories, and their influence are articulated in Table 7.

The US: A Foe, then a Friend of the World Bank

It is left out of many histories of the US influence over structural adjustment lending in the early 1980s that the relationship between the US and the World Bank was initially adversarial. Between January 1981 and early 1985, the US Treasury was unconvinced of the Bank's usefulness. The Reagan Administration preferred developing countries to use international credit markets, not the World Bank, for borrowing needs. When the Treasury changed its tune in 1986, the Bank had become politically and financially insecure after years of battling the United States for IDA funds. Bank dependence on the Treasury's goodwill was so profound that when the US (along with Japan and France; Germany and the UK abstained) failed to approve the Bank's budget in the summer of 1986, the Bank began its most significant and internally painful reorganization of the 32 years covered in this book (see Chapter 4).

In his first address to the Bank/Fund Annual Meetings in September 1981, President Reagan told delegates that "the magic of the marketplace" would solve global economic problems (Gedda 1981) and the debt-servicing difficulties of developing countries were not America's problem. One Deputy Secretary of the US Treasury argued that developing country problems were associated "with what I would bluntly call domestic economic mismanagement" (McNamar 1982, January 7). Other Treasury officials felt similarly: "I'm trying to be pragmatic and indicate to the other nations, both the industrialized and the developing, that there's no sense in calling on Uncle Sam to put up huge sums of money that are not going to be there. Because frankly, they don't have the votes any more in the United States. The era of open largesse for nations around the world in the United States has passed" (Edwards 1983). If multilateral development banks (MDBs) like the World Bank wanted to lend money, Treasury suggested "the willingness of borrowing countries to adopt and implement appropriate policies should be a prime consideration" (Treasury 1982, 68). For dissenting developing countries, the Treasury bottom line was "do it or else!" For a Bank dependent on US support, its perspective was difficult to ignore.

In 1982, the Treasury released a 194-page report clarifying its position on multilateral development banks. The US had three objectives: (1) In light of the Cold War, foreign aid should assist countries with strategic or political importance while encouraging an economic growth that leads to a "secure and stable world;" (2) MDBs should encourage low-income countries to participate in the international economic and financial system through their own development, in particular via "liberalized trade and capital flows;" and (3) humanitarian assistance should "[promote] overall economic growth and productivity in developing countries by pursuing programs targeted directly on the poor" (Treasury 1982, 3 of Executive Summary). For the Reagan administration, the path was clear: if you were a strategic ally, foreign aid might be forthcoming, and if you chose market-first reforms, the US would be pleased.

Underwriting the US perspective was a belief that MDBs do not effectively use their own resources. To force the World Bank's hand, Treasury stated its willingness to lower its capital allocation and to limit IDA considerations (Treasury 1982; Regan 1982). *This was a threat of the highest order which, at first, was not immediately taken seriously.* At least initially, Bank President Clausen (appointed by US President Jimmy Carter) argued for more IDA funding in an era where developing country needs were greater, not smaller. He viewed IDA funding as a "sound economic investment" for contributing countries (Farnsworth 1981). Clausen was blunt in his early disapproval of US disinterest: "That is not amputating a program. Who is the amputee? Not IDA the institution. But rather the human individual— multiplied by millions in the poorest developing countries—who is denied IDA assistance to enhance his own productivity and, hence, pry himself loose from the choking grip of poverty" (Clausen 1986 [1982], 120). When asked in his departing interview for *Bank's World* about his greatest disappointment as Bank President, he answered it was the Bank's inability to stop IDA-7's replenishment from dropping $3 billion from its IDA-6 amount of $12 billion (Drattell 1986).

With so many skirmishes, the Bank was eventually forced into a corner. It had to respond. To maintain US support, the Bank began to reorient its organizational and project structures. New development outcomes were economic growth, less state reliance, and increased private-sector involvement. The "good" reforms included "efficient resource mobilization and allocation within recipient countries," work on the "pricing and efficiency of services," and open trade. Such reforms also included improving fiscal deficits and encouraging floating exchange-rate regimes (Treasury 1982, 7). Treasury worried the Bank "*may have overemphasized redistribution considerations at the expense of sound economic policy reforms which would have represented the best approach to poverty elimination"* (Treasury 1982, 44, emphasis added). The US-led rebuke of ul Haq and Chenery had begun.

This turmoil meant that Clausen spent much of his tenure "putting the institution on a solid financial basis" (Rajagopalan 1993). While he successfully shored up the Bank's finances during a world recession, his dual burden of fighting US distrust as well as concerns about Bank finances meant Clausen unable to "substantively connect" (WB6) with an emergent PSM policy agenda. Although Mallaby (2004) argued that Clausen abandoned McNamara's poverty-first push, this book suggests US influence put Clausen in an untenable situation: Bank policy independence during a time of political and economic crisis was impossible when the Bank depended upon American goodwill. Although Clausen was a Carter appointee, he would try and toe Reagan's ideological line even if his statements did not fully encapsulate a neoclassical economics view (e.g., Clausen 1986 [1981], 8).

Despite an early 1980s burst of US-led anti-Bank rhetoric, signs of an American shift emerged as early as 1984. Structural adjustment was still the preferred Treasury perspective. But growing developing country debts encouraged Treasury to consider "a greater role in the debt strategy, supporting structural reforms … and helping catalyze private financing" (McNamar 1984). Highly indebted countries not only troubled a liberal order but countries in fiscal disrepair were also countries unable to borrow from commercial markets. The year 1984 was also when the Treasury began to positively link the Bank to US strategic interests. As noted by one Treasury official, "subscription to the IBRD shares is essential in order to maintain the U.S. veto power over amendments to the Articles of Agreement of the Bank" (Regan 1984b) even if the US did not support a capital increase for the IBRD (Regan 1984a).

With James Baker's arrival as US Treasury Secretary in February 1985, its publications focused less on convincing the Bank to implement American perspectives. Treasury had already won its structural adjustment argument (WB52). Instead, Baker brought a deeper understanding of why developing countries found the IMF politically unfeasible to engage and thus, Treasury reconsidered the Bank's role (Economist 1986a). At the 1985 Development Committee meeting, Baker shared the Treasury's position:

> The United States views the primary role of the Bank as supporting policies which encourage economic growth and revitalization in its developing member countries … The Bank's introduction of structural and sector adjustment programs has proved an effective means to help members both sustain growth and implement policy changes over the medium-term.
>
> (Baker III 1985b)

Elsewhere in that statement, Baker acknowledged the Bank's 1980 approval of a structural adjustment lending instrument and how, in Treasury's opinion, structural adjustment was a success. With rising Treasury support for the Bank, they now wanted the Bank's "fast-disbursing lending to support growth-oriented policies and institutional and sectoral reform" to create "a catalyst for commercial bank lending" (Baker III 1985a). It was not that clients should not focus on private sector borrowing *but that the administration understood that if countries were to borrow from commercial banks, then developing countries must be financially more secure so borrowing is possible.*

The first public mention of "privatization" by a 1980s Treasury official vis-à-vis the Bank was a speech on January 22, 1986 before the Bretton Woods Committee. In short order, privatization would shortly become "the" policy conditionality of structural adjustment (Baker III 1986). A *Christian Science Monitor* article from May 30, 1985 described an internal Treasury memo that called for

> an action plan to implement an active policy of privatization in the MDB programs. Among possible measures, the study suggests that in the short term these development banks not finance parastatals that compete with the private sector; that they limit their loans to "intermediate credit institutions" (also known as development finance companies) which in turn lend to the private sector, and that they require governments to have parastatals divest unused or dormant assets not immediately relevant to current operations.
>
> (Francis 1985)

In Baker's 1987 testimony before the US Senate, the administration's evolved perspective was clear. The US "cannot have it both ways, i.e. we cannot for long place more of the burden of fostering and enlarging the international economic system on the MDBs and other international organizations, and then refuse to support them adequately" (Baker III 1987, 7).[6] The US needed the Bank. To sell its new support to the US Congress, Treasury linked it to American jobs, strategic alliances, and what US leadership entailed. If developing countries are economically healthy, they can buy American exports. American exports lead to American jobs.

US Allies: UK and the G7 Group of Nations

As America's most important Cold War ally, with a Prime Minister (Margaret Thatcher) who shared Reagan's worldview, and as a former colonial power with global interests, the UK's support for structural adjustment is unsurprising. Its support also reflected its recent economic history. In the late 1970s, the UK experienced a fiscal crisis so acute that the government arranged an IMF stand-by

---

[6] As noted in Chapter 8, the US, Japan, and France's non-support of the Bank's 1986 budget set the stage for the Bank's 1987 internal reform.

agreement in 1977. The agreement allowed the UK to withdraw resources, if needed. The UK's fiscal crisis response was to rationalize government. Thatcher wanted government "efficiency" and public sector "accountability" (Humphrey et al. 1993). This view held that "public expenditure ... an essential part of the solution for economic and social policies, had now become part of the problem" (Humphrey et al. 1993, 9, referring to Deakin [1987]). The UK experience influenced Bank structural-adjustment policies. One Bank interviewee recalled the UK's stance as encouraging client nations to "get rid" of their large states (WB35). Reinforcing its agenda, the UK sent practitioners to brief Bank staff (WB12) and its Executive Director was changed to no longer come from its aid agency but instead, its treasury (WB16, WB42).

Other external actors also mattered. Between the 1975 and 1989 annual G7 meetings, the annual G7 statements reflected international economic and financial events. A major difference between the late 1970s statements and statements of the 1980s is that the former largely focused on the G7 member states. By the 1980s, the focus extended to developing countries. The G7 delegated its economic assignments to the World Bank and the IMF. The IMF was the G7's preferred organizational actor for monetary affairs (G7 1982). The Bank was to do everything else—from fiscal affairs and food issues (G7 1980) to solving African poverty (G7 1984). Shortly after the Bank approved structural adjustment lending, the G7 welcomed "the Bank's innovative lending scheme for structural adjustment" (G7 1980).

By 1981, the G7 desired Bank-Fund cooperation given the IMF's "recently expanded role ... in financing payments deficits on terms which encourage needed adjustment" (G7 1981). The Bank and Fund were to work on balance of payment issues. If developing countries defaulted on commercial bank loans, the G7 worried default would negatively impact a Western (non-Soviet) international economic order. In the early 1980s, this emergent consensus paired economic liberalism with democracy. Or, as the G7 stated in 1983: "We are the guardians of fundamental democratic values that have always united us" (G7 1983) since "promoting [developing countries'] economic development and thereby their social and political stability" (G7 1984) was important.

A Partial Ally: The International Monetary Fund

IMF had an early affinity for structural adjustment as its birds-eye macroeconomic focus fit structural adjustment lending purposes. The IMF's mission focuses upon fiscal and monetary stabilization so countries have a foundation for growth. Once stabilized, the Bank's job was to deepen reform and to spread the benefits from this growth. A charitable perspective considered the IMF's role as "creat[ing] the environment" for subsequent Bank assessment and work (Bank's World 1985, 16).

Innumerable articles have been written about the IMF and structural adjustment. For outsiders, the Bank and the Fund had the same perspective. But as the Bank adopted structural adjustment lending and deepened its involvement in public sector policy outputs, internecine squabbling between the two organizations increased. Such squabbling between the IMF and Bank of the 1980s is far less discussed.

When the Bank "failed" to sufficiently respond after the 1982 debt crisis (Rowen 1986; Economist 1986b) with long-term lending, the IMF increased long-term financing (Rowen 1986). This IMF stance directly competed with the Bank even if as one journalist noted, the Fund's support of medium- and long-term structural-adjustment-type policies predated the Bank (Kaletsky 1982a, 1982b). As the Fund re-focused on long-term lending, the Bank re-focused on short-term lending. Both institutions considered medium-term issues which further confused institutional boundaries (Chenery 1983). Nearly all interviewees for this book viewed the Bank–IMF relationship as important but conflicted.

In the early 1980s, and to help stem the potential for open conflict, the Bank President began to meet on a quarterly basis with his IMF counterpart (Tillier 1985) to discuss duty delineation even if conflict still occurred.[7] One of most publicized disagreements occurred in 1988. The Bank agreed to a US$1.25 billion loan to Argentina in exchange for structural adjustment reforms. The Bank and Argentina agreed to this loan *before* agreeing on an IMF program. The US Treasury, along with other donors, were not pleased. They thought the Bank should not "make loans without an IMF plan in place" (Kraske et al. 1996, 265). Although President Barber Conable (1986–1991) "denied that the agreement marked a shift in relations between the World Bank and the IMF," he was later forced to "insist that the Bank had not been pressed by the US to take a leading role in the financing" (Anonymous 1988; Kraske et al. 1996) and thus, all blame was appropriated to the Bank. This was particularly painful for Conable. James Baker, who had been described as Conable's "friend and patron" had just left the US Treasury and could not provide Conable political cover (Kraske et al. 1996, 265).

Distrust of the Fund extends to Bank staff. Multiple interviewees felt the IMF's early PSM reform tools were biased: the IMF wants "to simplify the basic issues and the basic problems down to numbers. Which is why 'civil service reform' equals reducing the wage bill ... [The IMF's] fundamental picture was

---

[7] In the mid-1980s, Brazil turned down a Bank project that would have helped its export industry. The reason? "The fear that the [Bank] program, when converted into *cruzeiros* would upset the accomplishment of the money supply goals set by the IMF and thus compromise the imminent debt renegotiations—strong circumstantial evidence of something less than full cooperation between the Bank and the Fund" (Hartland-Thunberg 1986).

the macro picture and the numbers … They want a summary of the economy … and complex issues such as incentives get translated into reducing the wage bill" (WB36, WB17). Or, the IMF's "here is the solution" attitude left Bank staff to sort out the "how" of reform (WB17). So, what should the IMF *not* do? One interviewee who had worked at the Bank and the Fund observed:

> Quite frankly, the Fund does not know about getting countries in order … Macroeconomists can tell you that you need to get in order and have some generalized ideas … so if you got a debt blow-out and then [the IMF tells you to] sell something that pays down your debt. But they don't know anything about privatization, they are macroeconomists, they are not lawyers, they are not microeconomists, they are not regulation economists, they are macroeconomists. They might give you a very good feel of the macro-dimension of the problem but they do not have the knowledge or experience with the adjustment that is required and that is what the criticism of the Fund has been about for many, many years. So, they put in place, back in the 1980s and 1990s, conditionalities into their Fund programs which are more specific than they had the expertise to devise … it's not their job. The [IMF's] job is to say you have a very big problem here and you have to fix it. And then, theoretically, if you look at how the system is set-up, the country figures out how to fix it and then writes to the Fund and asks for help. But in reality, the Fund drafts that letter.
>
> (WB54)

As early as 1966, the Bank and Fund agreed that the "balance of payments adjustments and exchange rate issues are in the sphere of the Fund, while development and investment programs are in the sphere of the Bank." And yet, by the 1980s, there was still "a large gray area … First, how efficiently resources are used. Second, how resources are mobilized. Third, the overall regime of trade and capital flows between nations. All are related, both to the near-term balance of payments and to the way development will occur" (Tillier 1985, 2–3). Soon thereafter, the Fund claimed leadership on technical issues of budgeting, expenditure control, and accounting, whereas the Bank and Fund shared fiscal, tax, and expenditures policies. The Fund handled macroeconomic issues and the World Bank handled microeconomic issues. But that distinction was never clean. As one Bank staff member observed, "We have a 'love/hate' relationship with them. If the IMF says a country's finances are in trouble, we cannot ignore their advice. That is a prerequisite for us. However, whatever they say, we are still obliged to do our own analysis to see whether they are any mitigating circumstances which would lead to a different view" (WB25). Today, overlap and contradictions still occur.

Under the Radar, a Battle Brews: Institutional Development Alternatives

So far, this chapter's stories match the commonly related history of the World Bank. This includes recollections about structural adjustment, the power of neoclassical economics in framing Bank responses, and the rise of the public sector as an anti-market barrier to economic growth. The US role and its vote share have been considered in many other scholarly publications. Less considered in such publications has been the G7, opposing Executive Directors, and linkages among the Berg Report, the departure of Chenery and ul Haq, the hiring of Krueger, and conflicts over the 1983 *WDR*. But overall, the overarching angle presented in the first half of this chapter (structural adjustment, US power) is familiar to Bank scholars (Harrigan and Mosley 1991; Williams 2008).

But it is exactly at this point that other stories must be told. Such stories are heard when researchers remember civil servants are not Weberian automatons in the service of authority and may, in fact, have power. This includes the power, as stakeholders, to create internal dissent about the supposed "neoliberal" direction of early PSM reforms. In the Bank, with thousands of highly trained civil servants, we should expect debate as one's expertise and experiences battle others with alternative views. The second half of this chapter outlines the alternative policy options that arose within the Bank's new PSM agenda. To recollect this policy battle, our attention shifts to Indonesia. One of the staff who recalled this debate had been located within the Resident Mission in Jakarta, Indonesia. While Indonesia was not the only flashpoint, the Indonesia Report was the most frequently mentioned start-point by interviewees when discussing sector policy change in the 1980s.

In the early 1980s, an Indonesian government department head suggested to the Bank that public sector reforms were needed. The Indonesian official observed that although his country had oil and other natural resources, *it did not have sufficient institutional and human resources to successfully implement its agenda.* Instead, its resources remained underutilized (Carey 1985). This include inefficiencies such as waste, leakage, corruption, and excessive reliance on external (non-Indonesian) consultants (WB6). Yet even if the Bank intellectually understood this desire for institutional development lending (Israel 1983) (WB6), Mission staffs were aware of new neoliberal trends back at Bank headquarters. This hamstrung the Indonesian office to offer alternative policy solutions to Indonesia (WB6).

The resulting "Indonesia Report" observed that the government failed to manage its natural, human, and financial resources. The report pinned Indonesia's "management problem" on "deficiencies in managerial skills, practices, and systems and the incompatibility of these with the requirements of modern organizations and future challenges" (World Bank 1985, 1). This was not a new idea. Earlier studies on Indonesia by the Ford Foundation acknowledged the "management problem." Between 1970 and 1980, Indonesia implemented civil service, procurement, and budgeting reforms. The Bank said that Indonesia's problems were caused by "weak planning and rigid budgeting, complex implementation procedures ... excessive centralization, weak coordination, inadequate civil-service policies, and poor monitoring and evaluation" (World Bank 1985, 8). The Indonesian government managers interviewed for the Report felt that civil servants were reviewed merely for their compliance to government orders rather than any thoughtful challenge to what they must implement. Budgeting, civil service, and centralization cultures prohibited civil servant flexibility at the government's lowest levels while performance was "evaluated against compliance with the rules rather than achievement of objectives." Report authors noted Indonesia's SOEs lacked strategic planning, monitoring, and evaluation capabilities and were unable to incentivize managers or make difficult decisions when the entity underperformed (World Bank 1985, 74). The report did not question whether importing business-management techniques was appropriate; instead, it was concerned that Indonesian civil servants did not view themselves as "managers" in the business sense (World Bank 1985, 22).

Indonesia: An Early PSM Agenda Battlefront

Both the 1985 Indonesia report and the 1983 *WDR* objectives focused upon PSM reform. Both reports acknowledged the SOE role in client economies and advocated training modules that emphasized market-oriented results, although the 1985 report focused on a particular country's context. *But that is where their similarities ended.* The 1983 *WDR* emphasized economic growth as the means by which poor countries might raise living standards. The *WDR* used technocratic definitions of efficiency improvements and dedicated discussion to removing price distortions rather than engaging complex in-country management shifts. The 1983 *WDR* implicitly preferred market-led solutions to development while the 1985 Indonesia Report preferred to work with local institutions. Whereas the 1983 *WDR* suggested top-down solutions on the assumption of trickle-down effects, the 1985 Indonesia Report acknowledged that centralization, formalistic rule-making, and excluding low-level bureaucrats in policy formulation led to government failures. Both documents highlighted a growing difference between those bankers who sought bottom-up administrative and managerial reforms and those whose macro-level perspectives emphasized broad (neoliberal) policy shifts. The latter group believed that if the policy was right, development would fall into place. Although the 1983 *WDR* claimed to understand that economic reform should be paired with institutional effectiveness (World Bank 1983, 126), its emphasis was on perfecting (neoliberal) policy rather than ensuring effective institutional implementation.

But despite increased headquarter-based agreement among the Bank's most powerful external actors and its Chief Economist that structural adjustment was the way forward, an interviewee recalled that decisions on whether a client should privatize or keep a SOE "was being done 'on the run' as countries were going broke" (WB35). This interviewee had been on missions to Liberia and Guinea, where Bank staff also arrived with food bags. "We [Bank staff] would spend a day sitting in front of these functionaries. They wanted the money" (WB35). If the client wanted the money, the Bank gave them the money. Doing so kept countries "alive" (WB35). Putting perspective on fiscal disarray, the interviewee emphasized how difficult it was to create "a framework to keep them efficient" (WB35). Efficiency was not a client-state's objective. It was survival. This on-the-ground reality could not be further removed from the economist offices in Washington DC where economic modeling was undertaken.

Moreover, even if the Bank had wanted to retain a birds-eye view, the "reality was they [the Bank] got sucked in more and more. [The] Bank started financing on both sides [state-owned-enterprise reform and privatization] little by little. *We gave support to African countries because if the Bank did not help ... free marketers would let [the client country] go broke*" (WB35, emphasis added). In other words, it *had become the Bank's moral duty to discourage country bankruptcy.* If the "free-marketers" held sway, countries would go broke, citizens would suffer, economic growth would be stalled, and poverty would increase. Simple identification of when neoliberalism became a Bank "answer" may skim over on-the-ground realities: client nations were suffering and the situation demanded a Bank response. By 1985, neoclassical economics and privatizing SOEs had become the dominant answer.

In 1983, the Indonesia Report was ready. However, it was not published until 1985 when it was published as a three-volume set, a length unusual for the Bank (World Bank 1985; WB6). What were the reasons behind the publishing delay? Starting with the 1983 *WDR* and more conclusively by 1985, Indonesia-type institutional development projects had become the poor cousin to structural adjustment. Institutional development carried less political support "back home" (at Bank headquarters). Between 1983 and 1985, Bank staff had coalesced around ideas that the "best" public sector reforms cut the state. In this view, public performance was hampered not by poor human resources and insufficient technical capacity to manage development (as argued in the Indonesia Report) but by a state's size and economic burden. If only the market was allowed to function, the argument went, then Indonesia's problems would, in theory, disappear. Interviewees called this the "quick fix" perspective (WB6). It was an increasingly dominant perspective in a Bank pressed by the US, UK, and G7 to reform developing country states. In such an environment, why would the Bank want to publish a Report that suggested complementary managerial and institutional reforms?

Other internal barriers also hampered quick publication. In the 1980s, the Bank's Resident Missions did not carry much "prestige" with Headquarters. Nor did many Headquarters staff have significant developing country experience beyond an occasional work trip (ul Haq 1982). This led to the sidelining of many field office suggestions. In addition, many early 1980s investment loans were used for the "hardware" of development, such as infrastructure-building or agricultural development. Today investment loans can include social and institutional requirements. In the 1980s, this was uncommon. The early 1980s the Bank was also not technically or structurally organized to handle "cross-sector" issues. Projects were to focus only on one sector. *Institutional development projects are explicitly cross-sectoral.* In other words, the Bank preferred to build a road without confusing a road building project with the institutional problems of a client's infrastructure ministry.

The battle also continued into the theoretical frame. The Bank's East Asia staff argued the report was not publishable "*because institutional development and public sector reform are not sufficiently analytical issues;* instead, the Bank should focus on trade and finance and because few people understood civil-service reform. How can the Bank analyze it?" (WB6, emphasis added) What purpose would the Indonesia Report serve if it undermined the macroeconomic management tools of the Bank, the ideological view of the regional chief economist, and ultimately, the Bank's Chief Economist? Institutional development projects were more difficult to implement than infrastructure projects. Indonesia Report authors observed that

> [i]nstitutional development projects (or components of projects) suffer from greater implementation difficulties than the physical facilities. The most fundamental constraint to success technical assistance for institutional development has often been the weak commitment and capacity of senior management of the target institution and the inadequate adaptation to on-going processes and cultural factors.
>
> (World Bank 1985, 8)

Other opponents, such as Ernie Stern, the Bank's Senior Vice President for Operations, felt that the issues raised in the Report were a "bottomless pit," were "too messy, too long-term," (as recalled by WB6) and required too many Bank resources. Stern believed the Bank had no "comparative advantage" in this issue. It was not that Stern did not understand that developing countries had weak institutions. He most likely did. But his preferred solution was greater private sector involvement. In Stern's own words, "we must be prepared for frustration because sometimes the availability of solutions is going to outrun the ability of the [client] institutions to implement them. *Time and again we're drawn into dependence on institutions that are weak. We've got to be very conscious of this weakness, and to minimize our reliance on institutions which cannot perform.*" (Bank's World

1984a, 15, emphasis added). This was different perspective from an earlier "free market" worry. The Bank, as designed, was unwilling to tackle such long-term and fundamental institutional shifts on its own.

We cannot deemphasize the Stern view. Multiple Bank interviewees recalled that Stern "ran the Bank" in the 1970s and 1980s (WB30, WB43, WB6, WB12).[8] As VP of Operations, Stern oversaw *all* Bank projects, including Indonesia. Nothing happened without Stern's approval—a sentiment that continued into the 1990s (see Chapter 5). Without Stern's buy-in, initiatives arising out of Indonesia would struggle to be operationalized (Bank's World 1983, 12). Moreover, Bank publications had discussed the institutional development problem as early as 1980. Institutional development programs required "substantial investments ... a slow and uncertain payoff ... [because] institutional changes require new structures, new technologies, new skills, and above all, changes in behavior" (Esman and Montgomery 1980, 210). By 1980, Bank-sponsored institutional reforms had "clear achievements" in just 25 percent of cases (Esman and Montgomery 1980, 210).

Yet despite anti-Report inertia, the report was published. How did that happen? There are two answers. One, the Bank was pushed by the Indonesian government to publish. And two, publication was encouraged by Edward V.K. "Kim" Jaycox and indirectly by Arturo Israel and Mary Shirley. During this period, Jaycox was Vice President for East Asia, which included Indonesia. Unlike his regional chief economist, Jaycox believed institutional development mattered. He provided high-level political cover to research and to publish the Indonesia Report. His commitment to institutional development was not a one-time event. As Vice President, Jaycox had tried and failed to create an East Asia-specific Public Sector Management Unit (PSMU). A few years later when Jaycox led the Bank's 1987 reorganization (see Chapter 4), he ensured regional vice presidencies had the right to create PSMUs.

Mary Shirley's role was more indirect. As a microeconomist, Shirley was one of the few Bank staff researching SOE improvement. Shirley was known for trying to "reconcile" (WB6) differing internal viewpoints by putting public sector language into economist-speak. Although not involved in the Indonesia Report, Shirley's employment within the Bank's first PSMU, her role as a 1983 *WDR* writer, and her professional relationship with Arturo Israel strongly influenced what the Bank understood to be public sector reform. So, who was Arturo Israel? Multiple Bank interviewees recalled Arturo Israel as the "godfather" of institutional development at the Bank (WB21). Israel, Shirley, and others such as John Nellis, pursued research agendas in which institutional improvements were understood

---

[8] It was an open secret that Stern (Head of Operations) clashed with Moeennuddin "Moeen" Qureshi (Muis 2000). Qureshi was Senior VP of Finance (1981–1987). He oversaw all Bank financial operations until his 1992 departure. In 1993, Qureshi became a short-term caretaker Prime Minister of Pakistan.

as complementary to, and not mutually exclusive of, neoclassical approaches. They were joined by other 1980s Bank staffers such as Sunita Kikeri, Barbara Nunberg, and Mammadou Dia, each of whom published relevant Bank papers. Even if these bankers were not a large group, they existed. *Yes, they ultimately were overpowered by the US, UK, and the G7 perspectives, but as Chapter 5 observes, their work provided the crucial intellectual underpinnings for the Bank's early 1990s addition of "governance" to its PSM agenda.*

Little External Actor or Bank President Support for Institutional Development

Unlike external support for structural adjustment and the "answers" provided by neoclassical economic theory, there was little external support for institutional development perspectives. Neither the US Treasury nor the US Executive Director publicly encouraged institutional development. In the 1980s G7 statements, there was only half-sentence mention (in 1981) of institutional development.[9] Although the G7 acknowledged that structural adjustment was "painful and courageous" (G7 1984), they wrote in 1988 that "the market-oriented, growth-led strategy based on the case-by-case approach remains the only viable approach for overcoming their external debt problems" (G7 1988).

Neither Bank President during the 1980s (Clausen and Conable) publicly supported alternative PSM approaches. In an organization like the Bank, staff members with alternative perspectives look to the top for guidance. If the President did not question structural adjustment, then opposing staff had uphill battles. In only one speech did Conable acknowledge that structural adjustment might be making poverty worse. Even though Conable reflected the Bank and Fund's view that "policy reform is in the best long-term interest of the poor" and that "distortions and misconceived economic policies harm them [the poor] more than others," he acknowledged that "poor people can get hurt ... in the transitional process of correcting past mistakes [of the developing country, not the Bank]. We have a special duty to encourage and finance measures which keep their short-term interests in mind" (Conable 1988). As observed in Chapter 5 and by the very late 1980s, the Bank was increasingly conscious (even if incrementally) of the impact structural adjustment had on the poor.

France and the Netherlands were less supportive of structural adjustment and privatization than the US or the UK. One interviewee described the importance of France's so-called "Nora Report" in framing the French view. The interviewee believed it was "not an accident" that the first regionally located PSMU existed

---

[9] Without referencing a lead institution, the G7 hoped to encourage "human resources, including technical and managerial capabilities" (G7 1981).

within Africa (WB35). There remained a strong French influence in its former colonies. The French preferred planned contracts in which SOEs and the government maintained a contractual relationship. According to a Bank interviewee, "we were dealing interestingly with the French tradition in French Africa and the British tradition in British Africa" (WB35). Several Nordic countries also opposed the privatization agenda (Maehlum 1994). One Bank and one non-Bank interviewee concurred: "The Nordics were very strongly pro-government and felt the Bank was going in the wrong direction. And they became more vocal about it as time went on … The Dutch executive director [Eveline Herfkins] was there for quite a long time [1990 to 1996] and she was very vocal in her opposition to what she saw as the Bank's mistaken move towards more emphasis on the private sector and trying to reduce the size of government" (WB12, WB43). Yet despite such questions raised by allied Executive Directors, the 1980s version of institutional development was not widely accepted.

Creating Some Space: Organizational Shifts

This lack of support from external actors and most internal actors for a institutional development project meshed with an internal organizational structure not conducive to amplifying its voice. Prior to the 1983 *WDR* the Bank had no department or unit focused on public sector reform. This contrasted with nearly every other sector of Bank interest.[10] Although Stern's Operations Department had a Project Advisory Unit, three of its staff would become key Bank PSM-sector researchers.[11]

But in 1983 with publication of the *WDR*, structures began to shift and the Bank created its first Public Sector Management Unit (PSMU). Originally led by Arturo Israel, it was staffed by just a few individuals. Three of Israel's advisors either contributed to the 1983 *WDR* and/or published within the sector.[12] Unfortunately for PSM institutionalization desires, the Unit was hampered by its location. Not part of the Bank's 1972 reform of its program and policy divisions, this Unit struggled to attract Bank attention since Bank projects were led by the program and policy divisions. If your sector is not "at the program table," then its sector projects are less likely to be considered. Instead, this Unit's role was to reviewed projects to ensure any PSM-like components fitted into Bank operational objectives. PSM reform was so new that Unit staffs were left to their own intellectual pursuits. Thus, any new impetus for PSM reform often came from client governments, as in Indonesia. Project staffs were often pressured by client-states to address public sector

---

[10] Sector Departments: Agriculture and Rural Development; Education; Population, Health, and Nutrition; Transportation and Water; Urban Development; Energy; Industry.

[11] Francis Lethem, Arturo Israel, and Nimrod Raphaeli.

[12] Geoffrey Lamb, Mary Shirley, and Samuel Paul. Lamb and Shirley contributed to the 1983 *WDR*.

failures. Project staff would tell Unit staff that certain client practices were failing and would ask Unit staff for assistance. Or, as one former PSMU staff member recalled, project leaders would become so exasperated by client complaints that Unit staff were told to "just come up with something!" even if PSMU staff did not know what the answer might be (WB12).

Among regional vice presidencies, none had PSM Units until 1985. A partial exception was an institutional advisor position within the Eastern and Southern Africa Regional Office. This office was newly led by Kim Jaycox, a recent transfer as Vice President from the East Asia region. As noted earlier in this chapter, Jaycox had supported publishing the Indonesia Report. His institutional advisor was to encourage (1) growth-oriented policy reforms, (2) improve public investment, and (3) consider "institutional and human resource development," which he defined as the ability "to institutionalize the capacity to manage the economy flexibly and be responsible to external and internal development factors and to improve the quality of government expenditure" (Drattell 1985, 3).

The limited internal structures for PSM in the first half of the 1980s would soon change. Two shifts occurred in the late 1980s. The first shift was the 1987 internal organizational reform (see Chapter 4). The 1987 reform was the Bank's most significant organizational reform since 1972. The 1987 reforms created important organizational space within the Bank to leverage and to expand the sector agenda. However, and given a reform link with lending incentive issues that cut across all 32 years of PSM/PSG policy, it is discussed in Chapter 4. The second shift was a nascent Bank literature on public sector reform. For Bank career development, research is an important, and perhaps more important task, than project work (see Chapters 4 and 9). It is to this early-to-mid-1980s research that we now turn.

Creating Some Space: PSM Research

By analyzing Bank PSM/PSG publications across 32 years, three observations specific to the 1980s arise (see Table 5). The first is that 1980s Bank staff engaged SOEs in their research. This included efforts to understand parastatal rationales, improve parastatal performance, and compare parastatal successes and failures worldwide (World Bank 1983; Nellis 1986; Shirley 1986). Others discussed lessons learned from contracts in SOE reform (Nellis 1991) or engaged single-country cases (Shirley 1989).

The second observation is that by 1985, staff realized that even an improved SOE will not "get the prices right." This led to decidedly neoliberal turns as SOE research moved from reform to privatization. Bank researchers were coalescing around an external actor view that the "state was a poor entrepreneur" (Nellis 1986, 42–45). Dissenting staff faced evidence that inefficient SOEs were significant drains on client finances. By 1987, divestiture (privatization) had become a key topic in Bank public sector research. This contrasts with the 1983 *WDR* in which page 85 of the *Report* (the only page where divestiture was mentioned) had caused consternation among client-states who believed divestiture violated the Bank's Articles of Agreement. But by the mid-to-late 1980s, those voices were muted. The neoclassical economic agenda had "won." As such, Bank staff began to write about divestiture benefits, problems, where it occurred along with alternatives to divestiture such as leasing, management contracts, and joint-ventures. Many client governments were unwilling to sell SOEs. Politically, governments faced opposing labor unions and academics as well as fearing a loss of their own authority (Berg and Shirley 1987).

The third observation is that by the late 1980s, there began a period of sub-sector topic diversification that continues today. New topics like financial management, civil service reform, tax reform, and public expenditure management had their origins in the late 1980s. Each retain importance in today's PSM/PSG work. Early financial management research focused on understanding where financial decisions were made and how the Bank should engage regulatory policies (Gelb and Honohan 1989). Another banker observed that because the Bank had prioritized public expenditure management issues, client countries were "unable to cope with the uncertainties inherent in the planning and budgetary processes ... [and] are forced to react with damaging, ill-thought-out, across the board cuts" (Lacey 1989, vii–viii).

In 1987, the Bank's *WDR* was focused broadly upon financial systems and in particular, financial deregulation. This *WDR* discussed fiscal policy initiatives, decentralized decision-making within client countries, tax reforms, and improved allocations of public monies (World Bank 1988). The report was not an indication that the "state mattered" to development (as the Bank formally "discovered" in 1997, see Chapter 6) but that good public financial systems assisted the market, strengthened public sector institutions, and provided fiscal transparency. However, as Lacey (1989) noted, only a few countries had the capacity to undertake such medium-term tasks and the Bank's own staff lacked the capacity to help.

Another early sub-topic was civil service reform. In a 1988, one well-known member of staff discussed relationships between pay and unemployment. She found countries spending too much on public sector wages, employing too many civil servants, offering low salaries, and with large salary differences between high- and low-level civil servants. She argued that the Bank's PSM agenda should move beyond short-term policy objectives and toward longer-term reforms (Nunberg 1988). In other words, staffs were too focused on "big issues" (privatization and cutting civil services) rather than "what to do next" once workers were eliminated. Finally, and as an indication of neoclassical economics' "one model for everyone" view and limited allowances for regional staff to do PSM research, very few regional or country-specific PSM papers were published before 1989. Beyond the Indonesia

Report, exceptions were rare (e.g. Pfeffermann 1987; Shinohara 1981; Middleton et al. 1987 ; Shirley 1989).

Conclusion: US, UK, IMF, and G7 Matter Most in the 1980s

This chapter began with a discussion of the international economic instabilities in the 1970s, the evolving Bank perspectives on economic development, and how the 1980s Bank focused on structural adjustment lending rather than an institutional development focus. Structural adjustment loans were broad, macroeconomic-focused policy prescriptions unconcerned with "messy" institutional development. Reflecting PSM newness and internal structural barriers to its institutionalization, Table 1 shows how PSM project approvals began to increase between 1980 and 1988. Between 1980 and the creation of the Public Sector Management Unit in 1983, 32 projects were approved at a rate of 7.8 PSM projects per year. Between 1984 and 1988, just over 36 PSM per year were approved. Of those 181 projects approved during that five-year period, 58 had PSM components which encompassed more than 50 percent of its project monies. This rapid increase would continue. During the three-year 1989 to 1991 period, 470 PSM projects were approved (156 per year) of which 74 of those projects were majority PSM. The creation of this sector, and which actors mattered in its creation, is one of the purposes of this book.

This chapter identified the US (along with the UK, IMF, and G7) as the key stakeholders influencing PSM policy creation and change during the 1980s (see Tables 4 and 7).[13] However, just because the US was identified as the most important external actor shaping the 1980s PSM agenda need not imply that the US *fully controlled* the World Bank and this agenda. In developing this new sector of interest, the Bank was aware of American demands along with demands originating from the G7, the IMF, the UK, as well as dissent from certain West European Board members and concerns about whether PSM policies and projects violated the Bank's Articles of Agreement (see Table 7).

The G7 Group of Nations' annual statements paralleled Bank actions. The Bank obtained political and ideological support from the G7; ideological and legal support from the IMF; and political, ideological, and financial support from the US and the UK. The 1970s and early 1980s international economic crises required coordinated action (see Table 7). Crises created space for the Bank's key external

---

[13] Sharma (2013) suggests that the Bank's adoption of structural adjustment lending was driven by flaws within the Bank's operational units and not, as many have suggested, external actors. While his study focuses on the creation of lending instrument and not the creation of a Bank sector, his willingness to look at internal organizational actors within the Bank between McNamara's Presidency and the 1980s resonates with one purpose of this book.

actors to strengthen their engagement with the World Bank and to encourage the Bank, as a tool of key external actors, to reflect their policy preferences.

If this book stopped its analysis in October 1989, then we might argue that key nation-states, in line with international relations' realist theory, control an IO's policy outputs. Alternative internal perspectives on institutional development were not the Bank's primary sector policy output. The Bank's international civil servants responded to the wishes of the organization's dominant shareholders. When alternative sentiments were raised (such as in the Indonesia Report or in SOE debates), the Bank did not stop "dissenting" civil servants from expressing their views. In many cases, dissenting civil servants published alternative perspectives to an evolving norm even if it is arguable that "dissent" at the Bank remained rather narrowly defined from a disciplinary sense.

During the 1980s, the Bank's external actors prioritized a neoclassical economics model and encouraged structural adjustment lending via reinterpreting (but not amending) the Bank's Articles of Agreement. Moreover, the Bank's Presidents, Chief Economists (Krueger, in particular), and Senior Vice President for Operations (Stern) also pushed for PSM policy outputs (see Tables 7 and 8). Within a few years, structural adjustment ideas dominated Bank lending to developing countries. Structural adjustment's importance made it more difficult for the Bank's institutional development or other non-privatization options to be heard. From a lending incentive perspective (see Chapter 4), institutional development was a long-term project with uncertain outcomes. Institutional development also required government ministry or department-specific contextual knowledge and policy solutions. In contrast, structural adjustment relied on economic models (or a scientization of economic policy, see Marcussen 2006) where its proponents could assume away any contextual differences.

But despite such trends, the internal seeds for ongoing dissent had been planted. Such seeds began early with staff choosing not to forget the ul Haq and Chenery focus on poverty reduction. The 1983 WDR report, the first such report on public sector reform, tried to mesh (often uncomfortably) Chenery and Krueger perspectives. Important member states such as Indonesia, the Bank office staff in Jakarta, and the "political cover" provided by Kim Jaycox as Vice President for East and Southeast Asia, led to publication (even if delayed) of the Indonesia Report. This Report along with ongoing internal sector dissent created a coalescing alternative to neoliberal perspectives. Such dissent was also the basis for new research which diversified the sector topic portfolio and paved the way for an internally driven alteration of what the Bank understand as PSM in the early 1990s.

New events were on the horizon. The 1987 organizational reform (Chapter 4) and sector topic additions broadened sector possibilities. The fall of the Berlin Wall and desires of key Bank member states to cement post-Cold War victories led to a "good governance" agenda to PSM in August 1991. The parallels between that agenda and institutional development are hard to ignore. New PSMUs created space for sector advocates to push for further policy changes. Although lending decisions were made by Country Managers, client countries, and the Board, this sector had a seat at the table. The next chapter explains how its "seat at the table" was institutionalized, how changing world events gave credence to institutional development (and structural adjustment) imperatives, from where "good governance" arose, and how, by October 1995, sector topic diversification led to new projects and publications.

4

Reforming the Bank's Structure

Lending Incentives and "Bureaucratic Genocide"

Institutions that wish to survive are institutions that will reform in response to an identified need or threat. IOs like the World Bank are no different. The previous chapter discussed not just the evolution of PSM and PSG at the Bank but also which stakeholders (external or internal) were or were not influential over such policy shifts and the when and why of their influence. Inseparable from such policy evolution and change is how the Bank, as an institution, views itself. Prior to its 1987 reorganization, the last major Bank organizational reform was in 1972 (Philipps 2009).[1] Much had changed in the world and in our understanding of development during the intervening fifteen years. While other important reforms occurred in those years (creation of the Bank's first Public Sector Management Unit in 1983) or the creation of new lending instruments (structural adjustment), these changes were no longer enough.

The reader will observe that most of the book's chapters proceed in an historical fashion: 1980 to October 1989 (Chapter 3) and November 1989 to 2012 (Chapters 5, 6, 7, and 8). In contrast, this chapter jumps backwards (the 1987 reforms) and forward (the 1992 Wapenhans Report). The importance of this reform and the Report required such a decision. Burying the 1987 reform within Chapter 3's extensive timeline would have muddied the reform's impact on PSM/PSG. While the reform is a product of external actor desires and, thus, mirrors the "external actors mattered most" conclusion of Chapter 3, the reform (perhaps unintentionally) also set in motion the internal organizational shifts which helped create the next 25 years of PSM/PSG sector and policy change. The reform helped institutionalize the power of international civil servants over this

---

[1] The 1972 reorganization was a "defining moment in the history of the Bank ... it turned the Bank from a specialist, sectoral, engineering-oriented investment bank relying on market signals into an institution defined by economic planning, broad based, development-oriented, and no longer preoccupied with isolated entrepreneurial investment decisions ... into a development institution with a strong planning bias" (Wapenhans 1993). The 1972 reorganization placed countries as an equal focus to technical/engineering units (each region now had two country departments and one technical) and as such, "inadvertently strengthening the public-sector and treating the private sector as a residual" (Wapenhans 1993). Because of this greater decentralization, the Loan Committee took on greater importance as a place for coordinating policies and projects for the Bank's clients (Wapenhans 1993).

Who Matters at the World Bank?. Kim Moloney, Oxford University Press.
© Kim Moloney (2022). DOI: 10.1093/oso/9780192857729.003.0004

sector's policy changes. As per Phillips (2009), the 1987 reform was "an event that changed the basic culture of Bank like no other, and disposed of the growth-based optimism and to some extent the idealism of the McNamara era" (47).

Just as burying the 1987 reform within Chapter 3 would be problematic, a similar concern is applicable for the 1992 Wapenhans Report. The Bank's decision (still to today) to not publish what is essentially an explosive Report[2] with ramifications for the core of how the Bank operates (within and outside of this sector), burying this Report in Chapter 5 would have diminished its importance. While the Report was written with the Bank's prior history (from 1947) in mind, it also highlights the organizational tensions, prerogatives, and unresolved operational debates which, in their best light, require further consideration. In their worst light, these concerns may affect the Bank's legitimacy (and accountability) as an institution. As importantly, Report findings highlight challenges faced not only by PSM/PSG sector specialists and units but other sectors too. Report findings will reverberate throughout this book's subsequent timeline. At times, the Report concerns will sit just below the surface while at other moments, its concerns will find a clear resonance for key moments in future chapters.

Of the two topics covered in this chapter, the 1987 reform has received limited attention. In Reforming the World Bank: Twenty Years of Trial—and Error (Philipps 2009), the author is focused on the lead up to the Bank's 1997 reforms under President James Wolfensohn. This includes a partial chapter on the 1987 reforms. However, for this book, it is the 1987 reforms which are more important for explaining PSM/PSG change than the 1997 reforms. Along with another brief mention of the 1987 reforms in Xu and Weller's (2009) book, I could only find two other chapters which partially (2–3 pages) discussed the reforms (Kerler 2007; Kraske et al. 1996). Kerler (2007) also noted that key Bank member states (US, Japan, France) were dissatisfied with Bank performance and demanded reform.

The 1987 organizational reform was both a response to external stakeholder demands and an output of newly powerful internal actors desirous of creating a Bank structure capable of responding to its needs. That the 1987 reform was partially led by Kim Jaycox, an early proponent of institutional development in the 1980s (see Chapter 3) is not coincidence. The resulting Bank structure dramatically strengthened PSM influence within the Bank. Interestingly, and as viewed from the still-evolving PSM agenda, the 1987 reforms appeared to neither strengthen nor weaken the theoretical viewpoint behind structural adjustment but, instead, did rearrange the Bank's structure in favor of more non-structural adjustment to PSM in important ways. Not to be forgotten, and perhaps ironically for Bank staff,

---

[2] I was leaked a copy of this report.

the reform created a situation whereby the staff became victims of the Bank's own neoliberal "structural adjustment" within the Bank. The 1987 reform was brutal in its management of individuals and their careers.

The second focus of this chapter is the 1992 Wapenhans Report (see also Adams 2015). That this Report was never publicly released indicated a conversation the Bank did not want publicly debated even if Report contents were well-known within the Bank. The Report focused on the incentives within the Bank's organizational structure to lend monies, to create policy, and to interact with client states. The Report identified the Bank's incentives and asked where they might hamper development outcomes. Its uncomfortable answers influenced the non-release of the Report. While one outcome of the 1987 reform was a restructured World Bank with new spaces, monies, and hiring incentives (and perhaps also a demoralized staff), an outcome of the Wapenhans Report may be impolitely (but accurately) described as simply bankers nodding their heads in agreement with what Wapenhans wrote but being unable or unwilling to alter incentives. Each outcome influenced what is or is not possible within PSM/PSG policy change outputs over the next two decades.

Changing the Bank's Organizational Structure: The 1987 Reforms

It is difficult to accurately discuss the Bank of the 1980s without referencing the Bank's 1987 organizational reforms. In a mid-1980s era when the Bank was advising client countries to cut budgets, retrench employees, and prioritize the free market, in 1987 the Bank also summarily "fired" all of its employees in an attempt to reduce Bank budgetary costs. A former Bank Vice President for Corporate Planning and Budgeting and former Director-General of OED/IEG stated in his interview with the Bank's Historian that the 1987 reforms were eerily similar to the Bank's own recommended reforms of client nations:

> In a way, it was like when we have very brutal conditions for adjustment loans. It was a similar process; very dogmatic and focused on shifting the Bank's work toward the higher place of macroeconomic adjustment. And, therefore, it's not surprising that the very people who designed the reorganization also were the people who enjoyed doing the brutal types of adjustment operations.
>
> (Picciotto 2000)

This dogmatic view of development also overtook the Bank, as an organization (Picciotto 2000). The internal reforms resembled the Bank's ruthless "cut the state" (in this case, "cut the Bank") advice that the Bank had provided to its clients.

There are conflicting stories about why the Bank undertook the reforms.[3] Some felt Conable did it to get Ernie Stern out of the Bank (Rotberg 1994; Kraske et al. 1996) because no one could "get the guy out of there, short of reorganizing the whole Bank to get him out" (WB12). Certainly it is true that the reforms removed Stern from his position as Senior Vice President for Operations to another Senior Vice President position (Finance). Others took a different view on Stern. An interviewee of the Bank Historian pointed out that Conable understood "that Ernie had more friends at the Bank than he [Conable] had, and that he wasn't about to move Ernie out of the Bank … He [Conable] needed Ernie, which was a wise and accurate assessment … I think that the reorganization, therefore, was meant to move Ernie out, over to Finance … [even if] Ernie … was totally disinterested in Finance" (Rotberg 1994).

A related but slightly different perspective viewed the reforms as a way to lessen the Bank's "approval culture" (and multiple project sign-offs) by shifting project units to the regions. The 1987 reform's decentralization of loan approval occurred in concert with the Bank's formal end to its Loan Committee (led by Stern). Prior to its transformation into the Operations Committee, the Loan Committee reviewed and approved all projects before reaching the Board for final (often rubber-stamp) approval (WB29).[4] By ending this Committee, removing Stern from its Head, and pushing Stern out of Operations, the view that the reform helped move a powerful internal actor had its merits.

Politically, Conable also had no choice. Conable wanted to "protect the Bank" given concerns about how the Bank's administrative budget had risen significantly since the 1970s. The Bank's then-Budget Director, Robert Picciotto, reflected that

> [h]aving been on the Hill working on budgets, he [Conable] knew how important it was. It clicked when there was a big budget overrun on the reorganization and the Board was so insulting that Wapenhans (then Senior Vice President for Administration) almost resigned … The budget at that time was unmanaged, and therefore, we had overruns and under-runs all the time. There was no budget

---

[3] In addition, Phillips cites a 1986 staff report "Streamlining Bank Procedures" (written by Steven Denning) as precursor to the 1987 reform (Philipps 2009, 37). However, this staff report is neither found on the Bank website or not via a general Google search. As such, my chapter summary is nearly entirely reliant on interviewee recollections, internal Bank documents, and a few newspaper articles.

[4] One Loan Committee project advisor [Abraham (Al) Raizen] said his job was to review "nearly every project submitted to the Loan Committee." "My function was generally a quality control one … I had to assure consistency in the approaches being taken by individual regions in terms of conditionality and applying the Bank's guidelines and policies." He reviewed an average of 250 projects per year (Bank's World 1984b, 19).

discipline. And the opacity of the budget process was the very reason that the Board supported the '87 reorganization."

(Picciotto 2000)[5]

In June of 1986, the World Bank's budget was opposed by the "United States, Japan, and France, with Germany and the U.K. abstaining. This vote of no confidence occurred two days before Barber Conable assumed office, which led him to ask Treasury Secretary Baker, who had prevailed upon Conable to accept the presidency, what are you doing to me?" (Gwin 1994, 77; Kraske et al. 1996).

In response to staff concerns that that a reform would reduce staff numbers, Conable wrote the following missive to staff:

> My personal view is that there will be some reduction but I don't want to quantify it. I don't want to get in a situation where we, in order to force manpower goals, have created bottlenecks in the Bank where we can't handle the load ... I personally think this institution is going to have to grow. But it will not be permitted to grow unless we can demonstrate we are capable of making the tough decisions that are necessary to keep ourselves lean. And so, a very large part of this is to tell our member countries that we are capable of internal reorganization–that we *don't* have to have imposed on us from outside, via our Board or anybody else, the desire to keep the bureaucracy under control here.
>
> (Bank's World 1987a, 22, emphasis added)

What is interesting about Conable's "answer" was not just his non-answer to staff questions but also his emphasis on how the Bank must show member states that it can keep its own "bureaucracy under control" and make the "tough decisions to keep ourselves lean." This answer is both a response to key external actor concern but also a reflection on whether the Bank can do to itself what it is asking other countries to do.

Other reasons for the 1987 reform included the Bank's over centralization and that the Bank "tried to do everything under the sun. We lacked focus" (Rajagopalan 1993). In a 1980s climate of budgetary cutbacks, donors were asking the Bank, "What did we build?" (WB19). Others concurred that the pressure for reform came from US and from the Executive Directors, in general (WB26). Wapenhans himself (the focus of the last half of this chapter) was not sure whether the need to reform came from "external pressure, or a deep conviction that the political goal of increasing the capital of this institution sufficiently to make it self-sustaining ... made it unavoidable" (Wapenhans 1993). More cynically, the reform may also have desired "to dampen the criticism from the US Treasury that the Bank

---

[5] The irony of such a Bank budget description is hard to ignore given the Bank's advice to developing countries.

was inefficient" and in particular, arose from a commercial bank disappointment that the Bank did not "bail them [commercial banks] out" (in terms of commercial bank loans to developing countries) in the early 1980s (Rotberg 1994).

"Bureaucratic Equivalent of Genocide"

When the Bank's key donors did not approve the Bank's June 1986 budget, the Bank reacted quickly. In the fall of 1986, the Bank hired an outside consultancy firm (Cresap, McCormick and Paget, now defunct) to assist (Philipps 2009). The firm's job was "to assess the Bank's current operations and recommend changes in its organizational structure and business processes" (Kraske et al. 1996). The hired consultants spoke with staff at all levels and then chose a dozen or so staff to sit on the Reorganization's internal Steering Committee. The consultant company's view was that Bank needed large-scale restructuring and it was best for the Bank to restructure from "within" and thus, a Steering Committee was created.

The consultants told Conable that Bank staff complained about "cumbersome, time-consuming procedures that took little account of the needs and wishes of borrowers" (Kraske et al. 1996, 254). Since Conable also believed the Bank's bureaucracy was to blame[6] and perhaps because of Stern's operational power within the Bank, Stern was excluded from participating in the reform process. Instead, it was Kim Jaycox (first Bank Vice President to create a regional PSM Unit and Indonesia Report supporter, see Chapter 3) who was selected to lead the Bank's Steering Committee for the 1987 Reorganization.[7]

Once President Conable agreed to the plan, the reorganization was "organized" in less than nine months. The first Steering Committee meeting was held in late January 1987. A second meeting on reorganization strategies occurred two months later and the implementation of the full reorganization plan began in June 1987. In late April, the steering committee submitted its report to Conable; in May, the Board approved the plan including a "separation package"[8] for 400 staff who would

---

[6] Conable concluded early that "the compartmentalized structure of the organization, the staff support available to him, and the way decisions were made in the Bank did not allow him to take charge. Specifically, he thought that a disproportionate amount of resources and decision-making authority was concentrated in the office of the senior vice president, operations [Stern's position]" (Kraske et al. 1996, 254).

[7] Here is why Jaycox was chosen: "At the consultants' recommendation, Conable decided to ground the exercise in the Bank itself, and he appointed a task force. Kim Jaycox, the recently appointed Vice President for Eastern and Southern Africa, who had impressed the consultants with his perceptive observations about what was wrong in the Bank, was chosen to head the task force" (Kraske et al. 1996, 254).

[8] Gwin (1994) wrote: "according to Conable, the Bank had to put together such a rich personnel separation package that he lost the support of the U.S. government for reorganization. The Bank staff considered the reorganization disruptive and, more seriously, without clear purpose or apparent benefit to programs. Indeed, many inside and outside the Bank claimed at the time that the reorganization led to a serious mismatch between the new tasks the Bank was being pressured to take on (in environmental

soon be asked to leave the Bank (Kraske et al. 1996). To say that the reform effort consumed much staff time, intellectual energy and psychological resources throughout 1987 is an extraordinary understatement.

As one of his first actions, Jaycox solicited 200 memorandums from staff asking "what [was] wrong with the Bank and what ought to be done to fix it" (Bank's World 1987b, 2). Jaycox claimed the major complaints were the following: "What have managers done for us lately? What is their contribution to the product? What is the value-added from all these reviews, quality control features and insurance policies that are part of the Bank's procedures? Where is the real responsibility— the accountability? How much time do I spend looking inward, in effect, working on the polish of the product, rather than on the substance?" (Bank's World 1987b, 2–3). Jaycox said that bankers wanted country-specific organizational structures but its then-current structure (created in the 1972 reorganization) made it "costly" to focus only on countries. The 1972 structure created situations where conflict resolution "involve[s] too many people, too many layers, and too much time. It is a very, very expensive" (Bank's World 1987b, 3). The "how to reorganize" debate became one of how the Bank could retain its technical units (and concurrent expertise) while encouraging a country focus. The Steering Committee answer was to create a matrix structure whereby one person monitors a country as opposed to a then-current situation where 4–5 persons at various layers of Bank bureaucracy monitored the country.

Echoing President Conable's concerns about staff size, Jaycox underlined in a staff newsletter that "there is no target to reduce personnel in this reorganization ... [despite] false information that someone got into the Wall Street Journal ... and reported as if it were fact" (Bank's World 1987b, 4). Unsurprisingly, distrust between staff members and the Steering Committee was high. In a Q and A with the staff association reprinted for Bank's World, Jaycox was asked if most Steering Committee members were former Bank Young Professionals,[9] like him. Instead of answering the question directly, Jaycox explained the task force recruitment process relied on Bank Vice Presidents (such as him, he had previously been a Vice President for East and Southeast Asia and also Eastern and Southern Africa) for recommending staff.

Willi Wapenhans, who became the new Senior Vice President for External Affairs and Administration after the 1987 reforms (and who wrote the Report covered in the last half of this chapter) recalled the "who was involved" question a bit differently: "Rather inexperienced, but ruthlessly ambitious younger managers, and some obscure outside consultants, were his [Conable's] advisors in the matter.

sensitivity, in eastern Europe and the former Soviet Union, and in private sector development) and the inadequate size and composition of the staff. Another problem observers believed, was too little sector-specific technical expertise as a result of reorganization" (Gwin 1994, 77).

[9] This recruitment program faces high entry barriers, is highly competitive, and once accepted, YP careers are put on a fast-track.

The experienced hands in the Bank were kept out" (Wapenhans 1993). Wapenhans recalled how his unasked for new Senior Vice President role was illustrative of the bureaucratic confusion that existed during that period:

> I was in [the reform] way over my head. I had not participated in the design and was brought in at a very late stage. There were some merits in the new overall design and its objectives, but lots of demerits in the details, especially the way in which the reorganization was to be implemented on the staffing side … The whole process was a foregone conclusion … To make matters worse, unbeknown to me, the newly appointed Vice President of Personnel, Bill Cosgrove, who was to report to me, and the very person in charge of designing the procedures for the implementation of the reorganization, had already been to the relevant Board committees. He had managed to commit the Board to the central features of the implementation plan. I clearly was to be the fig leaf covering the intimate parts of the shameful breach of compact with staff. At least, that's the way I felt. Now, one other thing happened. Immediately after I took the job, and before I was formally appointed, Conable started to fire people, senior managers. He did so in violation of every single rule in the existing book … It was pretty clear that ultimately I would have to hold the bag.
>
> (Wapenhans 1993)

Since many staff did not have individual contracts, Staff Association rules were their de facto contract and changes to its rules required time, sufficient notice, debate, and so on. However, that was not what occurred. Instead, "a new—the famous staff rule 509—or whatever the number was—was needed to be shaped, finalized, promulgated and communicated to become the rule that would govern personnel decisions during implementation of the reorganization but would then self-destruct" (Wapenhans 1993). Alternatively, per another description:

> [W]hat happened was almost like a coup d'état by a bunch of colonels … And the very people who designed the organization got all the plum jobs. And what they did was to eliminate, in the most elegant way, the entire infrastructure of the projects establishment which was the core of the Bank's professional leadership; they did so by eliminating one grade. Eliminating the 27 grade has to be the bureaucratic equivalent of genocide. We lost of a whole generation of development practitioners. When I saw this, I was flabbergasted, because what they were saying to people who devoted their life to this institution: "Either you get demoted, or you get out!" They got out.
>
> (Picciotto 2000)

Implementation began in early June 1987 and by late June, the Senior Vice Presidents and Managers had been named. A special June/July issue of Bank's World was published in which senior-level appointments were officially announced for each region and functional area such as legal, policy/planning/research, and administration (Bank's World 1987c). Notably, Ernie Stern, the former Senior Vice President for Operations between 1980 and 1987 became the new Senior Vice President for Finance, a decidedly less-prestigious post given that the former had shaped and managed the Bank's policy and project outputs. Of the staff not fired, most of the rest of the Bank's staff were in their new positions by October 1987 although several found no conclusion to their circumstances until the following year (Kraske et al. 1996).

The reform reality was that every staff member lost their job and then reapplied—everyone from secretaries to Vice Presidents. It was in one interviewee's words: "a free for all" and "the time of big tension within the Bank. Months went by with uncertainty about who was going and who was not going … Imagine sitting there wondering whether you were going to be left out. For some, it was a reason to celebrate. For some people, the package was much as a two-year salary" (WB33).[10] One former Bank staff member said the 1987 reforms were "one of the worst things to befall on this institution since its inception" (Rajagopalan 1993). Others felt Conable "came from Congress and was used to [managing] 5–10 people … [he] was under pressure from Congress to cut the Bank bureaucracy by 15–20 percent so he got a second-class consulting firm [to help]". The reforms were also variously considered a "management fad" (WB28), a "failure" (WB19), "traumatic" (WB6, Picciotto 2000) and "when we [the Bank] lost our innocence and virginity as an institution" (WB26). The Bank had failed to make a "business case" for reform and instead, just "cut jobs across the board" (WB26). In the end, about 5 percent of Bank staff lost their jobs (Philipps 2009).

Were the reforms effective? Jaycox noted that evaluating reform "efficiency" was impossible in an organization like the Bank, which is ironic given the Bank's interest in encouraging efficiency within client countries. Jaycox noted, "we are not the Ford Motor Company. We're not an assembly line, we don't have a standard product. Everything is tailor-made … some of the things we spend money on when we're not sure they'll be effective turn out to be extremely effective two years later when, for instance, things fall into place politically in the country" (Bank's World 1987b, 5).

One interviewee believed that the 1987 reforms "did not change the incentives within the institutions" (WB6). Such incentives would be discussed again, just five years later, in the Wapenhans Report. But for this interviewee,

---

[10] The most generous package was the so-called "Package B" with its three-year full-salary compensation upon departure. Some staffers, desirous of Package B, would allegedly not answer their home phone just in case human resources was calling saying that a position had become available.

The main thing it did—was a cultural break—before they [civil servants] joined the institution, they thought it was for life (like the Japanese system) and thus, you specialize in the arcane issues and in return, the World Bank gives you lifetime employment. The break of this contract, including everyone from developing countries, [who] had to move in 30 days, sell houses, and remove their kids from school, [many] had G4 visas … many were not rehired. After [the 1987 reforms], [there was] more temporary employment, fewer long-term hires … the Bank staff did reduce for a while but not for long. One of the conditions for these compensation packages was that you do not get re-hired, but some did, as consultants.

(WB6)

Another recollected: "On a given day, everyone was told they had 'lost' their jobs—started from the top-down" (WB19) and thus, "all professional staff were nominally fired on a certain date in early 1987 and had to re-apply for newly created positions" (Philipps 2009, 48). To re-build the organization, it was top-down exercise (WB19) where "Vice Presidents selected senior managers, senior managers selected middle managers, and middle managers selected junior managers and staff over a period of several weeks, or, in some cases, months" (Philipps 2009, 48). Thus, in the end, "anyone left over went into the 'pool' and there were generous pay-out options" (WB19). Often people would sit in an empty office and with no work program—many were discontented. People were rehired due to their work quality and personal network (WB19, WB26).

In the end, the Bank created "an aristocracy of macroeconomic managers, and a proletariat of professionals who do the work as task managers … they [macroeconomists] viewed projects and people essentially as commodities; fit for buying and selling among country directors. We lost a sense of loyalty and inclusion within the organization" (Picciotto 2000). The only benefit appeared to be that the Bank became less of a "lifetime career place". This is a controversial benefit for Bank staff who characterized the 1987 reform as a cultural loss (memory loss) that harmed the institution (WB6). Others felt the reforms were a version of "shock therapy" that changed staff "attitude [from one] of commitment to an attitude of compliance, in fact, an attitude of compliance in anticipation. The art of stargazing [i.e., staff replication of upper management thoughts] was perfected by staff and survival instincts were honed" (Wapenhans 1993). In the new Bank, there were 60 more managers than before (Kraske et al. 1996) and a doubling of Bank Vice Presidents from two to four (Philipps 2009).[11]

In terms of an evolving PSM agenda, the 1987 reforms appeared to neither strengthen nor weaken the theoretical viewpoint behind structural adjustment but did rearrange the Bank's structure in favor of more PSM in important ways.

---

[11] In a 1988 Staff Association report, the staff found "essentially the same problems as before: lack of direction, ineffective leadership, and unclear goals" (Philipps 2009, 49)

As Philips (2009) noted, the 1987 reform created an expectation "that economic policy reform rather than technical projects would become increasingly the Bank's business" (47). Infrastructure and agricultural development were no longer favored. As the next chapters relate, newly prominent negative lessons from structural adjustment would soon make waves. Other economic perspectives would alter the PSM agenda. The demise of the superpower rivalry between 1989 and 1991 was not yet on the horizon.

But with such post-1989 shifts via negative lessons, new economic perspectives, and the 1989–1991 events, the 1987 reform created structural space for more PSM and in particular, the institutional development version of PSM, along with emergent sector topics like public expenditure management and public financial management (see Table 5 and Chapter 3). The 1987 reform created new regional vice presidencies in which each region had the freedom to include or exclude PSMUs.[12] These PSMUs were staffed by persons whose understanding of PSM extended beyond a neoliberal perspective. Moreover, the new vice presidencies eased communication between the Bank's program and policy staff. They were no longer organizationally divided. Each technical unit could be incorporated into own regional vice presidency. This was important for PSM reform. An interviewee recalled that during the first eighteen months of Africa PSMU existence (before the 1987 reform), they were "begging for resources here and there ... asking the Belgian Executive Director, Saudi Arabian Executive Director, Kuwaitis, French ... each Executive Director for money. The topic was interesting but no one knew what to do about it. By the 1987 reorganization, they [PSMU idea] were 'popular' and every region of the Bank wanted to set up one of these Units" (WB35).

The reorganization allowed PSMUs to compete, for the first time, with other Sector Units (called "Technical Units") for project inclusion. Sector directors had to "sell" their services to country economists and directors (WB17). If a Country Director did not believe their client needed a sector's service, if they did not believe in the sector, and/or did not trust sector work, the Sector Director and their staff would not be hired. Sector Directors then moved to the next Country Economist or Country Director to sell sector services. Even if every Country Director did not "buy" a PSM sector idea (after 1987), it was far more advantageous to be within this program/project-making system than outside. This was a substantial improvement from the situation faced by Bank's first-ever PSMU in 1983 (see Chapter 3).

As noted in Table 1,[13] there were 57 PSM projects in 1987, 73 in 1988, and 117 in 1989. This 1989 project count for PSM equated to 47 percent of approved Bank projects in 1989. Table 1 also notes that from 1989 to 2012 (and also to 2020 via

---

[12] The Europe, Middle East, and North Africa Regional Office had a public sector advisor in 1987 but not in 1988 and 1989. The African and Latin American/Caribbean regions kept their institutional advisor positions after 1987.

[13] All tables referenced in this book may be found in the Appendix

the book's Postscript), no single future year would have a lower percentage of Bank projects with a PSM component than 1989. All of this occurred before the fall of the Berlin Wall and the collapse of the Soviet Union. It occurred before key states and their Executive Directors pushed the Bank to not lose their Cold War win. It also occurred four years before "governance" was added to the PSM agenda. This organizational shift via the 1987 reform set the stage for a more diverse understanding of PSM to emerge—whether it was privatization and structural adjustment or new projects in public expenditure management and public financial management or even institutional development—the 1987 reform gave fuel to the PSM agenda. With that fuel in its tank, PSM was no longer a Bank afterthought.

Yet, this story just relayed within this chapter has been infrequently told. The world-changing years of 1989–1991 starting just two years after 1987, quickly drowned out the reform as a notable event within most Bank scholars' timelines. The 1989–1991 events appeared to confirm for scholars of international relations that external actors (and events) alter Bank agendas. But for the PSM sector, it was the rearrangement of the Bank's structure with top-level Bank staff complicity (including that of the reform's lead manager who was also a PSM supporter, Kim Jaycox) which created organizational space for PSM project approvals to explode, for PSM sector work to infiltrate all Bank regions, and for a deepening of the sector's policy agenda. It is probably not accidental that Kim Jaycox, who helped pushed the Indonesia Report to publication (see Chapter 3), who led the 1987 Bank reform, and who prior to the 1987 reform (and afterward as well), was a Vice President of a region (Africa) that was first Regional Vice Presidency to add a PSMU.

The Wapenhans Report and Cementing Incentives

While the 1987 reform helped create the organizational space, budgetary resources, and hiring incentives to expand the Bank's PSM agenda, the 1992 Wapenhans Report attempted to understand how the Bank's organizational incentives influenced its outputs. The Report did not call for another reorganization; but it did become a still-unanswered clarion call that the Bank's "lending incentives" may hamper development outcomes. There are at least two dozen scholars who briefly mention the Wapenhans Report in their work (e.g., Annisette 2004; Thomas 2004; Bare 1998; Pincus and Winters 2018; Moore 1998; Nielson et al. 2006; Williams 2008). It is less common to detail Report specifics (Weaver and Leiteritz 2005). The general scholarly consensus is that the Report clearly links poor project performance to lending incentives and the Bank's culture. I do not disagree.

But given this book's purpose, the Wapenhans Report requires discussion. Similar to the 1987 reform, the Report matters for future PSM (and PSG) policy direction. It lays out the bureaucratic situation facing project managers, project evaluators, and sector policy staff. It places staff within an organizational incentives hierarchy that provides rewards not for sector policy performance but for lending or "getting money out the door" performance (Berkman 2008; Ravallion 2015). This chapter adds to prior analysis of this Report by detailing its impact on the PSM/PSG sector. There are at least three impacts.

The first is that while the 1987 reforms created organizational space for new PSM sector lending, the organizational incentives described by Wapenhans meant that any new organizational spaces must become quickly filled by projects. The project numbers from the 1987–1989 period, a period before the Cold War's end, indicate that this is what happened. PSM projects were created. The prior lending incentives were not overcome.

The second is that new priorities given to economic policies (in general) as PSM sector policies (specifically) meant that expansions of what is PSM sector policy to include public expenditure management, public financial management, and more civil service reform also meant more projects and more lending. The fall of the Berlin Wall and the end of the Cold War created a cascade of PSM (and after 1991, PSG) projects which further cemented the Bank's long-held lending incentives.

The third is that as noted in Chapter 9, poor project performance was considered a side issue both before and after the Report. While the short-lived Quality Assurance Group and another short-lived Results Secretariat attempted to alter a decades-long Bank affliction unsolved by the Operations Evaluations Department or OED (see Chapter 9), the first two had short organizational lives while renaming of the OED to the Internal Evaluation Group (IEG) in the early 2000s did not change its primary after-the-fact evaluative purpose. It is with the above in mind that this chapter's attention turns to the Report, its origins, its content, and its relevance to the PSM/PSG sector.

In February 1992, Bank President Lewis Preston and Ernie Stern[14] approached Senior Vice President Bill Wapenhans to lead a new "Portfolio Management Task Force." As Task Force Leader, Wapenhans would report directly to President Preston.[15] Wapenhans was to determine whether the Bank was learning from current and past program and project operations. The formal question, however, was whether Bank staff members, as then incentivized, were doing the best for the Bank's client countries.[16] On July 24, 1992, Wapenhans presented his report. Formally titled, "Effective Implementation: Key to Development Report," the Report is colloquially recalled as the "Wapenhans Report." Before submitting his report

---

[14] By 1992, Stern had returned to a "less exposed but once again powerful role in Operations" (Wapenhans 1993).

[15] Wapenhans later told the Bank Historian that he felt no interference from Preston or Stern (Wapenhans 1993).

[16] The Wapenhans Report was widely recalled by Bank interviewees despite never being publicly released. Some of my Bank interviewees tried while I was in their office to find a copy of the Wapenhans Report on the Bank's internal intranet. Each was surprised that they could not find it. Eventually, I obtained the Report from a non-Bank interviewee who had been leaked the Report.

to Preston, Wapenhans provided Stern with a courtesy copy. Wapenhans recalled that Stern "called me back the next day and said: "Don't change a word, I think this is a report the Bank needs" (Wapenhans 1993). In his letter introducing the Report, President Preston concluded that the Bank must consider the "successful implementation of approved operations outweigh[ing] new annual commitments as an indicator of the Bank's development effectiveness" (World Bank 1992a, 1; Annex E, emphasis added). In other words, program and project quality were to outweigh the Bank's "getting money out the door" incentive (see also Chapter 9).

The report was a thoughtful and at times, an unforgiving appraisal of Bank operations (Adams 2015). Based on client-country discussions, discussions and interviews with Bank staff and Task Force research, Wapenhans concluded that the Bank had room for improvement. If the 1990s Bank according to a 1989 speech by President Conable was to focus on development sustainability, then Wapenhans wrote that Bank must evaluate "success ... by benefits 'on the ground' ... not by loan approvals, good reports or disbursements" (World Bank 1992a, i). Since a Bank incentive is to loan money, he believed that the Executive Directors often prefer to not vote down a loan as it may never be seen again. Or, as noted by two scholars,

> Loans are already painfully slow in clearing all the procedural hurdles and borrowers despair of ever receiving one with less than a year and a half lead time. Executive directors are understandably interested in obtaining loans for their protégés without agonizing delays and thus will always lend a hand, and a vote, to their fellow-sufferers. Perhaps the greatest obstacle of all to board independence and increased power is the sheer bureaucratic guile of the Bank's top layers of management prepared to do battle against anybody who might try to manage the Bank in their stead.
>
> (George and Sabelli 1994, 216, emphasis in the original)

This "pervasive preoccupation with new lending" (and the bureaucratic muscle behind it) encouraged project managers to include loan conditionalities that made it easier to obtain Board project approval rather than conditionalities either beneficial to the project or country or, in some cases, even relevant to the project (World Bank 1992a, iii). A later interview with the Bank's Historian, Wapenhans underlined the incentive system's logic:

> If achievement is measured in terms of financial performance then, of course, success is measured in terms of piling up yielding assets. When the biggest success experience for the organization in the entire fiscal year is the release to the press of an Annual Report with yet another record year of new loan and credit commitments, another record year of net surpluses, and record allocations to reserves ...

That made for welcome news and reassuring publicity. [Such a practice] conditions the home arena, for Board members and their superiors, for those who sell
the Bank's bonds, and for those who procure taxpayers money in support of the
institutions. Not a negligible constituency that deserves some attention.

(Wapenhans 1993)

That is, lending continuance was more important than positive economic development resulting from the loans. Whether the sector focus was PSM or something
else, such Bank incentives made caring about developmental outcomes difficult.
For Bank Project Managers, this led to thinking in terms of "what was needed"
for a project to obtain approval and less about the project's assumptions, risks, or
whether there was "country commitment" behind the project. Project planning
and the project's suggested policy shifts were more important than project implementation or its supervision (World Bank 1992a). The Bank's project supervision
system was self-reporting and not transparent. As such, "too many projects receive
satisfactory ratings during supervision, only to fail on completion" (World Bank
1992a, 10).

When Bank staff were asked if their managers or Division Chiefs assisted them
in improving project quality, more than half said the managers did not have
enough time. Project and Task Managers felt "overload[ed] with administrative
tasks, project timetables and lending targets which, they believe[d], led to inadequate technical preparation and weak assessments of institutional implementation
capacity" (World Bank 1992a, 14). Even worse were staff beliefs that "supervision reporting serves to rate them rather than to facilitate managerial decisions,
and some report pressure—from managers—to minimize the number of project
projects through generous rating" (World Bank 1992a, 15).

If staff believed managers were more concerned with "lending targets rather
than results on the ground" (World Bank 1992a, 21), then we should not be surprised when lending incentives displace development concerns. No one, including
Executive Directors, wants a Bank unable to lend. Developing countries viewed
the Bank as a source of cheap money. This money, if obtained, can help achieve
government objectives. As such, client countries must then live with the consequences including loan payback even if a project became ineffective. At the same
time, the Report determined that the Bank's project negotiation process with client
states was considered "coercive" by Bank staff because it "impose[d] the Bank's
philosophy" rather than listening to client considerations (World Bank 1992a, 14).

Bureaucratic politicking among Project and Task Managers and their supervisors was tempered by staff belief that since the 1987 reorganization, there was more
space for dialogue. Even so, some staff felt that the Bank still had too few sector
specialists providing project advice. In the 1980s, the Bank believed ipso facto that
its project objectives were "right". Signing an agreement with a client state was
enough proof that implementation would occur. And yet, the Report noted that

just "22 percent of the financial covenants in loan/credit agreements were in compliance," which the Report labeled "gross non-compliance" (World Bank 1992a, 8). For Wapenhans, "[t]he high incidence of non-compliance undermines the Bank's credibility. It also indicates a lack of genuine concern about governance and a lack of realism at the time of negotiation. If staff and managers are prepared to tolerate high levels of continuous non-compliance, the question arises as to whether such covenants should be included in the first place" (World Bank 1992a, 20).

These failures coexisted with reductions in the Bank's portfolio performance. The project success rate was 66 percent in FY1989 to FY1991, down 21 percent from a decade earlier (World Bank 1992a, iii, 4). The Report argued that Country Directors and Division Chiefs "must be as accountable for managing each country's portfolio performance as for new lending" (World Bank 1992a, 18). Increased project complexity may also influence project failure. Projects could (and can still today) be co-financed; be banned under multiple loan instruments; require environmental, gender, or poverty considerations; contain multiple legal documents; or not even involve the project implementers in project negotiations. Such factors moved projects from a simple idea to ones that were difficult for the Bank and its clients to manage (World Bank 1992a). According to Wapenhans, "individual staffers may try to apply all policy prescriptions in each and every case. Even if a staffer knows better, a system of peer reviews adds compulsion because, invariably, the question is raised: 'How come you are not going to have environmental conditionality in this particular project? Is there no environment where your project is?' So, while the policy intent is to be preventive, its indiscriminate application is also in the career interest [of a project leader to comply]" (Wapenhans 1993).

When "problem projects" were identified, Project Managers found it difficult to obtain budgetary resources to restructure the project or to extend supervisory periods. Thus, the Bank infrequently restructured problem projects (World Bank 1992a, 9–10). If a problem project was identified, and if staff asked for more technical assistance, this was code for a "securing your rear-end mentality" given that "cutting losses was not a welcome option, neither in the Bank nor in the country concerned" (Wapenhans 1993). Legally, the Bank's Articles of Agreement defined project supervision as "supervising the procurement, disbursement and end use of IDA and IBRD funds" and (2) "monitoring compliance with loan/credit contracts". In other words, there was no legal commitment that the Bank must also "facilitat[e] implementation by helping Borrowers interpret and respond to the Bank's requirements" or "provid[e] substantive implementation assistance to Borrowers") (World Bank 1992a, 11). Implementation was not the Bank's task; it was the borrower's task.

In this environment, it is not difficult to envision how negative (development) cycles may perpetuate themselves or why incentives to think outside disciplinary boundaries were not encouraged. If a country's government officials know they will not be held accountable, and that the Bank has an approval culture not based on project quality or subsequent project follow-up but instead on getting money out the door, then "country commitment" was not required. Clients also understood that they did not have to comply with all Bank conditions. A client could take the low-interest money without much worry. Regardless of the fact that a country's subsequent generations must eventually repay the loan.[17]

In a 2005 book published by the World Bank, several former Country Directors recollected on their diverse experiences. Their insights reflect how personal and disciplinary politics frames policy outputs and the intersection of such politics with potential implications for post-project accountabilities. Acknowledging past difficulties with "impatience, intolerance, and sometimes nastiness among people at the Bank and with the appearance that our entire culture is designed to find fault in others," one staff believed for the most part, Bank staff are "well intentioned, competent, and professional, and everyone—I included—is entitled to make mistakes" (Lafourcade 2005, 164).

Years later, Phyllis Pomerantz served as the Bank's Country Manager for Mozambique just after the country concluded a decades-long civil war. This was exactly the type of situation where knowing a nation's politics might be important. But because Bank staffs often only interact with a client country's Finance Minister and top technocrats, broader sociopolitical understandings may be under-prioritized. Pomerantz observed that "in a number of instances, the marriage between the young technocrats of the government and the personnel of the World Bank was a happy one, and we learned from each other. But in other circumstances, our combined lack of political acumen and understanding caused big problems" (Pomerantz 2005, 55).

Given that the Bank's poorest countries (at the time) had limited access to other financing options (country-specific credit ratings became popular after the mid-1990s), the Bank called the shots. Whether the project was actually designed and implemented properly became a side issue (for perhaps the Bank and the country). Sensing such failures might become a Bank liability, Wapenhans brought in a former Bank General Counsel to evaluate this issue. Wapenhans' question and partial answer was simple: "If, in fact, the Bank is calling the shots and makes the decisions, did it create a contingent liability for itself, even if not enforceable, it is nevertheless there and difficult to deny" (Wapenhans 1993). Unfortunately, neither Wapenhans' 1993 interview with the Bank's Historian nor his Report directly answer the contingent-liability question.[18] It is likely that the Bank's internal

---

[17] Wapenhans observed, "In some instances, the Bank's IDA portfolio may account for up to 40 percent of total external indebtedness of a country, and 70 percent of the 40 percent are failing. That's a pretty troublesome mortgage to carry for that country" (Wapenhans 1993).

[18] Although hired 2–3 years after the Wapenhans Report, J.W. Muis' role as Bank Comptroller did attempt to introduce risk and other liability questions into Bank discussions. His post-departure interview with the Bank Historian on what he faced upon entering the Bank, the risk profile of the Bank, Bank unawareness of the risks it was taking, where money had been misappropriated, and a Bank culture that did not believe internal corruption was an issue (Muis 2000) make for hair-raising reading.

answer was kept from even the Report itself, just like the Wapenhans Report was kept from public consumption.

The Wapenhans Report was not focused on a particular sector. Yet, the Report makes several references to public sector reform. These included the Bank's poor performance in the "private and public sector reforms" (combined, not separated) where 23 percent of projects were weak. That compared to 17 percent for "industry" projects and 30 percent for environmental projects. Among the skill sets required within the Bank, its "availability of financial specialists ... and management specialists ... was disturbingly limited considering the incidence of managerial and financial problems in the portfolio ... and [more generally] with the [Bank's] economic and public administration skills" (World Bank 1992a, 18). During his 1993 interview with the Bank's historian, Wapenhans offered the following:

> Increasingly, managers were saying, if they only had enough staff to extend technical assistance, their portfolios would not be in the mess they were in. This was a loud and prominent call throughout the institution, and I began to suspect that there was something phony about this. Our encounter with the borrowers at the workshop should confirm my suspicion. Technical assistance is being extended whether it is wanted or not; staff enforce a contract by offering advice even when their qualification is in doubt. That is a highly problematic approach of the Bank and seriously questioned by the borrowers. In the first instance, the Bank is not necessarily the best source of technical assistance, in the second instance, under the guise of technical assistance the Bank may readily stand inclined to call the shots, and thirdly, it creates a situation in which the owner disowns the project, loses interest and commitment, or worse, blames the Bank for failure, perhaps even rightly so. The Bank, of course, accepts no liability even if the technical assistance extended turns out to be deficient. In the fourth instance, and rather importantly, one cannot expect that the Bank will—or could—provide the kind of staff continuity technical assistance requires.
>
> (Wapenhans 1993, n.p., emphasis added)

As such, if the Bank did not have enough skilled professional staff to deal with PSM/PSG reform, had a short-term lending interest, and if the Bank's policy solutions sometimes did not work, then the Bank's incentive culture may work against the Bank's mission.

To fix such problems, Wapenhans encouraged the Bank to increase its recruitment and training of specialist staff members.[19] In a 1994 report on the Bank's progress since 1992 in PSM/PSG, the authors noted that the Bank had fifty-two

---

[19] Wapenhans also noted, "It isn't that the Bank does not have technical skills. The Bank has still a large pool of technical skills amongst its staff. But the technical skills become less and less experienced— because of recruitment practices; they become more and more academic, abstract, and specialized as

sector specialists and that all regions now had PSMUs. In a footnote, the Bank observed that "[PSM/PSG] has been identified as one of the areas for emphasis in World Bank staff recruitment" and even so, the report was unclear where the specialists would come from, their training and professional backgrounds or even if they were staff or consultants (World Bank 1994b, 39–40, 61).

President Lewis Preston reviewed the Wapenhans Report in October 1992. Wapenhans recalled Preston and he going through the report page-by-page for a half day with Preston asking Wapenhans about this or that portion of the report. Wapenhans was asked by Preston what Preston should do next. There were two immediate items: (1) ask Country Managers to discuss their Country Portfolios and (2) ask the Regional Vice Presidents the same question. Just having a Bank President ask such simple questions for the first time might force its leadership to know their portfolios in detail. This was opposed to the usual reality where Bank managers knew little more than where in the project-approval timeline a project was located.

Upon reading the Report, the Bank's Board expressed two concerns: (1) the Board wanted to know why it had not known about these failure numbers, and (2) the Report implied the Bank will need to lower its "commitment volumes" and consequently, the Board wanted to know if that was what the Bank wanted. On the first issue, Wapenhans responded that the numbers had always been available. On the second, Wapenhans later recalled that it was the IMF and the Scandinavian Executive Directors who particularly wanted the Bank to keep lending. The developing country EDs did not disagree.

Common staff sentiment to his report was, "We agree with this a hundred percent, but this institution will never implement the report" (Wapenhans 1993). Similar sentiments were echoed among interviewees. One interviewee considered project supervision as a "thankless task" that had (and still gets) a "short shrift" (WB29). Others agreed that the Bank had done little since Wapenhans to change its culture: "I remember it being much more of a wake-up call that we really are wasting a lot of people's time and money with what we are doing because we are not doing things very well, at all. That I considered to be much more of a shock to our system than 'we are failing as a development institution,' I don't recall that leading to significant organizational changes rather just change in focus and changing things around in how do we manage information and looked at projects" (WB5). Interviewees agreed that "lending imperatives" or "getting money out the door" remains the Bank's primary interest, even today (WB25, WB29). Another interviewee correlated the Bank's incentive system with the Bank's financial constraints: "If the Bank does not lend, it does not get income to pay overhead … The World Bank

---

the bank hires younger staff with more highly specialized training … That's why I feel that to a considerable extent the Bank can cure this problem only by changing its personnel policies" (Wapenhans 1993).

is one of the few international financial institutions to actually be self-sufficient …
The Bank is an AAA institution—to money to borrow, you have to have lending …
[and importantly] part of the Bank's profit goes to IDA" (WB26).

Others commented that Wapenhans' observations about the approval culture
were not "new;" rather, Wapenhans was the first to publicly talk about the issue. Or,
as stated by one interviewee, "The brownie points [for staff] are for new projects—
not from managing a project over the years". The "smart task managers design
projects and hand them over and move on. And you don't know if the project was
a bad project until several years down the road" (WB25). It remained difficult to
assign project failure blame when more than one manager was associated with the
project. Or, as one civil society interviewee bluntly said, "nothing has changed"
since Wapenhans (WB51).

Conclusion: Internal Reforms and Reports Shape "Who Matters"

Since the last organization-wide Bank reform in 1972 and the 1987 reform covered
in this chapter, the world economic arena along with its development requirements has shifted. With that shift came alternative disciplinary perspectives and
developmental approaches. For this book's focus sector, this included new debates
between neoclassical economics and its structural adjustment versus institutional
development and later, good governance after 1991 (see Chapter 5). The ability
of the Bank's organizational structure to respond had become less clear. With US
disapproval of a June 1986 Bank budget, lingering concerns about the Bank's internal capabilities, management style, and its organizational structure came to a
head. Within a year, the Bank's structure was dramatically (and painfully) altered,
and perhaps with a bit of irony, the Bank was reformed in the same manner as the
painful reorganizations advocated by the Bank for its member states at the time.

This structure, through the initiative and role-prominence of Kim Jaycox (and
the temporary side-lining of Ernie Stern) along with increased internal agitation
against neoclassical economics and its approach to PSM sector policy, created
space in the chaotic year of 1987, for the Bank's regional vice presidencies to create
PSMU, for new sector-specific hires, and for bureaucratic inertia to encourage further sector developments. As per Table 1, this led to a substantial uptick in Bank
PSM projects. The overwhelming PSM (and PSG) needs of post-Soviet states only
further emphasizes the sector's institutionalization but, as noted by Chapter 5, via
new institutional economics.

Yet, as the 1992 Wapenhans Report indicates, all was not well within the
Bank. The innumerable incentives influencing staff and Bank behaviours discouraged emphases on project implementation and outputs in exchange for getting
money out the door. This meant that as sector policy deepened and the PSM and
PSG needs of the Bank's client nations multiplied, Bank staff were rewarded for

encouraging even more sector projects. The capacity of client states to manage that money or the conditionalities attached to it, led to uncomfortable ethical questions that were put aside for another day and in the short-run, not answered by the Bank, its client-states or its Board. The non-release of the Wapenhans Report to the public is as telling as its need to be written. Just as this chapter argued at its start that we cannot understand the 1980s Bank without understanding this 1987 reform and the 1992 Wapenhans Report, we also cannot understand the mid-1990s to 2012 Bank without understanding how the 1987 reform created crucial space for sector institutionalization and how the non-answers to the 1992 Wapenhans Report concerns continued to reverberate throughout the Bank. It is to these next decades that our attention turns.

5

Cold War Ends, Privatization Matters, and "Good Governance" Arrives (November 1989 to September 1996)

The 1980s structural adjustment focus continued into the early 1990s. Privatization policies dramatically expanded, particularly in the newly independent states of the former Soviet Union. But this expansion did not imply that institutional development (see Chapter 3) retained its 1980s *persona non grata* status. In August 1991, the Bank tentatively declared that "governance" also mattered. Governance analytically and operationally expanded the PSM agenda. Its addition to the Bank lexicon has been the subject of dozens of articles and books (among the many, see Crawford 2006; Grindle 2004; Santiso 2001; Kiely 1998; Erkkilä and Piironen 2014; Mkandawire 2007; Williams 2008; Thomas 2007; Guhan 1998; Doornbos 2001; DeFrancesco and Guashino 2020; Nanda 2006; Rose-Ackerman 2017).

This chapter adds to this literature in two ways. One, it notes that less discussed in this plethora of articles about good governance, its meaning, and its subsequent impact are the internal bureaucratic politics of this good governance addition, its link to an emergence of the good governance concept from the African continent (Mkandawire 2007), the 1980s institutional development work, and the 1987 reform. Two, also less discussed, is that by late 1991, neoliberalism, privatization, and structural adjustment coexisted with an emergent governance agenda. Each topic operated in parallel to a late 1980s rise of Bank work in financial management, public expenditure management, and civil service reform. Each are discussed.

As noted in Chapter 4, the 1987 reform created organizational space within the Bank for more sector projects. This sector topic expansion (see Table 5[1]) is linked to more sector project approvals. According to Table 1, between 1990 and 1996, 1466 projects with a PSM/PSG component were approved. This is 4.3 times more projects approved in the PSM/PSG sector than in the prior 21 years (1968 to 1989). The end of the Cold War and the addition of fifteen new Eastern and Central European member states further increased sector policy interests.

---

[1] All tables referenced in this book may be found in the Appendix.

Who Matters at the World Bank?. Kim Moloney, Oxford University Press.
© Kim Moloney (2022). DOI: 10.1093/oso/9780192857729.003.0005

By 1993, new institutional economics (NIE) replaced neoclassical economics as the dominant ideological paradigm within the Bank's PSM and PSG reforms (e.g., Nabli and Nugent 1989; Smyth 1998; Kumari 1995; Theobald 1999; Harriss et al. 1995; Williams 1999). NIE was viewed as more nuanced theoretical vehicle for economic development. It was less about "slash and burn" or "murdering efficiently" (see Chapter 3) but about understanding institutional incentives. Cutting the state was no longer the primary PSM objective. Sector policy was changing.

However, for this agenda to move forward, another reinterpretation of the Bank's Articles of Agreement and its "politics" was required (Sureda 1999; Bradlow and Grossman 1995; Shihata 1995, 2000a; Cissé 2012).[2] This reinterpretation allowed the Bank to legally accept a good governance addition to the PSM agenda. Article reinterpretations were encouraged by external actors desirous of cementing a democratic and market-liberal post-Cold War order. Good governance foci were viewed as crucial steps toward that future. By the mid-1990s, just 12 years after the 1983 WDR, PSM (with the 1991 addition of "good governance") had come to stay.

The Berlin Wall and the Washington Consensus

On November 9, 1989, the Berlin Wall fell. It was a symbolic end to the Cold War. The ideological triumphalism resulting from that November event was heralded as a potential "end of history" (Fukuyama 1992). The Berlin Wall's fall changed the international dynamic from a world where communism, socialism, and autocracy were contested political and economic alternatives to a world where democracy and market liberalism seemingly stood triumphant.

In this moment of global change, John Williamson and the Institute of International Economics (now called the Petersen Institute) held a conference in Washington DC to discuss the 1980s' economic development agenda. Williamson's ten-point "Washington Consensus" on "lessons learned" was published in 1990. Due to the Consensus's neoliberal bent, the "Washington Consensus" phrase would, like structural adjustment, become a catch-all phrase against which Bank opponents rallied. If the 1980s was a period of stark market-first ideologies, critics worried that the Washington Consensus had become America's (and thus, the World Bank's) first symbolic post-Berlin Wall statement about the new world order (e.g., Broad 2004; Broad and Cavanagh 1999; Soederberg 2001; Goldman 2008).

---

[2] The Bank's relative consistency in altering its interpretation of Article IV.10 of its Articles of Agreement for PSM/PSG sector expansion is not always replicated in other sectors of Bank work. For example, the "Bank contends that it has the authority to address human rights issues it wishes to address, such a female genital mutilation, while arguing that it does not have the authority to address other important human rights issues, such as the prevention of torture or the suppression of political dissent, because the latter are purely "political" issues that do not have a "direct" economic effect" (Bradlow and Grossman 1995, 431).

What did the Consensus actually say? Williamson observed a tentative late 1980s agreement within Washington's international development community: market fundamentalism was not working. Neoclassical ideals were facing backlash. The 1990s were to be about "rational economic policymaking" with policies encouraging "monetary discipline but not monetarism; tax reform but not tax-slashing; trade liberalization but maybe not complete freedom of capital movements; deregulation of entry and exit barriers but not the suppression of regulations designed to protect the environment" (Williamson 2000a, 255). There were ten Washington Consensus policies: (1) fiscal reform; (2) redirection of public expenditure priorities; (3) tax reform; (4) interest-rate liberalization; (5) competitive exchange rates; (6) trade liberalization; (7) liberalized FDI inflows; (8) privatization; (9) deregulation; and (10) secure property rights (Williamson 1990, 2000a, 2004).

The Washington Consensus' legitimacy among Bank staff came not only from its timing (the fall of the Berlin Wall) or its ideological perspectives (modified neoclassical economics), but also because major stakeholders agreed. The Consensus policies were implemented via the Bank's lending mechanisms. For many critics, Williamson's Consensus was no different from market neoliberalism. Its ideas became a rallying cry for a strengthening NGO movement (see Chapter 9). The term *consensus* also triggered a backlash because any consensus from Washington implied that in a newly unipolar world, economic development's ideological home remained in Washington DC and not elsewhere—certainly not within the world's poorest countries. Neoliberalism posited that economic growth was the best long-term approach for ensuring poverty reduction. But new research (see next sections) would soon show that trickle-down economics was not trickling down fast enough for Western powers concerned about member states reverting to a communist or socialist model.

It has been suggested that the Consensus never intended to have such a wide-ranging impact. Or that considering the Consensus as Fund and Bank "policy" misinterpreted its purpose. I have empathy with both views. According to its author, the Consensus was nothing more than an attempt to enumerate the policy reforms that were "widely held in Washington to be widely desirable in Latin America as of the date the list was compiled, namely the second half of 1989" (Williamson 2004, 1). That is, the Consensus is simply a document. It was largely not new. It was also only focused upon one region of the world. Many of its points reflected, as Williamson noted, what IFIs in Washington DC had already done throughout the 1990s.

But what was new was its creation of another tagline which like "structural adjustment" or "neoliberalism" became metaphors for increasingly vocal anti-Bank groups (see Chapter 9). The literal meaning of this Consensus is simply as an output from a conference. Structural adjustment is also just one of many lending instruments. Neoliberal is slang for neoclassical economics. But the literal origins did not matter. Each phrase became symbols of what was (apparently) wrong with the Bank (and Fund), their projects (including parts of the PSM agenda), and a Western order triumphant with a post-Cold War win.

Underplayed by critics was that three Consensus items were additions to (and corrections of) neoliberal paradigms: tax reform, redirections of public expenditure priorities, and property rights. Public expenditure priorities had been influenced not just by new Bank research in this sector topic (see Chapter 3) but also via *Adjustment with a Human Face* (WB52; Cornia et al. 1987) that argued structural adjustment was overly focused on social sector cutbacks. One practical result was that when "Anne Krueger's term expired and she was replaced by Stanley Fischer [January 1988 to August 1990], there was a distinct change in policy at that stage and those public expenditures were favored" and it was this new consensus, according to my interviewee, that the Washington Consensus attempted to capture in 1989 (WB52). The addition of public expenditure management reflected new projects at the Bank in this topic (see Table 5) in the late 1980s. Tax reform, in contrast, would not take off as a new PSM sector topic until the early 1990s (see Table 5 and later sections of this chapter).

It is a potentially moot point whether the Washington Consensus would have received as much critical publicity as it did if the Berlin Wall had not fallen. What mattered for Bank critics was that post-Consensus structural adjustment had not disappeared. Late 1980s additions to PSM topics such as public expenditure management and public financial management had neither become well-known and, once known, were not easy to mobilize against, since improved budget and financial transparency is not anti-poor. Thus, the argument was kept general. Critics asserted that structural adjustment negatively affected socioeconomic development. The trickle-down expectation of the neoliberal model was not trickling down, or at least not in the short-term. The fear that poor nations might slow or reverse their democratic and market-liberalism trends (and thus temper the Cold War win) pushed the Bank into reconsidering its prior market-first perspectives. By late 1991, the Bank had begun to recalibrate its state–market policy balance. The institutional development staff who had been critical of structural adjustment at the Bank were ready and waiting.

The Bank's Response to the Berlin Wall

The Soviet Union's collapse provided an opportunity for the Bank and its most powerful Board members to shape Eastern Europe in its image (Thurow 1997). Or, as President Clinton's National Security Advisor stated in 1993, "[The US] might visualize our security mission as promoting the enlargement of the 'blue areas' of market democracies" (Wade 2001a, 126). With the Cold War over, the Bank was deluged by new membership applications and more requests for advice than it could handle. Between 1992 and 1995, the Bank's membership expanded from

155 to 178 countries. New members meant new opportunities to lend money. The Berlin Wall's fall led to an all-hands-on-deck mentality within the Bank. It was no different for the Bank's PSM specialists. The sheer number of new countries joining the Bank and their immediate loan requirements increased Bank business. One interviewee recalled that period with particular vividness. The Berlin Wall's fall required the Bank to create a

> Country Unit for fifteen countries that [the Bank] did not have before. [There was a] parade of people searching frantically for who [among staff] had originally been from Ukraine, Turkmenistan … Language training efforts exploded into high gear. [It was] like being at Grand Central Station and watching the shingling board with arriving trains.
>
> (WB30)

Reflecting the scale of Eastern Europe's public sector inefficiency under the Soviet Union, many intra-Bank personnel transfers to the newly created Eastern and Central Europe region were former Africa-focused PSM specialists chosen for their professional experience (WB29). Eastern and Central Europe was now the Bank's priority region. Ambitious Bank staff wanted part of the action.

In short order, Mary Shirley and John Nellis' *Public Enterprise Reform: The Lessons of Experience* (Shirley and Nellis 1991) was published. It detailed the Bank's earliest SOE reform experiences in Eastern Europe. However, and unlike Bank prior experiences elsewhere, the former Soviet economies had SOEs as the *majority* of a state's economic activities. This difference had potential operational and policy ramifications:

> First … it makes the enterprise reform process exponentially larger, more complex, and important in socialist economies than in other countries. Second, it negates or calls into question at least one of the lessons of experience derived from capitalist and mixed economies: that privatization is but a means to an end. To illustrate the former effect, one can contrast the average of 75 public enterprises in the countries of sub-Saharan Africa (a region of heavy state intervention), to the 8,700 public enterprises with which Poland begins its transition process. Or one can note that while many developing countries administer some key prices, most socialist countries administer all prices. As for the second result, the fact is that the leaders and advisors of many socialist countries of Europe do not regard privatization and the creation of private property rights as a means toward the end of greater efficiency; they see it as tantamount to the destruction of the command system and hence as an end in itself … [O]n the political front, most reformers feel that they—and their suffering and demanding electorates—cannot tolerate a long wait. If the state sector remains dominant, it constitutes a base of operations for those who may want to restore the system of administered security.
>
> (Shirley and Nellis 1991, 72–73)

Staff observations that privatization was no longer a means to an end but the end itself was a hint that privatization, as understood in its mid-1980s version, was being updated. PSM policy change was happening and it was happening fast. Former Soviet satellites were not just privatizing a few industries, but the entire state. If the Bank did not work quickly, the Cold War's "win" might not last.

That the Berlin Wall's fall impacted PSM reform is hardly surprising. Both the Soviet Union and its satellite economies were almost entirely run by the public sector. This meant that prior understandings had "became a more complicated topic". It became a

> combination of how to liberalize economies (always a Bank issue) and how do that quickly. How do you train people to manage their public sector differently? It was a much more full-bodied, robust endeavor … You wanted to immediately integrate into the international economy, [but] had a sector heavily nationalized, [so] how to privatize it? *In the end, the Bank did it too fast. The Bank was under pressure to do it fast,* the IMF said, "you gotta get the economy in place." Bankers worried about how people would survive … [The] Bank made some mistakes but part of that also was the G7 pressure on the Bank to do it and to do it fast.
>
> (WB30, emphasis added)

This emphasis on complexities not predicted by neoclassical economic theory is shared with another insight from one Bank staffer who stated that he "could summarize my experience as country director in the Balkan states as the permanent education of an economist. My training in economics revealed its limitations when the solutions most often available were not second best, but fifth or sixth best" (Poortman 2005, 200). The false notion that there was a single-best or discipline-best model of development was echoed by others:

> A continuing, grave problem throughout the various strategic shifts the Bank has made … has been its propensity to continue to search for—and sometimes claim that it has found—the ultimate answers to development. This pattern reflects the surprising belief that there may be a ready-made, relatively simple, permanent, and definitive response to a specific problem of development that can be applied universally and the belief that, if it worked well here, it will work well there … Seldom were there real attempts at differentiating among countries and examining the different speed or the various degrees at which the countries were expected to adjust. It was as if only one pattern, one blueprint, or one correct path existed.
>
> (Lafourcade 2005, 182–183)

Finally, the fall of the Berlin Wall also forced the Bank to cooperate (some might suggest, "compete") with the European Union (EU) as liberalizing states sought EU accession. The Bank created a Brussels office to assist with Bank–EU relations

(WB31) and early on, Bank staff argued that the EU was not "ready" to guide countries toward accession (WB40). The EU "scrambled on what types of conditionalities to get them [Eastern European countries] to join Europe. It was not orderly, but now [the EU has] an 'encyclopedia of conditionalities'" (WB35). In the Bank view, clarity on EU accession requirements was not present until 1993 at which point, the Bank "let" the EU lead (WB35, WB36). Why such an agreement? It was felt that Western Europe was closer to Eastern Europe's problems and thus, the EU was better able to find "middle ground" than the Bank (WB40). Even so, the Bank's work in the newly independent states expanded rapidly. In cases where the EU's requirements did not emphasize a new Bank public sector subtopic such as judicial reform, the Bank would lead the reform efforts (WB40).

One Operational Result: Privatization Matters More

An operational outcome from the Cold War's end was an urgency for the Bank to continue structural adjustment. Privatization projects were emphasized. The *economic* imperative for this lending was established in the 1980s. The *political* imperative was strengthened after November 1989. By 1991, the Bank's privatization research had dramatically expanded. Bank research papers no longer debated whether privatization was right (as they did in the early-to-mid 1980s, see Chapter 3) but instead sought justifications, explanations, or reflections with privatization exercises. As long as newly independent states were in need of financial resources and FDI, the Bank and its donors held the upper hand. Although the Bank could have adopted a more nuanced strategy and/or have extended the period under which privatization was to occur, they did not. The strategic imperative to quickly transform the newly independent economies outweighed other objectives.

If there was any doubt about privatization's importance for economic development, a plethora of Bank-researched papers published during this period would emphasize this sector topic's importance.[3] In a paper analyzing 1100 privatizing transactions between 1988 and 1992, Bank researchers found positive links between privatization and increased FDI (Sader 1993). Other papers discussed the Soviet Union (Nellis and Lieberman 1994), evaluated the Bank's divestiture efforts (Kikeri 1990), and compared privatizations in Hungary and Albania with other socialist economies (Lee and Nellis 1990). By the mid-1990s, the Bank was analyzing the to-date "mass privatizations" of Eastern Europe. Papers discussed the processes, tools, problems, and issues of privatization sequencing along with

---

[3] My privatization references are brief. Brevity does not equate to minimal importance but instead, reflects that so much was written about privatization during the early 1990s that if I cited each Bank paper, citations would overwhelm the chapter.

country-specific reviews and privatization examples. Among the very few papers that discussed institutional development preferences or SOE reform (instead of privatization), their focus was on SOE modification through corporate governance (Pannier 1996), incentivization (Muir and Saba 1995), and performance evaluation (Jones 1991).

Key actors supported privatization. This includes the G7, US, and the Bank's President Lewis Preston (September 1991 to May 1995). In 1990, the G7 called for market-oriented reforms and investment liberalization in the newly independent states (G7 1990). Subsequent calls refocused on economic growth with a particular focus on Russia in 1993 (G7 1993). The US Treasury continued to prioritize pricing policies, the lowering of fiscal deficits, the promotion of market-based solutions, and the liberalization of trade and investment. In case anyone still had their doubts, Treasury officials reiterated in 1992 that "state control of economies is discredited" (U.S. House of Representatives 1992). Privatization was linked to client country debt reduction since privatization had the "dual benefits of reducing government financial obligations and allowing companies to act on market incentives" (Brady 1990). The first Bank loan to the Soviet Union was proposed in the summer of 1990 and signed in 1991 by the new Bank President, Lewis Preston. The US government wanted to immediately streamline the Soviet and the former Soviet bloc countries into Bank operations. In fact, "The U.S. administration was anxious to get the Bank and the Fund actively involved in the U.S.S.R., and in December 1990 the President of the U.S. asked the U.S. Governor [to the Bank] to explore the possibility of special associate membership for the Soviet Union "that will give Moscow access to the economic and financial expertise in those institutions" (Kraske et al. 1996, 275).

The Treasury also did not forget its 1980s wish for more private sector development in developing countries. Some at Treasury worried that multilateral donors were too focused on privatization at the cost of private-sector development (Hill 1991). The Treasury focus put the US in opposition to other donors who argued that greater state–market balance was needed. As noted by one magazine journalist,

Recent Bush Administration complaints that the Bank should lend more to the private sector are only a precursor of the controversy ahead. The *Bank's World Development Report* argued that there is no dichotomy between lending to build public schools and lending to privatize a steel mill, that "each has a large and irreplaceable role" in the "market friendly" development that the Bank advocates. But in the recent flap, which ended in a truce, [Bank President] Conable said that some of the other major donors "were concerned that the private sector was a goal [for the U.S. Treasury Department], not a modality." Japanese and European philosophical acceptance of a greater government role in national economies is likely to clash increasingly with America's free-market orientation.

(Stokes 1991)

Members of Congress such as Rep. David Obey [D-WI] felt that that George H.W. Bush Administration had a "narrow ideological agenda" and would pressure the Bank to consider fewer private sector loans (Rowen 1991). While Treasury, the US Congress, and Bank donors fought about the Bank's private sector focus, the Treasury was relatively absent from the Bank's debates about a new topic on the PSM horizon: governance. Unlike in the 1980s where the US was an important sector player, the Bank's 1991/1992 push for governance would arise from outside the US Government and outside the G7. The governance push was influenced by ongoing learning in Africa and the fast-moving events in Eastern Europe. It was also influenced by significant in-house Bank staff learning, a "scientization" (e.g., Marcussen 2006), and the incorporation of a new economic approach (new institutional economics) able to frame the Bank's emergent governance response. This is in stark contrast to its role in the 1980s.

In 1991, Lewis Preston became president of the World Bank. Preston did not challenge the prevailing structural adjustment and privatization sentiments. However, where he differed (and perhaps because the changed international environment allowed difference) was Preston's carefully worded support for good governance. Preston appeared to understand internal Bank concerns about governance (see forthcoming section) and would, two years after the Bank published its first report on governance, speak about how a state–market balance was essential for development.

Staff opinion on Preston was divided (WB6) and unlike McNamara, Clausen, and Conable, Preston kept to himself. Staff recalled that "no one saw him" (WB29). Noting some personal tragedies surrounding his presidency, one staffer recalled that "he was elderly, and I think he just sort of, let, really the place was being run by his subordinates [notably, Stern] rather than by him. I don't think that is unfair. I think he started out meaning to do more but he was dying. Plus, he was very depressed by it and his wife ... apparently went through depression because his son died. And so ... for him the Bank was not his first priority" (WB12). By February 1995, Preston announced he had cancer (Mallaby 2004). Ernie Stern was named acting president, and by June 1995 Preston had died (World Bank 2009b).

Small Policy Shifts toward Governance: Early Reports (1989 to 1991)

If the state were to be considered important to development, the Bank needed proof that modifying its 1980s pro-market, anti-state balance would lead to improved economic growth and poverty reduction. In a 1989 study, two IMF economists started to question whether neoclassical perspectives were enough to ensure development. Using what the authors called a "new growth analysis", they observed a growing consensus that not just capital, domestic savings, and exports mattered but that long-term growth required social expenditures (Otani and Villanueva 1989). *The emerging Bank perspective was not that neoliberalism was wrong; rather, it was no longer the whole story.*

Policy implications included that "any planning for adjustment policies should consider the adverse consequences for economic growth of cutting such spending" and that governments should reduce government expenditures (civil-servant pay and state-owned enterprises) while increasing tax collection, encourage export growth, tame population growth, and encourage low world interest rates to cheapen borrowing costs (Otani and Villanueva 1989). In keeping with the rhetoric of their decade, the authors still noted that developing countries must cut their civil service jobs and trim SOEs. As the early 1990s progressed, several internal Bank reviews of structural adjustment occurred. Summarizing these events was an article co-authored by Larry H. Summers (Chief Economist of the World Bank, 1991–1993) and Lant H. Pritchett. They wrote that "World Bank projects undertaken in poor policy environments themselves performed poorly" (Summers and Pritchett 1993a, 383). *The prior 1980s model was no longer enough. Sector policy change was needed. In response, microeconomists, institutional development supporters, and their allies of the 1980s raised their voices and would begin to lead this sector agenda forward.*

In 1989, the Bank published *Sub-Saharan Africa: From Crisis to Sustainable Growth*, a 322-page report that very briefly mentioned governance as critical to African development. This first high-level encouragement came via Kim Jaycox, the Bank's Vice President for the African Region, in early 1987 (Williams 2008). Shortly thereafter, Jaycox would serve as the staff lead for the 1987 reform (see Chapter 4) and be a force behind the creation of organizational space within the Bank for PSM unit expansion.

The 1989 Africa report would be the Bank's first-ever public reference to the governance term (World Bank 1989, 1991b). For one interviewee, a 1991 report co-author (see next chapter section), this 1989 predecessor was a "critical document" in the Bank's governance and PSM policy history (WB37). In President Conable's opening letter to the 1989 report, he highlighted links between poor economic growth and Africa's insufficient "good governance" (World Bank 1989). Not to be overlooked is that an analysis about African challenges became 'the' key initial report. It happened with the Berg Report in 1980 (see Chapter 3) and it happened again with good governance. The concept also, as noted by Mkandawire (2007) "diverges significantly from their own [African] original understanding" (276).

Unlike the Berg Report for which African scholars were not consulted (see Chapter 3), for the 1989 report, the Bank "did the then unusual thing of consulting African scholars and commissioning them to prepare background papers, apparently at the insistence of Africans within the Bank" (Mkandawire 2007, 276). This led to expectations that good governance should be a developmental term, a socially inclusive term, and a term that reflected democracy and respect for human rights which, as Mkandawire noted, was a combination leading to a predictably "lukewarm" response from IMF and Bank economists (266). Or as noted by another scholar, the 1989 report "created a stir" in the development community because of its open discussion of politics (Bräutigam 1991).

The reasoning for this "stir" reflected questions about the Bank's mission, its lending incentives, and who (within the Bank) should lead:

> First, it was felt that the focus on politics was distracting attention from the task of 'getting the macroeconomic fundamental rights' ... Second, the new focus did not leave much room for the [W]orld Bank. Its insistence on the importance of local initiatives, political accountability to the citizens, and the need to reconcile African traditions and institutions with 'modern' ones were not exactly the types of thing the World Bank could relate to in a quantifiable and operational manner
>
> (Mkandawire, 2007, 266)

That is, if the good governance term separates itself from the prior structural adjustment and potentially worse, from an economist and Bank lending perspective creates an unmeasurable concept, then how should the Bank proceed? That the Bank's institutional development performance in Africa had "the worst success record" was not unnoticed (Williams 2008, 109).

In the Report itself, Bank staff noted that Africa was experiencing a "crisis of governance" (World Bank 1989, 60). *Governance* was defined as "the exercise of political power to manage a nation's affairs" (World Bank 1989, 60). In this Report, good governance was linked to "political renewal," accountability, and transparency, including freedom of the press. This early governance definition would expand as the 1990s progressed not only fit the new term into the Bank's mission, its lending incentives, and how the Bank understood (often from an economic lens) development but also in response to the changing international economic environment and soon, the addition of new institutional economics to the sector agenda.

Another early report which influenced the upcoming good governance addition was written by Arturo Israel, the "godfather" of the Bank's early institutional development agenda (see Chapter 3). His 1990 report, *The Changing Role of the State: Institutional Dimensions*, unambiguously stated that the Bank must reconsider its stance on the state. On the report's first page he wrote: "The quality—not the size— of the state is what counts. And a prerequisite for changing the role of the state is an improved political process. Without that, any new development strategy will fail" (Israel 1990, 1). Israel's report laid down an intellectual gauntlet. The report shaped the Bank's subsequent shift. He made the following observations:

(1) "The argument that the size of the public sector needs to be drastically reduced has probably been taken too far, without really analyzing the full consequences of the shift;" (2) "*A crucial prerequisite for the successful development of the private sector is the existence of a modernized and highly efficient public sector, particularly in a number of key areas of policy management and regulation. The issue is the quality, not the size of the state;*" (3) "[T]he number of activities that the public sector can safely and effectively undertake is quite limited. To force additional functions on the public sector increases exponentially the chances of failure and poor performance;" and (4) "The change in development strategy also requires as a prerequisite a modernization and an improved performance of the political process. This point is seldom mentioned but it is crucial; otherwise, the new development strategy will fail."

(Israel 1990, 3–4, emphasis added)

Israel's voice and importance among the Bank's earliest public sector management specialists was not questioned by my interviewees. He was a prolific researcher (Heaver and Israel 1986; Israel 1983, 1987, 1989, 1990; Paul and Israel 1990). Although Israel was not a member of the Bank's "Task Force on Governance" (which would write the key early governance document: 1991's *Managing Development Report*),[4] Israel was one of just a few Bank staff members in the 1980s whose job description was focused on public sector management. He was a proponent of institutional management in the 1980s. His 1990 Report shaped subsequent governance discussions.

The next two reports indicating an ongoing PSM policy shift were published by the Bank but written by consultants—a trend assisted by the 1987 Reorganization. The first report was published by the PSMU of the LAC region. The author suggested that the Bank encourage greater efficiency via "modern management methods and techniques," improved public sector quality (although this was not defined), decentralization, and improved local-level participation in governmental affairs (Price 1991, 9–10). The second report linked governance with economic growth. Governance required accountability, openness, transparency, predictability, and rule of law, even though, at that time, there was a "dearth of research focused on the[se] specific variables" (Bräutigam 1991, 39). The difference between this report's language and that of the 1989 Africa report is notable. The former uses economist language to describe good governance. Economist-speak helped bankers "sell" policy change.

---

[4] The Task Force on Governance had thirty-one members (World Bank 1991b, 57), many of whom had published, were publishing, or would publish on PSM issues.

The 1991 *Challenge of Development WDR* set the stage for increased state-market cooperation even if the Bank was unclear on how it would occur. The *WDR* acknowledged that "macroeconomic stability certainly does not by itself lead to development but without it all other efforts are likely to be in vain" (World Bank 1991b, 109). *In the Bank's new view, they had not been wrong in its structural adjustment orientation but instead, the Bank was realizing that economic growth on its own was no longer a guarantee that development would occur.* In another surprise, the seventh chapter of the 1991 *WDR* began with a quote from John Maynard Keynes, an economist whose ideas were scarce in the 1980s Bank. The chapter argued that governments have multiple priorities, including economic growth, employment, and redistribution concerns. "Social consensus," the report argued, had been undermined by the government's need to obtain "the support of influential groups for the government" (World Bank 1991b, 129).

There are at least two ways to translate this last quote out of *Bankease*. The first was that the Bank did not blame itself or its policies for the lack of social consensus within developing countries but, instead, blamed internal client-country politics for client-country failures to address poverty. The second version was related: society-wide "social consensus" was undermined by societal elites. It was an "elite consensus" within developing-country governments which was required if those governments were to implement structural reforms, which at first glance, would have challenged one's elite status or at least changed the incentives favoring their status.

Moreover, the Bank asserted that poor "administrative capacity" and centralized decision-making structures within governments had widened intra-societal disconnections (World Bank 1991b, 130). The report pointed out that corruption was the byproduct of excessive state interventionism[5] and argued that countries with democratic characteristics and effective institutions were more likely to develop. It was not that equity considerations were antithetical to economic growth or that the Bank intended to warn about overzealous marketization; rather, the Bank was more worried about "overzealous redistribution" (World Bank 1991b, 131, 138–139).

Just because the Bank policies had begun to acknowledge the state's importance, this need not imply that the Bank trusted (or ideologically preferred) state motives. Yet it would be the post-Cold War environment and ongoing staff learning which helped ease the Bank into reconsidering the state. After 1989, "supporting the state" no longer automatically equated to a socialist or communist ideological tendency.

---

[5] Two points are needed. First, this was the earliest mention of corruption that I could find within a Bank report. In the Annex of *Managing Development*, the Bank published a two-page "box" on corruption (World Bank 1991b, 2930). For many Bank staff, however, it was not until President Wolfensohn's October 1996 "cancer of corruption" speech that it would be officially "OK" for staff to discuss the so-called 'C' word (see Chapter 6). Second, it is doubtful that the Bank's logic (at least in this report) that the state is the key cause of corruption is accurate. Corruption (with a big *C* and small *c*) also occurs via the private and voluntary sectors too.

For President Conable, "The easing of East-West tensions allowed [Conable] to speak up on issues that had long troubled those concerned with the alleviation of poverty: the level of military expenditures and the quality of governance" (Kraske et al. 1996, 276).

The new world order highlighted Western fears that if social expenditures were not increased and poverty were not reduced many of the world's poorest might turn away from the Bank, democracy, and market liberalism. To cement the Cold War's ideological victory, swift on-the-ground changes were needed. This included new shifts in the Bank's public sector management policies. The key sector document behind this policy change was *Managing Development: The Governance Dimension* (1991). The report was a tentative, small step forward. As this 1991 report was not a *WDR*, it did not have the policy stature (and widespread Bank approval) associated with *WDRs*. Still, it was the first time the Bank formally explained *with a clear reference to a cautious General Counsel legal opinion* that "governance" was developmentally important.

Managing Development: The Governance Dimension (August 1991)

The document that most clearly articulated the Bank's new policy shift from an exclusive PSM-only mindset was a 1991 discussion paper titled, *Managing Development: The Governance Dimension*. An accompanying book based on this 1991 report was published in 1992. The 1991 paper was written by a thirty-one-member "Task Force on Governance." It is quite unusual for the Bank to create such sector-specific task forces. But the approval and potential integration of this addition to the agenda was considered so important that such a Task Force was created. Not only was this report the first Bank report to discuss governance in detail but atypical of a Bank report, the potential political and legal ramifications arising from this short twenty-one-page report (with twenty-five pages of appendices) were potentially so great (and politically worrying) that the report necessitated an additional two-page memorandum from President Conable. In that memo, which was included in the final version, Conable cautioned,

> I want to emphasize that this is not a policy paper or a call for a new initiative. It establishes a coherent framework for efforts going on in different parts of the Bank, and reaffirms certain basic propositions: that efficient and accountable public sector management and a predictable and transparent framework for economic activity are critical to the efficiency of both markets and government interventions—and hence to economic development.
>
> (World Bank 1991b: President's Memo)

Given dozens of Bank discussion papers produced each year, it was (and still is) extremely unusual for a discussion paper to be preceded with a President's letter. It was even more unusual for a presidential letter to also reference a Bank legal memorandum.[6]

The legal memorandum was written by the Bank's General Counsel Ibrahim Shihata and dated December 11, 1990. The memo allowed the Bank to explore the governance issue in light of its Articles of Agreement and specified what the Bank could not do: (1) "the Bank cannot be influenced by the political character of a member;" (2) "it cannot interfere in the partisan politics of the member;" (3) "it must not act on behalf of donor countries in influencing the member's political orientation or behavior;" (4) "it cannot be influenced in its decisions by political factors that do not have a preponderant economic effect;" and (5) "its staff should not build their judgments on the possible reactions of a particular Bank member or members." So, what could the Bank do? The Bank could continue with "civil service reform, legal reform, accountability for public funds and budget discipline" (World Bank 1991b, 3, citing Shihata [1991, pp. 47–54]). Certainly "civil service reform, accountability for public funds and budget discipline" could be construed as political interference but for the Bank, the new line was legally sufficient.

The memo was important for its attempt to allay concerns that the Bank's new involvement in "governance" violated the Bank's Articles of Agreement. The Shihata Memo opened the door for the Bank to consider "small-*p* politics" because no longer were "all aspects of 'governance' precluded from the Bank's consideration" (Thornburgh et al. 2000, 9). In 1980, when the Bank approved a structural adjustment lending instrument, dissenting Board members suggested the Bank's Articles of Agreement are violated if the Bank entered into macroeconomic policy agreements with client governments. Similar arguments were raised a few years later when it was alleged that privatization interfered with a client country's political affairs. Yet again, a potential legal challenge was afoot. This legal memorandum from 1990 helped pave the way for the Bank to involve itself in governance without altering its Articles of Agreement. *A pattern has emerged: changing environment, new learning, member-state pressure, and the Bank's legal team must redefine its understanding of Section 10 of its Articles of Agreement.*

But what exactly was governance? The 1991 report defined *governance* as "the manner in which power is exercised in the management of a country's economic and social resources for development. The Bank's concern with sound development management extends beyond the capacity of public sector management to the rules and institutions which create a predictable and transparent framework for the conduct of public and private business, and also to accountability for economic and financial performance" (World Bank 1991b, i). This definition was different

---

[6] Most *WDRs* have a President's letter. This report was not a *WDR*. It was a Discussion Paper. None of the hundreds of Discussion Papers reviewed for this book contained a similar letter.

from the understanding of good governance contained within the *Sub-Saharan Africa: From Crisis to Sustainable Growth* report of 1989.

This definition also observed that "development management extends beyond the capacity of public sector management." The Bank's prior PSM projects in public expenditure management, financial management, and civil service reform were now part of a broader governance agenda. For the first time, the Bank also formerly linked the 1980s structural-adjustment reforms with its "related" PSM reforms (World Bank 1991b, 1). *In other words, structural adjustment and institutional development were no longer competing perspectives but instead, two parts of a whole that would soon include a new topic: governance.*

PSM was linked to the governance agenda. By 1994, the Bank considered PSM "the most visible of the four dimensions of governance" and defined the sector's new purpose as improving

> the capacity of governments to make and implement public policy, the effectiveness of public programs, and the strength of public institutions. The subject matter of public sector management is the means to achieve these—the civil service, the government budget, the public investment program, accounting, auditing, and other financial management systems, strategic planning and program evaluation, aid coordination, economic management agencies, the cabinet system, and other parts of the machinery of government that are essential to a well-functioning public sector. Public sector management is also concerned with the relationship between central government, agencies, and public enterprises, on the one hand, and between central and subordinate tiers of government on the other.
>
> (World Bank 1994b, 1)

This sector purpose is a near replica of the institutional development work from the 1980s. In some ways, it was an acknowledgement of an earlier Bank staff wish that the Bank assist institutional capacity improvement within client countries.

In Conable's introductory memo to *Managing Development: The Governance Dimension*, he diplomatically described the Board's conversations on governance as "lively and thoughtful" and that "governance is an emotive word, and more importantly, a potentially contentious issue internationally and within many of our member countries. It is not surprising that there were divergent views expressed by Executive Directors on the subject" (World Bank 1991b, President's Memo). In explaining Board disagreements, Conable noted,

> There remains some apprehension among our borrowing members that our staff might exceed the Bank's mandate in ways which could be interpreted as interfering in the political affairs of our borrowers. This concern, given the difficulty of drawing neat lines in this area, is understandable. I am confident that you will

respect the sensitivities and concerns of borrowers while not shying away from issues relevant to development performance when these need to be raised. Until our borrowing members achieve a greater level of comfort with dialogue on governance matters and our own experience with it matures further, it is advisable that delicate policy issues are discussed only by senior managers (directors and above). Technical issues, of course, can continue to be handled at staff level.

(World Bank 1991b, President's Memo)

It is also worth noting the Bank's new governance definition was not considered a violation of the Articles of Agreement. This may reflect the pressing reform needs of Eastern European states. But it also indicates the Bank either failed to understand that public sector management reform is not only a political act but also that it has political implications for a government. In other words, it may be impossible to take the politics out of public administration (Waldo 1984 [1948]). It is quite possible that bankers understood that reality but because they were forbidden to discuss "politics" via the Articles of Agreement such understandings were never publicly discussed. That staffers still could not publicly say the 'C' word (corruption) (see Chapter 6) provides support to the idea that staffers did understand that politics and administration were inseparable.

Conable noted that "delicate policy issues" should be discussed by senior staff members, whereas "technical issues" were for regular staff. The assumption (even if a false one) is that technical issues are inherently less political. Finally, Conable noted that the executive directors expressed concern that governance reforms are long term, require political commitment from client countries, and need to be viewed within the client country's context. In the 1980s, Stern had stated that institutional-development reforms were too long-term, too messy, and too unpredictable for the Bank (see Appendix, Chapter 3). Now, with the 1991 Report, such projects may not be off-limits. For the first time, the Bank acknowledged that even if "[Bank] programs and projects appear technically sound" they may fail if legal, institutional, decision-making, and incentive environments are not functioning (World Bank 1991b, i).

Project failure, the Bank asserted, could be influenced by institutional environments and thus, the Bank must work to correct unfavorable institutional environments. Institutional development was not the Bank's new phrase. Even if the problem description in this 1991 report had similarities to the prior decade's institutional development argument, to acknowledge "institutional development" was to suggest that perhaps, internal critics had a valid point. *Instead, good governance had become the Bank's new answer.* Nonetheless, and even with this new sector policy interest, the Bank acknowledged it lacked the "experienced auditors, accountants, lawyers, tax specialists, and management specialists" it needed to implement this shift (World Bank 1991b, 16). With the 1991 report, and the 1987 creation of PSMUs in the regional Vice Presidencies (see Chapter 4), hiring began in earnest.

Phrase Disagreement: "Governance" or "Development Management"?

With any Bank intellectual shift, staff perspectives are important. Bureaucratic politics and shifting internal stakeholder alliances can shape organizational and policy outputs. None of the staff interviewed about the 1991 report (including my four interviewees who helped write it) said that getting the report through the Bank's bureaucracy and obtaining management and Board approval was easy. Instead, they recalled the report as being highly controversial because it (1) argued that the Bank had gotten the balance between the state and the market wrong and (2) was perceived as asking the Bank to violate its Articles of Agreement by involving itself in the political affairs of its client countries.

One interviewee recalled that the Executive Directors were "mad as hell" (about the report) but only two executive directors voted against publishing the report: Saudi Arabia and China (WB30). Others did not recall it being "contentious" but did recall that General Counsel Shihata was careful to "draw the line on what we can and cannot do" (WB31). One interviewee remembered meeting with the Middle East and North Africa (MENA) Director and that afterwards, the Director was ready to "chew me up" and "spit me out" (WB30). The MENA region did not want to talk about good governance. Good governance was as politically impalpable for that MENA Director as it was for the Director's client countries.

The eighteen months that one interviewee spent working on the 1991 report were "exciting, migraine-inducing and rewarding" (WB30). The internal battle to write and publish the report perhaps reflected, as one later-day Bank report noted, that the 1991 Report was "the initiative of *mid-level Bank employees* with seemingly little in the way of support from their supervisors" (WB30; Thornburgh et al. 2000, 9, emphasis added). Even so, the report was published. If the report had had unequivocal support, the legal memorandum and the Bank president's introductory letter would not have been needed.

Unsurprisingly, intense bureaucratic politicking (and a bit of manipulation) was a Report feature. Because it was a Bank document,

> [that] meant drafts circulated to senior people. They would read/mark what they did not like and then traditionally, you take out what the senior people say. But Sarwar [who headed the Report] would selectively disregard them—he thought they'd forget it and so, he'd rephrase it. It went through seventeen drafts. Stern was still there—and Ernie changes governance to "development management" … but

> then in the end, Lamb [another coauthor] changed it back, the published version
> emerges as governance.
>
> (WB30)

Bureaucratic fights over the seemingly mundane, such as word choice, can be fraught if the battle resonates with larger ideological, political, and legal implications. Although "good governance" constituted a politicized reminder of what needed to be done, the "development management" term was a more technocratic and a term more palatable to a Bank senior leadership worried about either violating the Articles of Agreement or from moving too far from structural adjustment. In addition, "development management" was likely a non-accidental rephrasing of the 1983 *WDR* title "Managing for Development" and thus, would have felt more familiar and less political to a senior banker such as Ernie Stern.

With the Dutch executive director (Eveline L. Herfkens) pushing the Bank toward the consideration of governance issues and a need for legal clarity on that direction by Bank General Counsel Ibrahim Shihata, both Herfkens and Shihata helped shift the agendas. Even though Stern lost his old Operational VP role in the 1987 reform (see Chapter 4), his importance within the Bank had not diminished. He was still called upon to review this key report. In June 1993, a journalist with London's newspaper, *The Independent*, described the Bank with Stern: "The World Bank is run by a tricycle with only one wheel, insiders say. The 'tricycle' is the troika of managing directors at the Bank, of whom Ernie Stern is considered to be the most important. He is the wheel" (Thomson 1993). Moreover, when President Preston died in office (May 4, 1995), it was Stern who became the Bank's acting president during the three weeks until President James Wolfensohn's appointment on June 1st 1995.

Staff recalled that the report was also needed because of the Bank's belief that for its fifteen new Eastern and Central European members, the "big issue" was "governance" (WB30). If newly-independent states did not want a centralized mode of political control, then it was logical that the "what next" question, at least within Eastern Europe, required a new Bank response. In the end, the Report "made a difference" (WB30) and it was a "catalyst" (WB33) for technical assistance work. Projects that were not considered in the 1980s became important features of modern public sector policies (WB30, WB33).

Others believed that the Bank eventually grew into accepting "governance" as important but that the 1991 report was too "nebulous" since it never discussed the "day-to-day" reality. Thus, the Bank may have used the term governance to justify why second-generation PSM projects "were not going well" (WB23). For that interviewee, the first generation was the structural adjustment of the 1980s, the second generation was the new public expenditure management and financial management projects (begun at the end of the 1980s, see Chapter 3), and the third generation was governance.

Even though one interviewee wanted the Bank to integrate the second and third generations, he/she believed that the Bank just latched onto the governance idea as the solution for development (WB23). For this interviewee, governance was like

> dark matter in the universe. You can explain everything but what you see. And what you can't explain, you posit the new material as the explanation for what you are seeing. We discovered the second-generation reforms were more far more nu-anced, and required more consensus between us and the governments but [they] still did not work; therefore, the explanation must be dark matter. We just defined that as governance.
>
> (WB23)

Either way, the 1991 report linked public sector reform, institutional develop-ment, and governance work. With good governance, public sector issues were increasingly incorporated into the Bank's consideration of what mattered for development.

New Institutional Economics Becomes Theoretical Vehicle

Given questions about neoclassical economics and its potential partial inappropri-ateness for PSM policy, the Bank needed a new theory. In short order, the Bank's economists became enamored with New Institutional Economics (NIE) (Clague 1997; Olson 1997; Williamson 2000b; North 1995; Nabli and Nugent 1989; Smyth 1998; Theobald 1999; Harriss et al. 1995). In 1993, Douglass North won the Nobel Prize in Economics for his NIE work. The Bank, never an institution to ignore the latest economic thinking when it meshed with its evolving intellectual agenda, in-vited North's intellectual predecessor, Oliver Williamson (2009 co-winner of the Nobel Prize in Economics) to speak at its 1994 Annual Bank Conference on Devel-opment Economics. Williamson noted that, unlike neoclassical economics, NIE argued that institutions and in particular, state institutions, mattered for devel-opment. If neoclassical economics was about "getting the prices right," then NIE argued that it was time to get the "institutions right" (Williamson 1995).

As such, NIE quickly became the model under which the Bank could consider the state and not violate its Articles of Agreement. New institutional economists study the economics of organizations with a desire to "economize transaction costs" of organizations (Williamson 1975, 1985). Douglass North, a scholar who "had a lot of time for us [at the Bank]" (WB39) argued that human beings pos-sess unique mental models of their world that disallow the equilibrium expected by neoclassical economics. Instead, "multiple equilibria" exist and "incomplete in-formation" creates institutional "transaction costs" (North 1995, 18). These ideas helped the Bank modify and expand its development project. The resulting policy changes included (1) not simply transferring the Western model onto develop-ing countries (i.e., "privatization is not a panacea for solving poor economic performance"); (2) the assumption that politics creates institutional rules and thus, policy should focus on "polities that will create and enforce efficient prop-erty rights;" and (3) the idea that "adaptive efficiency," not "allocative efficiency," should drive policy" (North 1995, 25–26).

Institutions had risen in importance not necessarily because they were suddenly considered "good" but because improving the developing world's institutional ca-pacity was understood as necessary for economic growth. Again, it is hard to ignore this perspective's resonance with the "institutional development" of the 1980s. But for a Bank in which being an economist has currency, where economists were viewed themselves as representing the most important discipline, positing a theory upon which the economists could attach the next series of PSM polices and projects mattered. To claim "newness" or a "solution" to seemingly unsolved problem is not unique to the bureaucratic maneuverings of Bank civil servants.

NIE was melded into the Bank's governance agenda through new foci on policy environments and strengthened private property rights. NIE was used to justify decentralization as the method for lowering public sector allocation concerns to the lowest political levels. This includes more tax reform, service delivery improve-ments, and in response to 1980s critiques, also targeted social sector spending (Ahmad et al. 2005; World Bank 1998c). Other PSM policies influenced by NIE included expanded financial management reforms. No longer was the state the market's adversary (such as in the 1980s). Instead, the state, the market and the voluntary sector were increasingly considered as complementary.

Governance Addition Expands Public Sector Research

In the early 1990s, "technical" public sector management work such as budget-ing, public-expenditure management, civil-service reform, financial management, and tax administration were folded into the governance agenda. New governance components included new policies (and consequently, projects) in the rule of law, judicial reform, and decentralization. Even though corruption was briefly referenced in early 1990s reports, corruption did not enter the Bank's lexicon of acceptable project categories until the mid-1990s (see Chapter 6).

In the early 1990s, Public Expenditure Reviews (PERs) (later renamed "Partic-ipatory Public-Expenditure Reviews (PPER)) became a tool for evaluating client countries' expenditure capabilities (Pradhan 1996a; Toye and Jackson 1996). Its predecessor, Public Investment Reviews, had been part of Bank work as far back as the late 1970s (PREM 2001b). Public expenditure management research ex-panded rapidly in the intervening years. Some researched the Bank's experience in expenditure earmarking (McCleary 1991), its role in improving growth and equity in the Philippines (World Bank 1995c), or its role in reducing poverty in sub-Saharan Africa (Ferroni and Kanbur 1990). In the 1980s, financial management focused on small, one-off reforms. By the early 1990s the focus had changed (World Bank 1994b; Bartel 1996) as budgeting, accounting, auditing, and information systems were considered. By 1995, the Bank published its first *Financial Accounting, Reporting and Auditing Handbook* of best practices (World Bank 1995b).

Also changing was the Bank's earlier belief that civil service reform was simply a retrenchment formula (Nunberg 1992, 1995a; Nunberg and Nellis 1990). Even if the Bank wondered whether they had a comparative advantage in civil service reform and institutional development, internal advocates argued that if the Bank wanted improved government institutions, then civil-service reform must be part of that agenda. In the early 1990s civil-service reform projects began to consider "issues of improved performance and more effective management of human resources. Thus, current programs contain measures to strengthen personnel management in government and civil service ministries, install human resources management information systems, and in some cases, revise civil-service codes" (World Bank 1994b, 2). The new Bank mantra was to encourage client countries not to "manage less—but better" (Nunberg and Nellis 1990, 1).

In a review of Bank civil service reforms in sub-Saharan Africa, one of the Bank's longest-serving public sector staff, Mammadau Dia showed that prior Bank civil-service reforms focused on retrenchment and pay reform had failed because the Bank neglected to understand, at least in Africa, how patrimonialism influenced state employment. With governance's focus on accountability, transparency, and rule of law, Dia hoped such understandings might assist civil service reform projects (Dia 1993). Other early 1990s papers evaluated Western experiences in civil service reform, including the role of "control and planning," recruiting the "best and brightest," and how pay-based incentives encourage improved performance (Nunberg 1995a).

With the renewed interest in the state and its social expenditures, tax law and policy became new PSM/PSG sub-sectors. Broad developing country experiences in tax policy, reform, and administration were published (World Bank 1991a; Khalilzadeh-Shirazi and Shah 1991). Research also focused on the positive linkages between investment and tax policy, administration, and macroeconomic stability (World Bank 1990), including which tax policies fueled domestic investment (Shah and Baffles 1991). The Bank's first study in this area was published in 1992 as a multipart series with most written or co-written by Cheryl Gray.[7] Research focused on Eastern Europe and, in particular, the relationships between the rule of law and divestiture or private-market activity in Bulgaria (Gray and

---

[7] Gray later headed the Bank's first Public Sector Board. She led the writing of the Bank's 2000 and 2002 Public Sector Strategy reports (see Chapter 7).

Ianachkov 1992), the Czech and Slovak Republics (Gray 1992, Hungary (Gray et al. 1992a), Romania (Gray et al. 1992b), and Slovenia (Gray and Stibla 1992).

Although decentralization is less about public sector "management" than other topics, it soon became part of the Bank's new PSM/PSG agenda. The earliest Bank references to decentralization were published in 1983 (World Bank 1983) but it was not until the early 1990s that decentralization found its home. In 1991, the Bank created an Africa-specific "Municipal Development Program" under the premise that decentralization increased local participation and improved service delivery (World Bank 1994a). Decentralization research focused on improving ur-ban service delivery (Dillinger 1994), rural development (World Bank 1995a) or in reforming Poland (World Bank 1992b).

Reflecting growing economic differences among developing countries, the wealthier developing countries were increasingly able to seek capital market loans. Although these commercial bank loans were (and are) often at higher rates and less favorable terms than Bank loans commercial debts are often more politically favor-able to domestic audiences. They were not conditioned on a country completing a Bank or Fund-demanded policy shift before Bank or Fund loan disbursements. Some of the Bank's biggest borrowers (via amount borrowed per loan) were in-creasingly less likely to turn to the Bank for loans. In response, the Bank expanded research into public sector areas in which the Bank's middle-income countries might still borrow Bank funds. One such area was social security and pension reform (Arrau and Schmidt-Hebb 1995).

In just a few years the Bank's PSM policies had greatly expanded. Neoclassical economics was replaced by NIE. In the late 1980s, PSM topics like public expendi-ture management, financial management, and civil service reform were expanded. "Governance" became the new lingo and with it, new public sector topics such as judicial reform, tax policy, decentralization, and social security. Throughout it all, the key external stakeholders of the 1980s were largely absent. They did not direct the expansion nor did their statements mention such work beyond a desire post-Cold War, to cement its victories. Bank staff were free to find ways to cement that win. Project approvals in PSM (and PSG) increased as sector policies deepened and increasingly, became institutionalized within the Bank.

Less Involved Governance Stakeholders: G7, the US, IMF

In contrast to the conclusion of Chapter 3, the G7, US Treasury and the IMF were less involved in the addition of governance to the sector agenda than ei-ther a deepening of 1980s-style privatization in newly independent post-Soviet states (concurrent with the governance addition) or the 1980s' structural ad-justment. This was echoed by G7 and the US Treasury statements focused on structural-adjustment and the incorporation of former Soviet satellites than a newly emergent "governance" trend. A 1989 Bank-Fund concordat formalized institutional boundaries in public sector management while mentioning nothing about governance. NGOs (as noted in Chapter 9) would remain outside the governance agenda. *Unlike structural adjustment and privatization, two PSM topics led by the G7 and the US Treasury and their allies, good governance was led via policy learning (including at the IMF), the voices of the 1980s institutional development staff finally being heard, and new modes of discussing such reform via new institutional economics.* This space for more PSM (and PSG) was initially created by the 1987 reforms (see Chapter 4) and then given a further boost with the changing international environment between 1989 and 1991.

Many of the G7's early 1990s statements paralleled (*but did not precede, as in the 1980s*) the Bank's good governance developments. In 1990, the G7 observed that "open, democratic, and accountable political systems are important ingredients in the effective and equitable operation of market-oriented economies" (G7 1990). At the 1990 G7 meeting, the UK's Prime Minister at the time, John Major, stated that "strengthening the international order implies support for the policies of good government. All the evidence suggests that bad government is a factor in the poverty of developing nations" (Major 1990). Although that statement came from a particular G7 leader rather than the G7 as a whole, it was the first statement made at a G7 conference addressing governance.

By 1991, the G7 called for greater transparency and a "more efficient public sector" through "higher standards of management and including possibilities for privatization and contracting out" (G7 1991). Accountability was discussed at the 1991 meetings with *good governance* referenced in G7 statements from 1991 to 1993 and again in 1996. The 1995 communiqué mentioned the importance of civil society, "participatory development," and "rule of law" for the first time (G7 1995a) while the 1996 statement considered tax policy, expenditure management, and procurement policies as important to development (G7 1996). In 1995 the G7 prepared a special review of the international financial institutions. The report encouraged institutions to focus on the traditional structural policies. Concerned about external shocks and growing trade imbalances, the G7 report spent significant space discussing how the IMF (and to a lesser extent, the Bank) should encourage financial stability. The Bank and other multilateral development institutions were encouraged to ensure that developing countries provided "public goods" in an "economically sound" manner (G7 1995b).

Good governance and its PSM components were infrequently referenced by the US Treasury. Of the dozens of Bank-specific Treasury statements or releases, only a few discussed governance. The first appearance of the term *good governance* was Treasury Secretary, James Brady's, October 1991 speech before the Joint Development Committee of the Bank and Fund (Brady 1991b). Brady considered good governance as a complement, rather than a challenge to, privatization. The next mention was in 1993 by former Bank chief economist and then Undersecretary of the Treasury under President Clinton, Lawrence Summers (Summers 1993). At another joint Bank and Fund meeting in 1994, good governance, along with strengthening "administrative and institutional capacity," was encouraged (Bentsen 1994). Even as late as 1996, President Bill Clinton's Treasury discussed the benefits of "shedding" state-owned enterprises and how, after privatization, service delivery improved. In that particular statement, the Treasury pointed out how PSM and in particular, expenditure management, was the other side of the adjustment coin (Summers 1996).[8]

In 1989, the IMF and the Bank concluded a concordat agreement[9] that appeared, at first glance, to draw lines in the sand between how the Bank and the Fund could involve themselves in public sector management. The concordat left the Fund with macroeconomic policy-making along with the Fund's traditional "surveillance, exchange rate matters, balance of payments, growth-oriented stabilization" (Polak 1994, 42), whereas the Bank was to focus on long-term development (U.S. House of Representatives 1990). Although the IMF traditionally led advising on balance of payments, the concordat noted that Bank adjustment programs "deal with the efficient allocation of resources in both public and private sectors: priorities in government expenditures; reforms of administrative systems, production, trade and financial sectors; the restructuring of state enterprises and sector policies" (IMF-World Bank 1989, paragraph 10). Both institutions agreed the Fund would lead tax and customs *policy* (but not their *administration*) and would encourage statistical capability development. The Bank led on public enterprise restructuring (including privatization), corruption, decentralization, judicial reform, rule of law, and civil service reform. Financial management and public expenditure management were jointly undertaken.

But has the concordat worked in practice? The answer is that inter-organizational coordination remains low: "The Fund has its own sense of accountability and so does the Bank have its own sense of accountabilities. I think if there is a criticism to be made it is that there is no effective coordination device. There is not one between the two and for all of them. I suppose historically, the idea was that the UN would play that role, but the UN has trouble coordinating itself" (WB54).

---

[8] So if the Treasury did not really focus on governance or public-sector management, did it follow that the Treasury did not focus on any sector-specific issues and, therefore, we should not be surprised? Yes and no. Environmental concerns and the Treasury's support of the Bank's work in this sector were discussed repeatedly (Niehuss 1990; Brady 1991a; Bentsen 1993b; Shafer 1994), perhaps because the US Executive Director to the World Bank under President Bush was an environmentalist (WB43 2008). Even population growth and gender received a mention (Bentsen 1993a).

[9] There have been limited scholarly reviews of either the 1989 Concordat or a related Joint-Management Action Plan (JMAP) in 2007. For a short history, see (IEO 2020).

Instead, cooperation is based on "personality. Incentive alignment. Continued interest to cooperate. But, you know, it comes with costs. It's hard enough navigating your way through one bureaucracy but to do it through two" (WB54).

Similar views were expressed by others: "The IMF in some things has been extremely influential. And other things, not. It seems to depend on the personalities and if the people gel who work in a particular country, and then you know, they are very influential" (WB52). A 2007 report underlined these concerns and noted that the 1989 concordat's failures to closely define the division of responsibilities had practical and financial considerations. The 1989 concordat was considered a "negotiated statement, with ambiguity in parts of the text being the basis for reaching agreement," and that the distinction between the Bank and Fund's responsibilities remained "unclear" after 1989 (Malan 2007, 40).[10]

Conclusion: Shifting Actor Influences

With the Cold War over, the Bank's key shareholders sought to cement a market-liberal model in Eastern and Central Europe. The Bank's 1980s agreement on structural adjustment and privatization provided the ideological consensus to quickly create similar projects for the newly independent states. As the early 1990s progressed, Bank research on privatization expanded rapidly. As noted in Table 1, Bank PSM (and PSG) projects increased more than four-fold when compared to the prior 21 years of PSM project approvals.

Between November 1989 and 1991, the US held the most significant power, legitimacy, and urgency over the Bank's PSM policies. It did not stop Bank staff from using the 1987 reforms to expand and deepen PSM sector development. For the US and its allies, structural adjustment and privatization were the "how to grow" prescriptions for Eastern and Central Europe. The fall of the Berlin Wall was a political event that also became a potential international economic crisis. From the perspective of the Cold War "winners", a failure to incorporate Russia and former Soviet satellites into an emergent world order was a potential crisis requiring quick action. Successful incorporation would cement the Cold War win. As in the 1980s, an international economic crisis motivated key external actors to shape the major structural adjustment component of this sector's agenda.

However, the US role in PSM/PSG sector policy change must be nuanced. As structural adjustment expanded to include "good governance," the *G7 Group of*

---

[10] IMF historian (James Boughton) took that sentiment even further. Referring to the Concordatt phrase *aggregate aspects of macroeconomic policy*, Boughton wrote, "No one could say definitively what it meant, and all efforts to make it more precise failed. It provided the Bank with an excuse for asserting independence with respect to advice on lending conditions on whatever it might characterize as non-aggregative, and it provided the Fund with a reaffirmation of its macro policy, but in fact it was little more than an implicit acknowledgement that the institutions would continue to disagree" (Malan 2007, 41, citing Boughton (2001), emphasis added).

Nations and the US Treasury statements would concur with, rather than precede or encourage, such sector topic additions (see Table 4). US Treasury statements were quiet on good governance. This differed from the Treasury's lead agenda-setting role in the 1980s. Although the US Government and the G7 certainly had the power and legitimacy to encourage good governance, their most urgent issue was the economic restructuring of Eastern and Central Europe. Consolidating the Cold War "win" was their imperative. The Bank responded with an all–hands-on-deck effort. The Bank became an important lever over Eastern and Central European countries.

Table 9 and its fourteen external variables drawn from stakeholder theory neatly summarize external actor influences. By the early 1990s, the "control" of the Bank by the G7 and the IMF is less significant than the 1980s. A similar sentiment occurs for the US after 1991 and especially in PSM/PSG topics outside of privatization. Given President Preston's illness and the subsequent temporary replacement of Preston by Ernie Stern, this era and this sector lacked a clear interaction with the President. In Table 10, the main difference between the November 1989 to September 1995 era and the prior era is that the lead on PSM/PSG reform is the PSM Units and not DEC. In the 1980s, it was the opposite. The 1987 reform create organizational space for PSM Unit emergence. The exception to this claim is DEC lead role in reconsidering the neoclassical economics theory as a frame for Bank work and instead, integrating and championing NIE at the Bank.

Bank staff were the clear agenda leader on good governance and related sector topics like judicial reform or social expenditures (see Table 5). This allowed staff to increasingly redefine this sector's policy agenda. Yet, these shifts did not disagree with American strategic interests. This revised sector policy agenda was complex and by default, perhaps too detailed for strategic-level considerations of a G7 or US stakeholder. The Bank's expanded PSM/PSG agenda was an organizational and staff response to a changing world order. The fall of the Berlin Wall allowed a "supporting the state" perspective to no longer automatically equate to socialist or communist tendencies. Even though public sector staffs had long sought to change the Bank on PSM and institutional development, it took a broader confluence of external events for this shift to occur.

The new organizational spaces required staff to justify their purpose. As Eastern Europe and Russia began structural adjustment, staff understood that structural reform was not enough to ensure economic development. *It was not that the Bank believed that neoliberalism and structural adjustment were wrong; rather, the Bank came to believe that more was required. Good governance was consid-ered complementary to structural adjustment.* NIE became the theoretical vehicle to approach institutional issues. The international system's new strategic focus, client-country needs, World Bank analyses, and internal organizational shifts coa-lesced to strengthen and expand the public sector agenda. Bank lending incentives would be assisted by an expanded sector agenda. Sector agenda additions implied new lending.

Certainly, the Bank did not painlessly transition between structural adjustment and governance. The 1991 *Managing Development: The Governance Dimension* report was an important stepping-stone. It is likely not coincidental that good governance foci aligned with the US's strategic concerns in Eastern Europe and Russia. While the US may not have controlled, led, or even overtly influenced the Bank staff's new policy directions in good governance, the US certainly appeared not to disapprove of the expanded agenda. Although the 1980s Stern critique about the difficulty of institutional development work had not disappeared, the Bank realized that, despite such complications, institutional development (reframed as PSM/PSG) was beginning to matter. That NIE, with its more technical view of institutional activity, fit with dominant Bank staff perspectives only further encouraged sector policy evolution.

Even if Bank staff led sector deepening, they were independent of the Board. The Board has the final say and can force the Bank, if the Board is interested, to retract, change, or expand policies. The threat of Board veto or project disapproval concerns staff. No one wants to do a twelve- to eighteen-month project preparation just so the Board can disapprove. Bank staffs were freed to modify and expand the agenda but always with an eye to the Board's potential reaction. The 1991 Conable memo was an example of staff who needed to placate the Board while modifying the PSM agenda.

Like structural adjustment's controversial 1980 approval via a reconsidered (but not amended) Articles of Agreement, the Bank reinterpreted the Articles for the good governance addition. The carefully worded letter from President Conable and the attached legal memorandum preceding the 1991 Report indicated what was needed for the Bank to proceed into the good governance arena. It was no accident that in Conable's memo he explicitly linked "efficient and accountable public sector management" to "a predictable and transparent framework for economic activity" (World Bank 1991b: President's Memo). *Good governance was needed for structural adjustment's reforms to stick.*

6

The "C" Word Decloaked and the State Matters (October 1996 to December 1999)

After nearly two decades of structural adjustment and a half-decade of governance-related policies and projects, the Bank formally cemented a link between the necessity of the state and development between October 1996 and May 1997. *The state now mattered to development.* The prior Bank argument was that the state's best contribution to development was state minimization. In addition, after decades of Bank staff members observing corruption within client nations but forbidden by Bank practice to publicly name "corruption" or acknowledge its impact, the Bank's new President purposefully broke that taboo during an October 1, 1996 speech at the Bank and Fund's annual meetings in Washington DC. *This new rhetoric did not imply that structural adjustment had "lost" or that governance had "won" but instead, the neoclassical model was now an incomplete answer to "how one develops." The state mattered and if state mattered, then corruption must be publicly discussed.*

The Bank's internal dynamics also shifted in the last half of the 1990s. It had not been since Robert McNamara (1968–1981) that the Bank had a President such as James Wolfensohn. He embraced (and some say, led) these intellectual shifts, he publicly argued with the Bank's Board and the IMF, he spotlighted corruption within Bank client nations, and he "modestly" reformed ("modest" when compared to the 1987 reform, see Chapter 4) the Bank's organizational structure. The new emphasis on the state was matched with more office space, new staff, and more PSM/PSG.

The timid steps toward governance and greater Bank involvement in PSM in the early 1990s had become a torrent of activity by the mid- to late-1990s. As per Table 1, PSM lending continued to rise. Between 1997 and 1999, 771 projects with a PSM component were approved. These three years were part of a five-year period from 1996 to 2000 in which projects with PSM components encompassed between 81.7 percent and 82.8 percent of all Bank projects.

In short succession, Wolfensohn (1) legitimized anticorruption programs and projects (late 1996), (2) declared in the Bank's most widely distributed publication (*WDR*) that the state mattered (1997), (3) stated that the Bank needed to "move beyond" the Washington Consensus (1998). He also helped write the Bank's

Who Matters at the World Bank?. Kim Moloney, Oxford University Press.
© Kim Moloney (2022). DOI: 10.1093/oso/9780192857729.003.0006

first corporate strategy (Strategic Compact), initiated an organizational reform (matrix), and weathered a public and roiling debate with the IMF over the Asian Financial Crisis. The October 1996 to December 1999 period was a busy four-year period at the Bank, in this sector, and vis-à-vis an external financial crisis. Throughout it all, the PSM/PSG continued its upward trajectory. New interactions of the Bank President (with DEC) and the newly created PREM Network, Public Sector Anchor, and Public Sector Board were crucial to furthering PSM and PSG institutionalization and its topic diversification (see Appendix, Table 4).

Wolfensohn Arrived and the Bank Noticed

Unlike Robert McNamara, the Bank Presidents of the early 1980s and early 1990s (Clausen, Conable, and Preston) were considered weak Presidents by Bank staff. Each did little to buck the structural adjustment trends advocated by the G7, the US, Ernie Stern, and the Bank's Chief Economists. This does not mean that disagreements did not occur; rather that, based on publicly available information, the Bank's Archives, and my own interviewees, disputes often did not gather large press corps.[1] In addition, none of the three Presidents appeared to have McNamara's ability to take the organization by its horns and to forcefully lead it in a new direction. Wolfensohn, it was said, had the force of personality to do just that, although the following sections might temper the Wolfensohn enthusiasts who tend to claim that it was Wolfensohn alone who changed the Bank. Regardless of one's perspective, for the first time since the 1980 start-date of this book, the Bank had a President who could not be ignored (see Appendix, Table 11).

James Wolfensohn became Bank President on June 1, 1995 and served until May 31, 2005. That Wolfensohn had always wanted to be the Bank President was well known in Washington. After McNamara, the Bank Presidents had been men "who earlier spent long, illustrious careers cordially ignoring it" (Mallaby 2004, 40). Wolfensohn was different. Born in Australia, Wolfensohn had lobbied President Carter in the late 1970s to succeed McNamara as Bank President. To pad his candidacy, Wolfensohn gave up his Australian citizenship for American citizenship. But just as he obtained American citizenship, Carter announced Clausen as the next Bank president (Mallaby 2004, 74–75).

In the 1980s, Wolfensohn started a Wall Street firm. By 1990, he was asked to Chair the John F. Kennedy Center for the Performing Arts which allowed him to court Washington's Who's Who. When in 1994 the Bank presidency opened up, Wolfensohn lobbied hard. Mallaby reported that Wolfensohn called all of his

---

[1] The exceptions were Clausen's view that the US government should not rescind its IDA funding in the mid-1980s and Conable's public spat with the IMF over organizational boundaries between the Bank and the Fund.

friends including key Clinton supporters like Donna Shalala and Vernon Jordan. As the campaign heated up, Wolfensohn's lobbying was such that

> he was not calling a few friends, or even quite a lot of friends; he was wielding a vast switchboard of entangled lines that looped and curled and stretched around the world, each ending up with a devoted and distinguished associate in finance, music, or academic, or politics, or any of the dozen other areas that Wolfensohn's activities encompassed ... In short, Wolfensohn was playing the Washington game with an energy that amazed even the city's grizzled veterans. Jan Piercy [then US executive director] reckons she got calls from nearly every member of the Clinton cabinet, telling her why Wolfensohn was perfect.
>
> (Mallaby 2004, 85)

One Bank interviewee said Wolfensohn had the "vision thing," which was something that should not be "underestimated" (WB29). Others viewed Wolfensohn more callously: one interviewee stated that all the Board wanted was "a President that could live for two years. That was the number one requirement" (WB43, referring to Preston). That Wolfensohn was perceived to have a big ego and even bigger rolodex was not new. Mallaby recalled that staff worried that Wolfensohn was a "showboating newcomer, long on glitzy contacts and short on development experience" (Mallaby 2004, 85).

Wolfensohn's first trip for the Bank was to Africa. The trip impacted his presidency. Wolfensohn saw how countries had not progressed. He learned why middle-income countries such as South Africa refused to take Bank loans due to the "hassle" involved. Where debt relief had once been a sideline issue, under Wolfensohn its profile expanded. NGOs and other advocacy organizations had put debt relief on their agenda and an international campaign was brewing. He visited an unprecedented (for a Bank president) twenty-four countries in his first one hundred days and met with NGOs at each stop. Wolfensohn was seemingly frustrated by the Bank's slow bureaucracy. He felt the Bank's bureaucrats were afraid to make mistakes even as project quality suffered (Mallaby 2004, 161). The organizational impacts of such early forays were two related events: a modified organizational structure (the "matrix") and a Strategic Compact. Both events assisted PSM/PSG institutionalization within the Bank.

Wolfensohn and the "C"-Word Taboo

On October 1, 1996 at the Bank and Fund's annual meetings in Washington DC, President James Wolfensohn spoke about the importance of good financial management, public-expenditure management, and tax collection. But his most important statement was the following: "The Bank must talk more about 'economic and financial efficiency' and that conversation must include 'transparency, accountability, and institutional capacity. And let's not mince words: we need to deal with the cancer of corruption" (Wolfensohn 1996, n.p.; see also Best 2012; Berkman 2008b; Park 2012; Rose-Ackerman 1998; Marquette 2004, 2007). This was new. The taboo had been broken.

Cognizant of the Bank's Articles of Agreement, Wolfensohn underlined:

> The Bank group cannot intervene in the political affairs of our member countries. But we *can* give advice, encouragement, and support to governments that wish to fight corruption; and it is these governments that will, over time, attract the larger volume of investment. Let me emphasize that the Bank group will not tolerate corruption in the programs that we support; and we are taking steps to ensure that our own activities continue to meet the highest standards of probity.
>
> (Wolfensohn 1996)

In just a few sentences, Wolfensohn introduced a previously forbidden concept into *Bankease*, justified the Bank's work on it, and stated that its implementation would not violate the Bank's Articles of Agreement. The Bank would no longer ignore corruption. Bank staff members had long known that corruption might lead to distorted policy outcomes. But prior interpretations of its Articles of Agreement indicated that the Bank could not involve itself in the political affairs of member countries. Similar to structural adjustment, privatization, and governance, addressing corruption had been considered a violation of the Articles of Agreement. *Like structural adjustment, privatization, and governance of the 1980s and early 1990s, the Articles were not rewritten but instead, reinterpreted to mesh with the Bank's new priorities.*

The decision to discuss corruption was not made hastily, nor did Wolfensohn originate the idea. According to a NGO interviewee and a Bank interviewee, the US Government had long supported anticorruption efforts even if over the years, *the US voice had not been loud enough to ensure Bank action.* For my NGO interviewee: "The U.S. is always the lone voice in the Board on corruption in government and we [the U.S. Government] need to be selective in how we use them [the Board members] because (1) we don't want to use up their capital and (2) [it is] sort of like that dude nagging on the side. We can't, we don't want to get to that point." The Bank interviewee believed that an "external dynamic" encouraged the Bank to adopt an anticorruption agenda. This included not just a long-held American view[2] but later, an OECD's agreement to fight corruption[3] that influenced Bank behavior (WB37).

---

[2] US Foreign Corrupt Practices Act of 1977.
[3] OECD Convention on Combating Bribery of Foreign Public Officials in International Business Transactions.

As early as March 1996, Wolfensohn spoke with the head writers of the forthcoming 1997 WDR about his upcoming speech. Wolfensohn wanted an anticorruption focus to the Report. One of the 1997 WDR's key writers recalled meeting with Wolfensohn in March 1996. In that meeting, they agreed that corruption must be included in the 1997 Report even if, at that time, "corruption was [still] a closet word" (WB39). Wolfensohn was "very heavily involved" in making sure corruption was an important component (WB39). In June 1996, Wolfensohn said, very clearly, when the WDR head writers presented him with the outline, "I am going to make this speech; I am going to find the evidence for it. Make sure your report talks about how damaging corruption is to development" (WB39). So, they did.

Even so, some Bank staff disagreed about whether Wolfensohn's role was that important. Others resented that Wolfensohn was given credit for the "state matters" work that came afterwards. The Bank had previously published reports in which "corruption was acknowledged as important," and, thus, it was not as if "staff took the lead from Wolfensohn; instead, insiders wanted the Bank to consider corruption, but it did not go until Wolfensohn had given the stamp of approval" (WB20). One staff member said that Wolfensohn's work on corruption had a "huge impact" (WB31) while another said Wolfensohn shed light onto the anticorruption "profile" (WB36). A third said it was not until Wolfensohn made his speech that "corruption came to the forefront, [we could] openly talk about it. [It] became more legit" (WB40).

Staff knew that corruption impacted Bank policy outputs, but the Bank's legal mandate prevented corruption from being a topic for general discussion. Prior to 1996, corruption was referred to as the "'C' word" within Bank circles (WB13). Corruption was understood to exist but it could neither be mentioned nor considered in project formulation and implementation (WB13). Corruption was "an embarrassment" in the 1980s Bank and any staff who mentioned it were considered "troublemakers" (WB52).

By the mid-1990s, one NGO interviewee noted (with a bit of exaggeration) that corruption went from being the c word no one would discuss to becoming so important that "now [you] can be fired for saying corruption is not a major issue" (WB48). Explaining the historical basis behind the new anticorruption stance, one interviewee noted that in the 1990s,

> [Corruption] was so clearly in the air that it was a problem ... First, the fall of the Berlin Wall and the opening of the region. Second, [there was] a lot of academic research showing the costs of corruption. In the 1980s, it had just been kind of a rent-seeking and transfer with no economic costs. In the 1990s, more literature on the importance of institutions, and Douglass North won the Nobel

Prize, and problems of corruption and its costs. Transparency International was set up[4] and the whole civil society got going ... so when [the Bank] came along, [the corruption topic] had changed tremendously. [It was] hard to argue that it did not matter... It was in the air, you had the *WDR* [1997] that had just come out. I don't recall a contentious Board on [anticorruption] and I have been to a lot of contentious Board meetings ... Shihata [the Bank's general counsel] used to say you can't work on this because it is political.

(WB31)

Nonetheless, we cannot downplay the importance of new Bank leadership. This includes the now familiar discussion about whether the new PSM/PSG topic violates the Bank's Articles of the Agreement. This time the new topic was anti-corruption (Graham 2014). A Bank interviewee recalled an event between Wolfensohn and the Bank's General Counsel (Ibrahim Shihata): "Wolfensohn was told by [his] general counsel [that] 'You can't do corruption; it is in the Articles of Agreement.' [And Wolfensohn] said, 'Well give me the interpretation that allows me to do it.' You need an activist staff and management to push those boundaries" (WB1). In 2002, and with a quote often noted by other scholars of this era too, Wolfensohn reflected on how Shihata had introduced him to the topic and the impact of his 1996 speech:

When I arrived, the general counsel was giving me guidance on what it is that I could and couldn't do within the context of this, then rather-more-bureaucratic organization than it is now. He said very quietly to me: "Of course, we are not allowed to engage in politics, and you cannot mention the *c* word;" and I said: "What is the *c* word?" And he whispered in my ear: "That's corruption." And I said: "Why can't I mention corruption?" And he said that corruption is essentially political and it gets into the concerns of our Board members and we are a non-political organization. I took that for a few days, and then gradually started to redefine corruption as not a political issue but as an economic and moral and social issue, and an issue which addresses the very question of poverty. I gave a speech at the annual meetings in which I spoke about the cancer of corruption. That was literally the first time that a World Bank president had gone public using the word. It's preposterous, but it's true; and that's just a little over five years ago. Yet now we're operating in a hundred countries dealing with issues relating to governance and corruption, and it's done without a murmur on the part of our shareholders. In fact, they join us in talking about corruption. Now the *c* word is acceptable.

(Wolfensohn 2002)

---

[4] Transparency International was founded in May 1993 by Peter Eigen, a former Bank staffer, fed up with Bank inaction on corruption (see Chapter 9).

Shihata had served as the Bank's General Counsel since 1983. With Wolfensohn's arrival, the General Counsel role was shifting. For Wolfensohn, Shihata needed to be the General Counsel *for the president* and less so *for the Bank*. Shihata, who throughout the 1980s and 1990s, vigorously defended his interpretation of the Articles of Agreement, would retire in 1998.

Perhaps without surprise, not every Executive Director was happy with Wolfensohn's speech. Media reports quoted government representatives from Malaysia, Pakistan, and Bangladesh as concerned that the Bank's new agenda overinvolved the Bank in client politics, created difficult-to-evaluate contextual circumstances, and encouraged too much focus on *who takes bribes* rather than the developed-country officials or businesses *who give bribes*. That the Bank had entered into politically difficult waters was undoubtedly true.

By 1997, the Bank had published its first Anticorruption Strategy. Although one interviewee recalled the Bank's External Relations Department as worrying whether the Anticorruption Strategy was "too controversial," (WB31) events soon overtook Board preferences. In 1997, Bank and Fund's annual meetings were held in Hong Kong and corruption had become "the topic" of discussion (WB31). The strategy advocated four avenues of work: (1) "preventing fraud and corruption in Bank projects;" (2) "helping countries that request Bank assistance for corruption;" (3) "mainstreaming a concern for corruption in the Bank's work;" and (4) "lending active support to international efforts to address corruption" (Huther 2000, 1). Even though the Strategy was short on specifics, it was enough to move Bank research, projects, and policies on anticorruption forward. Anti-corruption was now part of PSM/PSG policies.

Organizational Impacts of the 1997 Anticorruption Strategy

Two internal organizational impacts arose from the 1997 Anticorruption Strategy. The first dealt with the Strategy's first avenue of work: "preventing fraud and corruption in Bank work" (Huther 2000, 1). According to Bank's own Integrity Vice Presidency (INT) history, the main motivator forINT's creation was a 1995 memo by a Bank employee "with extensive experience in Africa" who wrote "that the continent was rife with corruption and that Bank monies were being misdirected and squandered as a result" (Thornburgh 2000, 9). Prior internal Bank assessments found "some 20 percent or more of [Bank] disbursements 'leak' out of the system in one improper form or another" (Thornburgh 2000, 4). Therefore, the Bank had decided (or perhaps, had recently become politically able) to address those leaks. Shortly thereafter, Wolfensohn gave his "cancer of corruption" speech, which was followed a month later by a Controller's Office paper called the "C Word."[5] In

---

[5] None of my Bank interviewees had a copy of this paper. Nor could I separately find a copy. However, in a Bank Historian interview with its author, the paper is briefly mentioned (Muis 2000, 11–12).

early 1996, Wolfensohn "encourage[d] systematic addressing of the problem of corruption" in a meeting with the Bank's vice presidents (Thornburgh 2000, 10).

The first organizational impact was the creation of today's Institutional Integrity Vice Presidency (INT) which begun as a 1998 "Oversight Committee on Fraud and Corruption." Its independence has increased as its investigative arms have strengthened. Nonetheless, still limiting INT's effectiveness was the fact that the vice presidency has "no law enforcement powers either in the United States … or anywhere else in the world. This limits the ability to use certain investigative techniques available to many national investigative agencies, such as subpoenas, grants of immunity, and electronic surveillance" (Thornburgh 2000, 15). Instead, Bank staff misconduct is investigated as per the Bank's Staff Code. With a review of INT efforts by Paul Volcker in 2007 (Volcker 2007) necessitated, in part, by impacts of the Wolfowitz era (see Chapter 8) and multiple cases brought by INT staff against its leadership before the Bank's Administrative Tribunal, Chapter 9 will discuss impact (INT 2010, 13–17).

The second impact was to "mainstream a concern for corruption in the Bank's work" (Huther 2000, 1). Anticorruption became a multisector policy. Within PSM/PSG, anticorruption influenced both traditional structural adjustment and the administrative and civil service reform efforts such as public expenditure management, rule of law, increased public accountability, and auditing institutions. Operationally, staff worried that project-specific anticorruption work would be limited given anticorruption's home network (Poverty Reduction and Economic Management or PREM, see discussion later in Chapter) focused on policy advice, not lending.

Between 1997 and 2003, corruption-focused research papers quickly became the largest share of the publicly available, non-country specific, PSM/PSG publications. Nevertheless, mirroring the Bank's prior sector research, it focused on national-level policy shifts and less on specific departments or the bureaucratic behavior within those departments. Anticorruption research discussed causes, impact, and how it should be measured and evaluated. Published insights included learning that corruption was assisted by weak institutions, weak regulatory structures, and weak property rights. Bank researchers found that corruption reduced economic growth, harmed the poor, was more prevalent in countries with lower per-capita incomes, reduced procurement transparency, encouraged inefficient service delivery, harmed smaller enterprises, encouraged a large unofficial economy where tax collection became difficult, raised transaction costs, lowered private and public investment and lessened government legitimacy (Gatti 2003; Anderson 2003). Overcoming corruption required political commitment and specific institutional efforts including audit or oversight institutions, including ombudsmen. Simplified administrative procedures and improved laws and judicial actions also mattered, along with media campaigns, greater press freedom and citizen and NGO involvement to publicize abuses (e.g. Lederman 2001; Coolidge 1997).

With institutional backing, new research, and new projects emphasizing anti-corruption importance for the institutionalizing PSM/PSG sector agenda, the next step was to declare that contrary to the Bank of the 1980s, the state mattered for development. This declaration occurred with the 1997 *WDR*.

The 1997 *WDR*: The State in a Changing World

Wolfensohn's October 1996 speech was important. But as per the prior chapters, his speech had been preceded by a longer, if less public, PSM history. That history grappled with structural adjustment, fought for institutional development, debated privatization and SOE reform, and struggled with Washington Consensus implications. In many ways, a door into a "state matters" agenda was swung ajar with *Managing Development: The Governance Dimension* (1991). Wolfensohn simply responded to the times, saw a door open, and by giving his "Cancer of Corruption" speech, kicked door down, and led the Bank through it.

Seven months after Wolfensohn's speech, the Bank published *The State in a Changing World*. The WDR has either been the subject of or referent point for multiple studies (e.g., Pal 2012). This *WDR* was "devoted to the role and effectiveness of the state: what the state should do, how it should do it, and how it can do it better in a rapidly changing world" (WorldBank 1997b, iii). It proposed a two-pronged strategy (1) to not overextend the state and (2) to rebuild state capacity. The most effective state, the report argued, was a state with appropriate rules for private investment, its interaction with civil society, and ensuring that rules became reliable and predictable to undermine corruptive influences. Rules, as illustrated by NIE, were important for development. Rules could constrain the state while ensuring economic development. Good policy on its own was no longer enough to improve a country's development position. Instead, good policy combined with an "institutional capability" was considered important (WorldBank 1997b, 4–9). *The model had changed. This was no longer the Bank sector of the 1980s. The Bank had found a way, using the normatively acceptable (for the Bank) language of economics to bring a NIE twist to the institutional development argument of the 1980s.*

Why did the Bank's policy shift? Excluding the early 1980s PSM staffers who had argued for institutional development work, later-day PSM/PSG staff traced the state's resurgence to the "cancer of corruption" speech and the 1997 *WDR*. Of course, it was not as if in 1997 the state had suddenly become "good" and the market "bad;" rather, the Bank formally acknowledged with the 1997 *WDR* that the state was a valuable partner to the market and to development. To ensure the state did not become the inefficient behemoth that structural adjustment and privatization had tried to overcome, the World Bank modified its neoliberal rhetoric (informed by neoclassical economics) to include NIE's argument that not only do institutions matter but institutions are best managed by understanding incentives and rules. If institutions can be discouraged from overtaking society's economic functions, then the state had a place in the "what it takes to develop" equation.

But did that mean the Bank had forgotten the structural adjustment of the 1980s? No. While new state fundamentals included the natural environment and social service provision, the 1997 *WDR* did not imply the Bank's intellectual agenda favored states over markets. This view was echoed by US Treasury Secretary, Robert Rubin, in a 1997 speech: "U.S. leadership will remain vitally important in the years ahead. One priority, for example, is to continue to clarify the proper role of the state in the development process" (Rubin 1997). This US statement is an about-face from its 1980s and early 1990s rhetoric. For the US, public spending quality was important but so were fiscal choices and a state's legal and regulatory systems. Improved procurement systems, tax and banking reforms, and transparent financial management also mattered (WorldBank 1997b, 33). Encouraging a state to be accountable to its citizens was a new Treasury emphasis that mirrored the Bank's demand-side governance.

The mechanisms of how to improve state effectiveness were seemingly simple: contracting where necessary, encouraging performance-based actions, privatizing SOEs, and encouraging voice (WorldBank 1997b, 96). The 1997 *WDR*'s inclusion of "voice" was the first hint of an emerging perspective[6] that social capital, state-provided enabling environments for participation, and decentralization may encourage greater interaction between client governments and their citizens. The Bank believed in *espirit de corps* and that if only public sector institutions tried hard enough, they could create common understandings amongst themselves. Report authors cited Singapore's civil service as proof (WorldBank 1997b).

Acknowledging a break with the Bank's prior PSM work (at least in terms of training and technical assistance), the report noted: "This focus on institutions is very different from the traditional approach of technical assistance, which emphasizes equipment and skills and administrative or technical capacity. The emphasis here is on the incentive framework guiding *behavior*—what government agencies and officials do and how they perform" (WorldBank 1997b, 79; original emphasis). *The new theoretical battle lines were drawn.* NIE was to be the new-and-improved lens for understanding state underperformance. The old PSM work must be reframed using NIE.

Still, the Bank's new solutions were more than just nods to NIE. They were also indicative of the *WDR* staff's willingness to discard past public sector management work (and its specialists as we will soon see) as "less sharp" (interviewee words) than the Bank's economists. If the Bank was to incorporate the state into its intellectual agenda, then it had to do so on the terms best understood by the

---

[6] The focus on voice and participation became especially influential as the Bank would shortly bring in yet another branch of economics (political economy) to strengthen its theoretical basis for participatory approach relevance to development, see Chapter 8.

economists who had driven Bank policy since the late 1970s (Ascher 1983, 418–19, 425). *Reconciliation with non-economist perspectives was difficult, if not impossible.* The technical public administrative work of knowing a ministry, considering their management issues, and working with policy implementation and process issues was too complex and thus impossible to model. Without an economics model, such efforts were viewed as less valid to Bank economists. More practically, models not only help sell ideas and reforms to Bank staff but also to client nations looking for Bank expertise. Even though Ernie Stern retired from the Bank in 1995, many of his earlier comments about why the Bank disliked PSM work remained true into the late 1990s.

Who Made the 1997 *WDR* Happen?

President Wolfensohn played an important role in altering the Bank's perception of anticorruption's relevance, but less has been written about his 1997 WDR influence. One *WDR* co-author told me that Wolfensohn believed that the state *and* the market required each other. Wolfensohn realized that the Bank had to move beyond its narrow preference for just considering civil-service reform and that "different levels of the state"[7] were important, and as such, "we [the authors] widened the concept" (WB39). In the 1997 *WDR*'s Introduction, the Bank noted the *WDR* originated as a direct response to external factors including "the end of the Cold War and the collapse of command-and-control economies, the fiscal crises of welfare states, the dramatic success of some East Asian countries in accelerating economic growth and reducing poverty, and the crisis of failed states in parts of Africa and elsewhere—all of these have challenged existing conceptions of the state's place in the world and its potential contribution to human welfare" (Bruno 1996a, b, 1995). But was that all? Knowing who was involved is integral to understanding what was written.

Neither of the Bank's two chief economists during 1997 WDR formulation was a NIE scholar and yet NIE ideas are present throughout. As Chief Economist (1993–1996), Michael Bruno was considered a "practical, pragmatic economist" who understood that balancing the state and market was important. Whatever Bruno's pragmatism may or may not have been, none of the 1997 *WDR* coauthors who I interviewed (and I interviewed three of them) said more than that. Bruno's own publications during his tenure as Chief Economist reflected his interests in Eastern Europe and how deep crises impact inflation and economic growth (Bruno 1996c) rather than topics related to the 1997 *WDR*. Even so, his pragmatism might have been the perfect trait for his *WDR* task. Nonetheless, illness forced Bruno to leave

---

[7] This includes "decentralization, interface with civil society, the market, broader society" (WB39).

the Bank midway through the 1997 *WDR* process.[8] Bruno was succeeded by Joseph Stiglitz in February 1997.

Like Anne Krueger, who had become the Bank's Chief Economist halfway through the 1983 *WDR* process, Stiglitz entered the 1997 *WDR* process after it had begun. But unlike Krueger, Stiglitz "came on board at the end ... and we [the interviewee] had to force him to close the draft" (WB39). Acknowledging that "when you have that kind of change [from one chief economist to another], the *WDR* can suffer" (WB39), it appeared that whatever impact Stiglitz had was not as internally controversial as Krueger's impact fourteen years earlier. It also probably helped that he had been on the 1997 *WDR*'s External Advisory Team prior to his appointment as Chief Economist.

But when I asked a key 1997 *WDR* writer if the *WDR* writing team included the still-serving PSM staff folks from the 1980s and early 1990s in the Bank's first *WDR* on PSM since 1983, the interviewee responded that Barbara Nunberg (known for her civil service reform research) was not too involved and that they purposefully did not approach PSM specialists such as Mary Shirley. The key writer explained the reasoning as follows:

> [I] can always get a "Mary Shirley" but I know what the chapter will look like. She had a huge body of work already ... I deliberately picked people who had little experience, except Brian Levy[9] who came and sold himself to the team ... but the rest were people like me, who had no prior knowledge. We were all reading, we were all aware, most had come from [Bank] Operations. The idea was to have an idea that was fresh in its thinking, not people who are wedded to certain concepts.
>
> (WB39)

Also not involved was Arturo Israel who had given the *WDR* team his 1987 book, *Institutional Development: Incentives to Performance* to read. But the *WDR* contributor admitted that at the time, he had not understood Israel's book and its importance. It was only when Francis Fukuyama published *State-Building: Governance and World Order in the 21st Century* (2004) that my interviewee felt he finally understood what Israel was trying to say (i.e., the importance of transaction intensity and institutional design, WB39). My interviewee noted that the Chief Economist's office (under Bruno) preferred *WDR* writers with "no prior knowledge" and "little experience" in PSM rather than relying on the Bank's more experienced PSM researchers (WB39). It is imaginable that if such a big shift in Bank thinking was to be formalized, Bank economists wanted their disciplinary view to be most prominent. At no point prior to 1997 had technical PSM staff been allowed to fully drive the Bank's now-majority view on PSM/PSG. The neoclassical

---

[8] Bruno died of bone cancer a few months after leaving the Bank (WorldBank 1998a, 1).
[9] Levy later led the GAC Strategy team in the mid-2000s, see Chapter 8.

economists had led the 1980s sector policy interpretations and by the early 1990s, NIE was the star. *It is astounding, across both the 1980s and 1990s, that what was considered valuable PSM/PSG knowledge was acceptable only if it came from an economist.* Other disciplines were overlooked. Also overlooked were experienced sector staff whose work had eventually "won the day" by the mid-1990s were pushed aside, once again, by a Bank culture in which one discipline (and one or two parts of that discipline) mattered most.

The 1997 *WDR*'s authors knew they had to sell its ideas to the Board. India's official was initially opposed, in part because of the *WDR*'s inclusion of an India-specific text box discussing Indian failures (WorldBank 1998a, 1; Burki 1997). In the end, India's Board representative supported the report apparently only because it was "so well-written."[10] Representatives from Arab countries, and in particular, Saudi Arabia (the only Muslim country that represents itself on the Board) did not initially agree with the report but eventually came around. Russia's official apparently never had a problem, and China's representative was, in the end, the only "holdout." Anecdotally it appears that anticorruption conflicts at the Board level had been solved or at least so muted by May 1997 that a *WDR* interviewee only recalled general disagreements about whether the Bank should involve itself in state-centered activities.

Meanwhile, Ibrahim Shihata was still the Bank's General Counsel. It was Shihata who had written the legal memorandum that accompanied the 1991 governance report. For WDR writers, Shihata was considered a big "problem" for *WDR* approval:

> He opposed the [*WDR*] outline, the survey, and in the end, [we] tried to work with him, and that whole section on legal reform [in the *WDR*], he got one his lawyers to write that part, and in the end, he still opposed it. In the pre-meeting with Wolfensohn before the Board meeting, he said there will be problems [at the Board] ... I had a lot of respect for Shihata personally ... [but] on this particular report, he was not always helpful. I respect his opinion; Shihata also opposed Ernie [Stern] when they were going too far to the right in the 1980s. He had his views and he stuck to his views, he never changed them.
>
> (WB39)

In trying to explain Shihata's resistance to violating the Bank's Articles of Agreement on involving itself in a client country's political affairs, another interviewee observed that when these Articles were written, "we had all sorts of governments—Marxist, socialist, communist, capitalist" but that Shihata took the Articles of Agreement "to heart in the sense that [it was] a constitutional statement [for him]"

---

[10] This seems like a flimsy reason. But interviews of Executive Directors are nearly impossible. The ED's may not wish to publicly criticize the hand that feeds them since all but the US ED are paid by the Bank.

(WB27). Even so, Shihata was outmaneuvered. The state now mattered. While the Bank acknowledged that it must abide by its Articles, the Bank was moving forward. Contradictions between when or what is political involvement or whether public sector management and governance could technically be separated from political involvement were not solved, but instead, just discussed. It was time for the Bank to move on.

The 1997 *WDR* Impact on the Sector

One interviewee believed the 1997 *WDR* formalized a "shift in mentality in thinking *worldwide* ... to [viewing] governments as a necessary and important partner" (WB31, my emphasis), even though he/she personally was not convinced that the *WDR* influenced what the Bank was doing. The interviewee continued:

> [The *WDR*] is a big product, pulling on lessons from experience but does not feed directly into our [work] ... because projects are specific to a country's circumstance and *WDRs* are general, [the] conclusions are general, [it] plots the general trend which is valuable to have on paper. When you get to certain countries and specific cases and your counterparts [are in local] institutions, rarely are the broad lessons anything more than background ... I don't want to understate it, it was a nice *WDR* but I don't think there was a huge impact on the Bank except the idea was in the air that government matters and that we should do more public sector reform.
>
> (WB31)

Another interviewee agreed. Just to get a *WDR* through the Board, they become "so gray that they hardly have an influence because there is so much compromise" (WB34).

It may appear contradictory for a Bank staffer to believe the *WDR* influenced the world more than it influenced the Bank. When I add that this interviewee was a Bank PSM leader during their Bank career, his/her statements appear even more puzzling. Although this staff member noted that the 1997 *WDR* led the Bank to do more PSM reform, the Bank simply continued the civil service reform, financial management, and public expenditure management work that had defined earlier efforts. The rule of law and judicial reform projects that began in the early 1990s continued past 1997 (Barron 2005). Newer PSM projects such as pension reform or unemployment insurance would not take-off until the early 2000s. Since the early 1990s, the Bank had expanded its PSM/PSG work in both the number of projects approved and dollars spent. *In other words, the Bank did not need to publicly declare that the state mattered, it already did matter and the Bank's pre-1997 sector work had proven this claim.*

Operationally, an interviewee believed its impact would be limited because he/she (not a *WDR* writer but hired for his/her public management experience) believed the Bank's policy advice was not always linked to what client governments wanted to do. But even so,

> there was a tiny little catch, which, generally speaking, [was that] it did not work. For the second generation [of reforms] we had at least agreed what the problem was, or at least [what] the functional problem was and [we, the Bank] had people who could talk about it, but both us and the government were stymied with underlying political constraints. What the government said to us … ultimately was not what the government could deliver on, especially in major reform programs in weaker institutional environments. They just could not deliver. The political stakeholders were stronger than the formal officeholders.
>
> (WB23)

So, if PSM was about understanding political constraints, why did the Bank not pursue that angle? The interviewee said that the Bank "is driven by very, very short policy time scales. We need to show that we have done something." That was a familiar comment. In the 1980s, Ernie Stern argued similarly when it came down to the complicated institutional development reforms espoused by the Indonesia Report. PSM (with its longer timeframes) did not fit into short-term timeframes. When I asked why the Bank had such short time scales, the interviewee stated,

> I think it is likely largely to do with the internal career incentives, typically staff stay in their posts for 3 or 4 years while in that time scale cannot make differences in results, but can launch initiatives as a measure of how you are doing, initiative as in terms of a new approach. Let's announce a whole new way of doing things. At last, we've got to the bottom of it, and I will be long gone by the time you figure out that we are still in the same sticky mess.
>
> (WB23)

This view mirrors concerns from the Wapenhans Report (see Chapter 4). Bank incentives are not to "balance technical with political insights… [but] instead, announce a new initiative, which was … the GAC [Governance and Anticorruption Strategy, see Chapter 8]" (WB23). In other words, let us not solve the current conundrum and understand its complexities. Instead, let us introduce another initiative that still does not get at the fundamental problem among Bank advice, Bank timetables, and client-country unwillingness (or inability) to implement Bank suggestions. A Bank focused on short-term time scales would use the 1997 *WDR* to do exactly what it did: expand the number of public sector management and governance projects or at least the number of projects approved with a public sector management and governance component. Money out the door, observed the Wapenhans Report, was what the Bank needed to survive.

Beyond the Washington Consensus: Institutions Matter (1998)

Just a year after the 1997 *WDR*, the Bank's Latin American and Caribbean (LAC) staff published *Beyond the Washington Consensus: Institutions Matter*. The LAC region viewed the *WDR* agenda as "more determined by Africa and by transition countries" than by the middle-income LAC countries and thus, LAC needed its own report (WB34). LAC felt that its region's institutional development was "not as critical for the Bank" and, therefore, the 1997 *WDR's* focus "was not useful for the policy debates in LAC." WDR writers disagreed with this LAC characterization. Instead, one *WDR* writer noted that LAC concerns over the 1997 *WDR* were provided "too late" as the *WDR* process was "too advanced" (WB34).

Unlike the 1997 *WDR*, the 1998 LAC Report "never went to the Board [for approval]" (WB34). The LAC writers chose that path because they "knew that those reports that went to the Board took forever. [There were] all kinds of compromises and became so wishy-washy and the process was a pain. People who did reports on new thinking discovered that." Instead, LAC preferred a "'Viewpoint' or 'Work in Progress' report [so that the] LAC did not need Board approval" (WB34). Although my LAC Report interviewee acknowledged that such freehand publishing can create internal bureaucratic problems, the interviewee claimed that the 1998 Report escaped those issues due to Stiglitz's (as Chief Economist) support.

Even so, the 1998 LAC Report had a similar start point as the 1997 *WDR*. The region's view was that what had been "endorsed from Washington (i.e., the Consensus) were basically policy reforms, not institutional reforms. They were like open trade policies or privatization, but nothing about institutions ... we felt that that was an incomplete reform agenda" (WB34). The report's goal was to "put the importance of institutions again in the policy debate within the LAC and the internal political discussion in the Bank" (WB34). Noting that only one of the Consensus' original ten items dealt with institutions (property rights), the 1998 LAC report argued that institutional considerations matter. The Report was unequivocal about what worked in the 1980s (structural adjustment reform) and what did not (poverty reduction) (WorldBank 1998a, 2). Distinguishing between institutions and organizations, the report focused on the former. Institutions were the "rules that shape the behavior of organizations and individuals in a society," whereas organizations were "sets of actors who collectively pursue common objectives" (WorldBank 1998a, 15). The LAC staff perspective reflects NIE. That is, an assumption that if only the institution's rules were written properly, then the organization will be responsive.[11]

---

[11] Even if rules can encourage behaviors, it is far from proven that civil servants should only be obedient to rules (Friedrich 1940; Finer 1941).

In the 1990s, when a policy reached internal Bank consensus, indicator development often complemented the new policy's relevance. If public sector management and governance were to be incorporated into Bank projects, then the Bank needed a quantitative way to measure whether institutional development occurred. The 1998 Report proposed five indicators for measuring "institutional development," including "(1) the perceived risk of expropriation of property, (2) the perceived degree of contract enforceability, (3) the extent to which there are mechanisms for peaceful dispute-resolution or the perceived degree of the rule of law and order, (4) the perceived quality of public bureaucracies, and (5) the perceived incidence of corruption in government" (WorldBank 1998a, 25–31).[12] The indicators were a reminder of what the Bank still considered important: encouraging private markets to function.

In the report's final chapter, "Public Administration in Latin America and the Caribbean: In Search of a Reform Paradigm," the authors claimed that "the public administration of many countries of the region are typically inefficient, unable to deliver services to the most needy, and bastions of opportunistic behavior" (WorldBank 1998a, 124). To solve those problems, the authors considered various institutional models. But as worrying was their claim that there were only two public administration models for Western nations: the hierarchical model and new public management. In the former, they referenced Max Weber and his "idealized" hierarchical model. The authors wrote that Weber's model

> has worked well in the more advanced countries to circumscribe the freedom of politicians and public servants to act outside the public interest and to create a professionalized civil service … The hierarchical model is nonetheless under extreme pressure. It was born when government was small. In 1890, less than 10 percent of expenditures in today's OECD countries came from the public sector. But the role of the state expanded enormously—until the 1980s, at least—and by 1995 this share had grown to almost 50 percent … This growth has led to large public organizations that are difficult to control and easier for special interests to

---

[12] In the mid-1990s, World Bank Institute staff and a DEC economist created six governance indicators: voice and accountability, control of corruption, rule of law, regulatory quality, government effectiveness, and political stability. Published biennially between 1996 and 2002 and then annually, they have been subjected to several critiques (WorldBank 2002b, 2). Despite the widespread publicity given to the Governance Indicators and their use by scholars, NGOs, and the press, the Bank prefers to evaluate country performance using Country Policy and Institutional Assessments (CPIA). CPIA scores are the primary score for determining IDA eligibility even if CPIA historical scores and methods were initially not publicly available. The overall IDA Country Performance Rating determines a "resource envelope … but is not an entitlement" (WorldBank 2002b, 2007d, 2008a) from which future projects are determined. The CPIA calculates 16 indicators across four clusters. One cluster is "Public Sector Management and Institutions." Others are economic management, structural policies, and policies for social inclusion and equity. Within the PSM and institutions cluster, five indicators matter: (1) property rights and rule-based governance; (2) quality of budgetary and financial management; (3) efficiency of revenue mobilization; (4) quality of public administration; and (5) transparency, accountability, and corruption in the public-sector (WorldBank 2006, 5). Each indicator is worth 5 percent of a client country's CPIA score. Within each indicator, there are between two and four subpart indicators, which are 2.5, 1.67, or 1.25 percent of the CPIA score (WorldBank 1998a, 15–16). For an evaluation of CPIA, see (Thomas 2011; IEG 2010d).

"capture." It has led to inefficiency and inflexibility. And citizens, more distrustful of government than in bygone times, have expressed increasing dissatisfaction.

(WorldBank 1998a, 125)

It is surprising that the Bank considered the Weberian model *was* public administration until new public management came along. In doing so, Bank economists vastly underestimated public administration's disciplinary history including when and where small-*p* politics exists within an organization. A charitable perspective must suggest that the Bank knew of the politics-administration dichotomy and could not reference it, either due to the Bank's Articles of Agreement or perhaps due to the Bank's lack of desire to really involve itself within ministerial organizational affairs. But given the economist focus at the Bank, this is unlikely.

Noting that there was only a "small group in DEC working on institutional development," this well-placed interviewee recalled those researchers as "doing isolated work within the Bank. [The DEC] tried to put it more frontally within the LAC and at the Bank," (WB34) but it was not until Joe Stiglitz became the Bank's chief economist that the LAC could write its 1998 Report. Stiglitz "pushed it and liked it … Stiglitz took [the report] to heart, if he had not done that, it would not have gone well. In the end, the Bank is a hierarchical institution even if it feels anarchic. It is not very easy that a report coming from a region is going to change the way the Bank thinks about an issue, unless somebody more at the center takes it to heart" (WB34). These comments are telling on multiple levels.

First, my interviewee confirmed that prior to Stiglitz (i.e., Bruno and those before), institutional development was not a Bank priority. Second, for at least several years before the 1997 and 1998 Reports, there were "isolated" groups working within the Bank on PSM issues. And yet, points one and two conflict with the multi-sourced history of the prior chapters. In a big organization like the Bank, such histories can be lost. Third, although the interviewee claimed that Stiglitz's support was crucial to the 1998 Report's publication, it is unclear whether Stiglitz was responding to an intellectual agenda that he held prior to arriving at the Bank (doubtful) or, instead, whether once he arrived at the Bank he saw where the Bank was heading and thus, put energy into the 1998 LAC Report given progress already on the 1997 *WDR* when he arrived.

The Strategic Compact and More Reform

In 1997, the Bank published a "Strategic Compact" that was "in effect the first published corporate strategy of the Bank" (WB6) (Nielson 2006; Weaver 2010). Wolfensohn had come from the private sector. If private sector companies have corporate strategies, then so should the Bank. But since Bank clients differ dramatically, simple transference from the private sector to the Bank was impossible because the Bank cannot choose to ignore, say, Latin America—and the interests of these clients are not necessarily aligned with those of [the Bank's] shareholders. Instead, the Bank's shareholders want to be treated as a separate category of client as well: they aren't satisfied if it 'merely" relieves poverty successfully. The shareholders want the Bank to serve their foreign policy interests; they want it to promote a cleaner environment, human rights, and other values that their voters care about. This phenomenon of shareholders-cum-clients is common to most public bodies, and it frequently frustrates their efforts to emulate business".

(Mallaby 2004, 162)

In addition, unlike Corporate Boards, the Bank's Board meets several times a week, its Board reports back to home countries, and the Bank must often create "door-stop-sized reports to justify Bank's activities. No private sector chief executive is obliged to work with this sort of monster on his shoulder. In short, Presidents of the World Bank have little space for strategy. They have no choice but to spend much of their energy wooing outside NGOs and shareholders; if they fail to cover those bases, they will be besieged by demonstrators chanting 'Fifty Years is Enough' and they will be denied money for the soft-loan IDA kitty" (Mallaby 2004, 162).

The Strategic Compact's initial purpose was to restrain Bank spending. Even though the Strategic Compact was unpopular with the Board, it was passed. The US view contrasted with Wolfensohn's vision. Wolfensohn wanted to "spend more of the Bank's profits on administration" whereas the Board wanted Wolfensohn to retain President Preston's promises to cut staff. The irony was that Wolfensohn ran

an organization with a budget of $1.1 billion. Not a small sum, to be sure, but modest when compared to its shareholders' ambitions. The rich countries that sat on the Bank's Board thought nothing of making visionary pronouncements at their annual Group of Seven meetings, and then calling on the Bank to deliver on their promises ... [because during this period] in the public sector, austerity was ascendant. Schemes like Al Gore's reinventing government involved cutting thousands of jobs, if management theory was in vogue, it was the theory of "downsizing" and "delayering" not some theory of expansion. Housed in its new headquarters, suffused with a notoriously laborious, paper-shuffling style, the Bank seemed a prime candidate for belt tightening, or so the Bank's board members felt; they did not pause to wonder if the paper shuffling might reflect their own demands for documents and information.

(Mallaby 2004, 161–162)

Begun in April 1997, the Compact was an agreement "between the Bank and its shareholders: to invest $250 million in additional resources over a three-year period to deliver a fundamentally transformed institution—quicker, less bureaucratic, more able to respond continuously to changing client demands and global development opportunities, and more effective and efficient in achieving its main mission—reducing poverty" (WorldBank 2001, i–iv). A year later, Treasury Secretary, Robert Rubin, stated that he

[Looked] forward to full implementation of the Bank's new human resources policy, cost-cutting measures and improved internal procedures ... We urge the Bank to use the Strategic Compact to sharpen performance criteria for lending, to improve its own internal governance, and to strengthen its impact on labor, environment and microenterprise issues.

(Rubin 1998)

In 2001, the vice presidency that ran the Strategic Compact self-evaluated its efforts. The Report found ongoing implementation problems, including insufficient progress in "delayering and empowering of front-line staff," management-skill gaps, continuing redundancy, and ongoing morale problems (WorldBank 2001, 29–32). One of the Compact's biggest organizational shifts had been decentralizing Bank staff from headquarters to the field. In FY1997, there were just three country directors outside of Washington, by FY2000 there were twenty-nine. Country-based staff increased by 33 percent between FY1998 and mid-FY2001 while DC-based staff dropped by 5 percent.

Many of the "efficiency gains" expected via the Compact were not achieved and in some cases, "unit costs" increased (WorldBank 2001, 29, 45). In terms of the money allocated to the Compact, Mallaby noted that Wolfensohn's staff "were under extraordinary pressure to come up with proof that the quarter of a billion had been spent well" and thus, "not surprisingly, perhaps, the Bank's official data make the outcome look good," and so "the two key measures of the Bank improved— speed [project preparation time] on the one hand, and quality [project outcomes] on the other" (Mallaby 2004, 166–167). Identifying PSM as a targeted Bank sector by the Compact (others included Social Development, Rural Development, Financial Sector Development), the Report at least found an aggregate increase in adjustment lending for PSM between FY1995 and FY1997 and between FY1998 and FY2000.

The Matrix Organizational Reform: Reshaping "Who Matters"

The 1997 Matrix Reform sought to "address the issues of excess bureaucracy" where an appropriate rearrangement of "cross-functional integration, coordination, and standardization can increase productivity" (Philipps 2009, 59). Even though the Compact focused on the anticorruption portion of PSM/PSG, the matrix reforms help cement the PSM/PSG prestige within the Bank. This included creating new Sector Boards of which one was called the Public Sector Board. *For the third time in the Bank's history (1983 PSMUs, post-1987 reforms), institutional space was being created for PSM/PSG institutionalization.* Unlike the 1983 PSMUs which slightly opened the door, the 1987 reform threw it open while simultaneously throwing many other doors open. The 1997 reform was also important for the Bank as whole. But for this PSM/PSG sector, the 1997 reform was the equivalent to putting helpful door stops to keep open or to institutionalize the prior decade of PSG/PSM expansion. Having one's own place to work (with a budget to match) was an important victory for the sector. This included the creation of a new Sector Board and its related Anchor. Each of which were not isolated from the project leaders but instead incorporated into Bank decision-making structures.

However, and echoing comments about the 1987 reform, the matrix "was popular with the consulting company that [gave] recommendations ... it was an attempt to wrestle with the bureaucracy" (WB44). Originally led by a Bank Managing Director (Caio Koch-Weser) and a Bank Vice President for Finance and Private Sector Development (Jean-François Rischard), the Bank hired McKinsey Consulting to review the Bank's structure. After just a two-week review of Bank surveys of their client nations, the Bank and McKinsey agreed that the Bank should speed-up project preparation while encouraging project quality. To do so, the Bank needed "a management matrix" (Mallaby 2004, 153) that rivalled corporate best practice. According to Mallaby (2004), Wolfensohn went back and forth on whether he supported their recommendation. Although he eventually agreed, the "upshot was that the early management reforms were chaotic. There was never a clear moment when Wolfensohn sat down with his team, decided on a reform strategy, and laid out a timetable to implement it" (Mallaby 2004, 157).[13] In a latter-day review, the structure was seen as creating "a spirit of deliberate experimentation" that allowed "each region and network to design its organization relatively autonomously" (WorldBank 2001, 29).

With this reform, one of its two Managing Directors now managed four regions (LAC, Eastern and Central Europe, South Asia, and MENA) and two "knowledge networks," and the other Managing Director oversaw two regions (Africa and East Asia/Pacific), two "knowledge networks," External Affairs, and the Bank's Strategy Department. Knowledge networks were a Wolfensohn invention to replace the Bank's technical units. In the past, the technical units either were organizationally separate from the regional units (prior to 1987) or incorporated within the regions (between 1987 and 1995) but were not, until the mid-1990s reforms, intellectually united into a sector network across the regions. Each knowledge network was to be led by a Vice President. Each region also incorporates one or more sector specialists depending upon Regional Vice President objectives.

---

[13] Similar to the 1987 Reforms and the 1992 Wapenhans Report, there appear to be no publicly available Bank-written documents that either defended or explained the organizational reform. My interviewees, Bank organizational directories, and the occasional outside book (e.g. Mallaby's *The World Banker*) provided assistance.

The "network" in which PSM/PSG sat was Poverty Reduction and Economic Management (PREM). The PREM was considered the most powerful network because its objectives traditionally related more closely to the Bank's core mission.[14] Within the PREM, there are several Anchors where PREM's key objectives are institutionally located. The sector specialists within the public sector Management Anchor work for the PREM and not for the regions. The region's public specialists work for their regional vice president and not for the PREM even though cross-fertilization of ideas and projects is supposed to occur.[15] To further confuse reporting mechanisms, the PREM is the only Network that also reports to the Chief Economist who is also a Senior Vice President. This new matrix contrasted with the post-1987 system in which there was no cross-reporting or formalized discussion points for similar sectoral topics among regions and region-specific sector specialists and sector specialists within the Bank without a regional specialization.

The "Public Sector Management/Institutional Unit" is a PREM anchor. By September 2001, it was renamed the "Public Sector Group" or more colloquially, the "Public Sector Anchor." At some point in the late 1990s (no one seems to recall the exact date, but probably 1998), the Public Sector Anchor created a Public Sector Board whose purpose was ostensibly to direct PSM/PSG work within the Bank even if Board influence over each region varied.

Highlighting a Bank passion for hiring those with certain university pedigrees, one interviewee recalled the first Public Sector Board's members in the following manner: "Of the eight or nine members, one was [a] Stanford Ph.D., one was [an] LSE [London School of Economics] Ph.D., [and] five [were] Harvard Ph.D.'s, just a brilliant and committed group of really great people. The best we have ever had in the Bank" (WB31). In an attempt to determine if the Bank's first Public Sector Board members were staff members with public administration or public management experience or education, I asked if the Board's first members were all economists. The interviewee answered in the affirmative:

Yes. It was a great group, very committed. It was right when the reorganization took place and we had [Sector] Boards for the first time ... [previously] there were only three people in the Bank in public sector management, we started from scratch, and we had a budget. We had a big budget to build it up. We started with a blank slate. It was just a wonderful luxury to be able to start with a blank state, to hire people and determine what the network should do because it did not exist before. We had this wonderful Board [interviewee is referring to the Public Sector Board, not the Executive Directors] who was energetic and committed. It was a

---

[14] The other networks are the Human Development Network, Sustainable Development Network and the Financial and Private Sector Development Network.
[15] For example, I interviewed most current senior staff from the Public Sector "Anchor" and several PSM/PSG regional staff. Depending upon the region, one might have a law/justice subsector specialist and the next may not.

good time, huge support from the president, huge feeling that finally that were
getting at the things that mattered.

(WB31)

I am not sure why the interviewee falsely believed there had been just three people prior or why he/she felt that PSM/PSG was a "blank slate." *The interviewee's
perspective was telling in that, with just a few words, it dismissed the Bank's prior
fifteen+ years of PSM/PSG-related work.*

An important fact about the new matrix structure was that only the regions (and
their country directors) create and manage projects. The PREM (and the other
networks and anchors) do not lend. They "only" provide policy advice (WB29).
Therefore, the money that the Bank needs to push through its system incentivizes
and, consequently, provides more policy power to the country directors than the
sector board or its anchor (IEG 2013). Even with the matrix, dynamics among
the countries and regions and the technical units, networks, sector boards, and
anchors had remained unchanged since at least the 1970s. Moreover, as an IEG
evaluation of the matrix indicated, "attribution of impacts" due to the matrix are
"problematic because of changes in the external environment and overlapping
effects of other elements of the renewal strategy" (IEG 2013, xv). Or, as one interviewee who had worked inside and outside the Bank stated: "No one will say
they like the matrix. The countries [i.e., the regions] … that is where the money is,
that is where the rubber hits the road" (WB50).[16] Yet another acknowledgement
that the (dis)incentives noted by the Wapenhans Report (see Chapter 4) remained
unaddressed.

The Regions Speak: PSM and PSG

Despite increased Bank-wide prominence for this sector, each region viewed policy expansion. Even though the Bank may intellectually understand that Haiti
is not Chile, its regional reports preferred to "discuss issues and ideas that are
common to most countries" (WB34). One interviewee recalled democratic LAC
countries with leaders trying to be "imaginative and creative … cutting edge with
stakeholders [who had] a thirst for this [public sector management] stuff" (WB36).
Yet, public opinion surveys in the LAC region noted that while the citizenry wanted
more public expenditures, they did not trust the government's service delivery.

---

[16] This interviewee is blunt on PREM/Project Leader interaction: "The other issue with PREM, if
you really want to know about projects, you need to talk to [Task Team Leaders/Project Leaders] and
they are in the region. PREM, like OPCS [another part of the Bank], is a sideshow. All the operations
[project] folks hate them. They are a pain in the ass and whatever these guys come up with, the Ops
[project] people just laugh…. You will find more honesty with the [Task Team Leaders] than with
PREM. Especially with the higher levels of PREM." (WB50).

Thus, LAC-specific programs must work to reverse the LAC tendency for "taking resources form the poor and giving to the rich … [because in LAC] tax expenditures and social security are all skewed to the richer quintiles" (WB23). It was a situation made more difficult because several of the wealthier LAC countries simply rejected Bank loans (in favor of the private markets) when Bank conditionalities became unacceptable. That left the Bank with "no leverage, [and thus] we have zero conditionality on some countries of the region" (WB23). Even in countries that were poorer and/or smaller in size, the Bank was not always the biggest donor in town and thus, "the Bank has no traction" (WB23). Put another way, the Bank understood that if they were

> talking to Mexico, [and they] needed some help on social security reforms [and they'd ask] can you give us [Mexico] good practice on this and they will say, we don't want you to get into our health security and systems or broader public expenditure management, so they [Mexico] might target fairly explicit narrow area for your advice and support. Whereas in a country like say, Guinea-Bissau, everything is connected in some way—and we don't have the same degree of government counterparts who are able to tell you what they want and don't want and are not assertive in telling you to stay off from certain areas.
>
> (WB17)

In the MENA and South Asian regions, the Bank found client countries less interested in PSM reform. This was particularly true for MENA where certain countries were "prone to say 'political' when you [the Bank] uttered the word 'governance'" (WB36). Africa's PSM progress was "lagging," but for reasons different from everywhere else. Reasons included countries either entering or coming out of conflict or where priorities differed (WB36). In sub-Saharan Africa, the Bank felt "stretched" as there was "a much larger demand per country for good public sector advice" (WB17). Those regions were different from the so-called "vanguard" countries in Eastern Europe and Central Asia where the European Union and the Bank played "spearhead" roles in thinking "about assimilation ten years down the road" (WB36).

Another interviewee cautioned that just because the Bank thought PSM mattered, client country "interest" was a ruse. The interviewee described his experience at a Bank resident mission in Africa in the late 1990s. He observed that the African country (omitted to protect interviewee identity) suffered from general "economic mis-governance." To address it, the country convened a large forum attended by the country's president. At the forum, promises were made to tackle long-term problems. But in what the interviewee called a brilliant "countermove," the country appointed a so-called "Dream Team" that included former international civil servants but also in which the country's president shrewdly appointed as head of his public service someone well-known to Wolfensohn, a person the interviewee characterized as Wolfensohn's "close friend." The country's president thought "this would be a brilliant way to convince everyone that he was serious about reforming the public sector," (WB17) when in reality, the country planned to do very little.

Specific to sector topics, there were observable regional differences in civil service reform. Civil service reform was an important policy effort in sub-Saharan Africa but not in the LAC during the 1980s, 1990s, or 2000s (WB30). In addition, "traditionally, states in Latin America have at best been neutral and more traditional in taking resources from the poor and giving to the rich ... and if you look at the tax expenditures and social security, are all skewed to the richer quintiles" (WB23). I then asked the interviewee, "What does that lead you to do for projects?" The interviewee responded,

> Well, it leads us away from the premise that any simple cross-cutting civil service reform is likely to work and leads us toward more emphasis on case-by-case performance improvements ... It is a rather iconoclastic ring-fencing ... public administrator's think in terms of systematic and symmetrical at the same time, pay grading reforms happens across the entire sector, budget reforms across the sector. In LAC, it will be sector-by-sector, agency-by-agency and try to retrofit some logic around what's happened.
>
> (WB23)

The LAC and Eastern European countries were also moving "further ahead" in judicial reform than other regions. Several countries, such as Argentina and Guatemala, were just coming out of conflict, and as such, the judiciary played a larger role in state reclamations of itself (WB27). Among poorer states, most particularly Africa's IDA countries, reforming the rule of law or the judiciary seemed like a "luxury" when the post-conflict fragilities demanded that other needs be met first. For the Bank, that meant "a lot of stuff that took priority: roads, infrastructure, clean water, HIV/AIDS, the whole health issue, education, those are bigger amounts of money ... I think the jury is still out on whether or not there is a better way to approach it" (WB27).

Network and Anchor: Public Sector Management and Governance

To get off the ground, a project needs a focus. This is where the "knowledge networks" come into play. PREM staffers who report to their PREM boss (who then reports to his or her Managing Director and the Chief Economist) can provide advice on PSM/PSG work in all regions. Each knowledge network produces its own budget, analytical work, and publications (e.g., *PREM Notes* created in 1998). But just because a network exists or a country might appear to need PSM/PSG reform, there are no requirements that Country Director must involve a sector specialist (and thus, use part of the country director's project budget) from either the PREM network or the Public Sector Anchor. *This dominance of country directors over project priorities has been unchanged since at least the 1972 reforms.* Even though the PREM has its own budget, there is a dependency between the PREM and the regions as the latter do not have to internally "hire" or "borrow" PREM staffers knowledgeable in PSM/PSG for a project.

Although there was no hard-and-fast rule, the anchors tended to do less operational work (unless hired to do so by a region) and more of the "sit back and thinking about the sector" than the regions. The regions are closest to client-country needs while anchors were supposed to be closest to the latest sector ideas. Internal hiring (colloquially referred to as an "internal market"[17]) sits atop an unresolved cultural clash between regions and networks (see also Philipps 2009, 64–67). In a 2001 report, the internal hiring between the regions and the networks had led to "redundancies … [as] continuing concerns about the 'internal market' have increased fear and reduced trust … a deterioration from the 1999 Attitude Survey results (WorldBank 2000, 56).

While Wolfensohn tried to restructure the Bank into a "knowledge bank," some staff said the reforms created knowledge "silos" making it "impossible" for today's staff to have career movements across sectors and regions that was standard in the past (WB29) (IEG 2013). Just as generalization may have its costs, so does specialization. For one long-serving interviewee, the Bank's structure had become

almost a crisis for a number of years [as the Bank wanted] to try and balance the regional approach versus the global/network/anchor approach. In the end, it was resolved to give [project and program] budget to the regions [so there were] fiefdoms again … Obviously to drive a strong agenda from the center, you have to do that through sector boards and sector anchor, but overall, and over time, and today, the regions have the upper-hand and the center is left to do think-pieces and interface with global networks and economic reviews. The operational support is embedded within the regions … It was a tough issue. It was a good thing overall to move to the matrix—it allowed for knowledge management and sharing, but did not give [them], in my view, a powerful budget voice. This reflects the reality that the developing countries and regions themselves are more different [to each other] than two decades ago.

(WB6)

Applying the silo effect to project and task managers, another staffer observed that "private-sector people with MBAs tend to be the [project] task managers and [they do] not necessarily bring in their social development colleagues; it just may not occur to them to do so. It is probably not malicious; it just may not occur to them.

---

[17] The internal market presumes network (PREM) staff sell their knowledge product to the country directors who retain the lending purse strings and can chose whether to "hire" network staff for projects.

That is where the role of the manager comes in, is your team multidisciplinary, is it drawing in all the perspectives? [It is] more important … to have the bird's eye view" (WB27).

Conflict between Anchors and regional staff was common. When I asked if the Anchor is PSM/PSG's "intellectual leader" within the Bank, an Anchor interviewee explained the dynamic:

> People in [regional] division would contest [my question] with good reason. They will say, we [the anchor] are [removed] from the reality and they have a point there. We [the anchor] are not in the daily business, some of us cross-support" (WB10). The interviewee observed that the new GAC Strategy (approved in 2007) priorities put the anchor theoretically ahead of the regions but not "ahead in application … But in the regions, because so much driven by the countries that you are linked to, that is very different … So many of our [anchor] colleagues that used to be here [in the anchor], go onto the regions and subsequently tell us they do not have time anymore. They can question our knowledge because they say we [the anchor] are not aware enough of what is going on.
>
> (WB10)

However, not all Bank staff disagreed. One banker was positive: "From an operational perspective, from what the Bank does on the ground, I don't really have a problem with it [the matrix], I know some people feel quite strongly that [it] is very poor. For me, the matrix organization forces interaction among sector and country teams and it allows country teams who in theory have the best understanding of the country needs to kind of call a lot of the shots" (WB5).

Whatever infighting might have materialized over promotions or whether regions listened to the Anchor or vice versa, the fact was that prior to the matrix reforms, PSM's institutionalization was dependent upon a country director's decision to include a sector specialist. Although that logic remained partially true after the matrix, institutionalizing PSM/PSG led to more people, more money, and more ideas for doing sector work. With the 1996 speech, 1997 *WDR*, and the 1998 LAC Report along with a sector-helpful matrix reform, PSM/PSG had become the talk of the Bank.

The Asian Financial Crisis, the IMF, and the World Bank

Throughout the 1990s and early 2000s, the IMF continued to partner with the Bank on certain PSM/PSG subtopics. With corruption now on the agenda, the Fund created a Code of Fiscal Transparency for its client countries, and in 1995, Wolfensohn and the IMF's Managing Director (Michel Camdessus) signed a Joint

Guidance Note that required public expenditure management work to be annually and jointly reviewed (WorldBank 2000, 168).

Nonetheless, IMF and Bank conflicts, already noted in prior chapters, continued into the early 2000s. The biggest scandal between the two institutions occurred shortly after the 1997–1998 Asian Financial Crisis (Helleiner 2010). The IMF and the Bank's separate responses to the crisis provided a public platform for the Bank, Wolfensohn, the Bank's so-called *enfant terrible* (Mallaby 2004, 71) and future Nobel Prize-winning Chief Economist Joe Stiglitz to publicly separate the Bank from the Fund's poor handling of the crisis. Despite their public battles, the crisis ended up furthering the 1997 *WDR*'s and the 1998 Report's idea that the state, and as importantly, the state's relationship to the market, were important determinants of development success. Before discussing the Bank–Fund disagreement, the crisis is briefly reviewed.

In the summer of 1997, Asian financial markets collapsed. Causes included highly leveraged private actors, large current-account deficits, and insufficient regulatory oversight for its financial markets. Short-term capital and the desire for a quick profit had flooded these economies. The concurrent credit boom occurred within insufficiently regulated markets. Other crisis causes included new trade competition (e.g., from China) and the reversal of the yen's long-term appreciation in relation to the dollar. The specific trigger was a Thai devaluation brought on by overleveraging, a slowdown in exports, and overinvestment in property. In 1996, the Thai stock market dropped 30 percent and by early 1997, private capital investments had slowed and Thailand had to devalue the baht. The resulting contagion impacted others in East Asia due to their interlinked regional trade, financial markets, and exchange-rate movements. The impact was felt more severely in Indonesia, Malaysia, and South Korea, each of which experienced contractions, whereas Hong Kong, Singapore, and Taiwan weathered the storm. The social impacts included falling real wages compounded by drought and limited social safety nets. Job markets collapsed while prices rose and government revenues decreased, each negatively impacted social service provision (WorldBank 1998b, 1–17, 74; Radalet 1998; Sachs 2000). The need for more PSM/PSG projects was a natural post-crisis focus.

In response, the Bank pledged US$18 billion to affected countries and by September 1998, disbursed US$8 billion (Radalet 1998). The Fund extended even more money. The Fund committed US$35 billion to Indonesia, Korea, and Thailand and, by March 1998, had disbursed $19.4 billion. The IMF's packages were focused on stabilizing the exchange rate. The IMF viewed itself as a "quasi-lender of last resort" and hoped its packages would quickly restore financial market confidence, but by December 1997, this had still not happened (Radalet 1998, 29). Instead, "the IMF's own responses added to the risks of a sharply contractionary outcome encouraged greater economic contraction" (Radalet 1998, 30).

That increased risk led the US Treasury in January 1998 to force Korea into a nonmarket-based solution whereby debt servicing temporarily stopped.

For the G7, the Asian financial crisis was linked to "the importance of sound economic policy" and "transparency and good governance" (G7 1998). Increased transparency would provide "non-discriminatory national legislative and regulatory frameworks with a view to establishing equitable treatment for both government and private sectors as well as domestic and foreign entities" (G8 1999), a sentiment echoed a year later in Köln, Germany. Post-crisis, Deputy Treasury Secretary, Larry Summers, reflected on lessons learned, one of which was that "the emphasis of these programs [post crisis in Asia] has been at least as much on improving the quality of government intervention—to make it more transparent, less open to corruption, and more focused on the things that sustainable market-led growth depends on, but markets along cannot provide" (Summers 1998).

In the midst of this public disagreement between the Bank and the Fund, neither the G7 (G8) nor the US Treasury appeared to take a firm public stance on which IO should lead. This contrasted with statements in the 1980s in which the G7 delegated to the Fund. This difference may reflect new learning that macroeconomic adjustment alone (a Fund task) is not sufficient without sector-specific work (Bank task). As such, and in a 1998 statement, Summers stated that the IMF and Bank leadership understood the crisis and then discussed what should be done to prevent further crises without preferring one institution over the other. This statement is also notable its incorporation of "state matters" and "corruption matters:"

> The crisis brought out even more clearly what Jim Wolfensohn and Michel Camdessus [IMF Managing Director] had already recognized: that good governance is a core institutional underpinning for growth. With strong United States urging and support, both institutions have rightly been moving toward making reduced corruption as central to their assessment of countries as more traditional, narrowly economic concerns such as tariff reform and tax administration. Putting the fight against corruption at the heart of development programs is an economic as well as an ethical imperative. Corruption results in distorted allocation of resources. Adding new laws and supervisory systems will do little to safeguard stability if there is no credible—and honest—authority to enforce them. As we are learning, any country's capacity to take on major reform challenges such as those faced in Asia will depend critically on the credibility of its policy makers and public institutions—credibility that corruption fatally undermines.
>
> (Summers 1998)

Although this was not the first debate between the IMF and the World Bank on how to handle an unfolding crisis (Kranke 2020), this particular situation became undeniably public in 1998 (Komisar 2011; Wade 2001b; Stiglitz 2000). The IMF's stringent fiscal targets (i.e., requiring a surplus by 1998) along with its rapid reform push showed that the IMF was out of touch (Barro 2001). These policy errors gave more fuel to the growing anti-Bank and anti-Fund protests (Lemisch 2000) covered in Chapter 9. The suggestion was put forward that the IMF failed to correctly implement what the crisis-affected countries needed. The IMF's lead economist, Stanley Fischer, who served as First Deputy Managing Director during the Crisis, disagreed. He believed the Fund's response to be appropriate (Fischer 2005, 2003).

While another Bank President might have quietly offered behind-the-scenes cooperation or even a critique for the IMF, Wolfensohn was not that type of President. Instead, Wolfensohn and his Chief Economist Joe Stiglitz pursued a public warfare strategy against the Fund and Fischer. Since becoming the Bank's Chief Economist, Stiglitz had argued for a reversal of Washington Consensus type ideas.[18] For Stiglitz, the financial crisis proved that he had been right all along, according to Mallaby (2004),

> Stiglitz had helped to create a branch of economics that explained the failure of standard market assumptions; he was like a boy who discovers a hole in the floor of an exquisite house and keeps shouting and pointing at it. Never mind that the rest of the house is beautiful, that in nine of ten cases, the usual laws of supply and demand *do* work; Stiglitz had found a hole, a real hole, and he had built his career on it ... When the Asian crisis got under way, there was a lot of tumbling. The IMF, which had always annoyed Stiglitz by failing to incorporate his economic theory into its models, made a series of errors in the design of its bailouts.
>
> (Mallaby 2004, 193)

The crisis gave Stiglitz his opportunity to blast the IMF. Mallaby wrote,

> Stiglitz could not contain his glee. He lambasted the IMF, focusing particularly on two errors that resonated with the veterans of the Fifty Years is Enough campaign ... [H]e made much of the fact that the IMF-prescribed austerity in Thailand had bankrupted local companies, throwing people out of work, and he frequently implied that the IMF economists were too blinkered to realize that this might happen ... Stiglitz's second target was the removal of capital controls, which he presented as an IMF-prescribed free-market doctrine that laid countries open to speculative attack and made financial crisis possible.
>
> (Mallaby 2004, 194)

A Bank interviewee suggested that although Stiglitz was "80 percent right conceptually ... the way he went about it publicly was wrong" (WB34) as publicly abusing the Fund went against long-held traditions of decorum between the Fund and the

---

[18] Hence Stiglitz's backing of the 1997 *WDR* and the 1998 Report.

Bank. Even though Bank–Fund relations had "always been treated very delicately [because] a lot of what the Bank says is confidential, it is not. But that stuff [the fight between the Bank and Fund on East Asia] is confidential. You don't want the dirty linen washed in public. That only came when Stiglitz came in. Before that, [discussions were] fairly confidential and at a very high-level so as not to reveal that these two were actually at odds with each other, which they frequently were" (WB12). That Wolfensohn chose not to contain Stiglitz was telling. According to Mallaby, "Stiglitz talked as though the IMF were run by idiots. Wolfensohn allowed him to sound off to the press, blackening the IMF's name just when its crisis-fighting reputation was most precious. From time to time Wolfensohn would rein him in, but then Stiglitz would charge off again, and it was hard to avoid the conclusion that Wolfensohn was quite pleased about his pugilistic rudeness" (Mallaby 2004, 195).

So why else might have Wolfensohn and Stiglitz violated decorum? According to staff, in the crisis' aftermath, "the IMF took a hard line and Wolfensohn wanted to justify a meaningful role for the Bank. Originally, Wolfensohn had wanted the crisis countries to focus on poverty reduction, sustainable development. [But] due to changes in the development and intellectual climate, [Wolfensohn] took the high ground that the Bank is more about institutional development and [that] longer-term and multisector issues matter more" (WB6). The crisis gave an opportunity for Wolfensohn and Stiglitz to assert what the Bank had learned: institutional factors matter and the old, short-term, conditionality-filled, structural adjustment loans were passé. Moreover, Wolfensohn was upset about being "strong-armed" by the US Treasury in early 1998. That is, Wolfensohn felt frustrated that he "had been in no position to prevent the World Bank from being treated like a piggy bank" during the Crisis (Mallaby 2004, 195).

Wolfensohn insisted that the Bank, unlike the Fund, was concerned about poverty reduction and that "Wolfensohn would go to Indonesia and show how much he cared about the poor. He would not stand over Suharto [Indonesia's autocratic leader], his arms folded and his look frosty [i.e., like the IMF's Managing Director had done]" (Mallaby 2004, 195). Wolfensohn painted the Bank as a caring savior and as the only one truly interested in alleviating poverty.

By November 1999, the times had changed. Wolfensohn was pressured by the US to fire Stiglitz and ultimately, Wolfensohn let him go. According to Stiglitz, "there had been enormous pressure from the U.S. Treasury particularly from Larry Summers. Typically, it was a hierarchical thing. Summers would lean on Jim Wolfensohn and make his life unpleasant" but "No, I was never fired. Basically, I was told I could stay in the Bank, but if I did, I would have to circumscribe my thoughts. So I chose to resign" (Smith 2002). The Wall Street Journal reported the news differently: a new Chief Economist was arriving and thus, Stiglitz's "advisory post was eliminated" (Anonymous 2000).

Conclusion: Anti-Corruption, the State, and Internal Actors Matter

The three years and two months between October 1996 and December 1999 were jam-packed. The Bank had a new President, the 'C'-word was unmasked, there was a declaration that the "state matters," a publication of the Bank's first-ever corporate strategy, an organizational reform, and a public battle with the IMF over the Asian Financial Crisis.

The Bank's 1997 WDR declared that unlike the Bank's prior fifteen years, the state now mattered for development. It was an about-face whose time had come. The addition of PSG in 1991 to the PSM agenda was a huge step forward. This change was assisted with new economic models (in particular, NIE) and a trend toward internal stakeholders leading and then by the early 1990s, fully institution-alizing this sector's agenda within the Bank. The 1987 reforms (see Chapter 4) and post-Cold War demands further fueled policy agenda expansions. That the state mattered for development was not new to the institutional development staff of the Bank's 1980s but what was new was how, in the space of just three years, the state began to matter in ways previously unconceivable for many Bank staff until after the Cold War's end.

Compared to Bank Presidents of the 1980s and early 1990s, Wolfensohn was highly involved in this sector's changing policies (see Appendix, Table 11). It helped that the expanded agenda meshed with the Bank's key external actor de-sires along with broader international development paradigms espoused by the Bank and its nation-state allies. Although Wolfensohn fought the Board over his anticorruption ideas, he strengthened the PSM/PSG agenda. In addition, and al-though the Bank's Articles of Agreement were apparent legal barriers to the Bank's discussion of corruption, just as they were barriers with structural adjustment in 1979–80, privatization debates of the mid-1990s, and governance's addition in 1991, in the end, the Bank reframed the Articles' meaning. It is likely that part of the contentiousness of the subsequent Board discussions about corruption in 1996 and 1997 was not simply about the Articles of Agreement but a reality that it was corruption which greased client country wheels and if anticorruption be-came an emphasis, it was unclear what might happen to local power bases or even developing country stability.

Bank economists have long-preferred economic models that draw clear paths from the Bank's suggested policy intervention to economic growth. The policy-based lending exemplified by structural adjustment is one example. But to incor-porate the state into economic models, the Bank's economists sought models of institutional behavior. For an economist, NIE provided a sellable answer to client countries. The new answer was that institutional incentives, if properly aligned and understood, could improve economic development. Because the Bank "is driven by very, very short policy time scales" and a "need to show that we have done some-thing" (WB23, see also Chapter 4), a seemingly narrower focus on institutional incentives would provide the quick outcomes required by the Bank. This policy response contrasted with the old-style institutional development specialists of the 1980s for whom institutional development was a pseudonym for long-term projects with uncertain outcomes.

As a Bank beholden to its lending incentives and new realities that middle-income countries might not need as much assistance as in the past, the late 1990s was also a period where the Bank transformed itself into a "knowledge bank." This allowed its growing research activities to become another source of Bank survival. The Strategic Compact and the matrix reforms helped further this objective even if latter had less impact on PSM/PSG sector policy change than the 1987 reforms. Despite external actors having limited impact on this sector during these three years, the IMF and Bank interactions on the Asian Financial Crisis were notable. While these interactions had less to do with the PSM/PSG sector than either the 1980–1982 world recession (Chapter 3) or the Cold War's end (Chapter 5), the episode highlights how occasionally fractious the IMF/Bank relationship can become.

7

Two Decades Late

A Public Sector Strategy
(January 2000 to December 2003)

In 2000, nearly two decades after the Bank published its 1983 WDR, the Bank wrote its first PSM (and PSG) sector strategy. This is despite millions of dollars spent and hundreds of projects approved in which this sector played a major role. With 941 PSM projects approved between 2000 and 2003, the speed of PSM project dispersals was not slowing down (see Appendix, Table 1). With this increased PSM/PSG visibility, new within-sector divisions began to appear. The division occurred between the Bank's PSM technocrats focused on civil service reform, public expenditure management, and financial reform (renamed *supply-side governance*) and the newer *demand-side* priorities of service delivery, decentralization, anticorruption, accountability, rule of law, and judicial reform.[1] The divisions are highlighted here in concert with the 2000 Public Sector Strategy. These divisions, the 2000 Public Sector Strategy, and the 2003 Update to the Strategy are largely overshadowed by a scholarly focus on the next big crisis to hit the Bank: creation of the 2007 GAC Strategy and its link to President Paul Wolfowitz and his scandals. But such a jump is a mistake. The first Strategy and its update are telling reminders about how bureaucratic politics continued to shape the PSM/PSG sector. The GAC Strategy will be discussed in Chapter 8.

This chapter furthers the observation from the late 1990s period that external actors were largely absent and internal PSM actors mattered most. However, and unlike the late 1990s, the rush of activity involving President Wolfensohn and the PSM/PSG sector, which started in October 1996, had largely dissipated by late 1999. This left the Bank's civil servants to be the *de facto* sole owners of this sector policy agenda for the first time in this sector's history.

---

[1] That governance, an oft-political topic, took on economic terms such as *supply* and *demand* is telling. The Bank's technocrat staff members focused on the "supply side" while "demand-side" advocates viewed the state from the outside, e.g. the citizens. Although not stated by demand-side proponents, their view also appears to distrust the state and its bureaucratic apparatus. Instead, its focus encourages citizens to demand a responsive state and with improved service delivery. Political economy theories drove the demand-side approach. The disciplines of public administration and public policy continue to be overlooked.

Who Matters at the World Bank?. Kim Moloney, Oxford University Press.
© Kim Moloney (2022). DOI: 10.1093/oso/9780192857729.003.0007

The Bank's First Public Sector Strategy (2000)

As a symbol of PSM/PSG's internal institutional power, the Bank published "Reforming Public Institutions and Strengthening Governance: A World Bank Strategy" in 2000. This was the first Strategy for this sector—despite nearly two decades of advice and projects to developing countries. Written by a newly created Public Sector Board, the Strategy reflected on lessons learned and tried to provide future direction for the Bank. One Bank interviewee (who worked in a regional office and reflected the divide between the Anchor, the Sector Board, and the region) cautioned that because the sector strategy originated with the Public Sector Board rather than the regions, that I should be careful not "over interpret" the conclusions (WB40). Give region and country power: this may be true. Nonetheless, the 2000 Strategy was the Bank's first public sector management strategy. Given such a role, the Strategy does require some interpretation.

The Strategy was not a self-congratulatory fluff piece. At points, its authors were brutally honest with the Bank's PSM failures even if its evaluative components lacked the independence of the Bank's Internal Evaluation Group (see Chapter 9). The 2000 Strategy, more than any other widely distributed public sector focused document before or after its time, is arguably the Bank's most technically oriented examination of PSM.

If the early PSM years were about "core public sector" (supply side) tasks such as civil service reform, tax reform, public expenditure management and financial management, then the 2000 Strategy and its 2002 update reflected supply-*and* demand-side concerns. In the Bank's reconsideration of the state, there was reform within the state and its institutions (supply side) and then there was reform that responded or demanded something from the state (demand side). Supply-side PSM was considered the domain of the Bank's public sector technocrats whereas demand-side work focused on decentralization, service delivery, accountability, and similar areas. The terms *demand side* and *supply side* were borrowed from economics and became engrained in PSM/PSG *Bankease*.

No interviewed PSM staff who was knowledgeable about post-1997 sector change denied that there were internal differences among sector staff. Although staff members may not formally state their preference between supply- or demand-side, certain staff names were repeatedly mentioned as proponents of one side or the other. One Bank interviewee observed, "There is disagreement between the demand- and supply side of [public sector management]. Some people say, 'This is an extreme view. Do the treasury. [Do] public-expenditure management. Don't do the demand side.' The demand side, without doing that, you will not get anywhere. [In other words] tax reform is just technocratic crap. There is a tension that is still there, today" (WB40).

The main argument of the 2000 Strategy was that institutions, as identified in the 1997 *WDR*, must be brought to the forefront of development. The Strategy defined institutions in a broadly similar way to NIE in which institutions are the "rules of the game that emerge from formal laws, informal norms and practices, and organizational structures in a given setting. The incentives they create shape the actions of public officials. Institutions overlap with but are not synonymous with organizations; they are affected by policy design but are broader in scope and less subject to frequent change than most policy frameworks" (WorldBank 2000, xii–xiii). The Strategy referenced the importance of long-term institutional efforts, the need for better staff at the Bank who were working within this sector, and increased understanding of the political and institutional environments of client countries. Importantly, the Bank must "move beyond a *narrow, technocratic, supply-side approach* and work with clients and other partners to explore a broad range of mechanisms that promote *demand* for accountable, responsive, and effective public sectors" (WorldBank 2000, 22–25, my emphasis). In short, demand and supply sides of PSM/PSG should matter.

The demand-side was centered on improving voice and accountability. A second component focused on understanding the "rules and restraints" of the PSM game, including an emphasis on independent judicial, watchdog, and audit institutions and improved public budgeting. The third demand-side component introduced competition into service delivery, including competition from local governments, NGOs, and the private sector. All three components were to be assisted by decentralizing service delivery from the center to sub-national levels of government (WorldBank 2000, 37; original emphasis). To routinize its work, the 2000 Strategy asked the Bank to incorporate institutional assessments into its operational policies. The Bank hoped that by FY2001, such a policy would be finalized and incorporated into the Operations Manual. Today, there is still no such policy within the Bank's Operational Manual.

The 2000 Strategy asserted that previous Bank PSM projects had found limited success because of the project's technocratic preferences; short-term goals via structural adjustment, technical assistance or investment loans, and limited Bank staff capacity to understand, create, and implement PSM reforms. Echoing an early 1990s call for more PSM staff, the Strategy recommended hiring staff with expertise in "task management skills, broad skills in institutional analysis and assessment, and substantive expertise in specific areas such as budgeting, civil service reform, decentralization, tax administration, service delivery, judicial systems" (WorldBank 2000, 50–51).

But internal politics and the Bank's matrix made it difficult to hire staff: "The Bank's matrix structure implies that we may need special arrangements to recruit new staff. Regional budgets rest with the country directors, and there is inevitably a lag between their expression of 'demand' for work from the sector units and the ability of those sector units to expand their staff if demand exceeds current supply. Country directors are sometimes understandably hesitant to commit funding to tasks without commitment from pre-identified, well-proven staff. This situation can create impediments to expanding our staff skills in new and somewhat untested areas of high priority" (WorldBank 2000, 52). One potential response was for the Public Sector Anchor to "bring new staff into the Bank for an early 'tryout phase' and if the staff prove to fit well in operations, they can move to a Region after a period of time. To date, the anchor has had the funding to bring in two or three new staff per year, and the regional units have also been able to augment their staff, albeit incrementally and with some lag" (WorldBank 2000, 52–3).

The Strategy cautioned that "more [Bank] emphasis on evaluation and development impact is needed if the Bank is to have a deep and serious commitment to public sector reform in its client countries" (WorldBank 2000, 16). At no point between 1990 and 1997 did more than 40 percent of public sector management projects have a "substantial impact" on Institutional Development (WorldBank 2000, 17). Yet, after not quite reaching the 20 percent mark for "substantial impact" in 1997, by 1999 success had suddenly risen to nearly 60 percent, and in 1998 to 2000, nearly 70 percent of Bank public sector management projects were having a "substantial impact." Unfortunately, the 2000 Strategy did not explain why performance had dramatically improved. Instead, the Strategy discussed problems particular to PSM/PSG projects:

> projects are not likely to be successful when they fail to take fully into account the complex political and institutional realities on the ground—and thus the real incentives for implementation; the Bank has sometimes relied on models of "best practice" that may not be feasible in the particular country setting. Unrealistic optimism is a persistent strand of weakness running through Bank work, as reported regularly by OED and QAG; public sector management interventions have been hampered in the past by shortcomings in traditional lending instruments, which have made it difficult to address systemic problems in the public sector over the medium-term horizon needed for institutional change; problems within the Bank, including deficient staffing and weak incentives for timely and cost-efficient delivery of Bank products.
>
> (WorldBank 2000, 17)

By the 2003 Public Sector Strategy Update, PSM/PSG lending had risen even if more work was needed to link the sector to other Bank sectors (WorldBank 2003a, xi). Although more of the Bank's Country Assistance Strategies[2] considered PSM/PSG issues, not all of the country managers had chosen to include the sector's work within their agenda due to "country sensitivity" or because of "a lack of in-depth analytic work" by Bank staff (WorldBank 2003a, 5). OED's evaluation

---

[2] Country Assistance Strategies are the Bank's Strategy for each client nation. It is reviewed every couple of years and serves as a guide for where the Bank should lend within a country.

of sector projects found that projects with a "substantial impact on institutional development rose over time from a low of about 25 percent for projects completed in FY1995 to about 50 percent for those concluded in FY2000," which was not high enough if "institutional building was to be a central objective of Bank assistance" (WorldBank 2003a, 27). Between 1998 and 2000, over 80 percent of PSM projects were rated satisfactory by OED, in comparison to between 50 percent and 75 percent in 1995 to 1997 (WorldBank 2002a, 55). Among the fourteen Bank Sector Boards, the Public Sector Board had the highest percentage of projects "at risk" (at 23 percent) (WorldBank 2003a, xii–xiii).

By 2002, staffing shortages were being overcome. The Bank reported that it had "220 Bank staff formally mapped to the Public Sector Group" (WorldBank 2003a, 32). Unfortunately, the Strategy did not explain what "mapped" meant or whether a Bank staff member could also be mapped to other areas. Thus, "220" may not be 220 full-time PSM/PSG staff but instead portions of their time. Nor did the Strategy Update specify whether mapping had been conducted previously, and, if so, how the new "mapped" numbers compared to earlier years or if the 220 people had PSM/PSG backgrounds or experience. Even so, there remained skill shortages in "public expenditure management, for example, as well as revenue (that is, tax and customs) policy and administration, and e-government" along with "institutional and political analysis" (WorldBank 2003a, 38).

With a Strategy in Place, Sector Research Expands

The increased institutional and policy importance given to public sector management and governance was also reflected in Bank research. Public sector management's new importance led many of the Bank's older PSM emphases such as civil service reform, financial management, public expenditure management (from the 1980s), along with the rule of law and judicial reform (from early 1990s), to enter their own second generation of development research.

Of the Bank's long-established PSM topics, civil service reform struggled to adapt to a Bank view that successful work was measurable work and that Bank policy recommendations should reflect analytical rigor (WB11). This difference was due to the Bank's failure (or inability to fully embrace) the inherently long-term nature of civil service reform. Reflecting concerns since the 1980s, long-term projects led to larger uncertainties for the Bank, for the country director, and for the client nation about whether projects would be successful. The difficulty of selling the idea of long-term civil service reform has continually hampered its success.[3] Even today, "Reid [Gary] and Nunberg [Barbara] are struggling to keep

---

[3] In 2009, measuring civil service reform success was still difficult. The Bank acknowledged that "it is hard to say, empirically, whether the Bank's civil-service reform efforts have been successful" and that

the flame alive" even though it was "not always clear if civil service reform was working" (WB11). Country directors also worried that civil service reform projects "meddled in politics" (referring to Articles of Agreement concerns) and disliked that civil service reform projects often took "longer than people understand" (WB40).

If the 1980s civil service reform projects were a "first generation" given their focus on "how to downsize the government and attach conditions to adjustment lending," then such reforms were "a blunt and short-term tool. A quick fix type of approach—driven more by this ideology that developing countries were bloated—... It was crude—not trying to make sure that the best talent stays but instead, the best talent incentives were to leave the civil service" (WB6). The Bank "did not appreciate that there was a rationality/patronage to do this, people were willing to work for little money if it meant they could also obtain 'rents' [and the Bank] realized that they cannot address pay issues with too many people on the wage book" (WB20). The early Bank civil service reforms "didn't work. Africans found another hundred ways to get people on and off the rolls" (WB20). And when the number of civil servant staff were reduced, the savings were not sufficient to pay higher salaries to those who remained (WorldBank/IMF 2002, 14). In particular, African civil servants' real wages decreased over time, and most wage bill decreases were "unsustainable" (OED 1999, i). Even though the Bank's 1980s approach to civil service reform did change, "questions about how one chooses to retrench and retrain, many of those approaches are still used today" (WB20). The first generation's tools also included training and capacity building along with extensive downsizing (Nunberg 1995b, 30–9).

The Bank's second generation of civil service reform acknowledged that reform was not just a "technical" issue (WB20). In 1999, OED noted that "credibility and accountability of state institutions strained under the weight of cumbersome civil service rules, political interference, and cultures of nonperformance" (OED 1999, i). Governance environments mattered. That gave space for new civil service reform tools that encouraged governments to be "more transparent and accountable, in addition to being more efficient" (WorldBank/IMF 2002). There was a focus on data development and linking civil service reform to medium-term fiscal planning (WorldBank 1997a, vii). From the staff perspective, second generation civil-service reform

> help[ed] governments do a functional review of the government and see what are the parts of government where you could rationalize and which parts can be consolidated into core functions and from this, will emerge an understanding which parts of government are useful and are unnecessary and then you can

in comparison to other project sectors where OED found a 30 percent unsatisfactory rating between 1988 and 1997, civil-service reform's rating was 38 percent (PEFA 2009; IMF 2009; WorldBank 2009c).

be more tactful in how you cut because otherwise you start purely with sense of overall numbers and based on those numbers … [it was] meant to be more nuanced and give basis for more sophisticated approach to downsizing government. But problem is can do functional review but the political will to do this is often very difficult to master and governments have, you know, got into this and look around and see unionized civil servants and it becomes a difficult sell. And it takes an unusually bold government to proceed on this track. So [civil-service reform] … became a little more nuanced but had no further success in terms of actually getting government to think about [it].

(WB17)

Another involved PSM staff noted that there was "no point paying people with just a handshake if, in the end, the government still recruits more. This led to the conclusion that there were underlying management systems of public service to make it work properly—this included minimum structures, job descriptions, pay policies, how to deal with collapsed pay structures, how to deal with allowances, etc. Also, in the early to mid-1990s some were trying to put 'new public management' into it—but [the] Bank was never sure it was a good idea" (WB20).

Civil service reform research published between 1996 and 2003 reflected second-generation trends. A 1996 workshop on civil service reform in Francophone West Africa noted that civil services should be "competent, lean and efficient, while reflecting the concept of a State dedicated to public service and the values of loyalty, patriotism and equity" (WorldBank 1997a, 57–58). The Bank's civil service reform must be longer-term, cognizant of political and institutional factors, and move from a project to program approach in which non-lending services are included. OED found that, of the lending projects between FY1999 and FY2001, just four of sixty-two civil service reform projects were stand-alone civil service reforms because the Bank had come to prefer incorporating civil service reform into broader PSM projects or into other sectors, such as health (PREM 1999). Even so, state capacity improvements struggled to find a consensus within the Bank (de Janvry 2012).

In contrast, financial management was viewed as a technical exercise and thus, had greater popularity within an economist-dominated Bank (WB1). Projects focused on financial management were, in the words of one interviewee, "doing well" within the Bank (WB11). Financial management's popularity also "flows from the fiduciary responsibility of the Bank to protect its funds, and that connects to [the Bank's] imperative to keep lending levels up. If you [your client has] fiduciary problems, then it is difficult to keep lending levels up. This is close to the Bank's bread and butter" (WB1). Although "everyone loves" financial management, my interviewee cautioned that "everyone" also includes the client countries because they can "still be corrupt if [they] do it" (WB11). In its earliest years, the Bank's financial management efforts were focused on integrity of loan products and Bank projects [and that] governments commit to procedures for procurement, etc ... [The Bank then] dove into [structural-adjustment loans] in the 1980s—and budget support in the 1990s—not money to projects, but budget support for policy actions; therefore, How good are government financial controls, and is money in the budget used well? Therefore ... the Bank learned about government financial management systems as different from private accounts. They are driven by different considerations, like equality ... Then [the Bank] began to do financial management projects and modernization around financial computerization, modernization of the budget, and audit strengthening. [The] first [projects] were in South America—around the early 1990s in Colombia, Peru, and Ecuador. Then later, in LAC more generally.

(WB20)

That work has been supplemented by the Bank's belief that how governments prepare a budget within their specific institutional environment also mattered (WB17).

Bank staffing followed these generational trends. Between 1991 and 1997 the Bank had just a few staff with financial-management skills, and by 1998, there were many more staff members, even though the new staff members had "limited experience working in government" (WB17). After first commenting about financial management's staffing trends, an interviewee expanded into broader trends:

Some of the subareas, like financial management, economics, are more relevant than other public administration or anticorruption work but still, it is very suboptimal in terms of academic disciplines. The way the Bank corrects for this is to bring in lots of consultants. There are various groups, one large group is World Bank retired staff, and those are mostly economists and are not hired for their expertise but for their networks and their understanding of Bank operations and their institutional memory. Then there is another large group of people, junior people, who have just received their Master's or Ph.D.'s, mainly Master's, who get the degree in the area ... mostly U.S. degrees, but not all, some from Europe. They are also mostly economists. There is quite a large group of those people.

(WB1)

I then asked the interviewee if many political scientists or public administration scholars are found within these ranks. The interviewee responded,

Not many. You occasionally see a political scientist, increasingly the Bank is doing political economy studies, there was a time they [did] Institutional Governance Reviews, these are sometimes done, or at least have on the team, a political scientist, but the Bank calls them political economists. And sometimes they are economists.

(WB1)

In addition, the Bank created several instruments (some in cooperation with the IMF) to evaluate client countries' financial management situations. By the 1990s, Public Expenditure and Financial Accountability (PEFA) efforts were begun, which "assess[ed] the public financial-management landscape with twenty-eight indicators—[indicators] now adopted by others" (WB20).[4] This was followed by the creation of a PEFA Secretariat that "is a small shop, like one man and a dog" (WB20). The Secretariat sat within the Bank, had its own website, and was funded by the Bank, IMF, European Commission, Switzerland, UK, Norway, and France.

Public expenditure management research was limited during the late 1990s and early 2000s not because of topic unimportance but because effort was directed into completing client-focused Public Expenditure Reviews (Girishankar 1999). If the first-generation public expenditure management efforts of the late 1980s and early 1990s focused on budget allocation (and their sustainability), the second generation incorporated NIE and improved Bank-client collaboration (Pradhan 1996b; PREM 2001b). Although the Bank employed several public expenditure management staff before 1997, many left when the Bank was more focused on privatization rather than managing public sector expenditures (WB17). As the 2000s progressed, public expenditure management projects became a vehicle for discussing corruption with clients without having to actually say the word *corruption* (WB36).

On the supply side, social security and pension reform remained focused on the LAC region (Barbone 1999a) although sub-Saharan Africa was considered at least once (Packard 2001). Reform methods included privatization, pay-as-you-go, full capitalization, knowing how voluntary contributions plus mandatory-minimum disbursals and private management interact (James 1999) and how to transition from pay-as-you-go to fully funded systems (Edwards 2001).

In a 1999 report, the Bank sought to expand its tax research into revenue administration strategies and the integration of institutional factors in tax reform (Barbone 1999b; PREM 2000). Of the Bank's 120 tax projects, just forty-three had administrative features such as "revenue enhancement (40 percent), strengthening administrative institutions (37 percent) and promoting macroeconomic stability and growth (28 percent). Improving accountability taxpayer education and services was a major objective in very few operations (7 percent and 5 percent respectively), while no project had a major focus on strengthening voice and participation" (Mitra 2002).

On the demand side, decentralization research continued. Sector-specific discussions on decentralization's impact on the education sector were particularly popular along with legal issues (Patrinos 1997) and demand-side financing

---

[4] The twenty-eight indicators are split into three categories: budget credibility (four indicators); budget comprehensiveness and transparency (six indicators); and the budget cycle (eighteen indicators). The budget cycle is split into a further three sections including policy-based budgeting (two indicators); budget-execution predictability and control (nine indicators); accounting, recording, and reporting (four indicators); and external scrutiny and auditing (three indicators; (PREM 2001a, 1).

(Winkler 2000). Decentralization was thought to improve service delivery through allocative and productive efficiency, but it was decentralization's structural and institutional environment that seemed to determine whether service delivery improved. Fiscal decentralization (Fisman 2000) was negatively linked to corruption and positively linked to fiscal efficiency and stability (Spahn 1999). Decentralization's purpose varied regionally. In Eastern and Central Europe, decentralization was "the direct result of the transition from a socialist system to a market economy and democracy," whereas in the LAC decentralization came from "political pressure from the people for democratization" and in sub-Saharan Africa it was considered a "path to national unity" (Packard 2001; Edwards 2001; Gill 1997).

Conclusion: Internal Actors Matter Most

In the first years of the 2000s, the Bank further institutionalized its PSM/PSG agenda. Although external actors controlled the PSM/PSG during the 1980s and early 1990s, by the mid-1990s the Bank's internal stakeholder (staff) and boundary actor (President) had taken a sector policy lead. By 2000, the sector lead was firmly in the hands of Bank PSM/PSG staff (see Appendix, Tables 11 and 12). As PSM/PSG acceptability increased, sector-specific project lending increased. Internally, staff saw a President supportive of the sector, another reimagining of the purpose and meaning of the Articles of Agreement to accommodate the sector, new internal organizational structures and budgets favorable to the sector as well as expanded research.

The Bank's new matrix gave the PSM/PSG its own Board and an Anchor from which to interact with Bank regions. With a budget and staff of its own, the Public Sector Board drafted the Bank's first Public Sector Strategy in 2000. Even though the Board and the Anchor had internal policy importance, the real money and lending power still resided with the Bank's regions. It was not up to the Board or the Anchor (of any sector) to decide whether a developing country would or would not pursue PSM/PSG policies. Instead, the regions, their country managers, and the recipient client nations decided which sector policies were discussed. Moreover, if a middle-income country with other borrowing options or a politically powerful country such as China or Saudi Arabia did not want a PSM/PSG project, then the Bank did not do it. Therefore, although the Bank's new Board and Anchor were important new actors, the differences among regions and countries meant that, ultimately, lending power remained within the regions (WB6)—a sentiment unchanged since the 1980s and a sentiment relayed in the Wapenhans Report (see Chapter 4).

Personnel incentives only further strengthened such Bank preferences. Bank staff members only stay in a position for three to four years. Add-on that personnel incentives favored economics-based modeling along with how many projects a

Bank staff member ushered through to approval. Less important for promotion was a project's successful implementation because Bank staff members are often not held responsible for project failures (see Chapter 9). Yet despite such agreements about the public sector's importance, staff were divided over approach (supply side versus demand side) and whether regions or anchors were the more legitimate PSM/PSG actors within the Bank. That bureaucratic battles continued when budgets were flush and the internal political will was oriented toward approving more PSM/PSG remained important. Just as infighting occurs when resources are restricted, it also occurs when the conditions improved. Internal actors fought over sector agenda control and as such, the subsequent prestige and promotions that follow when one's ideas shape Bank agendas.[5]

---

[5] Interviewees noted that a well-received analytical policy paper may matter more for promotion than staff involvement in a successful project. Even project failures can be overlooked when staff are viewed as influential thinkers.

8

Becoming The Bank's DNA

Governance and Anti-Corruption
(January 2004 to June 2012)

By 2004, this sector had become *the* priority for shaping Bank projects. By 2012, the sector was not only the "DNA" of the Bank but also the first sector in Bank history to be elevated to a Bank-wide Council. With 2119 PSM projects approved between 2007 and 2012, this period had the highest average of PSM projects approved per year (353). This average is higher than the number of PSM projects approved in any prior single year (see Table 1[1]).

This chapter goes beyond the mid-2000s era overviews written by scholars of international relations or international political economy (e.g., Park and Weaver 2012; Weaver 2008; Balkvis 2005; Bazbauers 2014; Goldman 2007) by focusing specifically on debate nuances, which international civil servants held which side in the debate, and how intra-organizational actors influenced debates. Like prior chapters in this book, this chapter showcases the value of actor-specific analyses for understanding sector policy change and influence within the Bank.

Under Wolfensohn, PSM/PSG had risen in importance and was institutionalized within the Bank. With the arrival of Paul Wolfowitz as President in 2005, PSG (in particular) exploded in importance. Not just because Bank staff members had decided that governance mattered, but also because Wolfowitz explicitly desired expanded good governance work. Unfortunately for the Bank, Wolfowitz soon became embroiled within his own governance scandal and in June 2007, resigned as Bank President. This chapter details both the rise and fall of Wolfowitz as well as the debates which embroiled the Bank as it sought to redefine what it meant by PSG and anti-corruption. If the related scandals had affected another sector of Bank work, their coverage in this book would have been minimized. But, the scandal did not affect another sector. The scandal created a conversation about governance at the Bank as well as the Bank's governance and anti-corruption strategy for its client member-states.

---

[1] All tables referenced in this book may be found in the Appendix.

Who Matters at the World Bank?. Kim Moloney, Oxford University Press.
© Kim Moloney (2022). DOI: 10.1093/oso/9780192857729.003.0008

In this last historical era covered by this book, the prior demand side (PSG) and supply side (PSM) divisions would become more public (see also Yanguas and Hulme 2015). This was due to Wolfowitz's preferences for PSG projects (demand-side) over PSM (supply-side) but also the publication of a 2007 Governance and Anticorruption Strategy (GAC). The 2007 Strategy was dominated by a demand-side governance perspective in contrast to the supply-side approach of the Bank's first-ever Public Sector Strategy published in 2000 (see Chapter 7). However, by 2012 and the end of the Zoellick presidency, the debate would be less about which "side" of PSM/PSG mattered most rather a firm and unequivocal belief that the sector was critical to global financial crisis response, to lagging country performances, and that the sector mattered for all other Bank work.

A Controversial President: Paul Wolfowitz

On June 1, 2005, Paul Wolfowitz, a former Deputy Secretary of Defense under US President George W. Bush and an important strategist behind the US's 2003 Iraq invasion, became the Bank's tenth President. In the past, the US tradition of encouraging a citizen as the Bank's President had been accepted without much protest from G7/G8 members. But the Wolfowitz nomination was different. His background and unfamiliarity with development challenges was noxious to European leaders. But instead of publicly protesting his nomination, the "Europeans blinked" and Wolfowitz became President (WB45). Bank staff also did not like Wolfowitz. A *New Yorker* article from April 2007 referenced an April 2005 Bank staff survey that found that "nearly ninety percent of the staff opposed Wolfowitz's nomination" (Cassidy 2007; see also Park and Weaver 2012).

One Bank interviewee said that staff were "never going to like him because he was the neocon architect of the Iraq War … I worked in the private sector, if you did not like your boss, quit or suck it up. *[But at] the Bank though, there is this view that Presidents come and go but staff remain*" (WB4, emphasis added). With IBRD lending dropping 30 percent during Wolfowitz's tenure (but staff numbers only dropping 10 percent), the interviewee claimed that staff "have lots of time on their hands. Idle hands are the devil's playthings" (WB4). Others felt that Wolfowitz "said the right things and made the right moves" but then eight to nine months after he arrived, *U.S. News and World Report* published an article "characterizing the Bank as an institution awash in corruption that needed cleaning up … I think this was an outrageous article for many of us who are professionals and dedicating our careers to this agenda. And it marked a huge break [with Wolfowitz]" (WB28).

Wolfowitz's desire to halt Bank misappropriations became a Wolfowitz characterization to describe the entire Bank. The staff resented Wolfowitz for this view

(WB52).[2] When in 2006 a Bank staffer leaked that Wolfowitz had negotiated an extraordinary pay and promotion package for his Bank girlfriend, one interviewee wryly observed that if prior Bank President James Wolfensohn had done it, the leak would have been "swept under the rug," but in Wolfowitz's case, the initial leak fueled only staff resentment toward the President (WB47, WB52). During his first eighteen months, "about a dozen senior officials quit, including a managing director, the general counsel, the chief financial officer, and six vice presidents. Shengman Zhang, a Chinese national who was a Bank managing director for almost ten years, left in December 2005" because he was "bypassed, provoked and humiliated" by Wolfowitz and his top aides (Cassidy 2007). Zhang was what one Bank staffer called a "good Chinese, superb Chinese bureaucrat, very low profile, everything was pre-negotiated, there was never a conflict in decision-making" (WB13).

In short order, Wolfowitz "alienated constituencies that would have naturally supported him" (WB28). Adding fuel to the fire was that shortly after becoming President, Wolfowitz brought in his own team. On his second day on the job, Wolfowitz attended his first Executive Director meeting. At his second Board meeting five days later, the second item on the agenda was Wolfowitz's appointment of three senior staff including Robin Cleveland as Counselor to the President, Daniela Gressani as Interim Director for External Affairs, and Kevin Kellems as Senior Advisor to the President (World Bank 2005b, 2005c). The three followed Wolfowitz to the Bank from the Pentagon. According to an interviewee, there were "a lot of friends of Paul walking around" (WB28).

Robin Cleveland, in particular, was unpopular. Ms. Cleveland held "deep suspicions" about Bank staff (WB28) and "fired people for not being loyal," including a Belgian Vice President who did want to put Bank staff in Iraq (WB26). Staff members appeared particularly upset about how Cleveland (presumably with Wolfowitz's approval) forced Shengman Zhang to leave the Bank. Ms. Cleveland "ran all over him" (WB13). One Bank interviewee who recalled being teased by his/her fellow bankers for a "friendship" with Ms. Cleveland and yet, still stated that "Robin Cleveland could not stand [Shengman Zhang, a Managing Director] for two seconds. She told me within a week of her [Robin's] arrival that she will cut him off at his knees … Her way of [managing the Bank] was to shame everybody into it" (WB8).[3]

---

[2] One NGO, Government Accountability Project (GAP), helped publicize the Wolfowitz scandal (GAP 2007). One interviewee recalled walking around the Bank and seeing Bank staff spending lots of time watching for GAP website updates and contributing to its website (WB29).

[3] Two interviewees mentioned that since Wolfowitz had previously led Johns Hopkins SAIS (with its well-known neoconservative faculty), he brought many former SAIS students into the Bank because he thought they'd be "loyal" even if one interviewee was not certain that SAIS alums had a "compassion toward development issues" (WB52, WB26). As someone with a MA from SAIS (one partial origin of this book is an independent study under Professor Roett at SAIS), I can understand the interviewee concerns but disagree with its generalization about SAIS alums.

Although Wolfowitz would later resign from the Bank ostensibly due to his handling of a conflict-of-interest situation with his Bank staff girlfriend,[4] his tenure rankled the Board and staff even before the girlfriend scandal broke. This included his desire to turn off the lending spigot to corrupt clients along with his early expectation that he could circumvent the Board to do so. Additional conflicts included his desire for an Iraq-based Bank office (and his alleged attempt to conceal the death of a Bank consultant in Iraq), policy brawls with Prime Minister Gordon Brown of the UK and Angela Merkel of Germany, and Bank staff concerns that he would force a Bush-style policy of not funding health clinics that perform abortions (McKenna 2007; de Borchgrave 2007; Cassidy 2007; Kamen 2007; Yousefzadeh 2007). As if the above were not enough, there was more. This "more" involved the PSM/PSG sector.

Shortly after the girlfriend scandal hit the press, Bank staff released an open letter of complaint. This complaint was leaked to the press. In the letter, staff worried about the negative "impact of the current leadership crisis on the Bank's credibility and authority to engage with governments, non-government stakeholders, and donor partners on the GAC [Governance and Anti-Corruption] agenda" (World Bank Staff 2007). Staff warned that "the Bank's ability to 'practice what it preaches' on governance was 'eroding' and that 'in these circumstances, we cannot credibly implement the GAC strategy'" (World Bank Staff 2007). Initially signed by forty-six Bank staff involved in the GAC strategy, the letter was later signed by another 650 or so Bank staff (World Bank Staff 2007). When Wolfowitz tried to apologize to Bank staff for his behavior in mid-April 2007 (just one month after the GAC Strategy was approved and one month before the Board encouraged him to resign), *The Washington Times* reported that staff "heckled" Wolfowitz during a broadcasted apology in the Bank's atrium (de Borchgrave 2007). In the end, after weeks of saying, "I will not resign" he forced the Board into a "leadership crisis" because "there was no institutional mechanism for removing the President" (WB47). Six weeks after the Board asked him to resign Wolfowitz left the Bank on June 30, 2007.

The Executive Directors Intervene: Wolfowitz's "Governance"

A year earlier, at the April 2006 Bank and Fund Annual Meetings in Jakarta Indonesia, Wolfowitz announced that it was "a time for action:" The Bank

---

[4] Bank staff members expect to receive one, maybe two, promotions in their career. Young Professionals enter as an "F" grade. Specialists are a "G," Lead or Sector Managers are an "H," Sector or Country Directors are an "I," and Vice Presidents are a "J." Wolfowitz's girlfriend worked within the Bank's Gender Board. She had applied for an "H" position and although she was qualified, there were no "H" positions available that year so she was declined. Under Wolfowitz, her new contract required timed moves to H, then I, and then J grades (WB16).

must refocus its energies on governance and anti-corruption. Governance and anti-corruption are key components of the public sector governance addition to the sector's policy agenda after August 1991 (PSG, see Chapter 5) which was later reframed into economist-speak as demand-side governance (Chapter 6). Wolfowitz argued that "people need government that works" and that "an independent judiciary, a free press, and a vibrant civil society are important components of good governance. They balance the power of governments, and they hold them accountable for delivering better services, creating jobs, and improving living standards" (Wolfowitz 2006). He wanted the Bank to focus on country-level anti-corruption efforts including new investments in "judicial reform, civil service reform, the media, and freedom of information, and decentralization of public service delivery" (Wolfowitz 2006). Second, Wolfowitz signaled his desire to halt alleged misappropriations of Bank funds. Wolfowitz soon began pressuring Bank staff to create a strategy that addressed both goals.[5]

The first Wolfowitz objective was to increase Bank lending for good governance. This was a positive for sector policy institutionalization within the Bank. This led to the March 2007 Governance and Anti-Corruption Strategy (GAC) as a replacement for the previously updated Public Sector Strategy (see Chapter 6). But creating a new strategy was not simple. The battle took place on two fronts. The first battle had been percolating since before his presidency. This fight was over the appropriateness of applying a political economy perspective to PSM/PSG. The 2000 Public Sector Strategy and its update was technocratic with a supply-side focus.

Although the Strategy Update (see prior chapter) did partially consider demand-side ideas, it would be the 2004 *WDR* which further institutionalized demand-side ideas. The 2004 *WDR* (*Making Services Work for Poor People*) argued that only if developing countries' citizens can hold their governments accountable will public service delivery be improved. Although the Bank did not (and could not) associate the word "accountable" with "democratic" given its Articles of Agreement, the Bank argued that citizen participation was important if public services were to be responsive to their citizens. Although some Bank staff members might have wanted demand-side governance to overtake prior PSM work, others felt that the two approaches (PSM and PSG) were complementary. Nonetheless, the 2007 GAC Strategy largely became an institutional embodiment of the demand-side idea.

Although this battle was the most important for understanding this sector's evolving history at this moment in time, there was a second struggle over the Bank's internal governance that would become the more public of the two battles. This one involved Wolfowitz, his role as President, and questions about what was the core of the Bank's mission. When Wolfowitz observed that Bank funds

---

[5] See Chapter 9 for discussion of Wolfowitz' Integrity Vice President (INT). INT creation is contextualized in that chapter's discussion of Bank evaluative mechanisms.

were misappropriated by client countries, he not only *de facto* accused Bank staff members of ignoring corruption (and in some cases, encouraging it), but he aimed directly at the heart of the Bank's operations and its (dis)incentive culture (see also Chapter 4): if the Bank were to stop lending to developing but corrupt countries, then the Bank's lending portfolio would decrease. If PSM/PSG projects and policies were about improving a client country's public sector, should the Bank not lend money for such efforts?

With increasingly prosperous middle-income countries borrowing less from the Bank, cutting the Bank's lending portfolio would further impact the Bank's bottom-line. This includes limiting its purpose and lessening its importance as an institution. In a scenario in which client countries were borrowing less from the Bank, new questions arose. This included sector viability. In other words, it may be actually better to have "new priorities since [public sector management] is tough work. You are dealing with governments that do not want to address it because they are the problem" (WB31). This perspective has carried across the decades. From this perspective, the Bank was in a bind: dramatically force Bank client-states to cut funding or participate in a potential "helping" of corrupt state survival. Viewed from the Bank's incentive culture, Wolfowitz' salvo was perceived as an attack on the institution. Whether intentional or not, his questions hit at one heart of what it means to develop. Was it better to lend to corrupt countries in the hopes that some aid "gets through" to the poor or to improving that country's situation? Or would it be better to lend nothing at all? The eventual answer for the Board (but not for Wolfowitz) was that continued lending was most important. But to get there, more drama would ensue.

Worsening an already tense situation was a personal leadership style that rankled many. Cassidy (2007) detailed a tense eight-hour Board meeting over Congo-Brazzaville. A previously negotiated debt-reduction agreement had stated that if the country made certain economic targets, its debt would be reduced. Wolfowitz's view was that meeting economic targets was insufficient. He wanted to "restrict how the Congolese government could use the money it would save on servicing its debt" to which Bank Directors responded that Wolfowitz "was overstepping his authority" and in the end, "twenty-two of the twenty-four board members opposed Wolfowitz's demands, and he was forced to back down on some of them" (Cassidy 2007). As Wolfowitz shut down projects, staff complained that he never publicly provided the criteria for why some corrupt countries would have suspensions and others did not.

One of those early efforts was a project based in India (WB4). Wolfowitz had read an INT (see Chapter 9) report about corruption in a Bank-designed project in India. Then, rather "naively," Wolfowitz told affected staff that "let's not take them [new health projects in India] to the Board until you put together some risk mitigation measures [i.e., until you prevent what INT found] … [But] instead of [staff] saying, 'Yes, that sounds like a good idea, boss,' they went straight to the Board and the Board started, well, let's say, vocally objecting" (WB4). In short, Wolfowitz was trying to overturn Board decisions while *de facto* accusing the Board of approving projects where corruption was bound to occur. In another example, "Wolfowitz had read a headline that the president of the Democratic Republic of the Congo had spent US$180,000 on his hotel for two nights and Wolfowitz said, 'Why am I giving debt relief to a country like that?'… and the Board is saying, that is not how we do things around here. He [Wolfowitz] withholds the lending" (WB4). This effort to unilaterally stop funding projects and to do so without Board consent upset members of the Board. Adding to that problem were client states who did not want to talk about it for fear of how it looked at home (WB29). This was a perfect storm.

In the midst of this storm, GAC Strategy efforts plodded forward. The goal was to have a Strategy ready for Wolfowitz' intended March 2006 announcement about governance's importance and later, the September 2006 Bank and Fund meetings in Singapore. After several months of internal Bank deliberation and an early GAC draft, Wolfowitz's team was unhappy with staff progress. Wolfowitz and his team decided to take over the process and redraft the strategy on their own (Cassidy 2007). Certainly some staffers "sympathized" with Wolfowitz's office because the first GAC draft (ready in July 2006) looked like "the dog's breakfast" given that "every agency and every group [in the Bank] had input" and, thus, "there was a little piece for everybody and not much integrity" (WB28). However, and perhaps because the President's staff decided to redraft the Strategy late in the game, Wolfowitz's version was "hastily drafted and much more punitive," whereas the staff version was more developmental toward anti-corruption (WB28). Unfortunately, for Wolfowitz, the staff version had already reached the Board (WB28, WB32) and the strategy switcheroo was handled "clumsily" (WB28).

The Board met to discuss the strategy in August 2006 (WB28), a month before the Singapore meetings and five months after the Indonesian meetings. When Wolfowitz presented an entirely different GAC strategic platform than the staff version expected by Board, the Board was surprised (WB32), or more pointedly, "pissed that Wolfowitz was acting unilaterally" (WB10, WB38). This Board perception has a long history. As early as the mid-1980s, one staff member interviewed by the Bank's Historian noted that executive directors appear to defer to Bank staff because the staff are more well-versed in development than the Board (Please 1986). Please continued:

My own experience with most Board members is that they show enormous deference to the Bank staff and the Bank's management in terms of saying, Look, you people on the staff and management know more about development and the needs of developing countries than we on the Board do. We have our concerns and our problems, but you're the people we have to rely on for expert guidance. In the SAL [structural adjustment lending] discussion in 1980 and 1981, this occurred several times with me. They would say to me, This is a very private discussion. You can see we're unhappy, but if you people, who clearly know more about the needs and potentials of these countries, feel this is the only way to go at this stage to help them in a solid way, then okay, we'll go along. But recognize we're not altogether convinced. I think in a sense it was an interesting reflection about many Board members and in a sense a very healthy one; one that I think the Bank management and Bank staff should take seriously. Most Board members don't want to be seen as simply judging, double-checking on staff, but they want to have confidence that the Bank staff and management are not misleading them".

(Please 1986)

Further challenges faced Wolfowitz with the Board. One was that China and Saudi Arabia disliked the "demand-side" governance agenda (WB38).[6] Such demand-side approaches had previously rankled non-democratic Board members given its emphasis on participatory, citizen-focused activities with civil society and the media. This demand harks back to developing countries prior concerns about the Bank's Articles of Agreement initially via structural adjustment's addition to the Bank's lending portfolio and later, the additions of privatization, good governance, and anti-corruption.

The other problem was that when put under pressure by Board questions (including China and Saudi Arabia) about his Strategy, Wolfowitz *changed sides* at the Board meeting. He dropped his newer version (created by Office of the President staff) and then supported the Board's decision to keep the version creation by Bank staff. In doing so, he "destroyed any integrity that he had. The Board did not buy that for a minute. It was like, 'If you didn't write this paper, why did you give it to us'" (WB28)? In-between the August 2006 Board meeting and the Bank and Fund annual meeting in October in Singapore, the UK protested Wolfowitz's handling of the GAC strategy by withholding a £50 million payment to the Bank. It was not that the UK was "pro-corruption" but rather that the "UK is one of the few shareholders really committed to these … wacky little MDBs [Millennium Development Goals] that we have" (WB4) and thus did not want the Bank to stop lending to countries that were corrupt. Wolfowitz's version would have called such lending into question.

Perhaps unsurprisingly, the upcoming Bank and Fund Annual Meeting (held in Singapore) was one of the most "combative" Annual Meetings in recent memory with a "whole host of consultations to try and dig our way out of it" (WB28). Tensions became so heightened that the Bank's Development Committee had to remind Wolfowitz that the Executive Directors had "the right to determine how

---

[6] As noted by one interviewee, this is "because some countries do not like discussing demand-side governance, the Bank must always reassure them that the Bank is working within the confines of its agreements" (WB38).

the anti-corruption policy would be finalized and executed" and not Wolfowitz. In the Development Committee's Press Release, they wrote, "Given the importance of this issue … we stressed the importance of Board oversight of the [GAC] strategy as it is further developed and then implemented." In short, the Development Committee had given Wolfowitz its most public "reprimand" of a Bank president in recent memory (Cassidy 2007). An immediate outcome was a Board decision to broaden GAC Strategy discussions. By November 2006, the Bank had begun to consult with NGOs and governments on the Strategy (WB36). Six months later, in March 2007, the Bank published its GAC Strategy. On the question on whether the Bank would lend to corrupt countries, the answer was "yes." This answer was backed by the NGOs and governments with whom the Bank consulted (see also Chapter 9). It was not "'whether' but 'how' the WBG can stay engaged in countries with weak governance" (World Bank 2007b, 69).

The US only made a few public statements on Wolfowitz's evolving GAC Strategy or the Board's attempts to remove Wolfowitz. Of the few US statements, most were positive. On the GAC Strategy, a Treasury official stated, "[the] recent agreement by the heads of all the MDBs to collaborate on this [GAC] agenda is encouraging. We will urge them to be systematic in their approach, with clear and strict criteria consistent with a zero-tolerance philosophy" (Adams 2006). During Board–Wolfowitz negotiations, the same Treasury official commented that "the United States strongly supports President Wolfowitz's leadership on the anticorruption agenda" (Adams 2006). At the height of the Wolfowitz scandal, one early May 2007 statement came from a Bush White House Political Counselor who hoped that Wolfowitz would be given a "fair process and a fair hearing of the facts." By May 17, 2007, just days after the Board asked Wolfowitz to resign, President Bush stated, "I regret that it's come to this" (Aversa 2007a, 2007b).

A "Treaty" or a Political Economy "Victory"?

During the mid-2006 to early 2007 period in which the GAC Strategy was written, the public and personal dramas surrounding Wolfowitz were hard to ignore. The proximate cause of Wolfowitz's downfall reflected his own mis-governance. This included the attempted hijacking of the GAC Strategy from Bank PSM/PSG staff by Wolfowitz's personal staff. The near-term consequence was an October 2006 Board decision that the GAC required an external review and deliberation process. On March 20, 2007, the Bank's executive directors approved the GAC Strategy (World Bank 2007c). Eleven years after Wolfensohn's "cancer of corruption" speech, the GAC Strategy was to inform the Bank's "evolving agenda" on governance (World Bank 2007e, ii; Best 2012).

In response, the US Treasury

welcome[d] and supporte[d] the updated version of the World Bank group's [GAC] strategy. We applaud the Bank for an extensive public consultation process, which has helped to sharpen the GAC's approach and has opened the door to new partnerships. We are confident that the strategy will strengthen the Bank's role in helping borrowing countries promote good governance and fight corruption and in playing a leadership role with global partners. We believe the GAC rightly focuses on the most important issues: building effective and accountable institutions; country ownership; and government commitment to governance and anticorruption.

(Paulson, Jr. 2007)

Treasury's statement is interesting for two reasons. One, Paulson's focus on the "updated" Strategy (as opposed to the drafts over which the Board fought in mid-2006) and two, his praise of an external review process which had created new "partnerships." The US could have chosen silence after the GAC's publication (they were silent after the 2000 and 2002 Public Sector Strategy papers) but instead, Treasury desired to publicly commend the GAC Strategy. The contentiousness of the GAC process likely contributed to this Treasury decision.

Although some viewed the GAC Strategy as a "treaty among the Board, the President, and the Bank" (WB38), it had important objectives. Specifically, it sought "to scale up WBG support to countries to help them build transparent and accountable institutions capable of delivering public services, protecting public welfare, and ensuring a sound investment climate—so that poor people have great opportunities to move out of poverty" (World Bank 2007b, 11). Governance and anti-corruption efforts helped "develop capable and accountable states and institutions that can reduce poverty, promote growth, and contain corruption" (World Bank 2007b, 3). The GAC Strategy was not simply an update of the earlier Public Sector Strategy. It asserted that the Bank's prior approaches had been too one-sided. While the 2000 Public Sector Strategy (and its 2003 Update) were more technically specific and drew upon NIE, the GAC Strategy was a triumph for Bank staff who wished the Bank would pay more attention to demand side of governance and, in particular, political economy approaches (Best 2014; Yanguas and Hulme 2015).

The first part of the 2007 GAC Strategy took the perspective that "to make progress in reducing poverty, countries need good policies, a workable regulatory framework for markets and private-sector development, and reasonably efficient and effective provision of public services—all of which depend greatly on the effectiveness of the state" (World Bank 2007b, 3). The Strategy desired a "reasonably efficient and effective provision of public services" (World Bank 2007b, 3). Its understanding of "reasonably efficient and effective" service deliveries left equity or the state's role in redistribution unmentioned.

The Strategy was less about the Bank's prior PSM work in civil service reform, public expenditure management, or public financial management; instead, the focus was on governance in general (including efficient and effective service delivery) and anti-corruption in particular. For the political economists among the Bank's PSM/PSG staff, the GAC was a triumph. It was the realization of their decade-long complaint that the Bank focused too much energy on how governments functioned and less attention on the citizens or civil societies who created demand for government services.

Two months after the GAC was approved, the Bank held a special two-day conference in which participants answered prepared questions about how political economy approaches might assist the Bank's understanding of governance reform (World Bank 2007a).[7] The Bank's "lessons learned" came nearly exclusively from political economy and did not ask or consider whether conflicts did occur within client nations' public sector institutions. This leads to a broader "lessen" from this book. That is, staff with the dominant theoretical perspectives shape policy change: neoclassical economists of the 1980s, new institutional economics of the 1990s, and the political economy of the 2000s. Under-currents of dissent such as the institutional development of the 1980s or "supply side" under Wolfowitz or the broader links with Bank (dis)incentives via the Wapenhans report also influence what is or is not heard.

Other lessons from this conference included "[to support] improvements in capacity, transparency, participation, and accountability" and to "strengthen formal institutions of executive oversight and civil society efforts for better governance" (World Bank 2007b, 7). The latter option included efforts to address issues of financial management, civil service performance, corruption, local government work, capacity building, judicial reform, and assisting oversight institutions for public expenditures (World Bank 2007b). Financial-management projects were more likely to succeed than civil service reform or nationwide anti-corruption commissions (World Bank 2007b, 10).

Another important GAC Strategy statement reflected the Wolfowitz-Bank debate over whether the Bank should lend to corrupt countries. Writing that the Bank should not "make the poor pay twice," the GAC strategy publicly rebuked Wolfowitz. One interviewee was clear on his/her opinion of Wolfowitz's attempt to slow Bank lending to corrupt countries: "We [the Bank] will not have a black list of where we will not go" (WB32). Even if the Bank had fiduciary concerns,

---

[7] Questions included, "How do we [the Bank] use political analysis to guide communication strategy in governance reform?" "How do we secure political will—demonstrated by broad leadership support for change?" "How do we build broad coalitions of pro-change influentials?" "What do we do about powerful vested interests?" "How do we help reforms transform indifferent, or even hostile, public opinion into support for reform objectives?" and "How do we instigate citizen demand for good governance and accountability in order to sustain governance reform?" (World Bank 2007a, 1)

the GAC strategy asserted that withdrawing money from client nations would harm the poor. The Bank preferred to "create ways of providing support" to those countries (World Bank 2007b, 5). That view was (apparently) supported by the external review process, even if one staffer felt that the Bank "cherry-picked" among external views. The interviewee observed, "management responsible will highlight the [civil society] quotes where they want [the GAC strategy] to go and no, we want the Bank to remain engaged even if we find widespread corruption and our officials who are at the till, keep lending. And so, they [Bank management] grabbed quotes from all of these people saying this ... Do you think this is the unanimous view of the people in these countries? Keep lending to our government? Probably not. But that is the majority opinion put forth when [the Bank managers] come back with their external consultation" (WB4).

In some ways, both Wolfowitz and the Board partially achieved what they wanted (WB38). Wolfowitz saw governance's profile expand, while the Board (and the Bank staff) could continue lending in poorly governed environments. In doing so, the GAC agreed to "strengthen not bypass country systems" (WB32). This phrase was also found in the Strategy: "[The Bank] will strive to strengthen, rather than bypass, country systems—better national institutions are the more effective and long-term solution to governance and corruption challenges and to mitigating fiduciary risk for all public money, including that from the Bank" (World Bank 2007b, 5).[8] Of course, the "how" of successful aid provision in the most poorly governed environments was not easy, and the Bank only briefly addressed the issue in the GAC Strategy's Annex C. Operationally, the Strategy noted that "some elements of this strategy can become operational in the very short run, others will require revision of staff operational guidance or the development of new guidance" (World Bank 2007b, 34). As noted in Chapter 9, and even today, this task remains undone.

The GAC and the PSM Staff: With Us or Against Us?

In 2003, former Bank Chief Economist, Joe Stiglitz, wrote that the Bank "emphasizes the importance of 'governance'—the rules by which public and private institutions are governed—yet it has on its staff few people that know much about the subject beyond the ability to recite the latest mantra" (Stiglitz 2003, 125). Stiglitz may be right in that staff may "recite the latest mantra," but he underplayed

---

[8] Unlike years past, the Bank's Articles of Agreement were not "the fight" of the Strategy. By 2007, 16 years after good governance's addition and eleven years after anti-corruption's introduction, member states understood (even if not always supported) the Bank's version of "non-politics." Specifically, they said the Bank would "act within the constraints imposed by the Articles' general limitation on interference in a member's political affairs and on basing decisions on a member's political character or on noneconomic considerations" (World Bank 2007b, 6).

the extent to which Bank staff members fight, often bitterly, about that mantra. Of the many internal conflicts relayed in this book, the GAC fight appeared to be one of the most ferocious public fights over public sector management and governance. It is undoubtedly true that the GAC's recent formulation made the battle fresher in interviewees' minds, but given the GAC's interlinkage with press reports, Wolfowitz's personality and eventual departure, its publicness when compared to prior policy battles is hard to ignore.

One highly involved GAC interviewee (and economist) stated that the GAC created conflict because the "public sector people" preferred to define their work in "inclusive terms" while still doing "governance" work. In contrast, the governance folks preferred to "capture the public sector label to do governance work and not public sector work" (WB32). Another observed that "the public administration management discipline was an orphaned discipline in the Bank" and that even economists viewed "public administration management" (not the name the discipline uses for itself but instead, the economist's name) as having only one home: public expenditure management (WB2). That the entire sector is not the domain of public administration or public sector management but instead, a sector exclusively for economists is telling.

An interviewee related that his/her experiences working in Bank Region X (kept anonymous for interviewee protection) were guided by "really old-style public administration technocrats who are really quite happy in doing projects, no one challenges them" and that those public administration technocrats "feel intellectually insecure in the company of the economists" (WB32). Another Bank interviewee, who sided with the traditionalist camp (PSM specialists), observed there has been "an increasing fraction of those serving within the public sector group who have ... a background, whether it be training or experience in political economy analysis, whatever the hell that means, than we did ten years ago" (WB4). This disdain for the "other" (whether supply or demand side), including commentary on their disciplinary training, not only indicated the unique internal frictions of this sector during this era but may also remind readers of early 1980s debates about whether microeconomists with an interest in institutional development should have a voice in early PSM agendas. Both instances indicate an entwining of bureaucratic politics with perceptions about the value of certain disciplinary approaches.

One GAC-involved interviewee argued that a "major gain of the GAC strategy was the redesign of road projects to incorporate more transparency and more civil society" (WB32). For the interviewee, the "road project" phrase could have been substituted with another sector such as health or education or any other sector. The interviewee's point was that, prior to GAC, the PSM projects encouraged demand-side responsiveness across a client nation's ministries, be they the transportation or health departments. Prior projects were not focused on civil society but aimed to improve departmental functioning.

The GAC challenge was to ask the Bank's PSM specialists, "Why do you think any of this [their projects] will be implemented? Where are the incentives for results? What are the pressures for performance" (WB32)? This demand-side interviewee described the public sector management model of the 1990s and early 2000s as follows: "We take a very long time to get systemic changes; everything is connected to everything else. So, we have to run eight or nine years on supply-side improvements to the system and then, on year eight we will start to see gains. This is nonsense. This is not a workable way of doing development. [You will never] get the political continuity [in a client country] for eight years. And frankly, you cannot tell. In year eight you discover in this model, oh, actually what [we] were doing was funding boondoggles for international and local consultants" (WB32).

The Bank's economists also felt frustrated that the PSM portfolio was not performing well (excluding financial management and public expenditure management projects). One solution was to import political-economy solutions into the PSM agenda (WB24). Given "comprehensive reform will not work," the question was, "How can you proceed incrementally?" Thus, if the Bank worked with groups who will "pressure for performance in public administration" (WB32), then development is assisted. Yet for all of this anti-PSM or anti-supply side talk, the GAC interviewee stated that during Wolfowitz's tenure, "there was so much controversy and so many dimensions that the public sector agenda got somewhat short-shifted" (WB32).

Further politicizing these fights was that the Bank was undergoing leadership turmoil. Wolfowitz and the Board were fighting. The public sector agenda became, through no fault of its own, the headline item. Worse, for the supply-side technocrats, was that just when the sector agenda became the headline item, the Bank's President only wanted to expand the demand-side agenda. Distrust amongst staff and between the staff and the President was high. The question how the Bank could "expand strategically and selectively … in a way that is consistent with [its] capacity and budget resources" (WB28) was never far from any discussion.

When asked about disciplinary battles, one of my most senior Bank interviewees asked me to turn off the tape recorder before answering.[9] He/she agreed that the GAC and "technical public administration" folks were different groups within the Bank. The former focused on political economy and stakeholder analysis and included more economists than political scientists, many with NIE backgrounds. The latter group focused on public sector management and was dominated by former UK officials now working at the Bank. It was the interviewee's opinion that, despite those differences (and the GAC's approval by the Board), the GAC "does not go very deep within the Bank" and the Bank's Operations staff simply viewed the GAC as a public-relations idea. Although GAC advocates wanted the

---

[9] This was the only interviewee who asked me to turn off the recorder during one portion of our conversation.

strategy to go deep within the Bank, the reality was that client countries do not want to reform and the Bank cannot make them do it. When client countries do not want demand-side governance, the Bank country managers do not want to do it. Thus, the "people on the ground" (i.e., country managers) were not feeling well served. Another interviewee called the GAC a "revenge of the economists" who were upset that some "blue-collar types announced that they knew how to do projects" (WB23). The term *blue-collar type* was shorthand for technocratic supply-side PSM staff. The economists were worried that they would have to "rummage around this blue-collar business about how the public sector works;" instead, Bank governance advocates had only wanted to "talk governance without studying how it works" (WB23).

Operationally, supply-side PSM projects continued to be approved seemingly without GAC influence (WB31). This was in part because the GAC Strategy led to "fabulous confusion" among Bank staff. Despite the GAC Strategy being "elegantly written," there was "no agreed normative framework or clear sense of what should be done before what, what the points of entry are… [and] the closer you get to the framework there are 1,001 Power Points" (WB23). Or put more bluntly, the GAC Strategy created an "enormous cloud of uninformed discussion … pseudo-indicators, and a lot of conceptual nonsense, disconnected from operational work" (WB23).

But there were other perspectives. One interviewee preferred the phrase "internecine squabble within the public sector community" rather than "debate" among economic sub-disciplines or even between PSM and PSG advocates (WB28). This was important during the creation period of the GAC strategy, given it was like a civil war in which staff members had to declare sides (WB28). Others preferred to characterize the differences as a question of "taste" (WB41). Or to say that the GAC was a "milestone" for the Bank (WB10) because the GAC Strategy redrew the governance map for the Bank (i.e., parliaments were no longer "no-go" areas; WB10). The latter interviewee went as far as to say that after the GAC Strategy, one would be hard-pressed to find a Bank staffer who would say that the Bank had no obligation to "understand the politics of public sector governance" (WB10). Another interviewee pointed out that no matter where one stood, the reality was that the Bank's lawyers were still trying to figure out if the Bank's Articles of Agreement allowed staff to work with opposition parties or even oppositional in-country NGOs (WB29).

Demand Side Governance = More Research

This enhanced governance focus led to an explosion in Bank research and projects. Between 2004 and 2007 there were at least sixteen different public sector management and governance subtopics published between 2004 and 2012. In privatization and state-owned enterprise reform, short reports were published in 2006 and 2007 that took stock of what had been done and where state-owned-enterprise reform (privatization) was still needed. By the mid-2000s, power and telecommunications utilities along with water provision, banking, and the energy sectors were the most likely to still retain state ownership. Even so, the number of privatizations had been significant. The Bank calculated that "between 1990 and 2003, 120 developing countries carried out nearly 8,000 privatization transactions, raising US$410 billion in privatization proceeds," although just fifteen of those 120 countries "generated more than two-thirds of those proceeds" (Kikeri and Kolo 2007, 1). By the mid-2000s, financial management remained an important project lending area, even if research papers had somewhat diminished. Published papers included financial management's relationship to local government (Shah 2007) or incentives within low-income countries for financial management reforms (Stevens 2004).

Unemployment insurance research focused on regions or group of countries (Vodopivec 2004a, 2004b) or discussed new collaborations between the Bank and the International Labor Organization (World Bank 2007e). Studies on social security reform retained an LAC focus (Packard et al. 2004; Zviniene and Packard 2004). Tax and customs reforms remained ad hoc even if the former's research agenda widened slightly and the latter discussed customs modernization both as a broad topic and as a series of country-specific case studies (De Wulf and Sokol 2004, 2005).

The Bank's Legal Vice Presidency published a judicial assessment handbook that sought to move the Bank's ad hoc judicial reform projects into a unified assessment approach (Reiling et al. 2007). Another researcher explored the budget conflicts between the legislative and judicial branches when legislatures approve judicial budgets (Webber 2007). The legal vice presidency also began to annually publish an overview of the Bank's work in the legal and judicial arena. GAC Strategy discussions encouraged more research on corruption, including its measurement (Knack 2006). Others asserted that decentralized governments are less corrupt than centralized systems in the long run (Shah 2006; Gurgur and Shah 2005) and focused on how coalition-building can tackle corruption (Johnston and Kpundeh 2004).

In public expenditure management, the Public Expenditure Reviews continued as a formal review of a client country's state of affairs. Within this popular PSM topic, new considerations included social protection, safety nets, and general poverty-reduction spending (de Neubourg et al. 2007; Wilhelm and Fiestas 2005). The link between social accountability and civil society received an intellectual boost with the Bank's 2004 *WDR* on *Making Services Work for Poor People*, which described a framework for how citizen power can influence (and interact with) service providers directly (and thus, more efficiently according to the Bank) than via government (World Bank 2004).

As public expenditure management continued in importance, IMF-Bank cooperation remained fractious. In March 2006, the IMF's Managing Director (Rodriço de Rato) and Wolfowitz created a high-level committee to review Bank-Fund interactions. Their initial report, published in February 2007, was critical of the Bank and Fund's failures. The Review Committee considered the 1989 Concordat (see Chapter 5) as purposefully vague so as "to placate the interests of both institutions" rather than to clarify roles or propose initiatives for moving forward (Malan 2007, 41). According to a Bank interviewee, the Report thesis was, "create effective procedures for collaboration, don't accuse of each of not doing this or that; just get it done" (WB55).

The idea was that the "Fund considered itself more rigorous and disciplined, if not superior, compared with the Bank." Complaints also surfaced around the Bank's failures to consider revenue management, "conflicting advice ... on public financial management and taxation," the Bank's "failure to do enough" in civil service reform, pension reform, SOEs, and Bank and Fund failures to coordinate information flow for Public Expenditure Reviews (Malan 2007, 26–27). Another point of contention was that despite a 1998 Bank–Fund Agreement to consider staff interactions with the Fund as part of their performance assessments, in reality such considerations were underemphasized. Career progressions for which working "across 19th street" [in reference to the fact that the Bank and Fund are located across 19th Street from each other] which had been considered essential to senior management promotion was instead, de-emphasized (Malan 2007).

Seven months after the Bank–Fund Review Committee released its report, the Bank and the Fund released an action plan for moving Bank–Fund collaboration forward. The Joint Management Action Plan (or J-MAP) was published in 2007 (see also a later-day review, IEO 2020). J-MAP specified which units or job titles must incorporate Bank-to-Fund or Fund-to-Bank interaction into their job responsibilities. For instance, the Review Committee found that neither institution sufficiently communicated with each other. The solution included annual meetings between Fund and Bank country representatives to discuss upcoming programs, invitations to attend each other's meetings, debriefings, and co-drafting papers. For example, if the Fund asked the Bank for more analytical work, the Bank agreed to create a "cross-support window" to handle Fund requests. This is done while seeking funding from either institution's budget (including trust funds[10]) to further this analytical work and to train Bank staff to analyze "the sectoral/macro interface of aid and public expenditures as it affects the economy's supply side response and growth prospects" (Bank-Fund 2007, 23). In practice, the two institutions must not only share their key public expenditure management documents including concept notes and country- and sector-specific thinking, but allow the other institution to comment and to provide suggestions. Most important, given

---

[10] Despite pressures by the Bank to cooperate with the other IOs within the World Bank Group, one IEG report discovered that staff prefer to not engage in cooperative activities since "staff (*and their managers*) have limited control" (IEG 2010e, 11, emphasis in the original).

the Fund's focus on short-term policy shifts and the Bank's focus on the longer shifts, J-MAP established that "fiscal space" should not be discussed because "there should be no suggestion that there is a trade-off between short-term stability and long-term growth" (Bank-Fund 2007, 25).

A President Who Starts No Fires: Robert Zoellick

After the end of Wolfowitz' tumultuous run as Bank President, the Bush Administration needed someone whose reputation did not equate to controversy. The answer was Robert Zoellick, former US Trade Representative from 2001 to 2005 and Deputy Secretary of State from 2005 to 2006. Nominated to the role of Bank President on 30 May 2007, Zoellick became Bank President on 1 July 2007. One portrayal of Zoellick published in the *Financial Times* labelled him a "quiet revolutionary" who reoriented the Bank for a world in which its dominion over international development agendas was less secure than four decades prior (Mallaby 2012). Others believed he was a "lame-duck, one-term president" who has an "unfortunate combination of smart, arrogant, prone to temper tantrums, shy, and 100 percent secure in his own judgement" (Wade 2010, 52). Disagreement is not uncommon. At this point in the book, readers are forgiven for asking if *any* Bank President has been universally loved. The answer is an unequivocal "no." Zoellick was no different.

Just as the 1980–1982 global recession altered how the Bank's major external stakeholders viewed its purpose, Zoellick's arrival in the midst of a global financial crisis was an opportunity to use a crisis to refocus the Bank. His refocus did not engage in significant internal reform to the Bank's organizational structure. Instead, one remnant of the Wolfensohn reforms was the ongoing decentralization of Bank staff into the field. This reform continued into the Zoellick presidency. However, IEG evaluations published during Zoellick's presidency indicated that the reforms did not substantially improve project design, supervision quality, or project outputs if the project leader is in the field. In contrast, when a Bank country director is located in the country of emphasis and not a nearby hub, country-specific program outputs improved (IEG 2010b). In its management response, the Bank argued that the IEG underplayed decentralization benefits and that improved dialogues with member states, alignments with poverty reduction strategies, and faster crisis and post-crisis responses also mattered (IEG 2010b, 77–78).

Zoellick also used the crisis to re-envision the Bank's the next 50 years. This included new emphases on "securing development" in which security, legitimacy, and economy linked to good governance and where a state's "fragility and violence" or the "cycle of failed government" could be broken (Zoellick 2008a). This required the Bank to not just focus on how to improve good governance but what to do when governments fail. The prescription was more public sector governance (via local ownership, rule of law, state legitimacy, stable economies, and a focus on political economy), an emphasis on donor coordination (called "new multilateralism"), to recall that reform is not an overnight task, and to boost security for the people (Zoellick 2008a, 2008b).

By the October 2008 Annual Meeting of the World Bank Group, Zoellick had identified six themes: poor countries in Africa, fragile and post-conflict states, middle income countries, global and regional public goods, new opportunities in the Arab world, and knowledge- and learning-building (Zoellick 2008b). The themes did not sideline PSM/PSG but instead, "mainstream[ed] anti-corruption and good governance across all our activities" (Zoellick 2008b). This was reiterated four years later, near the end of his term as President, in his article for *Foreign Affairs* where he wrote, "promoting good governance and combating corruption are an integral part of the development" (Zoellick 2012, 74).

Despite using a crisis to encourage Bank staff to refocus on the poorest countries, Bank lending to middle-income countries rose during this period. The necessity of the lending was clear (global financial crisis) while also conveniently scratching that "we must lend to survive" itch. It is an "itch" that has been pervasive across the Bank's history (see Chapter 4). This book's sector of interest is no different. Middle-income countries, even in the midst of financial crisis reverberations, not only can borrow (with interest) but they can also borrow more given their economic size when compared to less prosperous countries (Winters 2011; Clemons and Kremer 2016). The necessity of Bank lending to middle-income countries and an increased competition to lend, forced the Bank to compete with multilateral institutions and private capital (Chang 2008).

Zoellick's presidency coincided with the arrival of a new external stakeholder with potential influence over the Bank as well as a shift in the Bank's Executive Directors. Although neither event would alter policy change within the Bank's PSM/PSG agenda, each is worthy of a brief discussion. The first is the emergence of the Financial Stability Board (FSB) in April 2009. The FSB was viewed by former US Treasury Secretary Timothy Geithner as the "fourth pillar" in post-WWII global architecture in which the other three pillars (Bank, Fund, and the World Trade Organization or WTO) were to be created immediately after WWII (Bank, Fund) or faced an aborted birth before being reborn as the WTO in 1995 (Wouters and Odermatt 2014, 50; Roger 2020). With a focus on global financial stability instead of the global economic or trade stability focus of the other three IOs, the FSB became party to meetings of the G20 and at times, the Bank/Fund Annual Meetings. Although the FSB is an informal, not formal, international organization (for definition discussions, see Vabulas 2019; Roger 2020). While interaction between the FSB and the Fund is necessarily closer than its interaction with the Bank, there are cooperative activities with only a peripheral engagement with PSM/PSG such as the IMF-World Bank's Financial Sector Assessment Program along with standards assessments (FSB 2010). This agenda is less about public financial management or public expenditure management (two long-term PSM/PSG topics) and instead, overall financial stabilities. As such, and for the sector focus of this book and its desire to explain policy change, the FSB had limited influence over sector policy changes.

In the decades preceding the global financial crisis, many countries previously labelled as poor or developing in the 1970s and 1980s had become middle- or high-income countries by the mid-2000s. Their economic growth and poverty reduction did not equate to an increased voice within the Boards of either the Bank or the Fund. While the drama surrounding Fund's quotas and vote shares has been amply described elsewhere, less attention has been paid to the Bank reforms. During the Spring 2010 Board of Governors meetings of the Bank and Fund, a voice vote led to a 4.59 percent increase in the vote share of developing and transitioning countries within the Bank's Board of Executive Directors. This reform was to create closer parities between developed country members of the Bank's Board (failing to 52.81 percent of votes) and its non-developed members (rising 47.19 percent of votes). Despite such shifts, the net benefit for non-developed states soon disappeared. This is largely due to the Bank's higher income states increasing their capital contributions (Vestergaard 2011; Vestergaard and Wade 2013, 2015; Wade 2011). While there is no counter-factual to imagine what might happen if non-developed states had had, in practice, greater policy agenda say so, the net effect for this sector of Bank work has been negligible.

The Bank's DNA: Public Sector Governance is Everywhere, All the Time

Zoellick did not diminish PSM/PSG importance (Güven 2012). The momentum for this sector was no longer an early 1980s tiny lapping of the shoreline but rather, a tsunami of sector projects everywhere, all the time. Sector lending continued between 2007 to 2012 period with 700+ projects in which PSM/PSG was the key sector. This occurred despite two IEG reports suggesting the sector governance was a mid-range performer either in general or when compared to the transport sector (top performer) or the health, nutrition and population sector (worst performer) (IEG 2010b, 2013). The reports were complemented by evaluations of GAC-specific resourcing implementation and country-specific engagement (Chatterjee 2011; IEG 2011b), country-level accountability institutions (Migliorisi and Wescott 2011) and creation of an updated GAC Strategy and Implementation Plan in 2012 (World Bank 2012).

With the creation of a GAC Council by 2008, sector importance was further institutionalized. The Council made PSM/PSG the first-ever Bank sector "to have a Bank-wide remit" (World Bank 2012, 53). *It is an extraordinary transformation of sector policy changes and ultimately, policy importance from before 1980 to 2012. By* placing Bank Vice Presidents within the Council and rotating the Bank's Managing Directors as Council Chairs, the message was clear: no part of the Bank was to be left untouched by this sector. Everyone should be thinking about public sector governance all the time. The Council's Secretariat engaged implementation concerns and diffused the GAC agenda across the Bank. The Council was housed within the PREM network and its Public Sector Units. In essence, the Council was an organizational amplification of the Public Sector Board. An amplification not received by any other Sector Board (see Table 14).

In terms of policy change within the PSM/PSG agenda, the only policy shift of any importance was the reality that PSG had become more dominant than PSM (see Table 5). Evaluative efforts followed this lead. This includes a report on the lessons of the Bank's post-2007 GAC implementation within client states. The report wrote that Bank should refocus on "tangible and time-bound governance improvements," utilize financial instrument innovations to prioritize institutional strengthening, place an increased emphasis on the "Bank's 'zero tolerance' stance on corruption," clarify roles across the Bank including with the GAC Council, and diffuse sector-specific specialists "across existing Bank networks" (IEG 2011b, xxii, xxiii). There was some movement of public financial management and legal/judicial reforms to a broader accountability portfolio in which country-level civil society development, information flows, human rights, media, parliamentary reform,[11] and security reform were bunched together (Migliorisi and Wescott 2011) but this was less a policy shift than an re-emphasis on "accountability."

Unlike prior eras, the sector agenda was proactively incorporated into other sectors. This includes additional funding for the Bank regions to incorporate GAC work via incremental budget increases as well as a short-term multi-donor Governance Partnership Facility (GPF) to "accelerate implementation of its GAC Strategy" (Chatterjee 2011, xii). This funding occurred despite a "flat real budget environment since FY06" (Chatterjee 2011, 10). Such increases have occurred despite the age-old warning that cross-sectoral or country interaction with sector-wide policies infrequently congeal—an observation not unique to this sector (IEG 2013). While Bank staff "reported almost universal commitment to the strategy's objectives" (IEG 2011b, xviii), many country offices felt GAC ideas were not new as their offices had been implementing its ideas "several years before the 2007 strategy" (IEG 2011b, 87).

In the Bank's management response to a 2011 evaluation of initial GAC strategy implementation, they desired an updated GAC Strategy. This is because Strategy implementation "did not match this [Strategy's] ambitious vision" (IEG 2011b, 99). In particular, disconnects between encouraging reform (present) and

---

[11] The Bank traditionally does not give assistance to parliaments. This reflects restrictions from its Articles of Agreement. More recently, however, the Bank has attempted indirect support, see (Migliorisi and Wescott 2011, 25–28).

accountability for change or no change (less present) remained stark. This includes a "muted" impact of budget increments as the non-strategic alignment of the GPF (which is outside Bank purview) with the Strategy (IEG 2011b). In 2012, this Strategy and its updated Implementation Plan were published (World Bank 2012).

The updated GAC Strategy incorporated lessons learned from the first five years of GAC Strategy implementation while understanding that slow post-crisis growth, new global emphases on accountability and the G20's increased importance altered the GAC environment. Nonetheless, and as noted by the new Strategy, the Bank's "commitment to governance and anti-corruption remains unequivocal" (World Bank 2012, 14). The GAC was to be "absorbed into the Bank's 'DNA'" (World Bank 2012, 62). With country-first emphases, the updated Strategy emphasized that GAC reforms are context-dependent, knowing that reforms should use (and improve upon) the capacity of country systems, incorporate GAC into country assistance strategies, and refocus GAC activities not just for the public sector but also the "private sector, procurement, and justice" (World Bank 2012, 22). Also crucial was the management of risk—to the Bank as an organization, to the Bank's fiduciary requirements, and to the Bank's need to show project and policy successes.

The Strategy also recommended GAC Council shifts. This includes creating Terms of Reference, encouraging Council accountability, being responsible for results and impact, and rejigging the Council's external advisory group in which its value-added remains. In addition, the updated GAC Strategy desired an alteration of its advisory authority to an executive authority with "strategic and decision-making authority" (World Bank 2012, 54). This decision-making power moved the Council from a coordinating body to one with potential authority over (or least potential conflict with) other sector-specific policies and projects. It also meant the Bank Vice Presidents as members of the Council must "demonstrate that they have cascaded GAC objectives down to the operational level, including Country Directors, Country Managers, and Sector Directors and Managers" (World Bank 2012, 54–55).

The publication of the updated Strategy, the further institutionalization of the GAC Council, and an unrelated end to Zoellick's presidency in 2012 are where this book's 32-year history of policy change within the Bank's PSM/PSG sector agenda comes to an end. This end point is chosen not because the sector would face less emphases in the years that follow (it did not, see Postscript) but because meso-historical studies must choose an appropriate end-date. With the diffusion of this sector's agenda into each of the Bank's sectors, countries, and operational units, its incorporation into post-2007 *World Development Reports*, the elevation of the sector into a GAC Council (the first to obtain that distinction), this book's purpose is complete.

Conclusion: Internal Actors Lead Sector Institutionalization

The PSM/PSG sector not only increased in importance between January 2004 and June 2012 but it became *the* sector of interest at the Bank. Several interrelated factors encouraged its prominence. The most important was that few, if any, bankers suggested that PSM/PSG did not encourage economic growth or poverty reduction. The Bank's belief in this sector's potential solidified as the disagreements of the 1980s and early 1990s were forgotten. By the mid-2000s, internal actors no longer argued about sector necessity but instead, disagreed over the best approach to PSM/PSG for client nations and, as interestingly, whether the sector's prescriptions should also apply to the Bank's own accountability.

During Bank President Paul Wolfowitz's tenure, there were significant differences of opinion on how this sector's policies should be formulated. That Wolfowitz also called out certain bankers and their staff members for lending to corrupt countries (and implicitly considered some Bank staff members as corrupt) further politicized this period. Despite growing divisions between supply-side (PSM) and demand-side (PSG) advocates, the divisions did not halt or slow lending (see Table 1). *If the supply-side approach was consolidated with the 2000 Public Sector Strategy, then the demand-side governance approach was consolidated with the 2007 GAC strategy.*

NIE continued to influence this sector's agenda. Its economists would align with supply-side PSM. To be sure, this association occurred in retrospect since before 2000 neither *supply side* nor *demand side* were words used within the Bank to label each perspective. If the update to the 2000 Public Sector Strategy initially incorporated demand-side ideas, then the 2004 *WDR* further institutionalized demand-side governance. Thus, the 2007 GAC Strategy would become the institutional embodiment of demand-side ideas. Although the Bank's Articles of Agreement disallowed the Bank from associating the word *accountable* with the idea of *democracy*, the Bank noted that citizen participation was important if a client state's public services were to be responsive to its citizenry.

Another source of conflict was the Bank President himself. Wolfowitz's desire to limit Bank lending to corrupt nations was not well-received. Bank staff alleged that the way Wolfowitz went about his ideas, including just stopping projects without Board consultation, left much to be desired. More important was Wolfowitz's interference with one of the Bank's most important internal incentives: lending (see Chapter 4). Lending was tied to the Bank's mission. The Bank's mission was to encourage economic development and poverty reduction within client states. Stopping or at least halting the lending spigot might make it difficult, in a Bank-centered world, for developing nations to develop. It also would make it difficult for the Bank to ask its member-states for increased IDA allocations.

Wolfowitz's critiques about client-country corruption would also have riled Bank recipients. That this message came from someone like Wolfowitz, an architect of an unpopular Iraq War, likely did not help. Although the Bank's clients may complain about Bank conditionalities, the Bank is one of the cheapest sources of developing country monies, worldwide. Given that the Bank had been experiencing a decline in middle-income country borrowings (which was and is a significant portion of Bank lending portfolios), Wolfowitz' calling out corrupt projects and countries might lead to less lending. This would bother interested bankers and the Board. The question became whether it was better to lend to corrupt countries or to wait until their institutional and fiduciary environments improved. The GAC Strategy's answer was that the Bank "will strive to strengthen, rather than bypass, country systems—better national institutions are the more effective and long-term solution to governance and corruption challenges and to mitigating fiduciary risk for all public money, including that from the Bank" (World Bank 2007b, 5).

Although the 2007–2009 Global Financial Crisis did reorient the Bank in certain ways, the PSM/PSG did not lose prestige. Instead, GAC became *the* sectoral centerpiece of Bank work. Sector elevation was cemented with the creation of a GAC Council in 2007—the first sector to ever receive such an elevation—and the further allocation of strategic and decision-making authorities to the Council with the GAC Strategy update in 2012. PSM/PSG, a sector with limited interest in an early 1980s "best state is a small state" Bank, had been transformed into a sector in which every Bank actor must engage.

While the G7 influence remained unchanged between 2005 and 2012, neither the G7 nor the US publicly commented during the Wolfowitz saga (see Table 13). The UK in the midst of the Wolfowitz GAC drama, did temporarily suspend monies targeted for the Bank. The IMF, somewhat chastened by the public beating it took over the Asian Financial Crisis of 1997–1998, returned to its former importance as countries struggled to respond the 2007–2009 Global Financial Crisis. Even if administrative and bureaucratic conflicts between the Bank and Fund had become increasingly common, the 2007 J-MAP agreement intended to resolve such issues. The influence of the US Executive Director and the Treasury remained unchanged from the late 1990s and early 2000s. Their influence over the evolving agenda could be slightly reconsidered as "control," if only because of perceptions that Wolfowitz, more than Wolfensohn or Zoellick, was in the pocket of the American president.

Although interviewees alleged that China and Saudi Arabia were not initially pleased with the 1997 *WDR* or even the 1991 Governance Report, the Reports were approved by the Board. However, when it came to a GAC Strategy with its demand-side governance, both countries increased their vocal protests. The Chinese Executive Director wanted the GAC to not focus on NGO or media efforts aimed at ensuring good governance, and at one point, the Executive Director stopped Wolfowitz from travelling to South Korea to discuss a topic they believed was outside the purview of the Bank's President. By 2012, with a partial diversion of Chinese interest into its newly created Asian Investment Infrastructure Bank and clearer understanding among Bank Board members that approving demand-side governance projects in Chinese or Saudi areas of regional influence may pose challenges, a détente of sorts, was reached. China's policy and operational influence within the Bank continued through this era. This includes influencing the appointments of Shengman Zhang who rose to one of three Managing Director positions (1997–2005) as well as a Bank Chief Economist (Justin Yifu Lin) from June 2008 to June 2012.

Few bankers wanted to stop the fast-moving lending train that was the PSM/PSG agenda. Like the other post-1991 eras, internal actors dominated its policy formulation and its expansion during the 2004–2012 period. This does not mean that the sector's current importance could not be reversed. That the Wolfowitz dramas brought this sector's debates to a more public arena is certainly true, even if their visibility neither increased nor decreased sector lending. Regardless, the public nature of the governance battle certainly raised the profile of the sector for the Bank's staff members and, by extension, increased the global awareness of the need for PSM/PSG.

9

Internal Evaluators and External NGOs

Broken, Distorted, or Ineffective?

This chapter charts the partial interaction of two sets of actors with PSM/PSG policy change: internal Bank evaluators of policies and projects as well as external civil society activists. This interaction is portrayed across 32 years of Bank PSM/PSG history. The chapter begins with a discussion of the Bank's Operations Evaluation Department (OED) later renamed the Internal Evaluation Group (IEG). The OED was created in 1973 in the years before structural adjustment and many years before "global civil society" was a term used to describe third sector activities.

The Bank's early evaluative system gave space for civil society to express substantial concerns about Bank policies. Civil society's ability to effect change within international organizations, including the Bank, has been hotly debated (Anderl et al. 2021; Edwards 2009; Ebrahim and Herz 2007; Paul and Israel 1990; Philipps 2009; Dellmuth and Bloodgood 2019). Whether or not one wishes to credit NGOs for altering the Bank's structural adjustment agenda or encouraging discussion of corruption depends on one's perspective. These debates are important.

But this book seeks to explain policy change within the one sector of the Bank's work: PSM/PSG. Despite sector importance, there is a surprisingly lack of discussion about whether and how NGOs did or did not support this sector's policy emergence. Following the pattern set in other chapters, the NGOs studied were identified by interviewees at the Bank, Fund, and other NGOs as the most relevant actors for this sector. Even then, at least two of the NGOs (Transparency International and the Bank Information Center reacted with puzzlement when approached for an interview. The latter because their work largely focuses on the environment sector and the former because despite founding leader's role in creating TI and interacting with the Bank's early PSG and anticorruption agendas, the TI of today interacts less with the Bank than it did in the early 1990s.

This chapter details why some NGOs like the Bank Information Center, 50 Years is Enough, and Public Sector International had limited-to-no sector policy influence at the Bank. In contrast, Transparency International and International Budget Project had some influence. Or how during the Wolfowitz and Bank staff spat over the GAC Strategy, questions were raised as to whether the interest of the Bank's

Who Matters at the World Bank? Kim Moloney, Oxford University Press.
© Kim Moloney (2022). DOI: 10.1093/oso/9780192857729.003.0009

staff in NGO opinions was genuine or instead, an instrumental use of NGOs to ensure that the staff "won" their debate against Wolfowitz.

This question of NGO influence leads to discussion of four internal evaluative actors created at the Bank during the 1990s to early 2000s period. The first two are the now-disbanded Results Secretariat and Quality Assurance Group. The second are the still-operational Institutional Integrity (INT) aka the Integrity Vice Presidency and the Inspection Panel. With the partial exception of the Inspection Panel, NGOs did not have a key role in encouraging each evaluative actor's creation or its operation. Instead, the first two disbanded given significant institutional lending imperatives, questions of measurement, and how to penalize poor performers. Each issue was noted by the Wapenhans Report (see Chapter 4). The latter two internal actors, while still operational, infrequently interact with the PSM/PSG section either due to their non-sector focus and lack of desire to split internal complaints into project or policy sectors (INT) or because the operational policies which are the bedrock of Panel interaction do not include PSM/PSG policies.

The output is an answer that internal evaluation actors and external NGOs have had limited influence on this sector's agenda and its policy changes. Although Transparency International, the International Budget Project, along with NGO interactions with the Panel and later, the Wolfowitz drama over the GAC Strategy did involve some NGO interaction, the reality is that the PSM/PSG sector is not home to significant and sustained civil society influence. Reasons for this output are highlighted throughout the chapter.

Early Evaluative Loops: Broken or Just Unpublished?

The Bank's OED was created in 1973 to evaluate Bank projects after their completion. Throughout the 1970s and 1980s, OED (renamed the Independent Evaluation Group or IEG in 2006) was the Bank's only formal internal feedback loop. The earliest OED reports were not made available to the general public with an external distribution just to other donors (Coronel 1986). By the late 1970s, OED had reviewed 100 percent of completed projects but by the early 1980s, this dropped to 50 percent. Although project-completion reports were to be written by Bank staff, 25 percent of projects had no completed reports by 1984 (World Bank 2003b, 48). During the mid-1980s, just half of the Project Completion Reports were submitted for an OED audit (Coronel 1986).

Specific to this book's sector, I found no OED documents published in the 1980s that evaluated PSM policies or its projects with the exception of one 1986 study on structural adjustment loans. That study examined fifteen structural adjustment loans in ten countries and found that just four countries benefitted from the loans, two did not benefit or were hurt by the process, and four showed mixed results. In trying to explain this result, then OED Director-General Yves Rovani noted that structural adjustment loans "are rather difficult to evaluate because structural adjustment involves the intersection of many variables about which we still have much to learn" (Coronel 1986, 5).

Two other early sector-specific evaluative studies were not written by OED but other Bank Units. A 1985 study by the Bank's Country Analysis and Project Unit (later made defunct through reorganization) reviewed twenty-two structural adjustment loan projects from the four years preceding the study. The authors concluded that not only were neoliberal prescriptions right, but structural adjustment should retain its big-project, big-reform focus. The report did not say that structural adjustment's distributional consequences were not Bank priorities: "[Structural adjustment loans] do not take explicit account of distributional consequences of their policy measures. Transitory conflict may exist between employment/income distribution and other objectives of the [structural-adjustment loans]" (Yagci et al. 1985, 20–21). Instead, distributional consequences were merely "transitory" issues.

The other evaluative effort was published in the Bank and Fund's joint journal in 1989. It was the first evaluation (that I could find) of institutional reform projects. The authors observed,

> Institutional reforms of the public sector, promoted by almost every adjustment program, have been slow. Some success has been achieved in holding back the creation of new enterprises and the growth of employment in them. Some public enterprises have reduced their losses, but largely through price increases permitted by their monopoly position, rather than through improvements in their efficiency. Efforts to improve resource use in utility companies have proved elusive and their financial losses remain high. Few of the reforms attempted have had much impact on planning, policy analysis, or debt management in the public sector … It is too early to evaluate the performance of enterprises because their privatization.
>
> (Thomas and Chhibber 1989)

With just three evaluative efforts, PSM projects (both structural adjustment and institutional development) appeared to run nearly blind. Without significant internal feedback, project and country team leaders could move to the next project before they knew if the last project failed or succeeded. The lack of publicly available reports suggests that the evaluative feedback loop that was supposed to strengthen and improve subsequent projects was broken, at least for this sector.

In an indication of tensions between the Bank's evaluative arm and the rest of Bank staff, other problems also existed. An early OED Director (Mervyn Weiner 1975 to 1984) recalled that "colleagues who had been asked to comment on draft reports concerning operations in which they had been directly involved … were deeply bothered by the way differences in views were handled. That there were differences is not surprising. Multiple observers inevitably have differing perspectives, especially when their views are shaped by varying experience. OED's staff and consultants at the time had little experience with Bank operations or direct knowledge of their history and context" (World Bank 2003b, 18–19). There were many problems. From budgetary and managerial issues to project-completion reports being written by the client countries to delayed project audits, to simply a Bank incentive structure that did not require (or seem to put too much credence into) staff evaluation. As the Bank's projects expanded and became more complex, the numbers of staff assigned to each project increased. Such increases made it difficult to pinpoint who should take the blame if a project failed. These faults were not limited to the PSM policies and projects but instead, were present throughout the Bank.

The OED's next Director-General (Yves Rovani) served from 1986 to 1992. He believed "the evaluative capacity of the Bank was being undermined to some extent" by weak presidential support. OED also had a "management problem" because "the department as such existed only on paper. There were no central administrative functions to speak of. There was no budgeting. There was no cost information. Common services were absent" (World Bank 2003b, 32). Culturally, OED staff members felt "very alienated. There was no team spirit. Many had been transferred to OED against their will. They were offended by the fact that they'd been moved to the M Building, which was way down near where the IFC is today" (World Bank 2003b, 46).

Under Rovani, OED was auditing just 40 percent of completed projects. OED also faced delays between project completion and when OED received the Project Completion Report. This was due to a 1980 decision to let client countries submit a project completion report. Rovani thought the idea was initially "well meant" (World Bank 2003b, 34):

> The borrowers were supposed to do a good job of reviewing them, and the re-ports would be sent to OED, and everybody would be happy. But the facts were otherwise. Anybody who had been involved in project supervision, as I have for a good part of my life, and who has seen the kind of reporting that comes out of borrowers or projects, could tell you that PCRs [project completion reports] would be handled in many cases *by a clerk in a backroom, to satisfy the letter of what the Bank was asking ... This decay mean that the whole [evaluative] system as conceived by McNamara ... was about to crumble.*
>
> (World Bank 2003b, 34, emphasis added)

Despite its best efforts, many interviewees agreed that the OED had little impact on the Bank or its PSM policies. And once OED had finished an audit, staff com-plained: "'Well, that's very nice, but we don't do this type of operations anymore,' or 'this is all very fine, but it's old stuff, you know. It's old stuff.' One reason they were right is that our studies took forever to produce" (World Bank 2003b, 35).

An exception was an OED report on Africa that indicated the Bank's work was "glaringly bad." The blame was put on Africa's poor institutional capacity. In this case, the OED report did influence the Bank to create a PSMU within the African Regional Office in 1985 (WB6, see also Chapter 4 and 5).

Another insight was that OED's results infrequently fed into new "learning" (WB30). Looking historically, an interviewee stated: "In the 1970s, on accountability the answer was Not to worry. We are a long-term development organization. No way to measure what is achieved. So, can't make a difference. It could be the weather, a government change; you are also one of 7-8 project folks" (WB26). Pointing to staff incentives, staff might say, "[OED] can say what they want to say, but I [as project coordinator] don't have to listen. If they are going to prize their independence, so will I." That view made it "tough" to "structure your evaluation units. If you want them to be part of your learning process, then [you] can't have them [with] independence. At the same time, independence allows scathing reviews but then again, no one has to read it" (WB30). Others were more succinct in their evaluation of OED impact. They said OED had "no impact" (WB25), that it was internally viewed by Bank staff to be the Bank's "Gestapo" (WB26) and/or its time lag was too great for OED feedback to impact subsequent projects (WB12).

Even so, how can Bank staff still ignore OED (IEG) even today? The answer is that the Bank's incentive systems remain off-kilter. The "fundamental problem in the Bank—and it continues today—is that staff, and by implication, managers, bear none of the risk of project failures... Essentially, if a project fails, it's too bad for the borrower but very little consequence for the Bank staff because they have either moved on or it just does not happen" (WB8). My interviewee continued,

I have never seen or heard of a person who was let go because their project was not satisfactory. Reputation counts. The Bank runs on reputational capital, not money. There is differentiation in people's salaries between levels but it's not that wide. I mean, it is significant, we are talking real dollars but, it's not like the difference between executive-level in the private sector and worker bee ... In my personal opinion the currency of the Bank is reputation ... If you are associated with a lot of projects that fail, there will be some reputational effect, but if you happen to also turn out really interesting analytical pieces, the project failures will show very little relative to the idea that you are smart. So, the smart people that succeed become managers; smart and clever tends to be defined internally to the Bank rather than the relative to the performance of projects on the ground. That is a pretty sweeping generalization and there will be important exceptions at either end. And significant ones ... So, for me, what has been the most fundamental point all the way through the experience I have had in the Bank is that *if a project fails, it's too bad for the borrower [but] not a real consequence for the staff.*

(WB8, emphasis added)

Further contextualizing his or her comments, the interviewed noted,

> Mostly where you see failure is in places where it is hard to count. A lot of quote failure may be due to not knowing how to measure success or failure, so you end up transferring a bunch of resources and whether or not they have done any good is not clear. And you have a lot of Bank staff, certainly in the 1980s, my experience, and a lot of my seniors, felt the Bank's mission was resource transfer and what happened to the resources was up to the borrower ... The implication of that is very straight-forward but the Bank seems to not have grasped. If the use of resources that the Bank has transferred is up to the borrower ... most of IEG effort or the QAG effort has been focused on Bank behavior *rather than understanding what determines bureaucratic political behavior and performance at the country level.*
>
> (WB8, emphasis added)

In other words, staff simply do not have to listen. One's Bank career does not end if a staff member is associated with a bad Bank project. OED/IEG independence from the Bank's President and the Executive Directors further separated any potential effort to sway its outputs. There is no number of evaluative improvements, new alternative methods, or scientization (e.g., Marcussen 2006) of the evaluation process that can alter this reality. Since multiple staff members are involved in creating, implementing, and monitoring a project (and since the mid-1990s even more staff members have become involved in the process), it is difficult to pinpoint which particular staff "caused" the problem. Further difficulties arise when Bank staff start projects but are promoted or move to another project before the original project finishes. Staff might also argue that even the best-planned project will not work if the client is only half-interested in the concept or is unable to prevent corruptive influences from diverting or altering project outcomes. Since the organizational reform of the mid-1990s (see Chapter 6), more staff than ever have been consulted on Bank projects. An outcome of greater input or "project design by committee" is that figuring out who should be blamed when the project fails remains far from clear. Perhaps it is no surprise given this evaluative environment that civil society's agitation grew increasingly vocal and began, in a small way, to influence the Bank.

Civil Society Enters Bank Conversations

The late 1980s and early 1990s were transformative for early anti-Bank NGO movements. Within a decade, global NGOs moved from unconnected issue groups into loosely organized movements, many of whom were sharply critical. The Bank and the Fund were viewed as *de facto* organizational representatives of the Washington

Consensus (Qureshi 1991; for a general discussion, see also Johnson 2014, 43–44; Ebrahim and Herz 2007; Park 2005).

Sporadic NGO-led protests about specific Bank projects began in the mid-1980s. NGO-led protests of Fund and Bank activities broadened in the early 1990s and by the early 2000s, protests had become regular features of Bank-Fund Fall and Spring Meetings. At the Prague Bank–Fund meetings in 2000, one estimate placed 15,000 protestors outside of where the meetings were being held. Both the Prague (2000) and Washington DC (2001) protests were so disruptive that the meetings were shortened (Malena 2000; Nelson 2000; Spiro 1995).

Scholars have debated the importance of anti-Bank NGO movements, their impact, and their dilemmas (Stackhouse 1994; Ferren and Montgomery 1994; Park 2005). Protestor wishes varied. Some anti-Bank and anti-Fund activists preferred to shout "World Bank, murderers," others wanted more "socially and environmentally responsible development," and still others preferred increased cooperation with the Bank (Moran 2000; Malena 2000). Some activists wanted the Bank and Fund to "dissolve" while others accepted the Bank's offer to meet with them (Economist 2000). Noting that protestors were well-organized but not part of an "intellectually coherent movement," *The Economist* wrote that the protestors "loath[ed] ... the established world order and ... the IMF, the World Bank, and the [World Trade Organization]—which they regarded as either running it or serving it" (Economist 2000).

It is likely true that anti-Bank protests encouraged the Bank to consider (at least theoretically) structural adjustment's implications. But despite such protests continuing into the early 2000s, structural adjustment and privatization had already become less important within the PSM/PSG policy portfolio (see Chapters 5–7). On the other hand, anti-Bank NGOs did publicize the plight of people to whom the NGOs felt had been left behind. By 1990 and 1991 the Bank began to quietly question whether the Bank's neoliberal emphasis was the only path toward development. Whether the proximate cause to that forthcoming shift was NGO publicity, increased social unrest in certain developing countries, or the opening provided by the Soviet collapse, change was afoot in the early 1990s (see Chapter 5). Or, as noted by an NGO interviewee, perhaps their influence would always be incomplete since the "The Bank ... is not capable of learning" (WB43). That is, outside advocacy can encourage Bank accountability but the reality was that "you create [a] mechanism, identify the problem, put some constraints on it, what the Bank learns is how to adapt to that, how to isolate it, learn how to deal with the problems" (WB43).

Although the G8 noted in 1999 that NGOs "have an important role to play" in international development (G8 1999), no other G7/8 or US statement mentioned

NGO protests. Even so, one of the first formal fig leaves to the NGO community occurred at the 1997 Annual Meetings in Hong Kong when Wolfensohn offered to meet with six NGOs (Bello 2000). It was alleged that Wolfensohn had co-opted the NGOs by bringing them into a Bank meeting since Wolfensohn had not really planned to implement their suggestions.

As such, the apparent NGO involvement in Bank activities "legitimized" the Bank and over time "these NGOs would develop a stake in maintaining the formal relationship with the Bank" (Bello 2000). By bringing in certain NGOs and not others, Wolfensohn could "split the Washington DC NGO community" (NGO Working Group 1995, 4). One Bank interviewee considered Wolfensohn's NGO outreach differently. That is, Wolfensohn "was a 'connector' … a believer in listening to the outside world. He tried to use the voice of NGOs and the clients to somehow clobber the Bank staff and [its] arrogance and difficulties to change the institution. In some ways … as an investment banker, he understood that client satisfaction was important. This put some pressure on the Bank to make changes" (WB6)

Wolfensohn's efforts were not new. Even if it was more public and more grand than prior Bank efforts. One early effort was an "NGO Working Group on the World Bank" which published its first statement on the World Bank in 1990.[1] In 1991, this Group's Saly Declaration engaged two issues: strengthening their anti-structural adjustment case and encouraging greater participation from the world's poor. By 1995, the Working Group had evaluated three Bank-written success stories of structural adjustment including Mexico, Senegal, and Sri Lanka. They argued that although structural adjustment's emphasis on privatization "contributed substantially to improving [the Mexican government's] current fiscal situation," the costs of further sequestering wealth in the hands of a few elite Mexicans, structural adjustment's social spending cuts, and failures of its tax reforms to lessen the "unequal distribution" of wealth were sufficient causes for concern (NGO Working Group 1995, 6). The Working Group recommended "in the wake of increasing protests against adjustment, a serious review of the Bank's policies must be undertaken. The lending process must respond to local development needs rather than impose a uniform series of macroeconomic policies globally; in other words, theoretical prescriptions of adjustment need to be radically altered to ensure policies derive from local realities. Putting this into practice requires a continuing interchange of ideas between grassroots groups, NGOs, the governments, and multilateral development banks" (NGO Working Group 1995, 22).

While such local-first rhetoric matters, the PSG agenda had begun to encompass many of those ideas in the early 1990s. In subsequent years, the Bank would publicly release its country assessments, encourage participatory rural approaches, create datasets like the Good Governance Indicators, and later, publish its CPIA

---

[1] I was unable to find a copy.

indicators. Its new public transparency had as much as to do with an evolving good governance agenda as it had to with Wolfensohn's matrix reforms and desires to transform the Bank into a "knowledge bank" (Goldman 2007; Enns 2015; IEG 2013).

Sector Policy Shifts: When NGOs Did Not Matter

But what about NGO interaction with specific PSM/PSG sector policy shifts? Did NGOs advocate in this sector? The answer is both "no" and "yes." This section and the next two sections explain this ambiguous answer. That is, with the partial exceptions of Transparency International, the International Budget Partnership, and the Wolfowitz-GAC Strategy debates, NGOs have had limited influence upon PSM/PSG policy changes during the 1980–2012 period. Moreover, the NGOs chosen for this section and the next were suggested initially by Bank interviewee and then later, the NGOs. When NGO interviewees were asked if there were any other NGOs who should be interviewed for their potential PSM/PSG influence, the answer was "no." In short, between 1980 and 2012, there were few sector-specific NGOs with an interest in PSM/PSG policy shifts.

One of the NGOs with potential influence was the Bank Information Center (BIC). In the early 1990s, the BIC strengthened its coordinating role among NGOs vis-à-vis the Bank and in particular, on environmental issues.[2] But did its coordination and influence extend to other sectors? No. While one Bank interviewee recalled that BIC "had a lot of access" during the Wolfensohn era, access need not imply that BIC used access to engage PSM/PSG change. By the late 1990s, BIC's anti-Bank advocacy had evolved from shaming Bank environmental efforts to trying to access largely non-public (at the time) Bank project documents. The goal was to obtain project details so that BIC advocacy could more effectively critique Bank projects. While one result of that focus, along with strategic lobbying of key Members of the US Congress during an IDA replenishment period, was the creation of the Inspection Panel in 1994 (discussed later in this chapter), another was BIC's increased interest in Bank transparency.

In response to Bank non-transparencies, BIC drafted a "Transparency Charter" in 2006. The Charter encouraged fuller disclosure of Bank activities (Batam 2006). The BIC conducted workshops in developing countries where civil society leaders, journalists, and other interested parties met to "create awareness about protection of rights, participation, transparency, and public accountability in governance

---

[2] Constructivists have studied the relationship between the Bank and environmental NGOs (Weaver 2008, 64–66) while others are more explicit in their critique of the Bank's environmentalism (Rich 1994). Still others explore which external and internal factors may favor an incorporation of environmental policy into the Bank (Le Prestre 1989). Similar discussions are largely absent for the PSM/PSG sector. This is despite PSM/PSG prominence within Bank lending.

and operations of the World Bank" (Anonymous 2006). Worried that developing countries were too reliant on the Bank to provide government statistics, BIC began publishing "tool kits" for NGOs and governments to interact with and understand the Bank. This included how to find Bank information, how to interaction with Bank Country Assistance Strategies, and to understand how the Bank makes policy, how it lends, and what the Inspection Panel can or cannot do (WB43, WB48).

Another early anti-Bank effort was the "50 Years is Enough" campaign. This movement believed that 50 years after the IMF and Bank were founded, they had done enough "development" and "harm" and thus, they should either be closed or at a minimum, operate under modified mission statements. Structural adjustment, privatization, and the Washington Consensus were rallying cries for anti-Bank activists who considered Bank policies as pro-West and anti-poor (Philipps 2009). At an NGO-led International Forum on World Bank and IMF Adjustment Lending in 1992, NGOs argued that structural adjustment was "undermining the well-being of families, food producers, workers and the natural environment, as well as the viability of fragile democracies, this movement is attempt to force a fundamental shift in development thinking in both the North and the South" (Hammond and McGowan 1992, preface). The Forum's output coalesced into a 1994 platform (50 Years Is Enough 1994) that would transform itself into a broad-based, multi-NGO protest movement (Development GAP n.d.; Hammond and McGowan 1992).

Both BIC and 50 Years is Enough had unique foci. The BIC wanted environmental reform and later, Bank transparency, while 50 Years is Enough wanted debt reform. Neither was focused on PSM/PSG in client countries, on PSM/PSG in the Bank's work, or even had an interest in improving client country public sectors. *It is arguable that it was easier to mobilize for the environment or debt relief but harder to suggest good governance was not a good idea. In addition, many NGOs in the 1990s and early 2000s focused on sweeping generalizations about the Bank and not the technical details of public expenditure reform, the details of civil service reform, or whether the Bank's financial management sequencing were appropriate.*

Sector Policy Shifts: When NGOs (Sort of) Mattered

There are three partial exceptions to the "NGOs do not engage PSM/PSG" rule: Public Sector International (PSI), Transparency International (TI), and the International Budget Partnership (IBP). However, as noted in the next section, there was one major difference: The Bank did not like PSI ideas but did accept TI and IBP ideas. The next paragraphs detail each NGOs interaction with the World Bank.

Founded in 1907, PSI is an association of public sector unions around the world. Its first position paper on the Bank's public sector reform policies was published in 1993. PSI worried "the public sector throughout the world has underdone radical surgery in the last decade" (PSI 1993, 7). PSI characterized the 1980s period as focused on "monetarism," "radical deregulation," and "privatization" and was concerned that public sector unions were "powerless" against such reforms (PSI 1993, 7–8). PSI was slightly optimistic that the Bank's 1991 *WDR* hinted that the state may have a role in development might become a Bank objective. But lacking faith in the Bank, PSI asked public sector unions to resist privatization. In 1995, PSI published "A Public Sector Alternative Strategy" for its trade union members. Unions and governments were asked "to cooperate as a counterweight to the globalization of the economy" by encouraging progressive reforms ("change not destroy"), union involvement, and a greater acknowledgement that the public sector must be "enhanced" in "directing and promoting investment and economic growth" (PSI 1995, 3, 6, 21).

In 1997, PSI found that "37 businessmen who already owned between them about a quarter of the country's [Mexico] gross national product were the main buyers in all but one of the sales or liquidations of nearly 1,000 enterprises" (PSI 1997c, 11). Similar allegations were made elsewhere. PSI suggested that former "*nomenclatura* and Mafia elements accumulate[d] the lion's share of privatized assets in former communist countries, especially Russia" (PSI 1997a, 3–4; WB41). The elite purchases of state assets worried PSI. For an association of public sector unions, privatization harmed workers and the poor. Newly privatized entities also did not employ public sector workers, the people that PSI represented.

As part of his outreach to NGOs, Wolfensohn used discretionary funds in the first years of his presidency to hire PSI trade unionists for three-month Bank contracts. One of PSI's national representatives received one of four available assignments. However, according to an NGO interviewee, "[Mr. X's] experience at the Bank was 'awful' because the Bank's public sector staff appeared to 'regard his presence as an intrusion'" (WB49). Instead, he had become simply the secretary of a female staffer and in the end, did very little. He was apparently "furious" about his treatment and wrote a complaint letter to Wolfensohn (WB49). The NGO interviewee reported that Wolfensohn was "embarrassed" and arranged for [Mr. X] to meet several senior Bank officials. The meeting outcome was to be a new Bank public sector contact point for PSI (WB49). However, when that contact point was created, the contact point was same female staff that had led to the PSI complaint. As such, a consultative progress appeared to exist, but in practice, consultation with incorporation of PSI concerns did not exist (WB49).

During the 1997 *WDR* drafting process, PSI suggested "hundreds of changes" (WB39) to Bank reports. Bank responses to PSI suggestions were at times "friendly" and other times "hostile" (WB49). One banker recalled PSI as being "very involved" in the 1997 *WDR* and that the World Bank "worked with them on the outline and ... we presented at their Annual Conference" (WB39). However, PSI's preference for the Bank to consult a country's public sector unions never went far. In other words, if the Bank consulted public sector unions, then privatization might never go ahead (WB49). The alternatives were clear: "Governments have to choose: either they want workers and their unions as part of the solution to current problems or they want them in united opposition" (PSI 1997b, 3). PSI called on the IMF and Bank to "be reformed and refocused towards good government, greater consultation with civil society (including trade unions), employment, human rights, core labor standards and poverty reduction" and that "unions should lobby their governments to use their voting strength on the governing bodies of these institutions to change their policies" (Mortisugu 2000). In the end, the Bank made the appearance of listening to PSI but because its public sector union emphases differed so dramatically from the PSM/PSG agenda—whether PSM of the 1980s, good governance of the 1990s, or supply- and demand-side in the 2000s—the Bank could not truly listen.[3]

In contrast, Transparency International focused on anticorruption. Anticorruption was a key component of Bank PSM/PSG agendas starting in the mid-1990s. TI was formed in 1993 by Peter Eigen. Eigen was a former Bank staffer. Eigen had left the Bank in the early 1990s to create TI given frustrations he had experienced with project corruption (WB4, WB50). One banker thought Eigen's idea was a "daring thing to do" given the "C" word [corruption] was not part of [the Bank's] mandate. If one came across it, [you] did not do anything about it. Eigen's impact [as TI] was on the rank-and-file of the Bank staff ... He promoted a vision. The Bank staff who knew him, aided and abetted him" (WB26). The TI agenda was to fight corruption. For the Bank, "this meant (a) to encourage the Bank to be the proper steward of its own money. To make sure its own funds 'reach their intended purposes' [quoting the Bank's Articles of Agreement], their fiduciary responsibilities" (WB50) and (b) the "Bank is a big player in many of the countries so it could be driving, promoting, governance reform in those countries" (WB50).

Unlike PSI, TI "was close to Wolfensohn" and TI "did the most pushing on the Bank" on anticorruption issues (WB31). Another Bank interviewee viewed TI even more favorably: Wolfensohn "raised the visibility of the issue—he made TI a 'partner'" (WB26) rather than the other way around. Either way, no other public sector NGO had as much high-level interaction as TI with the Bank. This includes sending 1997 *WDR* drafts to Eigen (WB39). By 1997, *The Economist* considered TI to be the "world's main anticorruption lobbyist" (Economist 1997). As a former Bank insider, Eigen knew the Bank's rules of engagement. His strategy was threefold: to encourage developing and developed countries to disengage from corrupt practices and to encourage organizations such as the Bank to have "strict

---

[3] By 1998, PSI had largely left the Bank's radar. Even a 2008 speech by Bank President Robert Zoellick to the International Labour Organisation did not focus on PSI-like demands (Zoellick 2008c).

accounting procedures" on their projects so that client country officials or even Bank staff could not profit from or siphon away development monies (McIntyre 1996).

The third NGO with partial PSM/PSG influence is the International Budget Partnership (IBP). Starting in the mid-2000s, IBP began working closely with the IMF and Bank on developing countries' budget transparency. IBP created a "Civil Society Budget Initiative" with the Bank and other NGOs to encourage developing country civil societies to monitor their country's national budget. This includes several years of testing budget transparency indicators with IBP, the Bank, and the Fund. Each created multiple interaction opportunities often on technical issues. These conversations have also led to close IBP interaction with the Bank's PEFA Indicators and the IMF's Fiscal Transparency Code (see also Moloney and Stoycheva 2018). This includes IBP advocacy that the Bank and Fund encourage client countries to allow citizens to access their national budgets including draft budgets and to create Auditor-Generals (WB43, WB48). In 2018, the IBP released its sixth iteration of indicators, a process began in 2006. That an NGO like IBP would, in 2018, actually host is a global release event for its indicators at the World Bank is in part, an indication of how far some Bank-NGO interactions had changed since the early 1990s.

Sector Policy Shifts: Who "Uses" Whom?

Civil society activism and anti-Bank protests of the 1990s and early 2000s did not always imply NGO influence over the Bank. As noted in Chapter 8, internal discord over the GAC Strategy and Wolfowitz' actions spilled out into the press. The resulting portrayal was of a Bank at war with itself. This created an opportunity for NGOs to opine about the Bank's internal turmoil. There are at least two ways to view the subsequent Bank-NGO action on this Strategy and on Wolfowitz. The first is to observe that late 2006 and early 2007 were the first time that the Bank had extensively consulted NGOs on the drafting of *any* Bank sector strategy whether PSM/PSG or not. It is possible this GAC Strategy interaction had been influenced by Wolfensohn's NGO outreaches a decade prior or perhaps also, technocratic NGOs like TI or IBP who could speak *Bankease*. Another view, and certainly a more cynical one, is that given the Bank staffs "war" against Wolfowitz (Edwards 2009), staff actually needed civil society to help them overrule Wolfowitz. Not only would NGOs back the staffs' GAC Strategy but they might also argue that counter to the Wolfowitz view, lending some monies to the developing countries (even if the countries were corrupt) was better than politically motivated decisions on which countries should receive Bank lending. Even so, not all NGOs were amenable to Bank consultation. One NGO interviewee wryly noted that any participating NGO to a Bank consultation risked being labelled an opportunist.

Why so? Because "no serious, genuine group will want to engage with the Bank because they would be afraid of being seen as getting in bed with the Bank" (WB50).

Nonetheless, the consultation progressed. In the Bank's first-ever world-wide consultation with NGOs, the Bank interacted with over 3200 "stakeholders" in forty-seven countries (twelve of which were donor countries) during a ten-week period between November 10, 2006 and January 26, 2007 on the evolving GAC Strategy (World Bank 2007b, 68). The Bank consulted fifty-one times (thirty-five were in developing countries) with "multiple stakeholders including governments, donors, civil society organizations, private sector, academic institutions, parliamentarians and other interested parties" (World Bank 2007b, 68). Boosting staff claims against Wolfowitz's attempt to block Bank funding for countries misappropriating Bank funds, GAC Strategy authors found that

> the message that perhaps came out most strongly was not "whether" but "how" the WBG [World Bank Group] can stay engaged in countries with weak governance, and how it can be a useful partner to countries in promoting GAC reforms. There was also widespread support that the WBG should engage more systematically in GAC work with a broad range of stakeholders, including civil society, media, the private sector and others outside the executive branch, including parliamentarians and the judiciary. Other main messages that emerged were that the GAC Strategy should put more focus on: strengthening country systems versus ring-fencing individual projects; improving transparency, participation and third-party monitoring of WBG operations; linking governance monitoring to governance reforms; and the WBG harmonizing its efforts with other donors and global actors.
>
> (World Bank 2007b, 69)

Whether such consultations formally moved the needle on the GAC or whether other factors such as Wolfowitz' personal scandals (see Chapter 8) influenced either the Strategy or Wolfowitz' departure, NGOs certainly had their say. And yet despite that say, there were no more NGOs exclusively focused on PSM/PSG sector policies by 2012 than in prior years. NGOs tend not to advocate for the public sector either in general or in specific terms. Instead, the "good governance" term first published by the Bank in August 1991 has become so diffused not only into Bank conversations but also into NGO, state, corporate, and foundation engagements. By the last years of the first decade of the 2000s, the semiannual protests before Bank and Fund meetings had all but stopped. The anti-Bank NGO movements had moved on.

Evaluation and Results: One Step Forward, Two Steps Back

Just as anti-Bank protests wound down, the Bank's internal evaluative efforts increased in importance. Less clear is whether such evaluations changed staff motivations, sector policies, and/or improved PSM/PSG projects. To explain, the next several sections analyze the Results Secretariat before discussing the Quality Assurance Group (QAG), the Institutional Integrity Vice Presidency (INT), and the Inspection Panel. Of the four, it is arguable that NGOs partially helped create the Panel but had limited influence on the other three evaluative outputs. There is limited information about the role of the Executive Directors encouraging each evaluative mechanism. It is expected that the IMF would have limited interest on what is an internal evaluative matter at the Bank. As such, the stories which follow are largely "within the Bank" considerations while the fourth, an Inspection Panel, had both inside and outside perspectives.

To relate our first story about the Results Secretariat, we must step back into Wolfensohn's presidency. In line with his effort to create a "knowledge bank," Wolfensohn was concerned with staff "decapitalization" and skill currency retention (WB29). Avoiding decapitalization was linked with his desire to improve Bank effectiveness and to have a results-oriented Bank. To do this, Wolfensohn led

a major effort to, if you will, update the management by developing a program called the Executive Development Program, which was designed by the Harvard Business School and the Kennedy School of Government and trained about 600 senior Bank managers. And in my view, I went through that in late 1990s with a whole lot of senior people, Harvard's major message that if you guys don't get a grip on your effectiveness, you will die. So, a huge theme in that [Executive Developmental Program] course was, how do we get a better grip? And in many ways, the Bank was trying to respond ... That's roughly the period that the Quality Assurance Group got its legs.

(WB8)

Course attendance at the Harvard program was viewed as a way to attack the Bank's "marshmallow middle" of senior managers and to potentially change Bank culture (Mallaby 2004, 165). The "Comprehensive Development Framework" (launched in 1999) tried to articulate cumulative lessons learned in development practice. The PSM subtopic of public financial management was highlighted as key. In other words, client countries tended to manage aid dollars and projects in governmental units separated from the rest of the government. With weak internal financial management, institutional fragmentation was the result. Managing for results suggested more Bank-led Public Expenditure Reviews and increased statistical capacity in client countries. However, and in 2000, a Bank Working Group concluded that its monitoring and evaluation remained a "persistent problem" (World Bank 2005a, 7).

It would not be until March 2002 when the broader international development community met in Monterrey Mexico to discuss aid effectiveness that movement on the "results agenda" occurred. The "Monterrey Consensus" committed world leaders to achieving the MDGs [Millennium Development Goals] and to acting with "sound policies, good governance at all levels and the rule of law" (UNESA 2002; Weaver and Moschella 2017). New to high-level international discussions on foreign aid was paragraph 43 in which foreign donors were to focus making aid more "effective." A month later, the Bank's Development Committee "underlined the importance of an enhanced focus on results" for the Bank and its clients (Development Committee 2002). Two and half months after Monterrey, the OECD-DAC and multilateral development banks convened to take stock of their results-focused approaches. By September 2002, the World Bank published its own report, "Better Measuring, Monitoring, and Managing for Development Results" which provided a framework for Bank action.

In its 2002 report, the Bank noted that its culture must be altered if results-oriented approaches at the project conception, implementation, and evaluation stages were to take hold. The Bank wrote that low-income countries' Poverty Reduction Strategy Papers needed revision if policy goals contained within the Papers were to be linked to detailed implementation plans and results-based analysis. Operationally, the 2002 Bank report recognized that "the two sides of the Bank's management matrix bear collective responsibility for achieving the desired results" (World Bank 2002c, 10). In the case of PSM/PSG, this included the Public Sector Board, the Public Sector Anchor, and the regions and countries with ongoing sector projects (IEG 2013). As a consequence, sector-specific strategy papers had to incorporate results-based considerations. The Bank's Annual Report on Portfolio Performance would also add the word *results* to its title and begin results-based reporting.

The Bank desired results-based reporting among all units and projects even if the Bank acknowledged that aggregating "different kinds of results" (across sectors and regions) would be problematic (World Bank 2002c, 11). Results-reporting would be limited to annual measurements "in terms of outputs and intermediate outcomes related to real-time actions, rather than program and country outcomes that will be realized only after long variable lags" (World Bank 2002c, 11). *This was an important statement. The wording disallowed the Bank from being held entirely responsible if long-term programmatic or country projects created imperfect outcomes.* The Bank viewed itself as just one factor within a country's development. This is true in any country but it is particularly true for middle-income countries for which development assistance was a tiny proportion of a nation's budget. The Bank worried that short-term results may not translate into long-term victories and that "results-padding" might distort on-the-ground progress (World Bank 2002c). The Bank also committed its human resources department to discovering how promotion might be more closely linked to results (World Bank 2002a, 64). In its 2002 Annual Review of Development Effectiveness, the Bank expected by fiscal year 2004, an "operational mainstreaming" of the Bank's "results focus" would be underway (World Bank 2002a, 34).

But was that just talk? My Results Secretariat interviewees provided a nuanced answer. The Secretariat was created in response to the Monterrey discussions (and later, the 2005 Paris Declaration on Aid Effectiveness). Located within the Operations Vice Presidency (but importantly, not in the PREM, the Sector Boards, or OED/IEG), the Secretariat functioned with a skeletal staff. By late 2008, the Secretariat had no more than four full-time staff. Still, the Secretariat continued to receive increased budget monies for its work (WB5, WB8), and when officials overspent the budget, the Secretariat was often able to obtain more money. Even so, my interviewee said, "the internal management of the budget in the Bank is one of the most disgusting things you could ever know" (WB8). To get more resources, my interviewee "leaned to get other parts of the Bank to use their resources" on results (WB8). This is because "you get money based on volume. Period. I think at the end of the day, volume has worked very nicely for them [the Bank] for sixty years, and it is going to continue to work nicely ... They [the Bank] don't want to change" (WB8).

Although my Results Secretariat interviewees were unclear as to which Executive Directors most encouraged a results-focused Bank, by 2008, the UK and US governments had become significant pressure points (WB5). That assessment (at least on the US side) was backed up by several Treasury statements in which results-based foci were encouraged (Adams 2006; Snow 2004; Paulson, Jr. 2007). Another influence was civil society, in general. Although the 50 Years is Enough coalition was mentioned as important by one interviewee, generalized NGO advocacy on whether the Banks loans were positively impacting their intended targets encouraged the Bank toward results-oriented agendas (WB5).

Hampering Secretariat prominence was that results management is not as "tangible" as financial management projects and reforms (WB5). Just as troubling was that most of my Bank interviewees had not heard of the Results Secretariat or if they did, they indicated the Secretariat did not impact their work. This may be because the Secretariat had difficulty figuring out who within project and sector teams should have results responsibility (WB5) or that the Bank has had "no shift in thinking ... that results is not something you do at the end of a project design, and instead, start out with" (WB8).

Operationally, the Bank had no easily transferable "model" of results management for developing countries. The Bank understood that creating developing-country Results Management Units would vary among governmental departments

(WB5). That may be because the "dominant view" among the Bank's senior management was that the "Bank's mission is resource transfer and what happened to the resources was up to the borrower" (WB8). Others wanted the Secretariat to quantify results into a simple number "like a profit/loss for the public sector" (WB8) but felt the Bank had become "hung up" in looking for a "single approach" or "a way to measure results" (WB8). It was "seductive" to think that there was "an" answer. So, what might be the equivalent for the Bank? The interviewee answered by stating the Bank "is lazy. It is far easier to count [loan] volume" (WB8).

The 1997 Executive Development Program and, in particular, Mark Moore's book on leadership and the public sector (*Trading Public Values*) also influenced the Bank's results agenda (WB8) even if the GAC Strategy "got going without any discussion about results. None. Zero" (WB8). If the Bank was committed to "results," GAC authors should have consulted the Secretariat. Without putting internal Bank incentives (such as losing one's job) toward results management, little will change. My interviewee asked, "Do you go home comfortably at night knowing you made a $100 million loan that added no value? Many people are. They are very comfortable ... There is very little accountability. [The Bank staff] are supporting huge families, both here [meaning Washington DC] and mostly back home ... [A lot] comes down to individual motivation and commitment" (WB8).

In its 2004 Annual Report on Operations Evaluation, OED concurred. The Report found that the Bank had not developed "a phased and costed plan showing how, and by when, different parts of the Bank would implement results management" and that more guidance to staff on results-based management was required including how incorporate results-based achievements fed into the Bank's human resources system (World Bank 2005a, x). In 2005, OED's Annual Report referred to another 2004 report prepared by Bank Operations staff that found only "marginal improvements" in the Bank's Monitoring and Evaluation Improvement Program (World Bank 2005a, 9). As importantly, the Bank acknowledged that even QAG (next section), the unit responsible for producing the Annual Report on Portfolio Performance, had to temporarily postpone its reporting for several years because "of the lack of relevant results-oriented M and E [monitoring and evaluation] in Bank operations" (World Bank 2005a, 10). Moreover, the Bank had not published advice to staff on how to modify their Country Assistance Strategies to include results-based monitoring. The Bank's advice to staff writing strategic sector papers was also silent on how to incorporate results-based considerations (World Bank 2005a, 17). Further prohibiting progress was the Bank's human resources department's desire to not consider results-based considerations as an immediate need but instead part of a "long-term reform agenda" (World Bank 2005a, 13, citing the World Bank's 2002 Results Report).

Operationally, the managing for results agenda also suffered from conflicting upper management signals, middle management's failure to provide operational guidance, and a host of traditional, incentive-based realities that limited staff proactivity (IEG 2012). As time moved on, and despite Bank Board members and Bank staff largely believing in OED's (later, IEG) organizational independence (IEG 2011a), staff had become increasingly sensitive to IEG evaluations. If the IEG found a certain project outcome that did not lead to a favorable result, staff could choose not to include that outcome in subsequent projects even if the outcome was desirable for the client country (WB14). Like QAG (next section), the Results Secretariat lifespan was short. Or as noted by one outside observer, the Bank gave "lip-service" to results because finding results was "hard" (WB51) whereas another view (this time from a banker) observed that no matter what, Bank results are "corrupt since they are not solving the lack of services to the poor people" (WB17).

Evaluation and Results: Getting "QAG'd"

Created in the late 1990s, the Quality Assurance Group (QAG) reviewed projects for "quality at entry" along nine criteria: strategic relevance and approach; technical, financial, and economic aspects; poverty, gender, and social development; environmental aspects; fiduciary aspects; policy and institutional aspects; implementation arrangements; risk assessment; and Bank inputs and processes (QAG 2006). In FY2003, QAG's main complaints about its surveyed projects included "inadequate results frameworks, unrealistic objectives, and lack of readiness for implementation" (QAG 2006). According to one staffer, QAG was formed because OED/IEG reports had become places where "the dead were burying the dead" since its reviews were written after project completion (WB15). By contrast, QAG focused on project and entry. Moreover, in an implicit criticism of OED/IEG, QAG was run by a panel of "experts" who take a random, stratified sample of projects to review (WB14, WB18). In FY2004-05, QAG sampled 125 (or 23 percent) of approved projects. This required project leaders to respond to QAG. On average, project leaders spent five staff-days to respond to QAG (QAG 2006).

QAG panelists were often senior Bank staff, current or retired. In certain instances, QAG reviews allowed for outside input, generally someone from an NGO, academia, donor group, or the private sector. The projects at entry were rated on a scale of 1 to 6 from "highly satisfactory" (1) to "highly unsatisfactory" (6). Just fifteen of eighty-five projects assessed in FY2003 were rated moderately unsatisfactorily (4) or lower (QAG 2006, 45). When projects are split by Sector Board, 94 percent of the Bank's PSM/PSG projects had a rating of moderately satisfactory or higher in FY2003 whereas 81 percent did in FY2004 (QAG 2006, 48).

Although the Results Secretariat worked with QAG to incorporate results-oriented actions (WB5), Bank staff members disliked being "QAG'd" as it was known internally (WB27). Staff "pushed back" when QAG was created as it felt like "another layer of review" (WB18). Furthering staff frustration was that QAG team members need not have experience with reviewed sectors or countries. One interviewee recalled a friend's Africa project in which no one on the QAG review team had been to Africa (WB14). Staff tried to avoid "bad QAG ratings" especially if they were cited for something easy to control (WB5). One interviewee, who had projects QAG'd, described the process as "terrible" (WB14). In his/her perspective, the QAG reviewer role is to be "critical" but that sometimes reviewers could be "unbelievably critical" and that "interrogation by these people [QAG staff members] is frightening" (WB14). Also, staff members would also appeal low QAG (and IEG) ratings even if a low QAG rating was more likely to reflect poorly upon the Project's Task Team Leader than a poor OED/IEG report (WB5). In the end, and perhaps emblematic of the stop-and-start of Bank evaluative efforts and the internal disincentives for result-based management, QAG was disbanded and not replaced.

Evaluation and Results: Institutional Integrity

In the 2007 GAC Strategy, the Bank's Institutional Integrity (INT) office was complimented for its "concern about fraud and corruption in Bank-financed projects" (World Bank 2007b, 56). The INT, established in 2001, "investigate[s] allegations of fraud, corruption, coercion, and collusion related to WBG-financed projects and to sanction firms and individuals found to have breached the fraud and corruption provisions of the Bank's Procurement Guidelines or the Consultants Guidelines. More than 2,000 external cases of alleged fraud, corruption, or other misconduct have been handled since 1999, and more than 330 companies and individuals have been publicly sanctioned, providing significant examples of issues in projects financed or managed by the Bank across countries" (World Bank 2007b, 56–57). The Bank's Articles of Agreement were used to justify INT's creation because the Articles require the Bank to know where its money ends up (WB4).

The 2007 GAC Strategy encouraged task team leaders to understand INT findings and to limit future investigations. The first INT Director (Susan Rich-Olson, appointed by Wolfowitz) was viewed as a disastrous first Director because she "terrorized staff and shut down communications with the rest of the Bank" (WB29). She assumed that Bank staff members were "on the take" and took the attitude that it was best for Bank staff to fear the INT rather than to foster a climate of cooperation (WB29). One outside NGO interviewee felt that she was a poor first choice because Rich-Olson had her own "conflicts of interest" and was "volatile and lacking in judicial temperament" (WB47). Later, the Bank's Administrative Tribunal would rule against her judgement to harass employees, causing further unnecessary scandal and embarrassment (Tribunal 2009). Despite the fiasco over Rich-Olson under Wolfowitz, the INT was making headway. Although only one interviewee admitted to having approached the INT about potential project fraud, a recent success was the indictment of a former Bank staffer who was given fifteen months in a federal penitentiary "for wrongdoing" (WB4). The interviewee said the Bank staffer was going to "spend fifteen months in the federal pens and then after that, his visa gets revoked and moves back to Calcutta. Does that make us popular? No ... [but] staff rate these announcements; we had 220 rate it as five stars" (WB4).[4]

INT's procurement discrepancy investigations were assisted by mid-1990s revisions of Bank Procurement Guidelines that allowed investigation of Bank-financed contracts. If fraud or abuse occurs, the Bank's Sanctions Committee (created in January 1998, later renamed the Sanctions Board) can debar guilty parties from accessing further Bank funds either temporarily or on a permanent basis (Thornburgh et al. 2000; Kohler and Bowra 2020). While questions have been raised about the integrity of this process (Hassett 2007), the US Senate Foreign Relations Committee has encouraged its efforts (US Senate 2010, 11, 34). As noted by multiple Bank evaluations (Leroy and Fariello 2012; INT 2010, 2011) and scholarly articles (e.g., Åhman 2020; Williams 2007; Dubois et al. 2019; Chen 2016; de Charzourne and Fromageau 2012), the Board has become institutionalized with clearer procedures on how debarment decisions are made.

Unfortunately, INT's impact on PSM/PSG policies and projects remains unclear as INT reports do not distinguish whether certain project and policy sectors are more likely than others to have issues. As such, and despite the publicity attributed to INT's creation, yet another potential feedback loop to PSM/PSG has had been limited. That does not mean that PSM/PSG projects are not influenced by INT's creation (they most surely are), but the "lessons learned" from INT's work may not be systemically (or at least not publicly) incorporated into future learning in PSM/PSG policies and projects.

Evaluation and Results: Inspection Panel

Perhaps unlike the Results Secretariat, QAG, or INT, NGOs had at least some influence over at least one evaluative actor, the Inspection Panel. The Panel helps ensure Bank compliance with its own operational policies. The Panel consists of three members with nonrenewable, five-year terms. The Panel is reliant on external actors (primarily NGOs and individual citizens) to submit claims for review. After determining whether the submitted complaint is reviewable, the Panel investigates and submits its report to the Bank's Board. From its inception in 1993 to 2012, the Panel formally investigated just over eighty complaints, and decided not to

---

[4] The interviewee was simply referencing staffers, in general, on G4 visas (e.g. Moloney et al. 2018). In addition, INT tried to improve communication with staff after Rich-Olson left. This interviewee is referring to Bank intranet "kiosks" where Bank staff can read (and rate) Bank news.

investigate another one hundred and twenty-five or so. The Inspection Panel does not deal with issues of corruption, fraud, contracting, or staff misconduct. Those issues were left to the Department of Institutional Integrity (now the Integrity Vice Presidency).

It has been suggested that NGO lobbying and oft-covered fiasco with Bank funding of the Sardar Sarovar Dam in India in the late 1980s and early 1990s, the Bank would not have created an Inspection Panel in 1993 (Pereira et al. 2017). In speaking about the dam, a Bank interviewee observed: "The Bank managed to mishandle that project in almost every way you can imagine from first completely messing up the environmental assessment and the resettlement of 100,000 people, massive protests in the valley led by extremely capable civil society leadership and it went to court in India and finally in very dramatic public appeals to the Bank leadership" (WB9). In response, President Conable convened an independent commission in 1991 (the Morse Commission) for the "first independent review of a World Bank project" (World Bank 2009a; Kraske et al. 1996).

Morse Commission outputs were unflattering. In one view, "the Bank largely disregarded its social and environmental policies and tolerated its borrowers' violation of the policies, [which] were soon confirmed more generally by an internal review of Bank projects. The Narmada policy violations were not an aberration, but a systemic part of the Bank's culture" (Clark 1999, 3). For the Bank, the dam failure indicated "[a] prevailing culture of volume lending at the expense of project execution" (Umaña 1998, 1). The Commission stated what the Wapenhans Report explained a few years later: Bank lending culture impacted project quality. However, another Commission output was that the Bank "realize[d] that at a certain point politically they could not stiff the international community[5] in building the standards and having some mechanism that would ensure that they were in fact meeting expectations" (WB9).

It is worth noting, however, that the Panel cannot investigate claims about the Bank's alleged malfeasance unless the complainant indicates that the Bank violated its operational procedures (OP) or bureaucratic procedures (BP).[6] But because

---

[5] The Bank's former OED Director-General agreed that "international NGOs" pushed the Bank toward a Panel even though OED had already proposed the idea: "In the early 1990s, given the declining trend that OED had documented in the development effectiveness of Bank-financed projects, Executive Directors sought to strengthen portfolio management and evaluation. In February 1993, four Executive Directors proposed to graft on to OED a quality management and inspection unit. That proposal was opposed by management and did not secure majority support from the Board. Eventually it was superseded *by an even more exacting scheme driven by international NGOs, for an Inspection Panel to investigate the Bank's alleged failures to comply with its own policies.* Management and the Board debated the Inspection Panel proposal at length; it was eventually endorsed in the context of an IDA replenishment negotiation" (World Bank 2003c, 64, emphasis added).

[6] The creation of Bank safeguard policies (via operational policies (OPs) and bureaucratic procedures (BPs)) in the early 1990s was an early lobbying success of NGOs concerned about Bank non-transparency within the environmental sector. With an IEG report on safeguards published in 2010 (IEG 2010c), a new effort to reform safeguards was begun. Later, questions were raised about whether prior safeguard gains were lost in the reform (Bugalski 2016; Bradlow and Fourie 2013).

there is no OP or BP on PSM/PSG, the sector is effectively eliminated from Panel investigation.[7] An interviewee who had extensive Panel experience noted, "if you are looking for projects that involved public administration or law or justice … the [Bank operational] policies for that, are incredibly weak or nonexistent" and in fact, "I would be hard-pressed to find a way to complain under Bank policies [for PSM/PSG]" (WB9). Specifically, the Panel is prohibited from responding to "actions which are the responsibility of other parties (such as the government, implementing agency, corporation, etc.) and which do not involve any action or omission on the part of the Bank" (Clark 1999, 11). Thus, although NGO advocacy helped create a potential feedback loop into Bank work with the Inspection Panel, NGO advocacy came from the environmental movements that declared victory upon Panel creation. For other Bank sectors such as PSM/PSG where NGO advocacy is far less prominent, the Panel was less useful.

Conclusion: Evaluators and NGOs Seldom Matter for PSM/PSG Change

In the 1970s and early 1980s, in an era before mass global civil society movements, the Bank did not publicly share many internal evaluation reports. Moreover, there is a consistent claim from before and after the anti-Bank protest era that OED (and IEG) evaluations have little impact on subsequent project planning. This is due not only to the Bank's incentive culture but also because a country or a sector may have moved on by the time a multi-year project ends and is then evaluated. This limits evaluative impacts. This may be especially true for PSM/PSG projects in which costs-benefits and economic rates of return are not easily calculated (IEG 2010a). Add-in the trade-offs between project quality versus project speed during crises along with coordination difficulties, any result-based emphases become difficult to calculate (IEG 2011c). Additional efforts to strengthen evaluations pre-Board approval (via QAG) or more broadly on an organizational basis (Results Secretariat) each have a short organizational life, the challenge of evaluation and Bank accountability has not gone away (Thomas and Luo 2011; IEG 2012). As noted in this chapter, PSM/PSG policy change was rarely driven by the Bank's evaluative mechanisms (see Table 15).[8]

In contrast, the answer to whether civil society influenced policy change within the PSM/PSG agenda depends on which NGO is being discussed (see Table 16). Certainly, the familiarity of an Eigen-created Transparency International with *Bankease* and its creation in a post-Soviet world in which "good governance"

---

[7] Writing an OP or BP on environmental reform (for example) is easier when there are international standards guiding what is or is not good environmental management. Similar safeguard standards do not exist for PSM/PSG.

[8] All tables referenced in this book may be found in the Appendix.

and, later, other demand-side practices were becoming dominant, does matter. TI's access to President Wolfensohn and the congruence of its message with the Bank's evolving PSM/PSG policies are important. In contrast, Public Sector International's core constituency had a different perspective than the Bank policies within this sector.

Others, like 50 Years is Enough, successfully mobilized civil society actors to protest the Bank's broadest ideological agenda. That some of this anti-Bank protest agenda was defined by opposition structural adjustment is also not unimportant. The push for the Bank to become more transparent, to publish its Country Assistance Strategies, to encourage participatory outreach, and depending on who you ask, to demand the creation of an Inspection Panel, are hard to overlook. The role played by civil society in cooperation with Bank staff during the Wolfowitz era may also matter too. Whether NGO roles in encouraging the Bank to continue lending to corrupt developing countries was truly as large and significant as the multi-stakeholder consultation might have suggested is less clear. The reality was the creation of an uneasy partnership. Staff used the participatory legitimacy attached to civil society to encourage the Bank to approve the staff version of the GAC Strategy.

The reality of several thousand protestors outside Annual Meetings for over a decade will influence staff. But whether the protests were enough to substantively alter the Bank's sector policy direction is harder to suggest. This is similarly true for the Bank's internal evaluation. Whether due to their initially non-public nature, latter-day evaluation delays, internal pushbacks against any evaluation criticism whether from QAG or OED/IEG or the Results Secretariat, and an ongoing lending culture, the evaluative impacts may be only partial, at best. In contrast, the quasi-judicial Inspection Panel is a mechanism whereby complainants may allege Bank violations of its operational policies. This is potentially useful if the sector has such policies. Since PSM/PSG does not, the Panel becomes a far less effective mechanism to influence this sector. Thus, and in the end, neither the internal evaluation actors nor NGOs have had as much influence on 32 years of PSM/PSG sector policy change as key member-states and the G7 in the 1980s and early 1990s and later, Bank staffs in the early 1990s to 2012.

10

PSM/PSG Sector Emergence, Policy Change, and Who Matters at the World Bank

This book explains policy change within the World Bank. The sector policy focus is public sector management (PSM) and public sector governance (PSG). The dependent variable is policy change within the World Bank's PSM/PSG sector. The independent variables are derived from stakeholder theory and a bureaucratic politics approach. Each independent variable is typical for stakeholder theory and its internal actors: a unit, a vice presidency, a board, a network, a region, a Council. This includes the internal evaluative actors that review Bank projects and policies during and post-implementation. The bureaucratic politics approach engages the organizational units, individual staff, and publications which articulate competing policy directions.

The book's focus is on policy outputs rather than the Bank's development outcomes.[1] The goal is to contribute to a theory capable of explaining IO policy change. Based on quantifiably observable increases in approved PSM/PSG projects between 1980 and 2012 (see Table 1[2]), two research questions were proposed: (1) Why did the World Bank's PSM/PSG increase (in project approvals per year) between 1980 and 2012? (2) Why and how did public sector governance policy objectives vary between 1980 and 2012?

To answer each question, this book opens up the "black box" of the World Bank. *It illustrates how the insertion of parts of the public administration discipline—and in particular, stakeholder theory and bureaucratic politics—can help explain policy change within IOs.* The public administration discipline helps to showcase internal battles, disagreement over policy design and influence, and where one or more actors had more or less influence than another. This includes debates over the

---

[1] As noted in Chapters 1 and 2, we cannot understand the policy outcomes of an IO's work if we do not understand how its policy outputs were created. This book does not suggest that outcomes do not matter. Outcomes absolutely matter but their discussion requires an altogether different book. For an excellent book on how one IO (OECD) can change public sector management outcomes in its member states, see (Pal 2012).

[2] All tables referenced in this book may be found in the Appendix.

Who Matters at the World Bank?. Kim Moloney, Oxford University Press.
© Kim Moloney (2022). DOI: 10.1093/oso/9780192857729.003.0010

creation of PSM as a policy sector in the early 1980s, leading up to the 1987 internal organizational reform and its impact on this sector, the end of the Cold War, and the early push in a post-1989 World Bank to consolidate its victory over the Soviet Union. This led to an aggressive effort to quickly integrate former Soviet republics while adding new ideas about good governance (PSG). With this expanding sector agenda encapsulated as part of the Bank's early 1990s sector work, key sector influencers like the US, UK, and G7, who had dominated the 1980s, had far less sector-specific influence after 1991.

With an agreement about anticorruption's importance (October 1995) and earlier additions of good governance (August 1991) to the sector agenda, questions arose about how far and how deep (and how political) the Bank wished to go. Competing economic theories and debates over supply-side versus demand-side governance soon dominated internal Bank discussions. The latter debate, with its origins in late 1990s conversations at the Bank, occurred outside the influence of external stakeholders like the US or the G7. It was only when then-President Paul Wolfowitz threatened an in-process GAC Strategy that external actors would *briefly* peer inside evolving sector policy debates. This momentary intervention in 2007 to quietly encourage Wolfowitz' departure was not delinked from staff discontent about his activities. By 2012, with the GAC firmly entrenched and its updated Strategy published, the sector became the only sector to be elevated to a Bank-wide Council. This is a dramatic difference to its 1980s origins. Throughout each sector development and policy change, the Bank's international civil servants, like civil servants within a domestic bureaucracy, are discovered to be a place where staff battle both each other and external stakeholders to determine "who matters" and how policy change occurs. Policy politics and individual politics are everywhere at the Bank.

This concluding section starts by evaluating the book's two framework components: stakeholder theory and the bureaucratic politics approach. Stakeholder theory was operationalized to evaluate external actors' behaviors, opinions, and their influence on policy change. Bureaucratic politics was combined with stakeholder theory to evaluate internal actors' behaviors, opinions, and influence on policy change. Although scholars do not have a theory of policy change within IOs, this book may help us achieve this objective. To further this theoretical objective, the next paragraphs also posit thirteen testable propositions. Each proposition is derived from the PSM/PSG policy changes shared in this book. Each is linked via Table 17 to the book's analytical framework and its variables (second column of Tables 7–16).

Departing International Relations to Explain Policy Change

International organizations do not exist without states. States create international organizations. International relations' realist theory helps scholars predict state influence within the international system. Since states create IOs, realist theory predicts that IOs simply respond to the international system's most powerful states (Mearsheimer 1995). In contrast, international relations' constructivist scholars have a different approach. Puzzled as to why IOs act contrary to realist predictions, early constructivist scholars attempted to encapsulate an IO's culture into its explanatory variable. This variable, if understood correctly, could predict when IOs would disobey state orders. It was postulated that such cultural behaviors were a deviation from or at the very least, counterproductive to IO missions. To justify this approach, constructivists drew on organizational sociology and in particular, Talcott Parsons' interpretation of Max Weber. This unnecessarily narrow perspective (and partial misreading of Weber) was the opposite of what the public administration discipline has long understood from before Weber's work was translated into the English. In its simplest form, civil servants cannot remove their small "p" politics from their policy preferences or advice.

Moreover, principal–agent theory (a frequent choice among scholars of international relations studying IOs) along with other theories and approaches (see the end of Chapter 2) each have limitations for studies of IO policy change (in the first instance) and for testing a theory of IO policy change anchored by a bureaucratic politics approach and stakeholder theory (in the second instance). Although institutional isomorphism may be the best of the alternative approaches even that had limitations. Instead, this book's analytical framework combined stakeholder theory with a bureaucratic politics approach to study 32 years of policy change within the Bank's most prescribed project sector: public sector management and public sector governance.

Since an IO's state "owners" play an important role in directing or encouraging policy shifts, stakeholder theory assists scholars in identifying and assessing whether external actors influenced the studied shifts (Mitchell et al. 1997; Pfeffer and Salancik 1978; Jonker and Foster 2002). Stakeholder theory does not assume that vote share prominence automatically equates to influence. Instead, stakeholder theory uses a checklist to assess external and internal actor influence. If realist theory assumes nation-state influence, then stakeholder theory helps assess the level of influence and to determine if influence was used to encourage policy change. A bureaucratic politics approach helps identify key internal stakeholders and in concert with stakeholder theory, assesses influence. Tables 7–16, shared at the end of each chapter, intersect with my book's analytical framework with each identified actor and time period.

The first "big picture" that arises from the tables and their accompanying text is the influence of the US, UK, G7, and to some extent, the IMF over the first 11 years of the PSM agenda. The subsequent rise in internal (non-evaluative) stakeholder influence over policy change within this sector after mid-1991 was not concurrent with a decline in PSM/PSG project approvals but a rising dominance of this sector via its own sector-specific projects but also its incorporation into other sector projects (see Table 1). This interest fed into sector-specific topic diversification too (see Table 5).

While the pre-1991 (external actor dominance) and post-1991 (internal actor dominance) sector influences may appear dichotomous, they need not be mutually exclusive. During the 1980s, perspectives counter to structural adjustment (via institutional development) were present. The confluence of such perspectives with new structural spaces created by the 1987 reform increased institutional development's influence. To be clear, this book does not argue that external actors were not present for this sector after 1991. Instead, their influence was frequently short-lived and not derived from sector debates. This includes (a) Board acquiescence (without a lengthy Presidential Memo as with the 1991 addition of good governance to the PSM agenda) to the addition of anticorruption, (b) the IMF-Bank responses to the Asian Financial Crisis were more about the egos of two feuding economists which spread into a limited display of public posturing by the two Bretton Woods "cousins" than an alteration of Bank's sector policy by the IMF or other IMF-supporting states, and (c) Board intervention during the Wolfowitz presidency had less to do with GAC appropriateness or its replacement of the 2000 Strategy than a response to an attempted usurpation of power by Wolfowitz and an increasingly public scandal.

The second "big picture" arising from the Tables is summarized into thirteen testable propositions shared in the next sections. Each is linked with this book's independent variables (see Table 17). The propositions arise from this book's analysis of policy change. The creation of a proposition is output from the book's analytical framework. Given that this book cannot possibly apply each applicable theory or concept excluded from its framework (see end of Chapter 2), one or more propositions may partially relate to an excluded theory, approach, or related literature. This may include, for example, a link between Proposition D and literature of IOs and crisis (Hardt 2014; Van Hecke et al. 2021; Olsson and Verbeek 2013) or links between Proposition E and when advocacy groups coalesce to encourage IOs to alter their direction (Dellmuth 2020; Dellmuth and Bloodgood 2019). It is expected that any intersection of propositions from this book's analytical framework with other literatures may be a particularly fruitful location for further efforts to create a mid-range theory of IO policy change.

Explaining Policy Change: External Stakeholders

The late 1970s and early 1980s challenged the World Bank to define what *development* really meant. At the time, many developing country states controlled significant portions of their economies. State control was an outcome of colonial histories and a need of many post-colonial leaders to consolidate enough power to manage their new states. At the same time, economies with significant state influence may create inefficiencies that hamper economic growth and poverty reduction while increasing their vulnerability to external crises such as the 1980–1982 world recession and the prior oil crises of the 1970s. In a global environment in which the US and Soviet Union angled for influence, it was against the strategic interest of the Bank's key external actor (the United States) and its allies (the United Kingdom and other Western European countries) to allow developing countries to economically collapse. Given this setting, the first proposition which may help scholars create a theory of IO policy change is following:

Proposition A: *The strategic, economic and political interests of an IO's key external state actors shape how an IO's policies are changed.*

In some ways, the first proposition is not unfamiliar to scholars of international relations. State power matters (variables E1 and E5 from Tables 7, 9, 11, and 13). But as noted in this book's mesohistorical study of PSM/PSG sector shifts, state power does not always matter. State interest in one area need not imply its concurrent interest in another (e.g., gender). For this sector, PSM was linked to economic stability, the Bank's mission, and the geopolitics of that era.

In addition, just because such state power mattered in one era of the Bank's sector history does not mean that it will matter in the next (see Table 4). This extends to external actor legitimacy. Throughout the book, the legitimacy of the external actor's claim over the Bank is unquestioned (variable E2 from Tables 7, 9, 11, and 13). Both the power to influence and the legitimacy of external actor relations with the Bank were derived from stakeholder theory (Mitchell et al. 1997).

Prior to 1980 the Bank paid little attention to policy-based lending or to a client state's institutional needs. But this changed with US (and IMF) encouragement to create its first policy-based lending instrument: structural adjustment. Between January 1980 and October 1989, structural adjustment lending rose in importance. It would define the 1980s' PSM policy agenda. In this period, the US and UK (along with the IMF and G7) were the Bank's key external actors. When multiple international political and economic crises affected the international system (1970s oil crises, developing country over borrowing, 1980–1982 world recession, and the Cold War), the Bank's key external stakeholders encouraged Bank staff members to adopt policies that might strengthen the fiscal and monetary health of developing countries. In the case of structural adjustment, the World Bank obeyed the sector directives of key external actors.

Realist theory also helps predict which external actor mattered. The answer during the 1980s was the US, UK, and G7. The Bank's sector policies matched G7 countries' concerns about the international economy. They used their power to create and influence this emergent sector's policy agenda. But as noted by international relations theorists, international economic crises may also shape state preferences. That two oil crises and a global recession in the early 1980s coincided with the Cold War heightened their importance. Recalling the stakeholder theory portion of this book's analytical framework, it was the "criticality" (Jonker and Foster 2002) and "urgency" (Mitchell et al. 1997) (variables E4 and E3 of Tables 7, 9, 11, and 13) of rising economic instability that encouraged initial policy shifts. This leads to a second proposition:

Proposition B: *Urgency of key state influence over IO policy change will increase during international crises if the IO's prior policy outputs were insufficient to respond to the crisis.*

However, and as noted in Chapter 2 and throughout this book, what international relations' theories often miss via their black boxing of IOs is that international civil servants and their politics can also influence policy debates. This includes a 1980s internal staff resistance to, and an intellectual disagreement about, neoclassical economics' importance. Despite the 1982 retirement of two high-level Bank staff (Mahbub al-Haq and Hollis Chenery) who cautioned against neoclassical perspectives, Bank staff still published reports suggesting SOE reform (rather than privatization) and institutional development were more appropriate. Moreover, Bank papers published before the 1983 *WDR* did not uniformly reflect neoclassical views. Bankers debated with neoliberal Bank Chief Economist Anne Krueger over the 1983 *WDR*. The 1985 Indonesia Report was an assertion of institutional development's importance to PSM. Subsequent Bank researchers also focused on institutional development. Such reports often had a more benevolent view of developing country administrative states than neoclassical objectives.

This book relays stories of sector policy change. It is about bureaucrats who debate each other as they vie for prominence. It is also a story about how internal resistance can be overcome and how one actor might matter one day and then a few years later, another actor matters more. In the 1980s, Bank's new development theory (neoclassical economics) required short-term policy shifts in the Bank's way of doing business. This theory provided "an answer" to external actor concerns about an international economic crisis. In the 1980s, the Bank was a tool for states to encourage particular developing country policy shifts. Longer-term reforms such as institutional development or SOE reform were deemed less desirable.

This meant that in some years, the Bank's institutional survival required its acquiescence to key state demands. With the early years of the Reagan administration largely hostile to the Bank, the Bank had to respond. Pfeffer and Salancik's tenth criterion on whether an organization will abide by external actors' demands is that "the organization desires to survive" (Pfeffer and Salancik 1978, 44). In the 1980s, the Bank desired to survive. This has not changed to today. However, it also important to recall that survival need not equate to simple obedience to an IO's key external actors. During the 1980s external actors such as the US, UK, and G7 mattered most for sector policy creation and its rising importance. Internal actors offered sector policy alternatives in the 1970s as well as the 1980s but struggled to be heard. The 1980–1982 international economic crisis forced the Bank's hand.

Starting with the Berlin Wall's fall in November 1989, accelerating through the August 1991 addition of good governance to the Bank's sector agenda, and the Soviet Union's dissolution in December 1991, there began an external-to-internal actor power shift over who mattered in the Bank's PSM/PSG sector. Crisis (as per proposition E2) was also present in this 1989–1991 period that is, the rapidity of the Soviet Union's dissolution and a desire to cement a market liberal world economy. As newly independent states arose from the Soviet rubble, the Bank was tasked with reshaping post-Soviet policies. The US and UK retained the power, legitimacy, and urgency (Mitchell et al. 1997; Jonker and Foster 2002) during a critical period to influence policy change. Cementing the Cold War win was strategically important for G7 nations. The Bank's key external actors used their collective muscle to ensure PSM reforms were central to post-Soviet independence. Worries about whether such states might return to a Soviet model or dissolve into anarchy were not far from the surface.

One Bank answer to this crisis was to rapidly disburse structural adjustment loans to Eastern and Central Europe. Soon, however, it became clear that market liberalism could not guarantee democratic liberalism. But to discuss democratic liberalism was to violate the Bank's Articles of Agreement. Instead, the Bank's new phrase was "good governance." Good governance and increased accountability would be linked via Bank research to its mission to improve economic growth and encourage poverty reduction. Achievement of the Bank's mission could be enhanced by this expansion of the PSM agenda to include public sector governance. Based on this identifiable international crisis, this era reconfirms Propositions E1 and E2 of the 1980s for the early 1990s.

Similar to the 1979–1980 introduction of structural adjustment lending, good governance also potentially conflicted with the Bank's Articles of Agreement. Debates among the Bank's Executive Directors, the General Counsel, and Bank staff were long and difficult. Certain regional Vice Presidents fought against publishing the August 1991 *Managing Development: The Governance Dimension* report. This Report outlined good governance's importance to development. In the end, the Bank's Articles of Agreement were simply reinterpreted to suit the times. This is an example of variable E13 which states: The Bank is capable of developing actions or outcomes that will satisfy external actor demands (Pfeffer and Salancik 1978). Such reinterpretations by the Bank of its legal obligations to satisfy changing external demands, leads to another proposition:

Proposition C: *When key state actors desire to modify IO policy agendas, a potentially contrary legal agreement may only pose a short-term barrier to motivated state actors.*

This proposition is also an assertion of key state power over the IO (Mitchell et al. 1997). It is one thing to use an international crisis to motivate a policy shift (Proposition B) and quite another to reinterpret an IO's Articles of Agreement when key states desire policy shifts. Since IOs sit within a semi anarchic international system without the separation of powers typical to democratic states (Moloney and Rosenbloom 2020), the "executive" (represented by the Executive Directors) is far freer to reinterpret Articles without considering legislative or judicial oversight.

During the early 1990s, other internal voices mobilized. Their influence would become greater than their prior limited importance in the early to mid-1980s. This includes new questions about the "fit" of neoclassical economics to PSM/PSG work, rising institutional development importance, the addition of civil service reform, public expenditure management, and public financial management projects to the sector policy agenda in the late 1980s, and the insertion of new institutional economics into sector policy discussions. With internal actor dominance after August 1991, their influence was further cemented by aligning with then-President James Wolfensohn's October 1995 announcement that the Bank would add anticorruption to its PSM/PSG agenda. External actor involvement on anticorruption was provided not because of an international crisis forced a policy shift but a growing *internal* realization that if the Bank wanted to effectively address public sector governance (and PSM), anticorruption activities were needed.

Without an international crisis or strategic consideration fueling a policy shift, key external actors may rely more heavily upon their power (e.g., vote or share size) to override others (e.g., China/Saudi Arabia) unconvinced of a new policy's importance or to encourage the Bank to engage in organizational reform as it did in 1987. However, what was witnessed instead was the following: simply obtaining resources (variable E6), recognizing that resources are important to Bank operations (variable E7), and acknowledging that alternative resources are not available (variable E8) (Pfeffer and Salancik 1978) did not always lead to external actor influence over post-1991 sector policy shifts. This leads us to Proposition D.

Proposition D: *Without an international crisis to fuel IO policy shifts, key states may, if necessary, rely upon their operational power (e.g., votes or budget shares) to override others unconvinced of a policy shift's importance.*

Similar to the Bank's introduction of structural adjustment, privatization, and good governance, key external actors' desire (in particular, the US) to lessen developing country corruption overrode any concerns that such anticorruption policies implied the Bank was violating its Articles of Agreement. The US provided the backing to this internal actor and boundary actor addition the PSG agenda. This gave extra weight to the sector policy shifts being led by internal actors. Just as with Proposition C, Bank Articles were not amended. Anticorruption projects just simply went forward. Increasing the acceptability of this addition to the sector policy agenda, was that Bank President James Wolfensohn's anticorruption interest gave additional legitimacy via former bankers like Peter Eigen and Eigen's new (at the time) Transparency International NGO. In other words, variable E10 (see Tables 7, 9, 11, and 13) implies that external actors can assess Bank compliance to their demands (Pfeffer and Salancik 1978). These lead us to another proposition:

Proposition E: *Non-state actors that support an IO's policy shift may be used by an IO, its leadership, and/or its other external state actors to legitimize policy shifts.*

Other implications of Proposition E may appear less sanguine. That is, the Bank's desire to survive (variable E14 of Tables 7, 9, 11, and 13) may lead to behaviors that appear manipulative. This includes Bank actions in 2007 to invite NGO responses to a potential GAC strategy and thus, create momentum against Wolfowitz' desires to alter Bank lending incentives.

At the same time, and despite NGO complaints about the Bank becoming louder and more organized by the mid-1990s, this did not imply that NGOs organizing against the Bank's environmental work (for example) were also interested in PSM/PSG. NGOs did not significantly influence PSM/PSG policy shifts for several reasons. The first is that the 1987 reforms, which gave this sector the institutional space to grow, occurred before many NGOs were sufficiently networked to protest Bank structural adjustment policies. The Bank's internal structure had already modified itself to (slowly) emphasize or build toward its later argument (via the 1997 *WDR*) that the state was beginning to matter for development. Second, NGOs' critiques were largely nonspecific. Structural adjustment, as a whole, was the problem. Specific PSM concerns were undiscussed. There was no acceptable response to NGO critics than to entirely rid the Bank of structural adjustment. Third, the Bank's addition of good governance, public expenditure management, and financial management to the sector agenda made it normatively difficult for NGOs to argue that such additions were inappropriate. Further assisting the Bank was that two of the three additions (public expenditure management and public financial management) were highly technocratic and not easy for Bank critics to mobilize around. This limited the public appeal of specific critiques. Since the Bank does not control external actor demands via variable E12 and the Bank also does not control the resources of external actors (variable E9) (Pfeffer and Salancik 1978), this leads to an additional external actor proposition specific to NGOs:

Proposition F: *If an NGO (or other critical non-state actor) seeks to influence IO policy change, the critical actor's success rate may increase if the policy critique is specific, technocratic, and not a radical departure from the IO's current operational realities.*

But what about TI, IBP, or PSI? Part of TI's rise reflected its access to President James Wolfensohn. As noted by one interviewee, bankers like to interact with former bankers. They speak the same language. Although Wolfensohn met with many NGOs during his tenure, TI was one of the few with semiregular access. TI's anticorruption focus coalesced with Bank internal discussions about how corruption hampered development. In the mid-2000s, the IBP interacted with the Bank and the IMF on technical issues around public expenditure management. IBP's technocratic focus jelled with Bank efforts to encourage budget transparency in its client states. Other than TI and IBP, the only other public-sector focused NGO that interacted with the Bank is PSI. PSI's focus is to protect public sector unions. Wolfensohn offered PSI short-term assignments at the Bank and asked PSI to comment upon Bank reports. But the PSI problem was similar to the anti-structural adjustment protestors: The Bank was not going to change its operational strategies and intellectual beliefs to accommodate perspectives (in this case, pro-union) that the Bank believed were contrary to its mission.

Explaining Policy Change: Internal Stakeholders

To increase case study reliability and validity, this book focused upon one particular aspect of the World Bank's work. For this book, the focus is the PSM/PSG sector from 1980 to 2012. Not only did the Bank's sector policies change between 1980 (introduction of structural adjustment), 1985–1986 (privatization emphasized), and 1987–1989 (new topics civil service reform, public expenditure management, public financial management) but they shifted again in 1991 (addition of good governance with multiple new topics), in 1996 (addition of anticorruption), in the 2000s (supply side and demand side debates), and in 2012 (cementing of GAC Council and sector as key to all Bank work) (see Table 5). Intellectual shifts also occurred as the Bank's primary economic model moved from neoclassical economics to new institutional economics and to political economy. Throughout, Bank staff not only desired greater influence over sector policy changes but would use their power to make additions to the sector agenda and to debate sector policy shifts. If necessary, staff were willing to "go public" as they did in 2006 and 2007 under Wolfowitz' presidency.

Stakeholder theory interacts with a bureaucratic politics approach to help understand the motivations, roles, and responsibilities of individual civil servants working within a particular sector. Rather than studying the institution as a black box, this book evaluates the *organization*, a *sector*, and *its bureaucratic and policy debates and behaviors*. We know from the public administration literature that civil servants debate and influence policy change. It is not a question of simple civil servant obedience to external actors. Civil servant influence is an inherent feature of bureaucratic life. The bureaucratic politics approach helps scholars highlight policy debates and to anticipate which internal actors may prevail.

From January 1980 to October 1989, the Bank's application of neoclassical economics and structural adjustment with client states had not taken place without internal debate. One staff cohort argued that Bank lending should focus on institutional development whereas others published papers suggesting that SOE reform was more appropriate than privatization. However, and by early 1986, research on SOE reform had been replaced by research on privatization. Institutional development had not fared well against Bank lending priorities. That is, to lend based on theoretically clear (even if highly optimistic and non-contextual) neoliberal models was preferable to potentially messy and long-term institutional development. In the 1980s, the Bank had no institutional development models acceptable to the Bank economists. As long-term projects with uncertain outputs, institutional development was discouraged by a Bank (and key external actors) which desired "immediate" results. The first two internal actor propositions (G and H) arise from the above discussion. Proposition G relates to a new corollary for this book. As noted in Chapter 2, this corollary is a modification of Betton and Dess (1985). Proposition H is an interplay of E3 and E4 with I3 and I4 (Jonker and Foster 2002).

Proposition G: *Internal debates may not be enough to counter external actor power over an IO if the perceived political and economic efficacy of the alternative policies is lower than the perceived efficacies of the current policies.*

Proposition H: *Internal debates may not be enough to counter external actor policy positions if key external actor policy urgency and criticality create short timeframes.*

Neoclassical economics offered, at least in theory, a fix to developing countries public sector imbalances. With external actors preferring a rapid response to such large state sectors, the "best" PSM policies were ones that offered seemingly quick fixes. But when does an IO desire short-term results? It may be inferred that short-term fixes may become an IO's objective when the organization's survival is threatened by key external actor desires to limit its operating budgets or when international strategic, economic, or political considerations of the key external actors force rapid policy change. Proposition I relates to E14 about the Bank's desire to survive (Pfeffer and Salancik 1978). It is articulated via variables I11 and I12 from the combined Models II and III of bureaucratic politics (Allison and Halperin 1972).

Proposition I: *Short-term results may become an IO's objective when the organization's survival is threatened by key external actors.*

If the organization is unable to respond to external actor desires, internal reorganizations may be a result. In the Bank's case, future sector policy shifts would be enhanced by the Bank's 1987 internal reform—the Bank's first major reorganization since 1972. Pushed into reorganization by the US (and to a lesser extent, Japan), the post-1987 organizational structure increased space for PSM/PSG sector policy expansion. By moving the PSMU (created in 1983) from the Operations Vice Presidency to newly created PSMUs within most regional vice presidencies, budget lines were assigned, and staff job descriptions included the determination of client countries' public sector requirements. Scholars may infer that internal reorganizations reflected ongoing policy shifts within the Bank even if the reorganization had not begun with the intention of favoring any particular sector. Internal reorganizations may expand or limit future policy possibilities and alter which internal actors become "reform winners" and which do not.

The addition of good governance (PSG) to the PSM agenda in late 1991 led to further expansion and institutionalization of PSM. This gave visibility to sector staff, many of whom had focused on institutional development just a few years earlier. This visibility was assisted via the 1987 reorganization reform. This leads us to Proposition J:

Proposition J: *Internal IO reorganizations may influence a sector policy's role, its expansion or diminishment, and its institutionalization or deinstitutionalization.*

For PSM, the 1987 Reforms strengthened the sector and gave a platform to reengage institutional development. Even though the 1987 Reforms (largely implemented by early 1988) predated the fall of the Berlin Wall, they raised the sector's profile in the eighteen months prior to this historical event. This increased the "sunk cost" of altering the sector, improved its communication structures, enhanced internal politics in favor of more PSM, and began to change institutional norms so that further topic additions and sector institutionalization could arise. Proposition J relates to variables I7–I10 from Betton and Dess (1985), the new corollary of Betton and Dess (variable I6) created for this book's analytical framework, and an increased legitimacy of PSM (and PSG) for the Bank's work (variable I2). With the end of the Cold War and a requirement that the Bank quickly incorporate post-Soviet countries into its work, criticality (variable I3) also increased.

With new public expenditure management research and modifications of structural adjustment's civil service reform perspectives, bankers were increasingly able to link accountability and governance with structural adjustment and economic growth. The new PSMUs were points of research and the location from which unit staff interacted with the country directors responsible for project generation. It is likely that without the fall of the Berlin Wall and subsequent Soviet collapse, this nascent institutionalization would have continued but at a slower pace. Instead, both external events when combined with the internal reorganization of 1987 sped-up sector expansion and its institutionalization.

This sector institutionalization continued into the next decades as new sector sub-topics were added (see Table 5). Between November 1989 and September 1996, the main PSM topic additions included civil service reform, public expenditure management, and public financial management (by 1989), good governance (by 1991), rule of law and judicial reform (by 1992), and tax reform (by 1993). Sector policy diversification continued as anticorruption was encouraged (by late 1996), pension and social security reform (by 2000), service delivery (by 2004), and re-emphases on demand-side governance (by 2007). This twenty-plus years of post-1987 sector sub-topic expansion coalesced with a mid-1990s Strategic Compact and a new matrix structure but also with staff efforts to institutionalize and to lead this sector policy change from within the Bank.

The legitimacy of increased sector visibility and its subsequent internal power to influence the Bank (variables I1 and I2) was assisted by external stakeholders who were less interested (if not fully absent) from post-1991 sector policy shifts. This leads to Proposition K:

Proposition K: *Internal stakeholders can increase sector policy institutionalization, sector power, and sector legitimacy even when external actors disengage from sector policy change.*

Bureaucracies infrequently act haphazardly. At the World Bank, in a policy environment full of Ph.D.s, new sector or topic policies often need substantial intellectual justifications (Ascher 1983).[3] This observation also explains why good governance led to sector expansion and institutionalization: Bank staff had an internal intellectual agreement that good governance improved economic growth and reduced poverty. Bankers understood that PSG (like PSM) would involve new research and by extension, new topics of interest. In the 1980s, developing country failures were viewed as policy failures rather than institutional failures. The

---

[3] Ascher (1983) observed that the Bank's civil servants are confident in their intellectual training: "For the international civil servant, the obvious (and much explored) competing loyalty is to the nation. For World Bank personnel, however, *identifications as professional experts and intellectuals promise better explanations of acceptance of or resistance to change* ... Furthermore, the status of intellectual, while it may liberate the staff member from the localism for which other international civil servants have been criticized, can also free the staff member from the "moral" obligation to comply with the wishes of superiors ... Many groups of well-educated individuals (such as university students) must choose between the professional and intellectual identities. This is not true, however, for those at the pinnacle of their professions, a situation enjoyed by many at the World Bank, particularly those most involved in the politics of defining the Bank's role and strategies. The top-level professional can hold these identities simultaneously, though not without strain, because he or she can be confident that mastery over one discipline of the ultimately convergent socioeconomic sciences allows him or her to approach the broad range of social issues, to set or refine the standards of the discipline, and to recognize the overlap of the disciplinary concerns with those of other disciplines" (Ascher 1983, 418-419, emphasis added).

structural-adjustment lending instruments were created to correct these identified policy failures. Structural adjustment and neoclassical economics were to provide short-term policy fixes. They tilted the state–market balance in favor of the market to encourage economic growth. A decade later, developing countries' failures would be understood not just as policy failures but institutional failures too. Good governance and its topics were created to address such institutional failures.

Between October 1996 and mid-1998, the PSM/PSG sector continued to institutionalize within the Bank. Institutionalization further strengthened internal actor control over sector policy changes. Sector expansion was assisted by an October 1996 speech by Bank President James Wolfensohn in which he stated that anticorruption efforts were necessary for development to be successful. No longer would Bank staff be forbidden from discussing the so-called "c-word." In its 1997 WDR, the Bank declared that the state "mattered" for development and in 1998, Bank staff wrote that it was time to move beyond the Washington Consensus. The transition from externally to internally led policy change was not a battle lost for the Bank's key external actors. The G7 nations already had their victory: the world was evolving into their desired economic and political order. Nor did this transition imply that external actors like the US had lost their structural power over the Bank. Vote shares had not changed. Nor had their legitimacy decreased. But after more than decade of key externally led guidance over this sector's policy shifts, the urgency and criticality of US involvement in this sector had lessened by the early 1990s. Key external actors stepped out of this sector's policy spotlight.

In addition, and not to be forgotten, internal reforms that favor a policy sector will increase its visibility within an IO, see Proposition I5 in Table 17. A further application of this inference occurred via the Bank's 1997–1998 matrix reforms. The reforms strengthened the PSM/PSG sector's placement within the Bank. The reforms created a Public Sector Board and a Public Sector Anchor. Both organizational units were placed within the Bank's most powerful lending network (PREM). It was the Public Sector Board that drafted the Bank's first Public Sector Strategy in 2000.

The main policy agenda shift between January 2004 and 2012 was the increased prominence of a demand-side (political economy) perspectives. Although the political economy thinking behind demand-side governance existed within the Bank good governance addition, its influence was not significant within the 2000 Public Sector Strategy. It would be until the mid-2000s that demand-side governance took over. Similar to earlier internal sector debates, political economy discussions with "supply side" governance occurred out of the public spotlight. The demand-side governance approach was strengthened with 2007 Governance and Anticorruption (GAC) Strategy. Interviewees, along with continued "traditional" PSM or supply side papers, suggested that a demand-side victory was far from complete. The GAC Strategy did not formally replace the 2000 Public Sector Strategy. Nor did the GAC Strategy replace PSM specialists who viewed political economy approaches as unrelated to PSM work. With the intellectual shifts from neoclassical economics to new institutional economics and to political economy approaches, Proposition L arises. This proposition is informed by variable I2 (legitimacy of economic theories for the Bank), variable I8 (the resulting communication structures as theory is disseminated across the Bank), and variable I9 (creation of institutional norms as a result of economic theory discussions) (Jonker and Foster 2002; Betton and Dess 1985):

Proposition L: *IO policy expansions and institutionalizations are assisted by internal actors' ability to intellectually justify the shifts.*

Unique to this sector, especially when compared to the prior twenty-seven years of sector policy shifts, was the level of public agitation attached to the GAC Strategy. The public battle was not about whether sector's policies should be "demand-side" or "supply side" (this was an internal battle) but about President Paul Wolfowitz, his management style, and how GAC Strategy would be approved. Wolfowitz demanded that the Bank put good governance and anticorruption high on its agenda. He also felt that a Bank President should be able to cut-off Bank clients whose corruption or financial mismanagement mocked Bank policy recommendations. Wolfowitz's actions also included his public dismissal of the Bank staff's draft Governance and Anticorruption Strategy. When the Board called him out on his Strategy switcheroo, Wolfowitz backed down and let Board discussion of the original draft to continue.

Wolfowitz's preferences also set off a noisy debate about the Bank's lending incentives and about what it means to "develop." This continued into the public sphere as Bank staff leaked information and shared gossip. At the next Annual Meeting, the Bank's Development Committee publicly reminded Wolfowitz of the relationship between the Bank's Executive Directors (who approved Bank projects and major policy shifts) and the Bank's President (who guides staff projects and policy creation). This rebuke by the Board of a President was without precedence. In the end, the lending questions were "resolved" via a rapid NGO "consultation" in which NGOs concluded that lending must continue. This leads to our final proposition and its link to two variables. The first is variable I6 (see Table 17) which suggests that given the importance of lending incentives, the Bank's internal environment will consider such incentives in its outputs. The second variable is E14 (see Table 17) in which the Bank's desire to survive requires it to lend.

Proposition M: *Lending and other operational incentives within an IO may be difficult, if not impossible, for internal actors to ignore.*

In the Wolfowitz fiasco, it also important to remind ourselves that the US was outnumbered by the Bank's other Executive Directors. It did not help Wolfowitz that he had tried to usurp Executive Director power by attempting to diminish their involvement in policy developments. It mattered that the Bank's organizational survival depended upon lending continuance. If the Bank does not lend, as noted by variable E14, the Bank does not survive. If the Bank does not survive, key states lose a vehicle for influencing developing country states and future sector shifts.

Shortly after Wolfowitz' departure, the Bank found itself confronting a global financial crisis, emergent middle-income countries with new non-Bank borrowing options, and a need to further envision the Bank's future. Robert Zoellick's presidency led to further institutionalization of PSM/PSG into the creation of a GAC Council. By 2012, the PSM/PSG sector had become the Bank's "DNA." It was the first sector (and still is the only one, in 2020) to be elevated as crucial for all Bank lending. From a sector born of international crises and ideological shifts (1980–1982 world recession, the rise of neoclassical economics), by 2012, the sector had not only survived several intellectual transformations, a Cold War end, and new sector topic expansions, but it had become *the* sector that nearly all Bank projects could not ignore.

Of course, Bank internal policy debates are about more than just ideology, approach, and preferences. Debate "winners" influence client state policy developments. But policy failure or policy inappropriateness does not negate the client states from repaying Bank loans. If a policy choice was "wrong," there is little recourse. Even if discoveries about poor Bank behavior are made, repayment is not overlooked. Assigning blame is difficult when multiple staff members create, implement, and evaluate Bank policies and projects. Similarly, it is not easy to determine how much blame should be assigned between the Bank and to the client country.

Until 1994, the Operations Evaluation Department (later the IEG) was the Bank's primary evaluative mechanism. As the importance of evaluation jumped to the top of external actor agendas, the Inspection Panel, the Integrity Vice Presidency, QAG, and a Results Secretariat were created. But within the PSM/PSG sector, these mechanisms generally did not feedback into policy change. Hampering this effort were the Inspection Panel, the Results Secretariat, and the Integrity Vice Presidency reports, which did not separate this sector's results when compared to other sectors. Interviewed staff considered the QAG review process to be arbitrary and overly aggressive while potentially relevant OED/IEG analyses were published long after project completion.

When asked about such problems, Bank interviewees claimed to be too overwhelmed with multiple project and research duties, an ever-expanding scholarly and Bank literature, and complex client demands. They complained about the lack of scholarly or Bank research about how IOs could reliably and comparably measure results across countries, contexts, and sectors. Even if such scholarship were available, this book has posited that Bank lending incentives may override such concerns (see Proposition I8). If a project or policy fails, should the Bank not lend until it finds another solution in a world in which there is often no single "right" development answer? For clients that may rely on low-interest IBRD loans or IDA grants to finance country needs, should countries really be obliged to take out higher-interest commercial debt until the Bank has designed the "right" policy? The answers are not easy.

Moreover, it may not be in the strategic long-term interest of the Bank's key external actors for the Bank to implement a comprehensive results management schema. Reflecting back on stakeholder theory and its observation that organizations like to survive (external actor propositions E1-E5 as well internal actor proposition I8), we cannot forget that the Bank is one of the few global development banks that the US and its G7 partners can, if they wish, control. Nonetheless, and given that there is also no single unassailably correct way to measure results efficiently, effectively, and equitably, this leaves the evaluation aspects of the Bank's work, both within and external to the PSM/PSG sector, constantly struggling to consistently and thoroughly influence feedback loops in sector policies and projects.

In Conclusion: Who Matters at the Bank?

The book's title asks: Who Matters at the World Bank? For the PSM/PSG sector, the answer varied across the 32 years covered by this book. In the 1980s, external actors and in particular, the US, UK, and the G7 (and to some extent, the IMF) mattered most in the creation and early contouring of PSM sector policies. This continued until the good governance concept was added to the Bank's sector agenda in August 1991. From that point on and with few exceptions, internal civil servants largely controlled and influenced policy change within the PSM/PSG sector. The Bank had moved from little-to-no interest in PSM in 1980 to not only becoming the Bank's "DNA" but also the first-ever (and still only) sector "to have a Bank-wide remit" (World Bank 2012, 53, 62). In doing so, sector policy topics multiplied, research deepened, and projects with a PSM/PSG component became dominant.

This book also answers how one sector of the Bank's work rose to prominence against all odds despite different forces seeking to alter its objectives and to influence its outputs at multiple points in time. This task was assisted by evaluating when, where, why, and how PSM/PSG sector policy change occurred and who influenced policy change. Influence was evaluated by the power, legitimacy, and urgency of the external, boundary, and internal stakeholder's claim on the organization, whether the organization is controlled by an external actor, considerations about the influence of an internal environment's size and importance, the explanatory power of bureaucratic politics, and identifying when and where internal actors may outweigh external influence (Mitchell et al. 1997; Pfeffer and Salancik 1978; Betton and Dess 1985; Allison and Halperin 1972).

A clear advantage of stakeholder theory and the bureaucratic politics approach to explaining policy change is their additive power. The more characteristics attributable to an actor at a point in time, the more likely the actor will influence policy change. Through process tracing, archival research, interviews, Bank document reviews, and importantly, no limitation of the dependent variable, this book's analytical framework allowed an estimation of actor power, legitimacy, and urgency over sector policy shifts. Tracing sector policy change across a mesohistorical timeline of 32 years increased the number of observations along with the reliability and validity of this book's findings. One output is the creation of thirteen propositions on policy change that may further our understanding of policy change within other IOs, other sectors, or even across multiple IOs.

This book's analytical focus and its understanding of civil servants are familiar to scholars from the discipline of public administration. However, this disciplinary approach need not negate nor even operate in a mutually exclusive fashion from international relations' realist theory. But rather than forcing two disciplines into an unhappy marriage of IO policy change, stakeholder theory and bureaucratic politics may be a potential bridge between the realist and the public administration scholar. This is important. In 1998, Checkel reminded scholars to "avoid the charge that they are reducing one unit of analysis—agents (states, decision makers)—to the other—structures (norms). In doing so, scholars have overlooked how norms arise in the first place (and the role of agency and power in the process), and how, through interactions with particular agents, norms change over time" (Checkel 1998, 340). Checkel desired a middle-range theory capable of connecting the dots. Stakeholder theory and bureaucratic politics help scholars connect those dots and as such, they help us step toward answering Checkel's call for a mid-range theory capable of explaining IO policy change.

If published fifteen years ago, this book's suggestions for mid-range theory development might have been one of only a few to offer an approach to understanding IO policy change potentially capable of modifying realist understandings of IO behaviors. But the constructivist challenge to realist theory beat me to the punch. Since my primary discipline (public administration) has largely ignored civil servant behaviors and policy change within IOs, the book had to first address the elephant in the room: constructivism (Weaver 2008; Barnett and Finnemore 2004). This discussion linked to scholarship whose work (Vetterlein 2007; Allan 2019; Makinder 2020; Sharma 2013; Williams 2008) which was not anchored within the public administration discipline or its concepts but which starts to bridge gaps between international relations and public administration. When combined with Xu and Weller's work linking the public administration discipline with IOs studies (Xu and Weller 2008, 2009, 2015, 2018; Weller and Xu 2010,

2015), my book's analytical framework and analysis continue that trend (Fleischer and Reiners 2021; Bauer et al. 2017; Moloney and Rosenbloom 2020). It is a trend which is part of a growing literature on international public administration, transnational administration, and global policy written by scholars of public administration and public policy (e.g., Knill and Bauer 2016; Bauer and Ege 2016; Ege et al. 2019; Bauer and Knill 2007; Patz and Goetz 2017; Bayerlein et al. 2020; Stone 2008; Stone and Ladi 2015; Stone and Moloney 2019a, 2019b, 2019c; Moloney and Stone 2020; Moloney and Stoycheva 2018).

In doing so, the surprise may be that realist theoreticians were not necessarily wrong (as suggested by constructivism) but instead, their answers did not fully explain all IO behaviors. IOs can (and often do) respond to the will of their key member states. This book draws on (a) the assumptions embedded within the public administration discipline (e.g., Dwight Waldo, Herbert Simon), (b) analytical sociology (e.g., Peter Hedström, Arthur Stinchcombe), and (c) the 1960s to early 1980s work by scholars of international relations who sought to understand IOs behavior (e.g., William Ascher, Robert Cox, Ernst Haas, and Harold Jacobsen). The output is an actor-specific understanding of how international civil servants, civil servant groups, and policy sector groups *are actors capable of influencing policy change.* If my book's analytical framework emphasized internal *actors* and their power interacting with external actors and their power via just two of the public administration discipline's many concepts and ideas, then constructivists emphasized a different (but complementary) organizational *culture.*

Constructivists offer organizational culture as the explanation for why IO may not obey state owners. However, in the public administration discipline, culture is not automatically viewed as an impediment or even a key independent variable for policy change. This does not mean that culture does not matter or that a bureaucracy cannot incorporate positive or even negative traits. Instead, the public administration discipline suggests that civil servants' sector policy preferences may reflect a policy politics in which their individual policy preferences, actor constellations, and organizational structures influence policy change. For IOs like the Bank, this includes intellectual agendas too.

Moreover, civil servant policy politics or bureaucratic politics are not the only influence upon policy change. External actors may also influence policy change whether states, other IOs, or even NGOs (e.g., Clark and Dolan 2021). *For the public administration scholar seeking to understanding IO policy change, the influence of internal actors upon IO outputs is not an either-or influence on whether a culture is good or bad or whether the IO staff actors simply act "disobediently" to state interests.* This argument has also been observed by Xu Yi-Chong and Patrick Weller in the last decade (Xu and Weller 2009, 2018; Weller and Xu 2015). Instead, this book attempts to empirically center Xu and Weller's argument with my interest in the public administration discipline, international civil servants, and IO policy change via one sector of one IO's work across 32 years of its sector policy history.

Stakeholder theory's ability to operationally interact with international relations theories and to also interact with public administration's long-held understanding of the politics-administration dichotomy is important. Stakeholder theory allows actor influences to be evaluated and to create potential explanations for policy change. To the best of my knowledge, neither stakeholder theory nor the bureaucratic politics approach have been used in prior IO studies. This book's offering is not just to scholars of international relations but also to scholars of public administration to reach out and to see what each may offer in understanding IO behaviors (e.g., Moloney and Stone 2020; Fleischer and Reiners 2021; Bauer et al. 2017).

The World Bank is an IO that affects the lives of hundreds of millions of people. The Bank influences intellectual debates about what development is and how development should be undertaken. Although the Bank may be the most important voice within development arenas, it is not the only voice. Other multilateral and bilateral donor institutions have voices and their client states can and do listen. Just as the World Bank's policy change histories may infrequently have just one narrator or one truth, other perspectives not chosen for this book (see Chapter 2) or left unexplored may not only have value but may be further highlighted via comparative IO research. It is also possible that if the Bank chose to release more documents (in particular, comprehensive Executive Director meeting minutes or its internal administrative budgets across the decades), such documents may further challenge, change, or contextualize this book's findings.

If there is to be a theory of IO policy change, the theory must incorporate more than what has been offered by scholars of international relations. This book's framework is both *complementary* to international relations' scholarship on IOs while also sharing just two of the many perspectives from the public administration discipline with potential relevance to IO studies. IOs exist within an international system that is difficult for many domestically focused public administration scholars to systematically assess. The *realpolitik* and regime theories guiding modern international relations are irremovable from IO studies. And yet, and as noted repeatedly in this book, disciplinary understandings from public administration are also irremovable from debates about international civil servants, their power and influence, and IO policy change. Understanding relations among and between internal and external actors via historically contextualized knowledge is crucial to creating a theory of IO policy change.

Postscript: An Update to 2020

In 2012, the PSM/PSG sector had become the Bank's "DNA" but also its first-ever (and still only) sector "to have a Bank-wide remit" (WorldBank 2012b, 53, 62). In its analysis of the 2013 to 2020 period, this postscript seeks to answer three questions: (a) Did the PSM/PSG sector retain its prominence? (b) How have a new President and an organizational reform altered this sector at the Bank? and (c) Given COVID-19, what might be the Bank's future? Given such objectives, readers are asked to treat my answers with caution as each is only a broad update and is not an output of the detailed multi-actor internal and external analyses of the rest of this book.

PSM/PSG Sector Still Prominent? Yes.

Between 2013 and 2020, the PSM and PSG sector did not lose its prominence at the Bank. As noted in Table 1, after a "dip" to being part of "just" 2/3 of projects approved in 2011 and 2012, the creation of the GAC Council and acknowledgement of the sector's Bank-wide remit led to increases in sector-included project approvals from 2013 to 2020. By 2017, 85 percent of approved Bank projects had a PSM and/or PSG component. Not only has the sector not gone away but most sectoral work links to the PSM/PSG agenda. A similar scan of sector topics appears largely unvaried from the early 2000s with the exception of a new topic in regulatory and competition policy. Using the search criteria which was used to create Table 1 but for the 2013 to 2020 period, regulation and competition policy (1275 projects), administrative and civil service reform (1109), SOE restructuring and privatization (888), and "other" public sector governance (721) are prominent.

New President, New Problems, New Agenda Items

With Robert Zoellick's departure as Bank President in July 2012, Dr. Jim Kim became the Bank's President. He served until February 2019. With a career in medicine, public health, and civil society (Dr. Kim was a founding director of the Partners in Health NGO), his background was unusual for the Bank (Moss 2012). But his choice was also politically necessary: President Obama wanted someone he "could present as an outsider" (Rice 2016) since the vacancy had been filled through the Bank's first-ever "outright 'competition' for the job" (Park 2019). With the exception of President Conable (former member of the US Congress), nearly all prior Bank Presidents had significant economic, finance, treasury, banking, and/or trade experience. McNamara and Wolfowitz came from the defense establishment. Dr. Kim was different. He was the first Bank President to have had decades of experience in public health and international development, to be a physician, and to be an anthropologist. He was also the first to have previously led an academic institution (Dartmouth College).

His selection was initially seen as a victory for NGOs who believed their voices were infrequently heard by the Bank as well as by public health experts who viewed the Bank's public health work as playing second fiddle to the World Health Organization and to an increasingly powerful Gates Foundation (e.g., Storeng 2014; Loewenberg 2015). For Kim, the Bank's 1993 *World Development Report* was a "catalyst in global health and development policy" (Kim 2013, E33) which ushered in a "golden era" of interest in global health, in the WHO, and in the creation and mobilization of multiple transnational public private partnerships (Huckel-Schneider 2019). He wanted to increase its impact at the Bank.

In his article for *Foreign Affairs* in 2018, Kim emphasized the links between human capital development, public health, and economic growth. From a PSM sector perspective, the importance of human capital for development had been emphasized by the Bank's institutional development experts as early as 1985 (see Chapter 3). It was not new. But Kim's emphasis was broader. It was about education and workforce training as well as understanding links between more education and decreased criminal activity, fewer social and economic inequalities, increased social participation, and improved intrasocietal trust. Given that "human capital doesn't materialize on its own," Kim noted that it "must be nurtured by the state" (Kim 2018, 96). When states are misaligned with their citizens, human capital development suffers. His solution is one that the Bank of the post-1990s period knows well: increased transparency, human capital metrics, and comparative benchmarking (Edwards 2018). But he also desired to close tax loopholes, to improve public expenditure management, and to emphasize health and social services delivery. Each were Bank lessons from prior decades too.

But there is at least one trait Dr. Kim shared with many Bank Presidents: a desire to reform the Bank. As noted by one observer, the Bank in 2012 was facing an "existential crisis" (Moss 2012). That is, its IDA clients would soon graduate and need the Bank less, the remaining low income states have sociopolitical environments where Bank advice has struggled (e.g., fragile and conflict-prone states), and the Bank needed to increase its understanding of global public goods (Kanbur 2016; Kopiński and Wróblewski 2021). A further warning sign was increased competition for the Bank. This competition concern was one influence on the last major reform: Wolfensohn's matrix structure. But this concern was heightened after the global financial crisis. There was new capital available for developing countries to borrow from commercial banks, from China, and from a new Asian Investment Infrastructure Bank (Moss 2012). Each challenged the Bank's desire to survive and to continuing the Bank's role as leader of the global development agenda.

Kim's attempt to reform the Bank in 2014 was contentious from the start. Like the 1987 Reform, Kim hired outside management consultants for advice. The intended output was a redesign of Wolfensohn's matrix into a structure that emphasized Kim's preferred "global practices." If the matrix continued the Bank's decades long prioritization of Country Directors, the latter gave policy sectors the lead (Girishankar 2013). Within months, staff were in an uproar. It did not help matters that the Bank's Chief Financial Officer had allegedly received a US$100,000 bonus just as Bank staff were being asked to tighten their belts (Edwards 2019). From the start, reform implementation was flawed. In an IEG evaluation published in 2015, the author noted that the "central change management team was dispersed when the reform became effective in 2014. This caused discontinuity in reform implementation" and, in a comment reminiscent of the Wapenhans Report of 1992, Kim's reform "did not change incentives, behaviors, and organizational culture" (Heltberg 2019). With the newly-created global practices not effectively communicating, the output was an "unmanageable" situation for Bank Country Directors (Provost 2014). The reform was so ineffective that by 2017, much of the 2014 reform efforts were undone. Country directors, once again, were in charge of which projects and which sector of lending would go forward (Edwards 2019).

An Unremarkable Year, then COVID-19

In April 2019, just ten months before COVID-19 hit, David Malpass became the 13th World Bank President. Like those before him, Malpass had finance and treasury experience. On the 75th anniversary of the Bretton Woods conference and in one of his first speeches as Bank President, Malpass noted 2019 that "strong country programs" will retain importance (Malpass 2019a). It was a suggestion that Bank staff understood: that is, despite the Kim reforms, country directors still mattered. A few months later, at an event held by the Center for Global Development in Washington DC, he observed ongoing good governance and human capital challenges in developing countries, noted the importance of global public goods, and spoke briefly about the challenges facing fragile states (Malpass 2019b). All in all, it was an unremarkable start to a Bank Presidency.

But then COVID-19 hit. The pandemic has not only altered how client needs were prioritized and which lending instruments were chosen but also the Bank had to manage itself, often from quarantine. The Bank's strategy on COVID-19 was two-fold: (a) initial emergency support; and (b) increase vaccine financing as well as vaccine deployment operations (WorldBank 2021b, 2020). It is certainly true to suggest that COVID-19 is altering the Bank's future. This is particularly true the world's poorest countries who may take years to recover. It is also true for the Fund. A record of 100+ countries sought IMF assistance in 2020. It is unclear whether predictions a few years earlier about IDA graduations will remain on hold or if for some IDA graduates, COVID may push their economy back to an IDA status.

Looking to the future, PSM and PSG are unlikely to fade away. No longer toiling away unnoticed in a back corner, it is a sector that links to everything the Bank does from infrastructure to health to gender to global public goods. As IDA countries recover from COVID-19, the challenges identified at the start of Kim's presidency remain. The securing of finance for Bank operations remains as crucial today as it was in 1980. With alternatives to Bank financing on the rise, its ability to survive requires innovations in its lending instruments, its modalities of work, and new partnerships outside the institution. Each are necessary if the Bank is to retain its role as the leader of global development agendas.

Appendix

How the World Bank Operates

This Appendix overview is written to assist students, practitioners, and scholars unfamiliar with the World Bank Group. It answers four questions: (1) What is the World Bank? (2) How is the World Bank organized? (3) How is the World Bank funded? (4) How is the World Bank governed?

What is the World Bank?

According to the 2013 Union of International Associations (UIA), there are 803 international governmental organizations (UIA 2013).[1] Among IOs, no less than ten are classified as multilateral development banks (MDBs). The MDB label is exchangeable with an International Financial Institution (IFI) label.[2] There are two global MDBs: the IMF and the World Bank. Regional MDBs include the European Bank for Reconstruction and Development, the Asian Development Bank, the Inter-American Development Bank, the African Development Bank, and more recently, the Asian Investment Infrastructure Bank as well as the New Development Bank. Smaller regional MDBs include the Islamic Development Bank and Caribbean Development Bank.

Among MDBs, one of the largest and most important (staffing, budget, influence) is the World Bank. Its mission is to encourage economic growth and reduce poverty with a particular focus on less developed countries. The World Bank, along with its counterpart, the International Monetary Fund (IMF), can resuscitate a developing country's financial situation and (in)directly impact domestic politics. The importance attached to the Bank's policies requires that we understand how its policies are created, considered, and changed.

As a global actor, most states are members of the World Bank. Along with the IMF, the International Bank for Reconstruction and Development (IBRD) was founded at a 1944 conference in Bretton Woods, New Hampshire. Attended by forty-four countries including the US, a conference purpose was to find consensus for a post-World War II international economic order.[3] Today, there are several Bretton Woods Institutions: the IMF and the World Bank Group (and its two constituent parts, the IBRD and the International Development Association (IDA)), the Multilateral Investment Guarantee Agency (MIGA), the International Finance Corporation (IFC), and the International Centre for the Settlement

---

[1] Others calculate the number of IOs differently. This includes the Correlates of War database which in its 2020 iteration, counted over 500 IOs (Pevehouse et al. 2020).

[2] No MDB / IFI is a commercial bank or an investment bank.

[3] Discussions about creating international financial institutions began as early as late 1941 when the then-US Treasury Secretary asked Harry White (a Treasury employee) to "prepare a memorandum" on how to establish an organization that "should provide the basis for postwar international monetary arrangements." The so-called "White Plan" and its iterations were debated throughout WWII (Bank's World 1986a, 5).

of Investment Disputes (ICSID). Membership in IDA along with the IFC and MIGA are conditional on whether or not a state is also a member of the IBRD. Each Bretton Woods institution is headquartered in Washington DC with its main office located between two and six blocks from the White House.

The IFC was created in 1956 and today has 185 member states. The IFC supports and invests in private sector enterprises in developing countries. A key difference between the IFC and the World Bank is that the former invests in private enterprise whereas the latter largely interacts with government policies. By the late 1980s, the Bank added private sector development activities to its portfolio even if the Bank does not veer into IFC territory in directly supporting foreign direct investment. Instead, the Bank can assist client countries'[4] public sectors increase country attractiveness to foreign or domestic private sector developments. The ICSID was established in 1966 and today has 164 member states. The institution arbitrates legal disputes between foreign investors and its member states. MIGA was established in 1988 and today has 181 member states. MIGA helps insure certain select foreign direct-investment projects for currency transfers, expropriation, war and civil unrest, and breaches of contract. Using its country-specific knowledge, MIGA can lower private borrowing costs, settle disputes, and encourage social and environmental standards.

The IMF was jointly established with the IBRD at the 1944 Bretton Woods conference. The IMF observes the macroeconomic management of its member countries[5] and where needed will provide loans and advice. The purpose of today's World Bank is to increase economic growth and reduce poverty in its member states. The duty lines and scope of influence between the two organizations can become muddied. For PSM, overlap can lead to public disagreements and a need reestablish mission boundaries (see Chapter 5 on the Concordat and Chapter 6 on the Asian Financial Crisis).

Countries cannot be members of the World Bank without IMF membership, although a country may choose IMF membership without World Bank membership. Even though both organizations were founded at Bretton Woods, the IMF is not part of the World Bank Group. The IMF has its own managing director, traditionally a European appointed by European governments whereas the IBRD's and IDA's president traditionally has been an American citizen selected by the US Government.[6] The IFC, ICSID, and MIGA are part of the World Bank Group and receive a portion of their operating expenses from the Bank's annual budget, but each has its own organizational structure.

World Bank Organization

There is no "World Bank" as a singular IO. Instead, the IBRD (189 member states) and IDA (173 member states) are two formal IOs with separate Articles of Agreement. Together, they are colloquially understood as *the World Bank* or more familiarly as *the Bank*. The IFC, MIGA, and ICSID are generally referred to by their acronyms. When combined, all five IOs (IBRD, IDA, MIGA, IFC, ICSID) are members of the World Bank Group.

---

[4] Bank staff call developing country states *client countries*. This term is also used in this book.

[5] The IMF publishes reports about the fiscal and monetary health of all member countries including wealthy countries.

[6] The IBRD's Articles of Agreement do not state that the President must be appointed by the US. The Articles of Agreement indicate that the Bank's Executive Directors choose the President, but in reality, the US preference to have a US citizen as President has remained unchanged (Shihata 2000b). Although President James Wolfensohn's birth citizenship was Australia, he obtained American citizenship about fifteen years before becoming Bank President.

Even though the World Bank is not a "bank" (as the term is commonly understood), its name stuck because no one at the Bretton Woods conference had a suitable alternative name.[7] The IBRD's first project—a postwar reconstruction loan to France—was approved in 1947. Many of today's developed countries were early IBRD clients. Between 1947 and 1959, 27.7 percent of approved IBRD project loans went to Australia, Austria, Belgium, Denmark, Iceland, Finland, France, Italy, Japan, Luxembourg, the Netherlands, and Norway. The remainder was loaned to 30 countries some of which are considered as developing today (World Bank 2008d).

As anti-colonial independence movements succeeded in the late 1950s and 1960s, many newly independent states sought developmental finance. The IBRD identified a need for specifically targeted multilateral aid programs for developing countries. The organizational response was to create the IDA. Founded in 1960, the IDA's first loans were approved in 1961 for four countries: Chile, Honduras, India, and the Sudan (IDA 2009). The IBRD and IDA share the same President, Executive Directors, and Board of Governors. The primary difference is which countries receive their aid, the concessionality of that aid, and how each organization is funded. IDA countries are mostly the poorest of the poor.

In 2021, seventy-four countries were classified as IDA countries. IDA classification requires a Gross National Income (GNI) per capita of US$1205 or less. Since its creation in 1960, IDA has "graduated" 46 countries to IBRD status. In three of those cases (Egypt and Philippines in 1991, Indonesia in 1993), the countries re-entered IDA before re-graduating in 1993 (Philippines), 1999 (Egypt), and 2008 (Indonesia). In another eight cases, countries graduated, returned to IDA classification and as of mid-2021, have not re-graduated. These eight include Cameroon (exited in 1981, re-entered the IDA classification in 1994), the Republic of Congo (exited 1982, re-entered 1994), Cote d'Ivoire (exited 1973, re-entered 1992), Honduras (exited 1980, re-entered 1992), Nicaragua (exited 1981, re-entered 1991), Nigeria (exited 1965, re-entered 1989), Syria (exited 1974, re-entered 2017), and Zimbabwe (exited 1983, re-entered 1992) (IDA 2021a).

In contrast to IDA arrangements, IBRD loans are not concessional. IBRD countries are typically understood as middle income or higher countries although in nearly all cases since 1960, the highest income countries do not seek World Bank assistance. In-between IDA and IBRD categories are the IDA's "blend" or "gap" countries. Such countries have a per capita gross national income above the IDA cut-off but their small size (often a small island-state but not always) makes each country particularly vulnerable to global economic shifts. Loans to blend countries have a shorter maturity than IBRD loans. If the IDA country is not a blend/gap country but is considered a "small economy" their loan maturities and grace periods are longer than regular non-small IDA countries (IDA 2021b).

This book, like the many others studying the Bank, considers the IBRD and IDA to be one institution. This is both analytical convenient but also a reflection of staff careers. Not only do Bank staff move freely throughout their careers between the two organizations, but as mentioned above, both report to the same administration. Projects can be prepared by staff from one or both institutions. There is no Managing Director or Senior Vice President specifically for IDA; rather, these administrators serve "the Bank" (IBRD plus IDA)

---

[7] As the Belgian delegate to Bretton Woods observed on July 21, 1944, "So novel was [this institution] that no adequate name could be found for it. In so far as we can talk of capital subscriptions, loans, guarantees, issues of bonds, the new financial institution may have some apparent claim to the name of Bank. But the type of shareholders, the nature of subscriptions, the exclusion of all deposits and of short-term loans, the nonprofit basis, are quite foreign to the accepted nature of a Bank. However it was accidentally born with the name Bank, and Bank it remains, mainly because no satisfactory name could be found in the dictionary for this unprecedented institution" (Bank's World 1986b, 14).

as a whole. For instance, it is possible to be a Bank Vice President for Latin America and the Caribbean and for the regional portfolio to include IBRD and IDA-eligible countries. Still, PSM/PSG project choices do differ across countries and not always cleanly along IDA versus IBRD lines. Country- and region-specific differences have increased as wealthier countries require different policies than the poorest countries. For example, interviewees suggested that Middle East and North African countries are less amiable to civil service reform and anticorruption projects (WB28) while Latin America's IBRD countries prefer technical assistance over sector-wide projects (WB34).

Bank Funding

Knowing the origin of the Bank's money helps to partially explain to whom the Bank responds. Most of IBRD and IDA project and program money and its administrative budget[8,9] come from member state contributions or the Bank's leveraging of member-state guarantees (to obtain further financial resources from international markets). IBRD money is a guarantee authority from a member state's capital commitments to the organization. The Bank also retains callable capital which allows the Bank to ask its member states to pay what they promised. To date, the Bank has yet to call in that capital. Bank member states must provide three percent of their guarantee, in cash, to the Bank (Klutznick 1988). According to the Bank's own analysis in 2008, "this [guarantee system] has been done at a relatively low cost to taxpayers, with governments paying in $11 billion in capital since 1946 to generate more than $400 billion in loans" (World Bank 2008b).

This raises a logical question. If only a tiny portion of the Bank's annual financial requirements have been paid to the Bank, where does the rest originate from? The short answer is that the difference comes from the world's financial markets. The IBRD issued its first bond

---

[8] During fieldwork, I was given three hours of access to the Bank's Resource Management Unit to copy administrative budget numbers. When I asked to return and continue what would have become a likely sixty-hour task, my contact wrote that his/her unit supervisor prohibited further viewing of internal budget documents and had also disallowed any not for attribution interview. This was only one of two interview declines. As to why the unit disallowed access, I received this email: "This unit is not a Federal model entity like OMB [US Office of Management and Budget] or in a [sic] traditional Federal agency CFO. In the Federal realm more emphasis is placed on the budget process and related documents. The process is extremely time consuming and never ends. OMB's budget process, policies, and laws, the president, and Congress keep up the intensity ... Here at the Bank there is no iron triangle or executive and legislative branch ... As such, priorities are given to the managing directors from the executive directors and we allocate 'the administrative budget' to help fulfill those priorities. As such we are called 'resource management' and not 'management and budget'" (7 July, 2008). Thus, the Bank merely allocates the budget to priority, oversight is limited, and the potential interviewee could not imagine my interest. When subsequent interviewees were asked how budgets were determined, most expressed little understanding. Although ED meeting minutes provided little help for this book, one set noted that administrative budgets must be managed "within a band of plus or minus 2 percent" and they require quarterly Board approval (World Bank 2005d). Administrative budgets could have provided a key analytical assist to triangulate and to track money and therefore, suggest potential policy sector changes.

[9] During my Research Management Unit visit (see immediately prior footnote), the employee indicated that his/her office's collection of the annual administrative budgets (which only went back to the 1980s) was the *only one* available. He/she was uncertain if the Bank's storage archives (held at an abandoned salt mine in Pennsylvania and not accessible to the public) had earlier budgets. Even the employee was astounded by those two facts. Given limited public oversight of Bank budgets and the limited budgetary information relayed in annual financial statements, preserving detailed administrative budget memories appears to not be a priority. When my fieldwork was updated for this book, public access remained unavailable.

in 1947 (World Bank 2008c) and obtained a AAA credit rating in 1959—a rating the institution has likely maintained (World Bank 2008b).[10] In testimony before the US Congress in 1982, the Treasury Department observed that the Bank had never drawn upon its reserves nor had it altered its "gearing ratio … [which] is fixed in the World Bank's Articles of Agreement at a very conservative one-to-one ratio, in contrast to the fractional reserve system used in commercial banking" (Dawson 1982).[11] Although this ratio has been considered a "lending straitjacket" (Rowen 1984), the IBRD has used its AAA credit rating to secure the best terms for its client states. This includes an IBRD ability to borrow at rates just above US treasury bond rates (World Bank 2008b).[12] The Bank may make a profit via its investments and the returns on loans provided to clients. This profit is redistributed to the IDA budget. Before July 1982, the Bank lent at fixed interest rates. In response to global interest rate volatility in the early 1980s, the Bank began to offer variable rate loans (Clausen 1986 [1982]; Tillier 1984).[13]

In contrast to IBRD, nearly all IDA funding is replenished every three years. The latest pledges (for IDA-19)[14] were made in December 2019. To fund its loans, grants, and administrative expenses, the Bank approaches governments to replenish IDA funds.[15] The pledged amounts constitute the vast majority of IDA funding. This equaled US$23.488 billion in IDA-19 given by 56 countries of which the UK (12.07 percent of contribution for IDA-19), Japan (10.0 percent), and the US (9.31 percent) provided the most. A tiny remainder comes from investment income redistributed to IDA. In IDA-19, this additional amount equaled US$134 million. The amount contributed by each member government is not fixed. It is possible that a member state will donate more to the overall IDA replenishment than their voting shares might indicate. For example, during a time of IDA crisis (see Chapter 3 on the US, Chapter 4 on the 1987 Reform), IDA-6 (FY1982–84) received pledges of US$12 billion but IDA-7 (FY1985-87) pledges were just US$9 billion. Triennial replenishment requirements may put IDA funding in the crosshairs of prevailing donor sentiments. Since the Bank's governance structure allows certain countries to have a greater voting share than others, the Bank is predisposed to listen to its largest shareholders during and after IDA replenishments. Moreover, just because a country pledged a certain number of dollars at the

[10] It is surmised that the Bank has continually retained its AAA rating although conclusive proof is not publicly accessible. In one recent analysis, the Bank's current credit rating is made available to the public but its "historical credit rate and its historical investment performance were not available" (Moloney and Stoycheva 2018).

[11] I could not find a more recent citation. A one-to-one ratio means that the Bank holds $1 in savings for every $1 it borrows. The fractional reserve system references a requirement that US commercial banks must retain a fraction of their liabilities in reserve. During the Asian financial crisis (1997–1998), the Bank's President, James Wolfensohn, worried the Bank might "soon be lending beyond its prudential limits." Wolfensohn further stated, "I'm not going to be the one who endangers the AAA credit rating of the Bank" (Mallaby 2004, 208) given that every prior Bank President jealously guarded the AAA rating.

[12] One late 1980s rumor about the Bank's triple-A credit rating required Standard and Poor's to issue a statement that it would be "unlikely" for the Bank to lose its high credit rating (Reuters 1987). Among eight MDBs with credit ratings, only the African Development Bank was rated aa+ by Standard & Poor's while the IBRD, IDA, and IFC had AAA credit ratings (Hay 2021).

[13] Rate is determined twice yearly via "average cost of a pool of IBRD borrowings" (Clausen 1986 [1982], 110).

[14] "IDA-19" refers to IDA's nineteenth replenishment cycle since 1960. Since at least the early 1980s replenishment cycles have covered three fiscal years. The Bank's fiscal year runs from July 1st to June 30th.

[15] Only Switzerland and the US require legislative input before allocating monies to the IDA (Stanton 1986).

start of the replenishment period, there is no requirement that during the three-year disbursement process that the donor country will deliver. This is no different from the UN's appeals to the world community after a humanitarian tragedy.

In the last fifteen years, trust funds have provided additional monies. They are separate from IDA pledges and IBRD capital commitments. By creating a trust fund, donor countries do not expect a reduction in their IDA commitments or IBRD capital commitments. Trust funds "are financial and administrative arrangements with an external donor that leads to grant funding of high-priority development needs, such as technical assistance, advisory services, debt relief, post-conflict transition, and co-financing" (WorldBank 2008e, n.p.). Their importance has increased over time. For example, the UK, Netherlands, and Norway created a $75 million trust fund in 2006 that specifically targeted the PSM/PSG sector.

Bank Governing

The Bank has a Board of Governors. The Board meets once a year at the World Bank and IMF's Annual Meetings. Each Governor is a member state's Minister of Finance or Treasury or in some cases, a senior official from their bilateral aid agency. The Bank's Charter gives the Governors power over the World Bank Group. However, for the Bank's daily operational life (budgets, policies, projects, reforms), the Governors ceded power several decades ago to the Bank's Board of Executive Directors (EDs).

The IBRD Board of Executive Directors has twenty-five members who also serve *ex officio* as IDA EDs. As of mid-2021, the seven permanent EDs for the IBRD include the US, Japan, the UK, Germany, Saudi Arabia, China, and France. The EDs retain offices within the World Bank complex. Each ED holds two-year terms that can be renewed at the discretion of the government(s) they represent. Each of the seven permanent members represent only their own government. Russia previously represented only itself but in recent years, represents itself and Syria. The rest of the EDs represent their own country plus others. This "representation" ranges from three countries (Angola, Nigeria, South Africa) for one ED and 22 countries for another. By IBRD voting shares, the seven main members hold the largest shares (43.17 percent, combined) with the US retaining the largest (15.9 percent) followed by Japan (7.47 percent) and China (5.07 percent) (IBRD 2021). At the IDA, the same seven represent their own countries with the US having the largest vote share (9.97 percent) followed by Japan (8.36 percent) for a combined share among the seven of 39.84 percent (IDA 2021c).

Tables

Table 1 PSM/PSG Projects approved (1968–2020)

Year	PSM/PSG Projects (1968–2020)				
	Total Projects with any PSM/PSG Component Approved/Year	All Projects Approved in All Sectors	Projects with PSM Approved as % of All Project Sectors	Projects with ≥ 51% PSM/PSG per Year	% of PSM/PSG Projects with ≥ 51% PSM/PSG per Year
1968	1	81	1.23%	1	100%
1969	0	112	0.00%	0	N/A
1970	0	138	0.00%	0	N/A
1971	1	121	0.83%	1	100%
1972	2	146	1.37%	2	100%
1973	3	189	1.59%	3	100%
1974	2	187	1.07%	2	100%
1975	2	204	0.98%	2	100%
1976	5	219	2.28%	5	100%
1977	1	217	0.46%	1	100%
1978	4	249	1.61%	4	100%
1979	6	234	2.56%	6	100%
Total (1968–1979)	*27*	*2097*	*1.29%*		
1980	6	262	2.29%	6	100%
1981	7	235	2.98%	7	100%
1982	10	256	3.91%	10	100%
1983	8	256	3.13%	8	100%
1984	11	213	5.16%	10	91%
1985	14	266	5.26%	10	71%
1986	26	236	11.02%	6	23%
1987	57	247	23.08%	17	30%
1988	73	221	33.03%	15	21%
1989	117	248	47.18%	11	9%
1990	170	238	71.43%	31	18%
1991	183	257	71.21%	32	17%
1992	192	274	70.07%	49	26%
1993	187	249	75.10%	39	21%
1994	241	312	77.24%	60	25%
1995	222	284	78.17%	49	22%
1996	271	327	82.87%	51	19%
1997	244	292	83.56%	54	22%

Continued

Table 1 *Continued*

	PSM/PSG Projects (1968–2020)				
Year	Total Projects with any PSM/PSG Component Approved/Year	All Projects Approved in All Sectors	Projects with PSM Approved as % of All Project Sectors	Projects with ≥ 51% PSM/PSG per Year	% of PSM/PSG Projects with ≥ 51% PSM/PSG per Year
1998	259	316	81.96%	61	24%
1999	268	328	81.71%	58	22%
2000	261	318	82.08%	68	26%
2001	254	339	74.93%	76	30%
2002	222	310	71.61%	55	25%
2003	204	356	57.30%	62	30%
2004	284	432	65.74%	79	28%
2005	285	415	68.67%	83	29%
2006	281	442	63.57%	87	31%
2007	351	532	65.98%	105	30%
2008	357	550	64.91%		
2009	338	561	60.25%		
2010	384	646	59.44%		
2011	372	572	65.03%		
2012	317	465	68.17%		
Total (1980–2012)	*6476*	*11,255*	*57.54%*	*Data not available after 2007 as new Bank project database does not specify % of monies within a project targeting one or more Bank sectors of work.*	
2013	363	486	74.69%		
2014	391	581	67.30%		
2015	313	467	67.02%		
2016	321	440	72.95%		
2017	457	540	84.63%		
2018	388	453	85.65%		
2019	340	394	86.29%		
2020	526	617	85.25%		
Total (2013–2020)	*3099*	*3978*	*77.90%*		
Total (1968–2020)	*9602*	*17,330*	*55.41%*		

Note: Column B, E, F (1968–2007) from 2008 Projects Database. Column C plus rest from 2020 Projects Database.

Table 2 Reviewed documents

Document Series	Years Reviewed
Annual Reports	1947, 1975–2012
Annual Reports on Portfolio Performance	1993–1996, 2002, 2004–2006
Bank historian interview transcripts	Various
Bank Swirled (satirical staff newsletter)	1984–2008
Bank's World (staff newsletter)	1982–1989
Development Committee documents	1993, 2000–2012
Inspection Panel reports	1993, 1996, 1998, 1999, 2003
Integrity (INT) reports	2003–2004, 2007
OED/IEG reports or documents	1982–2012
PREM Notes (series began in 1998)	1998–2007
QAG reports	2001–2006
Staff directories (not public after 2002)	1970, 1974, 1979, 1982–1996, 1998–2001
World Bank research reports	1978–2012
World Development Reports	1978–2012
G7(8) communiques, statements	1976–2012
IMF statements, speeches, reports	1976–2012
NGO activities, reports, statements	1976–2012
US Treasury speeches and press releases	1979–2012

Table 3 Interviewees, organization, and category

Number	Organization	Organization Type	Category
WB1	Bank/IEG	World Bank	Internal
WB2	Bank/IEG	World Bank	Internal
WB3	Bank/WBI	World Bank	Internal
WB4	Bank/INT	World Bank	Internal
WB5	Bank/Results	World Bank	Internal
WB6	Bank/General	World Bank	Internal
WB7	Bank/IEG	World Bank	Internal
WB8	Bank/Results	World Bank	Internal
WB9	Bank/IP	World Bank	Internal
WB10	Bank/PSM Anchor	World Bank	Internal
WB11	Bank/DEC	World Bank	Internal
WB12	Bank/PSM	World Bank	Internal
WB13	Bank/General	World Bank	Internal
WB14	Bank/PSM Civil Service Reform	World Bank	Internal
WB15	Bank/PSM	World Bank	Internal

Continued

Table 3 *Continued*

Number	Organization	Organization Type	Category
WB16	Bank/PSM Anchor	World Bank	Internal
WB17	Bank/PSM AFR	World Bank	Internal
WB18	Bank/General	World Bank	Internal
WB19	Bank/General	World Bank	Internal
WB20	Bank/PSM Civil Service Reform & Fin Mgmt	World Bank	Internal
WB21	Bank/PSM AFR	World Bank	Internal
WB22	Bank/PSM	World Bank	Internal
WB23	Bank/PSM LAC	World Bank	Internal
WB24	Bank/PSM Eastern Europe	World Bank	Internal
WB25	Bank/General	World Bank	Internal
WB26	Bank/General	World Bank	Internal
WB27	Bank/PSM Law & Justice	World Bank	Internal
WB28	Bank/PSM MENA	World Bank	Internal
WB29	Bank/General	World Bank	Internal
WB30	Bank/PSM AFR	World Bank	Internal
WB31	Bank/PSM Anchor	World Bank	Internal
WB32	Bank/PSM Anchor	World Bank	Internal
WB33	Bank/PSM	World Bank	Internal
WB34	Bank/PSM (via 1998 Institutions Matter only)	World Bank	Internal
WB35	Bank/PSM AFR & EE	World Bank	Internal
WB36	Bank/PREM MENA, LAC	World Bank	Internal
WB37	Bank/AFR and EDI/WBI	World Bank	Internal
WB38	Bank/PSM and DEC	World Bank	Internal
WB39	Bank/1997 Report; IEG Director	World Bank	Internal
WB40	Bank/ECA	World Bank	Internal
WB41	Bank/2004 co-director	World Bank	Internal
WB42	Institute for International Finance	Commercial Bank	External
WB43	Bank Information Center	NGO	External
WB44	Bretton Woods Committee	NGO	External
WB45	Center for Global Development	NGO	External
WB46	Development GAP	NGO	External
WB47	Government Accountability Project	NGO	External
WB48	International Budget Project	NGO	External
WB49	Public Services International	NGO	External
WB50	Transparency International	NGO	External
WB51	American Enterprise Institute	Think-Tank	External
WB52	Heritage Foundation	Think-Tank	External
WB53	Institute for International Economics	Think-Tank	External
WB54	IMF	IMF	External
WB55	IMF	IMF	External
WB56	Bank's GAC Secretariat	World Bank	Internal
WB57	Bank/1987 and PSM	World Bank	Internal

Note: This is a blinded version. The non-blinded version with interviewee names has been shared with Oxford University Press.

Table 4 Who matters most in PSM/PSB policy change (by actor, by chapter)

Chapter	Years	Who Matters Most in Influencing PSM/PSG Policy Change			Who is Present but Matters Less in Influencing PSM/PSG Policy Change	Who Is Not Present in Influencing PSM/PSG Policy Change
		External Actors	Boundary Actor	Internal Actors		
Chapter 3	January 1980–October 1989	US, UK, IMF, G7 Group of Nations	Does not provide substantial publicly accessible comments	Anne Krueger as Chief Economist (as proxy for US/UK); Ibrahim Shihata; Ernie Stern	Mahbub Ul Haq and Hollis Chenery (both exited the Bank in early 1980s), PSM Unit/staff, Microeconomists, Kim Jaycox as East Asia VP (Indonesia Report in 1985)	Bank President, NGOs, Internal Evaluators
Chapter 4	*1987 Reform*	*US*	*Bank President (authorization only)*	*Kim Jaycox as Reform Leader, as PSM Unit Supporter, and as person who pushed the 1985 Indonesia Report to completion.*		
	Wapenhans Report (1992)	*Provides no substantial publicly accessible comments*	*Bank President (authorization only)*	*None as Report not implemented*		
Chapter 5	November 1989–September 1995	US and UK (until 1991) and nearly exclusively upon continued structural adjustment and privatization.	Largely absent	Ernie Stern, Kim Jaycox, DEC, PSM and PSG specialists	Bank President	US (after 1991), G7, IMF

Chapter 6	October 1996–December 1999	Largely absent	Bank President & DEC (1995/1996 only)	PREM Network, Public Sector Anchor, Bank President	Bank President after 1996	US, G7, IMF
Chapter 7	January 2000–December 2003	Largely absent	Largely absent	PREM Network, Public Sector Anchor	DEC, Bank President, IMF (in relation to Asian Financial Crisis only)	US, G7
Chapter 8	January 2004–July 2012	The Board intervened in the GAC Strategy given Wolfowitz' strategy switcheroo, evolving scandals, and staff uproar	Bank President Wolfowitz (on GAC Strategy)	PREM Network, Public Sector Anchor	US, DEC, Bank President Zoellick	G7, IMF
Chapter 9	*External NGOs and Internal Evlauative Actors*	*TI (mid-to-late 1990s only); NGOs (in general with 2007 Wolfowitz/GAC); IBP (late 2000s and early 2010s with public expenditure management topic only)*	Largely absent	N/A	*OED/IEG prepares evaluations but policies/projects already moved on; Public Sector International (NGO); Bank Information Center (NGO); 50 Years is Enough (NGO)*	*Inspection Panel, QAG, Integrity, Vice Presidency, Results Secretariat*

Table 5 PSM/PSG sector topics by era

Chapter	Years	Sector Topics
Chapter 3	January 1980–October 1989	From 1980–1984, archtypical "structural adjustment" focused on exchange rates, interest rates, state owned enterprises, and unclear PSM topic differentiation with IMF. By 1985, the addition of privatization. By 1988, new additions of civil service reform (first generation), public expenditure management, and public financial management.
Chapter 5	November 1989–September 1995	The above plus "good governance", social expenditures, tax reform, decentralization, judicial reforms.
Chapter 6	October 1996–December 1999	No longer archtypical "structural adjustment". Fewer privatization projects. Civil service reform (2nd generation). Rest of the above sector topics are retained. Anticorruption, accountability, participatory objectives, service delivery, social security, and pension reform are added.
Chapter 7	January 2000–December 2003	Topics become divided into "supply side" (public expenditure management, public financial management) and "demand side" governance (the early 1990s good governance plus anticorruption). Very few archtypical "structural adjustment" and privatization projects. Rest of above sector topics are retained.
Chapter 8	January 2004–July 2012	Same as Chapter 7 but with an emphasis on demand side governance. Added umployment insurance.

Table 6 Top project sectors (1947–1979)

Years	No. of Projects	Most Common Project Sector	Second Most Common Project Sector	Third Most Common Project Sector
1947–1949	21	Transportation adjustment (4); Economic management (4)	Agricultural adjustment (3)	Forestry (2); Electric (2); Hydro (2)
1950–1954	91	Railways (13)	Agricultural adjustment (10)	Economic management (9); Electric power (9); Hydro (9)
1955–1959	140	Railways (23)	Hydro (18)	Electric power (15)
1960–1964	227	Highways (43)	Hydro (28)	Irrigation and drainage (25)
1965–1969	371	Highways (68)	Hydro (27)	Telecommunications (25)
1970–1974	781	Highways (93)	Financial sector development (59)	Agricultural adjustment (53)
1975–1979	1310	Agricultural adjustment (133)	Irrigation and drainage (115)	Financial sector development (107)
Total Projects:	2,920			

Note: Column B, E, F (1968–2007) from 2008 Projects Database. Column C plus rest from 2020 Projects Database.

	January 1980 to October 1989				
	External Actors			Boundary Actor	
External & Boundary Actor Matters?	G7(8)	IMF	US ED	Other EDs	President
E1 [External/Boundary Actor] *power* to influence the Bank	Yes	Yes	Yes	Yes	Yes
E2 *Legitimacy* of the [External/Boundary Actor] relationship with the Bank	Yes	Yes	Yes	Yes	Yes
E3 *Urgency* of the [External/Boundary Actor] claim on the Bank	Urgency	Urgency	Urgency	Yes for UK ED	Yes, especially during the 1987 reform period
E4 [External/Boundary Actor] *criticality* over the Bank	Yes	Yes	Yes	Yes for UK ED	Yes
Is Organization Controlled by External/Boundary Actor?					
E5 Bank is aware of [External/Boundary Actor] demands	Yes	Yes	Yes	Yes	Yes
E6 Bank obtains some resources from the [External/Boundary] making the demands	Yes—Political, Economic, Financial, Ideological	Yes—Legal, Ideological	Yes—Political, Economic, Financial, Ideological	Yes—Political, Economic, Financial, Ideological	Simply agrees with G7(8), IMF, US/UK EDS
E7 The [External/Boundary Actor] resources are critical or important part of the Bank's operation	Very Indirectly	Largely indirectly	Yes—Political, Economic, Financial, Ideological	Yes	When political will is needed, yes.
E8 The [External/Boundary Actor] controls the allocation, access or use of the resources; alternative sources for the resources are not available to the focal organization	Very Indirectly	Only in so much as any Bank member-state must also be a member of the IMF too	Directly and Indirectly. But its superpower status, largest voting share, and ability to influence Bank direction matter.	Yes, theoretically	Has influence, yes. Controls, no.

Continued

Table 7 *Continued*

External & Boundary Actor Matters?	January 1980 to October 1989					
	External Actors					Boundary Actor
	G7(8)	IMF	US ED	Other EDs	President
E9 Bank does not control the allocation, access, or use of other resources critical to the [External/Boundary Actor] operation and survival	The Bank does not control	The Bank does not control	The Bank does not control	The Bank does not control	Not relevant.
E10 The actions or outputs of the Bank are visible and can be assessed by the [External/Boundary Actor] to judge whether the actions comply with its demands	Yes, but that task is too detailed for Presidents & Prime Ministers	Actions are visible but IMF does not formally review Bank outputs	Yes, but see President column	Yes, but see President column	Yes, of all external/boundary actors, President will know the most. EDs are fed information by President/staff.
E11 Bank's satisfaction of the [External/Boundary Actor] requests are not in conflict with the satisfaction of demands from other components of the environment with which it is interdependent	Yes	Often true	No, at least not until the NGO movements began to rise in the late 1980s.	Yes	Yes, same as the 1980s
E12 The Bank does not control the determination, formulation, or expression of the [External/Boundary Actor] demands	The Bank does not control	The Bank does not control	The Bank does not control	The Bank does not control	It is interactive and iterative process between the President and staff.
E13 The Bank is capable of developing actions or outcomes that will satisfy the [External/Boundary Actor] demands	Yes	Unlikely given rising concerns about each IO's "territory"	Yes	Yes	Yes
E14 The Bank desires to survive.	Yes	Yes	Yes	Yes	Yes

Table 8 How internal actors matter (Jan 1980 to Oct 1989)

	January 1980 to October 1989		
	Key Internal Actor Entities		
Internal Stakeholder Identification (Jonker & Foster 2002)	PSM Unit & Its Evolution	Chief Economist/DEC	General Counsel (Shihata)
I1 [Internal Actor] *power* to influence the Bank	Limited until after the 1987 reform	Significant as Bank's intellectual leader	From his arrival as General Counsel in 1983, Shihata had power (and used it) to caution the Bank against violating Article 4.10 of the Bank's Charter
I2 *Legitimacy* of the [Internal Actor] relationship with the Bank	Limited until after the 1987 reform		The General Counsel is the Bank's top lawyer
I3 *Urgency* of the [Internal Actor] claim on the Bank	Urgent given 1980–1982 world recession		Constantly urgent as each new PSM topic was added to its sector agenda
I4 [Internal Actor] *criticality* over the Bank	Less so until after the 1987 reform		The General Counsel is the Bank's top lawyer
Size of Organization (Betton & Dess 1985)			
I5 The larger the organization, the more that an organization's internal (bureaucratic) environment influences output	PSM Unit was tiny when compared to other sector bodies within the Bank.	The Chief Economist was the intellectual leader of the Bank. DEC staff had internal power especially as the Bank switched from an infrastructure/agricultural Bank (pre-1980) to one focused on structural adjustment.	Yes, the General Counsel had more to monitor especially as PSM/PSG policies expanded in importance

Continued

Table 8 *Continued*

	January 1980 to October 1989		
	Key Internal Actor Entities		
	PSM Unit & Its Evolution	Chief Economist/DEC	General Counsel (Shihata)
Internal Stakeholder Identification (Jonker & Foster 2002)			
Moloney Corollary to Betton & Dess (1985)			
I6 The more important a particular component of an organization's work is for the organization, the more that an organization's internal (bureaucratic) environment influences output	The PSM Unit was largely unimportant actor within the Bank from 1983 to 1987. Its outputs (institutional development, SOE reform not privatization) and its employees (often microeconomists) had limited influence.	The Chief Economist mattered. Anne Krueger could not be ignored. The replacement of Hollis Chenery with Anne Krueger altered sector intellectual agendas.	Yes, likely.
When Internal Factors may Outweigh External Factors (Betton & Dess 1985)			
I7 "sunk cost of firms" I8 "communication structures" I9 "internal politics" I10 "dominance of institutional norms"	Bank came "on board" to structural adjustment slightly later than the IMF, even if internal "push back" or "alternative views" were (weakly) heard		The early 1980s was a testing ground for early potential violations of the Articles of Agreement via structural adjustment and privatization. The legal norm was being reinterpreted to reflect a changing institutional expection about PSM's growing importance
Bureaucratic Politics Model II & III Combined (Allison & Halperin 1972)			
I11 Captures "organizational innovation"	Inaccurate critique	Inaccurate critique	Traceable and constant effort by Shihata to caution against politics violations of the Articles of Agreement
I12 Lauded for "efficiency" in "explaining incrementalism"	Efficient explanation of step-by-step incremental sector policy shifts	Efficient explanation of step-by-step incremental sector policy shifts	Efficient

Table 9 How external and boundary actors matter (Nov 1989 to Sep 1996)

| Internal Stakeholder Identification (Jonker & Foster 2002) | November 1989 to September 1996 | | | | |
| | External Actors | | | | Boundary Actor |
	G7(8)	IMF	US ED	Other EDs	President
E1 [External/Boundary Actor] *power* to influence the Bank	Yes, Cold War victor.	Remains high, but with the 1989 Concordat, PSM/PSG areas of responsibility are more distinct	Yes, Cold War victor.	Yes, there is power but non-US ED use of that power is largely unmentioned by Bank staff and related literatures	Conable help diplomatically smooth tensions over the PSG addition to PSM. For Preston, he was ill during most of his tenure.
E2 *Legitimacy* of the [External/Boundary Actor] relationship with the Bank	Unchanged from the 1980s, did more than the US ED on legitimizing governance, but G7(8) statement did not *precede* the Bank's.	Unchanged from the 1980s but Fund also experienced necessity of "all hands on deck" in post-Cold War early years	Did not want to lose the Cold War "win"	Yes, legitimate but largely unmentioned by Bank staff and related literatures	High due to role position.
E3 *Urgency* of the [External/Boundary Actor] claim on the Bank	Yes, Cold War victor.	In Eastern Europe and former Soviet Russia, high urgency. Elsewhere, not so much	Did not want to lose the Cold War "win"	Largely unmentioned by Bank staff and related literatures	For Conable, PSG was departure from prior PSM. Preston's illness/absence hampered his effectiveness
E4 [External/Boundary Actor] *criticality* over the Bank	In Eastern Europe and former Soviet Russia, plus governance	As Bank partner to address macroeconomic issues from Soviet collapse	Yes	Largely unmentioned by Bank staff and related literatures	High due to role position. Conable's diplomatic touch in the 1991 report is notable.

Continued

Table 9 *Continued*

Internal Stakeholder Identification (Jonker & Foster 2002)	November 1989 to September 1996				
	External Actors				Boundary Actor
	G7(8)	*IMF*	*US ED*	*Other EDs*	*President*
Is Organization Controlled by External/Boundary Actor?					
E5 Bank is aware of [External/Boundary Actor] demands	Yes	Yes, Concordat helped lessen tensions	Yes	Yes	Yes, for both. But few demands from President in this sector given his illness.
E6 Bank obtains some resources from the [External/Boundary Actor] making the demands	Yes—Political, Economic, Financial, Ideological	Yes, same as the 1980s.	Yes—Political, Economic, Financial, Ideological	Largely unmentioned by Bank staff and related literatures	Yes
E7 The [External/Boundary Actor] resources are critical or important part of the Bank's operation	Indirectly	Directly and Indirectly	Yes—Political, Economic, Financial, Ideological	Yes	When political will is needed, yes.
E8 The [External/Boundary Actor] controls the allocation, access or use of the resources; alternative sources for the resources are not available to the focal organization	Very indirectly	Only in so much as any Bank member-state must also be a member of the IMF too	Indirectly but more than others due to remaining superpower status and largest voting share	Yes, theoretically	Has influence, yes. Controls, no.
E9 Bank does not control the allocation, access, or use of other resources critical to the [External/Boundary Actor] operation and survival	The Bank does not control	The Bank does not control	The Bank does not control	Bank does not control	Not relevant.

E10	The actions or outputs of the Bank are visible and can be assessed by the [External/Boundary Actor] to judge whether the actions comply with its demands	Yes, but that task is too detailed for Presidents & Prime Ministers	Yes, same as the 1980s.	Yes	Yes	Yes
E11	Bank's satisfaction of the [External/Boundary Actor] requests are not in conflict with the satisfaction of demands from other components of the environment with which it is interdependent	Yes, same as the 1980s	Yes, same as the 1980s.	Yes, they can be in conflict.	Largely unmentioned by Bank staff and related literatures	Yes, same as the 1980s
E12	The Bank does not control the determination, formulation, or expression of the [External/Boundary Actor] demands	The Bank does not control	Unclear although Concordat attempted greater clarity	The Bank does not control	Largely unmentioned by Bank staff and related literatures	It is interactive and iterative process between the President and staff.
E13	The Bank is capable of developing actions or outcomes that will satisfy the [External/Boundary Actor] demands	Yes	Yes, same as the 1980s although "demands" might be too strong of a word.	Yes	Largely unmentioned by Bank staff and related literatures	Yes
E14	The Bank desires to survive.	Yes	Yes	Yes	Yes	Yes

Table 10 How internal actors matter (Nov 1989 to Sep 1996)

Internal Stakeholder Identification (Jonker & Foster 2002)	November 1989 to September 1996		
	Key Policy-Making Entities		
	PSM Unit & Its Evolution	Chief Economist/DEC	General Counsel (Shihata)
I1 [Internal Actor] *power* to influence the Bank	1987 reform and PSM/PSG sector topic expansion meant more PSM units, more staff, more projects, more policy expansions	Significant as Bank's intellectual leader	Shihata had power (and used it) to caution the Bank against violating Article 4.10 of the Bank's Charter
I2 *Legitimacy* of the [Internal Actor] relationship with the Bank	Increasingly seen as highly legitimate internal actor after 1991		The General Counsel is the Bank's top lawyer
I3 *Urgency* of the [Internal Actor] claim on the Bank	Urgent given new PSM/PSG prominence, necessity of incorporating post-Soviet states, relevance of good governance for development		Constantly urgent as each new PSM and PSG topic was added to its sector agenda
I4 [Internal Actor] *criticality* over the Bank			The General Counsel is the Bank's top lawyer
Size of Organization (Betton & Dess 1985)			
I5 The larger the organization, the more that an organization's internal (bureaucratic) environment influences output	Less relevant	Less relevant	Yes, the General Counsel had more to monitor especially as PSM/PSG policies expanded in importance

Moloney Corollary to Betton & Dess (1985)

16	The more important an particular component of an organization's work is for the organization, the more that an organization's internal (bureaucratic) environment influences output	Yes, the 1987 reform created space for the PSM (and PSG) sector to fill. New PSM Units in Bank regions created new projects. New projects led to sector topic deepening and thus, even more projects. With the Wall down, PSM/PSG became even more important. Did not want to lose the Cold War's win	Yes, DEC and its economists authored many of the PSM/PSG documents. But they did not drive authorship or sector deepening like they did in the 1980s. PSM staff were more prominent.	Yes, as PSM and PSG rose in importance, Shihata was there to remind staff, the President, and the Board that the Articles of Agreement could not be violated

When Internal Factors may Outweigh External Factors (Betton & Dess 1985)

17	"sunk cost of firms"	The new "sunk cost" was steering a structural adjustment dominated Bank to new PSM topics and to the PSG addition. But once PSG was agreed upon, research agenda/projects expanded.	Less relevant	There is a "sunk" cost in terms of the Articles
18	"communication structures"	More internal actors (multiple units, new topics) in communication	No change from 1980s	Shihata was not shy in communicating his concerns. This includes direct interaction with legal memoranda and events around the introduction of PSG

Continued

Table 10 *Continued*

| Internal Stakeholder Identification (Jonker & Foster 2002) | November 1989 to September 1996 | | |
| | *Key Policy-Making Entities* | | |
	PSM Unit & Its Evolution	Chief Economist/DEC	General Counsel (Shihata)
I9 "internal politics"	1987 reform create space for PSM/PSG agenda. Lending incentives further enforced this expansion. Colds War's end required respondent Bank to restructure economies.	No change from 1980s	Lots of politics with Shihata views
I10 "dominance of institutional norms"	Neoliberal still most important. Changing though as new "norm" via NIE/governance was on the rise.	DEC leads NIE shifts	He was trying to keep the Bank away from politics
Bureaucratic Politics Model II & III Combined (Allison & Halperin 1972)			
I11 Captures "organizational innovation"	Bureaucratic politics approach is especially effective in this era to captured organizational and policy innovations	Publication tracing and interviewee comments about DEC/NIE helped capture this NIE emphasis	Traceable and constant effort by Shihata to caution against politics violations of the Articles of Agreement
I12 Lauded for "efficiency" in "explaining incrementalism"	Efficient	Efficient	Efficient

Table 11   How External Actors Matter (Oct 1996 to Dec 2003)

Internal Stakeholder Identification (Jonker & Foster 2002)	October 1996 to December 2003				Boundary Actor
	External Actors				
	G7(8)	IMF	U.S. ED	Other EDs	President
E1 [External/Boundary Actor] *power* to influence the Bank	Indirect even if its 1997 statement encouraged MDBs to tackle corruption	By the late 1990s, its influence upon PSM/PSG was indirect. The exclusion was a flare-up between the Bank/Fund (and their Chief Economists) about the Asian Financial Crisis	Same as before. But this does not mean that the power was actualized to alter the PSM/PSG agenda	Yes, there is power but non-US ED use of that power is largely unmentioned by Bank staff and related literatures	Always had power, Wolfensohn chose to use it and to help reshape the PSG agenda
E2 *Legitimacy* of the [External/Boundary Actor] relationship with the Bank	Same as the 1980s	Same as the 1980s	Same as before. Yes, it is a legitimate relationship. But this does not mean that the US ED also attempted to alter the PSM/PSG agenda	Yes, legitimate but largely unmentioned by Bank staff and related literatures	High due to role position

Continued

Table 11　*Continued*

Internal Stakeholder Identification (Jonker & Foster 2002)	October 1996 to December 2003				
	External Actors				Boundary Actor
	G7(8)	IMF	U.S. ED	Other EDs	President
E3　*Urgency* of the [External/Boundary Actor] claim on the Bank	The G7 was not commenting on the "details" of PSM/PSG	Conflicting views on how to handle the 1997/8 Asian Financial Crisis	US switching to Bank transparency, anti-corruption in clients, and results management within Bank.	Largely unmentioned by Bank staff and related literatures	The increased state/corruption focus was likely never "urgent," but instead Wolfensohn saw the lack of progress on development, understood why MICs were not choosing Bank loans, etc; plus, urgency of not lending money to the IMF, didn't want to the be first Bank president to lose the AAA
E4　[External/Boundary Actor] *criticality* over the Bank	Yes	Yes, new efforts ot have IMF/Bank jointly review public expenditure management topic	Yes	Largely unmentioned by Bank staff and related literatures	Yes, defining issue, especially the MIC stuff and the AAA stuff
Is Organization Controlled by External/Boundary Actor?					
E5　Bank is aware of [External/Boundary Actor] demands	Yes	Yes, this includes a G7 critique of the IMF's response to the Asian Financial Crisis	Same as before	Yes, especially in the late 1990s period	Yes, absolutely. Wolfensohn was not shy.

E6	Bank obtains some resources from the [External/Boundary] making the demands	Yes—Political, Economic, Financial, Ideological	Yes, same as the 1980s with a new resource: politics/prestige. This is due to the Bank's "victory" over the IMF in the Crisis	Same as before	Largely unmentioned by Bank staff and related literatures	Yes
E7	The [External/Boundary Actor] resources are critical or important part of the Bank's operation	Yes, and the G7 was being critical of the IMF and the G7 was reaffirming the importance of transparency and good governance	Yes, but not so critical that room for political manuvering could not be found.	Same as before	Yes	Yes, Wolfensohn was "heard" more than Clausen, Conable and Preston
E8	The [External/Boundary Actor] controls the allocation, access or use of the resources; alternative sources for the resources are not available to the focal organization	Very indirectly	Only in so much as any Bank member-state must also be a member of the IMF too	US is but one actor of many, but on PSM/governance's new detail, U.S. seems absent other than approving projects as before; Rubin in-line with Bank sentiment, not leading it	Yes, theoretically	Has influence, yes. Controls, no.
E9	Bank does not control the allocation, access, or use of other resources critical to the [External/Boundary Actor] operation and survival	The Bank does not control	The Bank does not control	Bank does not control	Bank does not control	Not relevant

Continued

Table 11 *Continued*

| | | October 1996 to December 2003 | | | | |
| | | External Actors | | | | Boundary Actor |
Internal Stakeholder Identification (Jonker & Foster 2002)	G7(8)	IMF	U.S. ED	Other EDs		President
E10	The actions or outputs of the Bank are visible and can be assessed by the [External/Boundary Actor] to judge whether the actions comply with its demands	Yes, but that task is too detailed for Presidents & Prime Ministers	Yes, same as the 1980s.	Increasingly so. Even if not, is the USG really going to stop the Bank's focus on the state? Highly unlikely.	Yes		Yes
E11	Bank's satisfaction of the [External/Boundary Actor] requests are not in conflict with the satisfaction of demands from other components of the environment with which it is interdependent	Only with the NGOs, and with the IMF	The Bank/Fund were in public disagreement	Yes, it could be considered in conflict with certain developing country Eds.	Yes, they can be. MENA region suggesting that PSG and anti-corruption involved the Bank in political affairs. China more willingno to push back against certain PSM/PSG in Asia		Not everyone agreed with Wolfensohn's anti-corruption/Asian Financial Crisis stances
E12	The Bank does not control the determination, formulation, or expression of the [External/Boundary Actor] demands	Bank does not control	Bank does not control	The Bank does not control	Largely unmentioned by Bank staff and related literatures		It is interactive and iterative process between the President and staff.
E13	The Bank is capable of developing actions or outcomes that will satisfy the [External/Boundary Actor] demands	Yes	Yes, same as the 1980s although "demands" might be too strong of a word.	Yes	For many countries, yes. But not everyone always		Yes
E14	The Bank desires to survive.	Yes	Yes	Yes	Yes		Yes

Table 12 How Internal Actors Matter (Oct 1996 to Dec 2003)

Internal Stakeholder Identification (Jonker & Foster 2002)	October 1996—December 2003		
	Key Policy-Making Entities		
	PSM Unit & Its Evolution	Chief Economist/DEC	General Counsel (Shihata)
I1 [Internal Actor] *power* to influence the Bank	Unchanged from early 1990s	Significant as Bank's intellectual leader. But by late 1999, far less relevant for future PSM/PSG development	Shihata had power (and used it) to caution the Bank against violating Article 4.10 of the Bank's Charter
I2 *Legitimacy* of the [Internal Actor] relationship with the Bank	Highly legitimate internal actor and by late 1999, the key actor for PSM/PSG development		The General Counsel is the Bank's top lawyer
I3 *Urgency* of the [Internal Actor] claim on the Bank	Unchanged from early 1990s		Constantly urgent as each new PSM and PSG topic was added to its sector agenda
I4 [Internal Actor] *criticality* over the Bank			The General Counsel is the Bank's top lawyer
Size of Organization (Betton & Dess 1985)			
I5 The larger the organization, the more that an organization's internal (bureaucratic) environment influences output	LAC did not like 1997 WDR. Further evidence of ability to re-interpret Articles of Agreement, Matrix reform strengthens PSM/PSG, debate on supply/demand side emerges	Yes, but still need a Chief Economist to agree	Yes, the General Counsel had more to monitor especially as PSM/PSG policies expanded in importance

Continued

Table 12 *Continued*

Internal Stakeholder Identification (Jonker & Foster 2002)	October 1996—December 2003		
	Key Policy-Making Entities		
	PSM Unit & Its Evolution	Chief Economist/DEC	General Counsel (Shihata)
Moloney Corollary to Betton & Dess (1985)			
16 The more important a particular component of an organization's work is for the organization, the more that an organization's internal (bureaucratic) environment influences output	Absolutely true here. The more important that the sector becomes, the more that staff may bicker about its details, e.g., supply/demand side.	Yes, helps with Stiglitz on Board; easier to get an organizational reform that favors your sector when PREM is the only network directly reporting to the Chief Economist	Yes, likely.
When Internal Factors may Outweigh External Factors (Betton & Dess 1985)			
17 "sunk cost of firms"	Amount of "sunk" growing. States mattered, then reforms, then Strategy. Corruption mattered, then Strategy. Research/projects increased; yet, not all country managers included PSM/governance due to "country sensitivity"	Helped that PREM now reported to the Chief Economist	There is a "sunk" in terms of the Articles
18 "communication structures"	Favoring these ideas, President in line, external actors making favorable noises even if external actors not leading it	Helped that PREM now reported to the Chief Economist	Shihata was not shy in communicating his concerns.

I9	"internal politics"	Strengthened favoring PSM/governance sector; lots of infighting, i.e. between supply and demand, between Anchor/Regions, between technocratic and others, etc.	Helped that PREM now reported to the Chief Economist	Lots of politics with Shihata views
I10	"dominance of institutional norms"	the state mattered (probably the only thing that everyone agreed upon ... the "how" was not always agreed upon)	Chief Economist making sure that "state" does not veer off from Bank-accepted ideas like neoliberalism and neoinstitutionalism	He was trying to keep the Bank away from politics

Bureaucratic Politics Model II & III Combined (Allison & Halperin 1972)

I11	Captures "organizational innovation"	Bureaucratic politics approach is especially effective in this era to captured organizational and policy innovations	DEC was innovating (e.g., Governance Indicators) but largely not involved in PSM/PSG institutionalization. This lack of innovation is captured well	Traceable and constant effort by Shihata to caution against politics violations of the Articles of Agreement
I12	Lauded for "efficiency" in "explaining incrementalism"	Efficient	Efficient	Efficient

Table 13 How external actors matter (Jan 2004 to Jul 2012)

| Internal Stakeholder Identification (Jonker & Foster 2002) | External Actors | | | | Boundary Actor |
| | *January 2004 to July 2012* | | | | |
	G7(8)	*IMF*	*US ED*	*Other EDs*	*President*
E1 [External/Boundary Actor] *power* to influence the Bank	Largely disinterested in this sector.	Same as the 1980s	Yes, but silent throughout GAC battle; only after GAC approved did Paulson make statement; Treasury focusing on Results. Treasury absent on GAC under Zoellick	Chinese did not want GAC to say "NGOs and media;" Chinese & Saudi Arabia disliked demand-side governance	Yes, absolutely.
E2 *Legitimacy* of the [External/Boundary Actor] relationship with the Bank	Same as the 1980s	Same as the 1980s	Same as before. Yes, it is a legitimate relationship. US ED support for GAC is rather sanguine and provides no comment on Wolfowitz	Yes, legitimate but largely unmentioned by Bank staff and related literatures	Legally, Wolfowitz had legitimacy. Politically, he struggled to gain traction at Bank; DevCmte reprimand at Singapore meetings. Zoellick was different and had no revolutionary ideas for this sector.

E3	*Urgency* of the [External/Boundary Actor] claim on the Bank	Disinterested in this sector	Yes, reports of PEM disagreements rising, new J-MAP to address it	Unchanged from the 1980s, but the US does not always find every issue urgent	Yes, the DevCmte made it urgent when they felt their power being usurped by Wolfowitz	Governance was not an "urgent" issue since it was already an approved issue. Moreover, by Zoellick's time, sector had become "DNA" of the Bank.
E4	[External/Boundary Actor] *criticality* over the Bank	Same as the 1980s	Same as the 1980s	Unchanged from the 1980s	Appears to be assert themselves more and in particular, Saudi Arabia and China.	Unlikely given anti-corruption's acceptance but it became again critical given Wolfowitz's desire to cut funds to corrupt countries
Is Organization Controlled by External/Boundary Actor?					
E5	Bank is aware of [External/Boundary Actor] demands	Yes	Yes	Yes	Yes	Yes
E6	Bank obtains some resources from the [External/Boundary] making the demands	Yes	Yes	Yes	Yes	Yes

Continued

Table 13 *Continued*

Internal Stakeholder Identification (Jonker & Foster 2002)	January 2004 to July 2012				
	External Actors				Boundary Actor
	G7(8)	*IMF*	*US ED*	*Other EDs*	*President*
E7 The [External/Boundary Actor] resources are critical or important part of the Bank's operation	Yes	Yes	Yes	Especially China's resources, G7(8) resources	Yes
E8 The [External/Boundary Actor] controls the allocation, access or use of the resources; alternative sources for the resources are not available to the focal organization	Yes—Political, Economic, Financial, Ideological	Yes—Political, Economic, Financial, Ideological	Not quite "control" but definitely has "strong influence"	Not all countries have the same influence	Has influence, yes. Controls, no.
E9 Bank does not control the allocation, access, or use of other resources critical to the [External/Boundary Actor] operation and survival	Yes	Yes	Bank does not control	Bank does not control	Bank does not control
E10 The actions or outputs of the Bank are visible and can be assessed by the [External/Boundary Actor] to judge whether the actions comply with its demands	Yes	Yes	Yes, increasingly so	Yes, increasingly so	Yes, can be assessed, but no ED mechanism to rid the Bank of a President

E11	Bank's satisfaction of the [External/Boundary Actor] requests are not in conflict with the satisfaction of demands from other components of the environment with which it is interdependent	Same as the 1980s	Yes, they are in conflict, especially within the Bank's PSM/governance units	Yes, especially with Wolfowitz	Yes, especially with Wolfowitz	Yes, they were in conflict. Especially as it related to whether or not to lend to developing countries. Less so under Zoellick
E12	The Bank does not control the determination, formulation, or expression of the [External/Boundary Actor] demands	Bank does not control	Bank does not control	Bank does not control	Bank does not control	Bank does not control
E13	The Bank is capable of developing actions or outcomes that will satisfy the [External/Boundary Actor] demands	Yes	Yes	Yes	Yes, although not always	Yes, but Bank did not want to. Staff did not like Wolfowitz, Board did not want to budge on lending. Zoellick steered boat, did not revolutionize it.
E14	The Bank desires to survive.	Yes	Yes	Yes	Yes	Yes

Table 14 How internal actors matter (Jan 2004 to Dec 2012)

Internal Stakeholder Identification (Jonker & Foster 2002)	January 2004–July 2012		
	Key Policy-Making Entities		
	PSM Units & Its Evolution	Chief Economist/DEC	General Counsel
I1 [Internal Actor] *power* to influence the Bank	Unchanged from early 1990s	Significant power but largely unused to shape PSM/PSG in this era	Shihata retired from the Bank in 2003. New General Counsel largely uninterested in using his power to influence the Bank in this particular sector.
I2 *Legitimacy* of the [Internal Actor] relationship with the Bank	Unchanged from the early 2000s	Legitimate but largely unapplied for shaping PSM/PSG in this era	The General Counsel is the Bank's top lawyer
I3 *Urgency* of the [Internal Actor] claim on the Bank	Unchanged from early 1990s	Less urgent for this sector	Less urgent for this sector with the post-2003 General Counsel
I4 [Internal Actor] *criticality[1]* over the Bank		Less critical for this sector	The General Counsel is the Bank's top lawyer
Size of Organization (Betton & Dess 1985)			
I5 The larger the organization, the more that an organization's internal (bureaucratic) environment influences output	Yes, especially with GAC Strategy, its Update, and GAC Council creation	No new info, less important to sector policy shifts	Yes, but post-Shihata, the General Counsel largely disappears from public discussions about this sector

Moloney Corollary to Betton & Dess (1985)

16	The more important an particular component of an organization's work is for the organization, the more that an organization's internal (bureaucratic) environment influences output	Yes, especially with GAC Strategy, its Update, and GAC Council creation	No new info, less important to sector policy shifts	Yes, but the style and views of the person in the position also appears to matter

When Internal Factors may Outweigh External Factors (Betton & Dess 1985)

17	"sunk cost of firms"	Hard to stop a moving train, i.e. stopping funds for projects that were an important part of the Bank's portfolio	Chief Economist/DEC have less importance in driving this sector in this era than any prior era	There is a "sunk" in terms of the Articles
18	"communication structures"	Yes, communication structures were overrun by Wolfowitz' stoppage of funds to corrupt countries. Less relevant during Zoellick presidency.	Chief Economist/DEC have less importance in driving this sector in this era than any prior era	General Counsel disappears from public discussions about this sector agenda
19	"internal politics"	Did not like Wolfowitz from the start; GAC mess with the Board/Wolfowitz; the political economy vs technocrat battles. Battles were largely over by Zoellick presidency.	Chief Economist/DEC have less importance in driving this sector in this era than any prior era	General Counsel disappears from public discussions about this sector agenda

Continued

Table 14 *Continued*

| | | January 2004— July 2012 | | |
| | | Key Policy-Making Entities | | |
Internal Stakeholder Identification (Jonker & Foster 2002)	PSM Units & Its Evolution	Chief Economist/DEC	General Counsel	
I10 "dominance of institutional norms"	Yes, to keep lending went against Wolfowitz attempt to stop lending; economists seeing themselves as best; Zoellick's creation of the GAC Council fully institutionalized the sector	Chief Economist/DEC have less importance in driving this sector in this era than any prior era	General Counsel disappears from public discussions about this sector agenda	
Bureaucratic Politics Model II & III Combined (Allison & Halperin 1972)				
I11 Captures "organizational innovation"	Innovation is shown	Disappearance from sector agenda means Chief Economist/DEC attentions are elsewhere	General Counsel disappears from public discussions about this sector agenda	
I12 Lauded for "efficiency" in "explaining incrementalism"	Efficient	N/A given above	N/A given above	

Table 15 How evaluative actors matter for PSM/PSG agenda (1980–2012)

Internal Stakeholder Identification (Jonker & Foster 2002)	January 1980—to October 1989	November 1989—September 1996		October 1996—December 2003	
	OED/IEG	OED/IEG	Inspection Panel	OED/IEG	Inspection Panel
I1 [Internal Actor] *power to* influence the Bank	Limited as project and policy evaluations are frequently after the fact	Limited as project and policy evaluations are frequently after the fact	Yes, insomuch as no Bank staff wanted their projects to go before the Panel	Limited as project and policy evaluations are frequently after the fact	Unchanged from the early 1990s
I2 *Legitimacy* of the [Internal Actor] relationship with the Bank	Its independence from Bank control increases its legitimacy	Unchanged from the 1980s	Highly legitimate especially given Panel support from external NGOs	Unchanged from the 1980s	
I3 *Urgency* of the [Internal Actor] claim on the Bank	Limited as project and policy evaluations are frequently after the fact	Limited as project and policy evaluations are frequently after the fact	Initially urgent as Panel is created and staff realize importance of clearly applying Bank operational and bureaucratic procedures to Bank projects	Limited as project and policy evaluations are frequently after the fact	Prior early 1990s urgency becomes routinized
I4 [Internal Actor] *criticality* over the Bank					
Size of Organization (Betton & Dess 1985)					
I5 The larger the organization, the more that an organization's internal (bureaucratic) environment influences output	In the early 1980s, % of projects evaluated fell as project approvals increased	Potentially, Wapenhans highlighted how staffers just apply every policy prescription (old 210), or just try and lend money and not be supervised.	The Panel is a small part of Bank operations.	No change from 1980s	No change from Panel creation in the early 1990s.

Continued

Table 15 *Continued*

Internal Stakeholder Identification (Jonker & Foster 2002)	January 1980—to October 1989	November 1989—September 1996		October 1996—December 2003	
	OED/IEG	OED/IEG	Inspection Panel	OED/IEG	Inspection Panel
Moloney Corollary to Betton & Dess (1985)					
16 The more important an particular component of an organization's work is for the organization, the more that an organization's internal (bureaucratic) environment influences output	Evaluations not impacting new PSM projects and policies	Wapenhans highlighted issues but OED remained largely non-response. OED may require empowerment from above to take on Wapenhans' suggestions.	Bankers had to ensure that Bank operational and bureaucratic procedures were followed. No staffer wanted their project before the Panel.	OED evaluates PSM/ governance more	No change from Panel creation in the early 1990s.
When Internal Factors may Outweigh External Factors (Betton & Dess 1985)					
17 "sunk cost of firms"	Lend over evaluate. Sunk "cost" of needing to money out the door if the Bank wanted to show mission success and to survive as an organization. This did not change in the 32 years covered by this book.	New "sunk cost" was trying to steer Bank to care about outcomes/project & program quality via Wapenhans but lend over evaluate remained dominant	Panel creation is a new sunk cost	The higher the PSM/governance cost became, the more that OED evaluated it. Lend over evaluate remained.	No change from Panel creation in the early 1990s.

I8	"communication structures"	Lend over evaluate	Wapenhans was "known" but Report not easily found. Bank is less concerned about client governance, compliance	Staffs wanted to avoid being a part of it.	Staff had access to OED reports. They were communicated.	No change from Panel creation in the early 1990s.
I9	"internal politics"	Lend over evaluate	Wapenhans, "pervasive preoccupation with new lending"/Scandinavian EDs & IMF wanted the Bank to keep lending, developing country EDs did not disagree	Staffs wanted to avoid being a part of it.	But just because OED staff reports were communicated did not mean that post-project evaluations influenced next projects. Politics of project preparation and approval often overtook OED lesson-giving	No change from Panel creation in the early 1990s.
I10	"dominance of institutional norms"	Lend over evaluate	Wapenhans Report was kick in the arm that maybe outcomes matter more than money out the door. But this norm was not overcome. Thus, evaluative units stayed out of spotlight	Panel challenged a prior cultural norm that careful attention to Bank operational and bureaucratic procedures did not matter	Uninvolved, simply evaluated project outputs. Not empowered to challenge norms. At the same time, OED/IEG institutionalization within the Bank was not going to be challenged.	No change from Panel creation in the early 1990s.

Continued

Table 15 *Continued*

Internal Stakeholder Identification (Jonker & Foster 2002)	January 1980—to October 1989	November 1989—September 1996		October 1996—December 2003	
	OED/IEG	OED/IEG	Inspection Panel	OED/IEG	Inspection Panel
Bureaucratic Politics Model II & III Combined (Allison & Halperin 1972)					
I11 Captures "organizational innovation"	Inaccurate critique. OED was an innovation. The Bank's OED was an early leader for IO evaluation.	Captured organization talking about its problems & its need for innovation (Wapenhans)	Unclear, since this innovation was put upon the Bank from outsiders	OED could encourage such evaluation even if I am not "capturing" it with OED and the Bank	The Panel evolved as the Bank's operational and bureaucratic procedures were increasingly implemented as the Panel institutionalized.
I12 Lauded for "efficiency" in "explaining incrementalism"	Yes, but given few OED reports on the PSM sector in the 1980s, its reports were not a key "go to" for shifts in this era	Yes, OED/IEG published evaluative reports which assist any review of what were the incremental policy shifts in a Bank sector.	Efficient, but more from NGO views since I did not capture internal debates on IP creation	Yes, OED/IEG published evaluative reports which assist any review of what were the incremental policy shifts in a Bank sector.	The Panel evolved as the Bank's operational and bureaucratic procedures were increasingly implemented as the Panel institutionalized.

Table 15 *Continued*

Internal Stakeholder Identification (Jonker & Foster 2002)	January 2004—December 2012				
	OED/IEG	QAG	Results Secretariat	Inspection Panel	Integrity VicePresidency
I1 **[Internal Actor] *power* to influence the Bank**	Less limited in the past as IEG undertakes more sector-specific reviews in the midst of policy application	Yes, but only if one's project has been QAG'd		Unchanged from the early 1990s	Yes in the Wolfwitz years as it was politicized. Afterward less so as it evolved
I2 *Legitimacy* of the [Internal Actor] relationship with the Bank	Unchanged from the 1980s	Never obtained significant internal legitimacy			Yes as way for the Bank to be seen as an accountable IO to the international community
I3 *Urgency* of the [Internal Actor] claim on the Bank	More urgent and critical especially for midsteam sector-specific reviews in which IEG report with potential concerns cannot be left unaddressed	If your project was QAG'd, responses were needed urgently		Prior early 1990s urgency becomes routinzed	
I4 [Internal Actor] *criticality* over the Bank		Its criticality was not accepted by Bank staff			

Table 15 *Continued*

Internal Stakeholder Identification (Jonker & Foster 2002)	January 2004—December 2012				
	OED/IEG	*QAG*	*Results Secretariat*	*Inspection Panel*	*Integrity VicePresidency*
Size of Organization (Betton & Dess 1985)					
15 The larger the organization, the more that an organization's internal (bureaucratic) environment influences output	Renamed IEG. More involved in sector reviews. However, ability to influence future output of Bank remains as indirect as before	QAG is a small part of Bank operations.	Secretariat is a small part of Bank operations.	No change from Panel creation in the early 1990s.	This part of the Bank is a small component but it has a big public face vis-à-vis its investigation of project-related corruption and procurement. Even so, its focus is not specific to the sector.
Moloney Corollary to Betton & Dess (1985)					
16 The more important an particular component of an organization's work is for the organization, the more that an organization's internal (bureaucratic) environment influences output	OED strengthened in terms of staff allocation, new evaluative methods, and more sector and sub-sector evaluative analyses.	No banker wanted to be QAG'd. Active avoidance of such pre-approval evaluations.	Rhetorically, results measurement mattered. In practice, however, the difficulty of measurement and a Bank unwilling to go to this path.	No change from Panel creation in the early 1990s.	Less about specific sector than about implementing good governance within Bank operations during latter years

When Internal Factors may Outweigh External Factors (Betton & Dess 1985)

17	"sunk cost of firms"	Growing in importance as its evaluation sophistication grew. But lend over evaluate remained.	Short-lived sunk cost for project staff to QAG-proof their work.	Not yet sunk cost but instead, battle against other sunk costs/incentives	No change from Panel creation in the early 1990s.	Deepened its work in investigating corruption and other irregularities potentially linked to Bank work
18	"communication structures"	Staff had access to OED reports. They were communicated.	Direct communication with Bank staffs involved in chosen project	Unclear	No change from Panel creation in the early 1990s.	Rich-Olson assumed staffs were on the take. When combined with staff resentment about the GAC strategy, communication misfires were the result.
19	"internal politics"	But just because OED staff reports were communicated did not mean that post-project evaluations influenced next projects. Politics of project preparation and approval often overtook OED lesson-giving	Disliked being "QAG'd"	Politics disfavored results secretariat institutionalization	No change from Panel creation in the early 1990s.	Internal politics was not necessarily opposed to INT's creation but staff did oppose the management style of its early leadership

Table 15 *Continued*

Internal Stakeholder Identification (Jonker & Foster 2002)	January 2004—December 2012				
	OED/IEG	QAG	Results Secretariat	Inspection Panel	Integrity VicePresidency
110 "dominance of institutional norms"	Uninvolved, simply evaluated project outputs. Not empowered to challenge norms. At the same time, OED/IEG institutionalization within the Bank was not going to be challenged.	Staff preferred the prior normal of quiet internal project evaluation and not the QAG spectacle	Battling against incentive cultures to get money out the door. Staff worried that poor results would affect promotion.	No change from Panel creation in the early 1990s.	INT was a new creation. Its focus on the "other" (contractor, procurement partner) helped assuage concerns that INT was going to be the Bank's internal police.
Bureaucratic Politics Model II & III Combined (Allison & Halperin 1972)					
111 Captures "organizational innovation"	Innovation not shown but instead, increased OED evaluations	The bureaucratic politics knew that QAG was an organizational innovation and staff did not like this particular innovation.	Was not capturing org innovation; Bank hesitant to innovate so that results really mattered	Not as relevant since Panel fully institutionalized by this point.	Not as relevant for this sector even if INT is an organizational innovation when compared to other IOs
112 Lauded for "efficiency" in "explaining incrementalism"	Yes, OED/IEG published evaluative reports which assist any review of what were the incremental policy shifts in a Bank sector.	Yes, the bureaucratic politics helps explain incremental movements on evaluative efforts, on internal politics on projects, and on how staff can align against new ideas	Yes, the bureaucratic politics helps explain incremental movements on evaluative efforts, on internal politics on projects, and on how staff can align against new ideas	Continued to explain incrementalism.	Not as relevant for this sector

Table 16 How NGOs matter for PSM/PSG agenda (1980–2012)

Internal Stakeholder Identification (Jonker & Foster 2002)	January 1980 to October 1989		November 1989 to September 1996	
	NGOs, in General: BIC	*NGOs, PSM/PSG focused*	*NGOs, in General:* BIC, 50	*NGOs, PSM/PSG focused: TI, PSI*
E1 [Insert External Actor Here] *power* to influence the Bank	No	No PSM/PSG-related NGO in existence	Still small, but growing. Protests became Annual Meeting feature; NGOs/Sarwar important for IP creation	Limited. "PSI who"? TI was just getting started.
E2 *Legitimacy* of the [Insert External Actor Here] relationship with the Bank	Yes		Not all believed NGOs were legitimate.	Legitimacy from the Bank perspective? Extremely limited for PSI, less limited for TI.
E3 *Urgency* of the [Insert External Actor Here] claim on the Bank	None		Yes, protests gathering; "urgency" not NGO legitimacy that pushed Inspection Panel forward, i.e. NGOs got the US Congress to hold IDA monies.	No urgency, still the "C" word
E4 [Insert External Actor Here] *criticality* over the Bank	None		No, excluding NGO ability on the IP issue to hold up IDA replenishment funds.	None

Continued

Table 16 *Continued*

Internal Stakeholder Identification (Jonker & Foster 2002)	January 1980 to October 1989		November 1989 to September 1996	
	NGOs, *in General:* BIC	NGOs, *PSM/PSG focused*	NGOs, *in General:* BIC, 50	NGOs, *PSM/PSG focused: TI, PSI*
Is Organization Controlled by External Actor?				
E5 Bank is aware of [Insert External Actor Here] demands	Barely. A bit more so in the late 1980s	No PSM/PSG-related NGO in existence	Yes (even Weaver would agree)	For TI, yes.
E6 Bank obtains some resources from the [Insert External Actor Here] making the demands	Only minimal pushback		Legitimacy from the NGOs (but not clear that the Bank wants their legitimacy)	Not yet.
E7 The [Insert External Actor Here] resources are critical or important part of the Bank's operation	No		Not normally.	Not yet.
E8 The [Insert External Actor Here] controls the allocation, access or use of the resources; alternative sources for the resources are not available to the focal organization	No		No, except that BIC and allies were able to get the US Congress to agreed with them on need for Inspection Panel.	No
E9 Bank does not control the allocation, access, or use of other resources critical to the [Insert External Actor Here] operation and survival	Bank does not control		Bank does not control	The Bank does not control

E10	The actions or outputs of the Bank are visible and can be assessed by the [Insert External Actor Here] to judge whether the actions comply with its demands	Not until environment movement/BIC started distributing Bank documents in the late 1980s	Yes and no, dependent on what Bank/clients want published work and/or reliant on bankers removing documents for NGO viewing.	Not yet since corruption is still c-word at the Bank.
E11	Bank's satisfaction of the [Insert External Actor Here] requests are not in conflict with the satisfication of demands from other components of the environment with which it is interdependent	Unless the other external actors do not consider the NGO perspective as valid	Yes, they would be in conflict if about intellectual direction. Perhaps not, if about increasing Bank accountability.	Yes, they would be in conflict with TI objectives until Wolfensohn's October speech. Yes, always in conflict with PSI public sector union stance
E12	The Bank does not control the determination, formulation, or expression of the [Insert External Actor Here] demands	Bank does not control	Bank does not control	Bank does not control
E13	The Bank is capable of developing actions or outcomes that will satisfy the [Insert External Actor Here] demands	Probably not entirely	Probably not entirely	Potentially, but not until bankers bought into the TI stance. Bank is unable to agree to PSI's public sector union stance
E14	The Bank desires to survive.	Yes	Yes	Yes	Yes

Table 16 *Continued*

Internal Stakeholder Identification (Jonker & Foster 2002)	October 1996 to December 2003		January 2004 to December 2012	
	NGOs, *in General: BIC,* 50	NGOs, *PSM/PSG focused: TI, PSI*	NGOs, *in General: BIC,* 50	NGOs, *PSM/PSG focused: TI, PSI, IBP*
E1　[Insert External Actor Here] *power* to influence the Bank	TI, IIE, BIC potentially "heard" by the 1997 WDR writers	TI were definitely "heard" but PSI was not since PSI's comments on unions would have rankled Bank staff.	NGOs in general focused on Results	Technocratic NGOs like IBP increase influence within public expenditure management topic within PSM/PSG
E2　*Legitimacy* of the [Insert External Actor Here] relationship with the Bank	**Bank decided legitimacy** not anyone else;	To the Bank? Only TI.	Consulted on GAC; Legitimacy of environment NGOs wanting Bank results largely assisted by Monterrey and Paris	Consulted on GAC Update
E3　*Urgency* of the [Insert External Actor Here] claim on the Bank	Urgency? Unlikely. See—>	Politically within the Bank (and also outside of it now), TI's message was gaining currency. PSI? Not.	Urgent if only because NGOs agreed that lending should continue in Bank consultation on World Bank (2007d)	Unlikely
E4　[Insert External Actor Here] *criticality* over the Bank	No defining event, perhaps the Wolfensohn speech	No defining event, perhaps the Wolfensohn speech	Critical for that moment only during staff versus Wolfowitz friction on the GAC (2007)	Only critical for 2007 GAC only given staff versus Wolfowitz friction

Is Organization Controlled by External Actor?

E5	Bank is aware of [Insert External Actor Here] demands	Yes, the Bank asked for them with the 1997 WDR	Yes, the Bank asked for both to provide advice for 1997 WDR	Yes. Also the Results Secretariat is aware of environmental NGO desires to improve Results	Yes
E6	Bank obtains some resources from the [Insert External Actor Here] making the demands	Yes, advice on its 1997 WDR & Corruption Efforts	Yes, the Bank asked for both to provide advice for 1997 WDR; TI advises on anticorruption too	GAC (2007) commentary in era of staff versus Wolfowitz friction	For IBP, technical cooperation
E7	The [Insert External Actor Here] resources are critical or important part of the Bank's operation	No, the NGO's resources are not critical but the agenda is increasingly becoming critical to the Bank's operation	No, the NGOs resources are not critical but the IT agenda is increasingly critical to the Bank's operation and to a lesser extent, Bank legitimacy	Not normally	Only for IBP in sense that their technical exchange is cooperative
E8	The [Insert External Actor Here] controls the allocation, access or use of the resources; alternative sources for the resources are not available to the focal organization	NGOs do not control	NGOs do not control	NGOs do not control	NGOs do not control

Continued

Table 16 Continued

Internal Stakeholder Identification (Jonker & Foster 2002)	October 1996 to December 2003		January 2004 to December 2012	
	NGOs, in General: BIC, 50	NGOs, PSM/PSG focused: TI, PSI	NGOs, in General: BIC, 50	NGOs, PSM/PSG focused: TI, PSI, IBP
E9 Bank does not control the allocation, access, or use of other resources critical to the [Insert External Actor Here] operation and survival	Bank does not control	Bank does not control	Bank does not control	Bank does not control
E10 The actions or outputs of the Bank are visible and can be assessed by the [Insert External Actor Here] to judge whether the actions comply with its demands	Yes, increasingly so	Yes, increasingly so	Yes	Yes
E11 Bank's satisfaction of the [Insert External Actor Here] requests are not in conflict with the satisfaction of demands from other components of the environment with which it is interdependent	If the Bank considered _all_ NGO actors, then yes. If only the NGOs that the Bank itself "legitimates," then no	PSI is in conflict, TI for the most part is not in conflict.	If the Bank considered _all_ NGO actors, then yes. If only the NGOs that the Bank itself "legitimates," then no	PSI left the "attempt to influence the Bank" scene, TI achieved its Bank influence objectives, IBP is cooperative on technical public expenditure management discussions
E12 The Bank does not control the determination, formulation, or expression of the [Insert External Actor Here] demands	Bank does not control	Bank does not control	Bank does not control	Bank does not control
E13 The Bank is capable of developing actions or outcomes that will satisfy the [Insert External Actor Here] demands	For the one's legitimized by the Bank, potentially. For the one's on the outside, likely not while at the same time, the Bank does not want to be beseiged by protestors (old 252)	For TI, perhaps (although TI interviewee was not so certain). For PSI, no.	Probably not entirely	For IBP, yes via technical cooperation of public expenditure management objectives
E14 The Bank desires to survive.	Yes	Yes	Yes	Yes

Table 17 Linking the book's analytical framework to future propositions for research

Variable	External & Boundary Actor Matters?	Proposition(s)
E1	[External/Boundary Actor] *power* to influence the Bank	A, C
E2	*Legitimacy* of the [External/Boundary Actor] relationship with the Bank	A
E3	*Urgency* of the [External/Boundary Actor] claim on the Bank	B, H
E4	[External/Boundary Actor] *criticality* over the Bank	B, H
E5	Bank is aware of [External/Boundary Actor] demands	A
E6	Bank obtains some resources from the [External/Boundary] making the demands	D
E7	The [External/Boundary Actor] resources are a critical or important part of the Bank's operation	D
E8	The [External/Boundary Actor] controls the allocation, access, or use of the resources; alternative sources for the resources are not available to the focal organization	D
E9	Bank does not control the allocation, access, or use of other resources critical to the [External/Boundary Actor] operation and survival	Variable matters for explaining policy change but does not lead to new proposition
E10	The actions or outputs of the Bank are visible and can be assessed by the [External/Boundary Actor] to judge whether the actions comply with its demands	E
E11	Bank's satisfaction of the [External/Boundary Actor] requests are not in conflict with the satisfaction of demands from other components of the environment with which it is interdependent	Variable matters for explaining policy change but does not lead to new proposition
E12	The Bank does not control the determination, formulation, or expression of the [External/Boundary Actor] demands	
E13	The Bank is capable of developing actions or outcomes that will satisfy the [External/Boundary Actor] demands	C
E14	The Bank desires to survive	E, I, M
New	*The Bank is more likely to listen to an [External/Boundary Actor] demands if the demands are given in language that the Bank understands*	F

Continued

Table 17 *Continued*

Variable	Internal Actor Matters?	Proposition(s)
I1	[Internal Actor] *power* to influence the Bank	K
I2	*Legitimacy* of the [internal Actor] relationship with the Bank	K, L
I3	*Urgency* of the [Internal Actor] claim on the Bank	J
I4	[Internal Actor] *criticality* over the Bank	H
I5	The larger the organization, the more that an organization's internal (bureaucratic) environment influences output	H
I6	The more important a particular component of an organization's work is for the organization, the more that an organization's internal (bureaucratic) environment influences output	G, J, M
I7	When internal factors outweigh external influence: "sunk cost of firms"	J
I8	When internal factors outweigh external influence: "communication structures"	J, L
I9	When internal factors outweigh external influence: "internal politics"	J
I10	When internal factors outweigh external influence: "dominance of institutional norms"	J, L
I11	Captures "organizational innovation"	I
I12	Lauded for "efficiency" in "explaining incrementalism"	I

References

50 Years Is Enough. 1994. "Original Platform of 1994". 50 Years is Enough. Accessed Feb 16. http://www.50years.org/about/94platform.html#top.

Abouharb, M. Rodwan, Cingranelli, David. 2008. *Human Rights and Structural Adjustment*. Cambridge: Cambridge University Press.

Adams, J.W. 2015. "Reform at the World Bank". In *The Politics of International Organizations: Views from Insiders*, edited by YC Xu and P. Weller, 58–81. London: Routledge.

Adams, T. 2006. "Statement by Under Secretary for International Affairs". In *Advance of the Meetings of the G7, IMF and World Bank*. edited by Timothy D. Adams. Washington, DC: U.S. Treasury.

Agarwala, R. 1983. Planning in Developing Countries: Lessons of Experience. *World Bank Staff Working Papers, No. 576;* Management and Development Series, No. 3. Washington, DC: World Bank.

Ahmad, J., Devarajan, S., Khemani, S., Shah, S. 2005. Decentralization and Service Delivery. *World Bank Policy Working Paper*. Washington, DC: World Bank.

Åhman, J. 2020. "Facts, Evidence and the Burden of Proof in the World Bank Group Sanctions System". *Journal of International Economic Law* 23 (3): 685–702.

Alimi, D. 2015. "'Going Global': Policy Entrepreneurship of the Global Commission on Drug Policy". *Public Administration* 93 (4): 874–889.

Allan, B.B. 2019. "Paradigm and Nexus: Neoclassical Economics and the Growth Imperative in the World Bank, 1948-2000". *Review of International Political Economy* 26 (1): 183–206.

Allison, G.T. 1971. *Essence of Decision: Explaining the Cuban Missile Crisis*. Boston, MA: Little, Brown.

Allison, G.T., Halperin, M.H. 1972. "Bureaucratic Politics: A Paradigm and Some Policy Implications". In *Theory and Policy in International Relations*, edited by Raymond Tanter and Richard H. Ullman, 40–79. Princeton, NJ: Princeton University Press.

Anderl, F., Daphi, P., Deitelhoff, N. 2021. "Keeping Your Enemies Close? The Variety of Social Movements 'Reactions to International Organizations' Opening Up". *International Studies Review* 23 (4): 1273–1299.

Anderson, J., Kaufmann, D., Recanatini, F. 2003. Service Delivery, Poverty and Corruption: Common Threads from Diagnostic Surveys. *Background Paper for the 2004 WDR "Making Services Work for Poor People")* (DRAFT). Washington, DC: World Bank.

Andrews, M. 2014. *The Limits of Institutional Reform in Development: Changing Rules for Realistic Solutions*. Cambridge: Cambridge University Press.

Annisette, M. 2004. "The True Nature of the World Bank". *Critical Perspectives on Accounting* 15 (3): 303–323.

Anonymous. 1988. "IMF, World Bank Hold Annual Joint Meeting". *Facts on File World Digest*, 7 October.

Anonymous. 2000. "World Bank's Stiglitz Dismissed from Post of Adviser to Chief". *Wall Street Journal*. Accessed Jul 10, 2021. https://www.wsj.com/articles/SB956872641509953487.

Anonymous. 2006. "Public Awareness of Projects Emphasized". *The Statesman*, 7 November.

Arrau, P., Schmidt-Hebb, K. 1995. Pension Systems and Reforms: Country Experiences and Research Issues. *Policy Research Working Paper*. Washington, DC: World Bank.

Ascher, W. 1983. "New Development Approaches and the Adaptability of International Agencies: The Case of the World Bank". *International Organization* 37 (3): 415–439.

Ascher, W. 2003. "The World Bank and U.S. Control". In *The United States and Multilateral Institutions: Patterns of Changing Instrumentality and Influence*, edited by K.A. Mingst and M.P. Karns, 78–94. London: Routledge.

Atkinson, C. 1981. "World Bank Report Seen as Aid Plan". *Washington Post*, September 2, D8, Business and Finance.

Aversa, J. 2007a. "White House: Give Wolfowitz Fair Hearing". *USA Today*. http://www.usatoday.com/money/economy/2007-05-09-3701887316_x.htm.

Aversa, J. 2007b. "Wolfowitz to Resign from World Bank". *Houston Chronicle*. http://web.archive.org/web/20070519040810rn_1/www.chron.com/disp/story.mpl/ap/fn/4814948.html.

Baker III, J.A. 1985a. *Statement of the Honorable James A. Baker, III, Secretary of the Treasury of the United States before the Joint Annual Meeting of the International Monetary Fund and the World Bank*. Seoul, Korea: World Bank.

Baker III, J.A. 1985b. *Statement by Secretary of Treasury James A. Baker, III at the IMF Interim Committee Meeting on Use of Trust Fund Reflows (Speech)*. October 6.

Baker III, J.A. 1986. *Remarks by the Honorable James A. Baker, III, Secretary of the Treasury before the Bretton Woods Committee* (Speech). Washington, DC: U.S. Treasury.

Baker III, J.A. 1987. Statement of the Honorable James A. Baker, III, Secretary of the Treasury. *Subcommittee on Foreign Operations, Committee on Appropriates*. Washington, DC.

Bakir, C. 2009. "Policy Entrepreneurship and Institutional Change: Multilevel Governance of Central Banking Reform". *Governance* 22 (4): 571–598.

Balint, T., Bauer, M., Knill, C. 2000. "Bureaucratic Change in the European Administrative Space: The Case of the European Commission". *West European Politics* 31 (4): 677–700.

Balkvis, P. 2005. "Wolfensohn to Wolfowitz: What does the Change at the Top of the World Bank Mean for Labour?" *Transfer: European Review of Labour and Research* 11 (4): 633–638.

Bank's World. 1983. "Valedictory excerpts from a speech by Warren C. Baum, Vice President in the Senior Staff Resources Program". *The Bank's World*, 10–12.

Bank's World. 1984a. "The Evolving Role of the Bank in the '80's". *The Bank's World*, 13–15.

Bank's World. 1984b. "An Institution within the Institution". *The Bank's World*, 19.

Bank's World. 1985. "An Interview with Richard D. Erb: And Now a Word from the IMF". *The Bank's World*, 14–16.

Bank's World. 1986a. "Harry Dexter White's Role in Founding the Bank and the Fund: The White Plan". *The Bank's World*, 5–7.

Bank's World. 1986b. "How the Bank Came to be Called a Bank". *The Bank's World*, 14.

Bank's World. 1987a. "As We Go to Press …" *The Bank's World*, 23.

Bank's World. 1987b. "Chairman of the Steering Committee Speaks to Staff Association: Kim Jaycox on the Reorganization". *The Bank's World*, 2–6.

Bank's World. 1987c. "Senior Appointments in the Reorganized Bank". *The Bank's World*.

Bank-Fund. 2007. Enhancing Collaboration: Joint Management Action Plan (Follow-Up to the Report of the External Review Committee on IMF-World Bank Collaboration). Washington, DC: International Monetary Fund and the World Bank.

Barbone, L. 1999a. Pensions and Social Security in Sub-Saharan Africa: Issues and Options. *Africa Region Working Paper Series*. Washington, DC: World Bank.

Barbone, L., Das-Gupta, A., de Wulf, L., Hansson, A. 1999b. Reforming Tax Systems: The World Bank Record in the 1990s. *Policy Research Working Paper*. Washington, DC: World Bank.

Bare, J.F. 1998. "Of Loans and Results, Elements for a Chronicle of Evaluation at the World Bank". *Human Organization* 57 (3): 319–325.

Barnett, M.N., Finnemore, M. 2004. *Rules for the World: International Organizations in Global Politics*. Ithaca, NY: Cornell University Press.

Barro, R.J. 2001. *Economic Growth in East Asia before and after the Financial Crisis*. Washington DC: National Bureau of Economic Research.

Barron, G. 2005. *The World Bank & Rule of Law Reforms*. London: LSE DESTIN.

Bartel, M. 1996. Integrated Financial Management Systems: A Guide to Implementation Based on the Experience in Latin America. *LATPS Occasional Paper Series*. Washington, DC: World Bank.

Batam, J.A. 2006. "Secretive Institutions: Campaigners Urge 'Massive Shift' to Transparency". *The Guardian*, 18 September, 21, Financial Pages.

Bauer, M.W. 2002. "The EU 'Partnership Principle': Still a Sustainable Governance Device Across Multiple Administrative Arenas?" *Public Administration* 80 (4): 769–789.

Bauer, M.W. 2012. "Tolerant, If Personal Goals Remain Unharmed: Explaining Supranational Bureaucrats' Attitudes to Organizational Change". *Governance* 25 (3): 485–510.

Bauer, M.W., Ege, J. 2016. "Bureaucratic Autonomy of International Organizations' Secretariats". *Journal of European Public Policy* 23 (7): 1019–1037.

Bauer, M.W., Knill, C., ed. 2007. *Management Reforms in International Organizations*. Baden-Baden: Nomos.

Bauer, M.W., Eckhard, S., Ege, J., Knill, C. 2017. "A Public Administration Perspective on International Organizations". In *International Bureaucracy: Challenges and Lessons for Public Administration Research*, edited by M.W. Bauer, C. Knill, and S. Eckhard, 1–12. London: Palgrave Macmillan.

Bauer, M.W., Ege, J., Schomaker, R. 2018. "The Challenge of Administrative Internationalization: Taking Stock and Looking Ahead". *International Journal of Public Administration* 42 (11): 904–917.

Bauer, M.W., Bayerlein, L., Ege, J., Knill, C., Trondal, J. 2019. *Perspectives on International Public Administration Research: A Rejoinder to Johan Christensen and Kutsal Yesilkagit*. Oslo: ARENA.

Bayerlein, L., Knill, C., Steinebach, Y. 2020. *A Matter of Style? Organizational Agency in Global Public Policy*. Cambridge: Cambridge University Press.

Bazbauers, A.R. 2014. "The Wolfensohn, Wolfowitz, and Zoellick Presidencies: Revitalizing the Neoliberal Agenda of the World Bank". *Forum for Development Studies* 41 (1): 91–114.

Becker, M. 2019. "When Public Principals Give Up Control Over Private Agents: The New Independence of ICANN in Internet Governance". *Regulation & Governance* 13 (4): 561–576.

Béland, D., Orenstein, M.A. 2013. "International Organizations as Policy Actors: An Ideational Approach". *Global Social Policy* 13 (2): 125–143.

Bello, W. 2000. "World Bank, IMF Disempowerment 'Cost-Effective' Alternative to Reform?" *BusinessWorld*, 26 September.

Bendor, J., Hammond, T.H. 1992. "Reconsidering Allison's Models". *American Political Science Review* 86 (2): 301–322.

Bentsen, L. 1993a. Remarks by the Honorable Lloyd Bentsen Secretary of the Treasury at the Afternoon Session of the Interim Committee (Speech). Washington, DC: U.S. Treasury.

Bentsen, L. 1993b. Statement by the Honorable Lloyd Bentsen, Secretary of the Treasury. *Foreign Operations Subcommittee, Senate Appropriations Committee*. Washington, DC: U.S. Treasury.

Bentsen, L. 1994. Statement of Treasury Secretary Lloyd Bentsen at the Development Committee of the World Bank and the International Monetary Fund in Madrid Spain (Speech). Washington, DC: U.S. Treasury.

Berg, E., Shirley, M. 1987. Divestiture in Developing Countries. *World Bank Discussion Papers, No. 11*. Washington, DC: World Bank.

Berger, P.L., Luckmann, T. 1966. *The Social Construction of Reality*. New York, NY: Anchor Books.

Berkman, S. 2008. *The World Bank and the Gods of Lending*. Sterling: Kumarian Press.

Berkman, S., Boswell, N.Z., Bruner, F.H., Gough, M., McCormick, J.T., Pedersen, P.E., Ugaz, J., Zimmerman, S. 2008. "The First Against Corruption: International Organizations at a Cross-Roads". *Journal of Financial Crime* 15 (2): 124–154.

Best, J. 2012. "Bureaucratic Ambiguity". *Economy and Society* 41 (1): 84–106.

Best, J. 2014. "The 'Demand Side' of Good Governance: The Return of the Public in World Bank Policy". In *The Return of the Public in Global Governance*, edited by A. Gheciu and J. Best, 97–199. Cambridge: Cambridge University Press.

Betton, J., Dess, G.G. 1985. "The Application of Population Ecology Models to the Study of Organizations". *The Academy of Management Review* 10 (4): 750–757.

Biersteker, T.J. 1990. "Reducing the Role of the State in the Economy: A Conceptual Exploration of IMF and World Bank Prescriptions". *International Studies Quarterly* 34 (4): 477–492.

Birdsall, Nancy. 2003. *Why it Matters Who Runs the IMF and the World Bank*. Washington, DC: Center for Global Development.

Braaten, D. 2014. "Determinants of US Foreign Policy in Multilateral Development Banks". *Journal of Peace Research* 51 (4): 515–527.

Braaten, D., Orozco, M., Strand, J.R. 2018. "Voting for Green? U.S. Support for Environmental Projects in the Multilateral Development Bank". *The Journal of Environment & Development* 28 (1): 28–53.

Bradford, A., Gadinis, S., Linos, K. 2018. "Unintended Agency Problems: How International Bureaucracies are Built and Empowered". *Virginia Journal of International Law* 57 (2): 159–220.

Bradlow, D.D., Fourie, A.N. 2013. "The Operational Policies of the World Bank and the International Finance Corporation: Creating Law-Making and Law-Governed Institutions?" *International Organizations Law Review* 10: 3–80.

Bradlow, D.D., Grossman, C. 1995. "Limited Mandates and Intertwined Problems: A New Challenge for the World Bank and the IMF". *Human Rights Quarterly* 17: 411–442.

Bradshaw, York W., Huang, Jie. 1991. "Intensifying Global Dependency: Foreign Debt, Structural Adjustment, and Third World Underdevelopment" *The Sociological Quarterly* 32 (3): 321–342.

Brady, N.F. 1990. Statement by the Honorable Nicholas F. Brady. Subcommittee on Foreign Operations, Committee on Appropriations. Washington, DC: U.S. Treasury.

Brady, N.F. 1991a. Statement of the Honorable Nicholas F. Brady, Secretary of the Treasury. Subcommittee on Foreign Operations, U.S. House of Representatives. Washington, DC: U.S. Treasury.

Brady, N.F. 1991b. Statement of the Secretary of the Treasury, The Honorable Nicholas F. Brady at the Meeting of the Development Committee of the World Bank and the International Monetary Fund. Washington, DC: U.S. Treasury.

Bräutigam, D. 1991. Governance and Economy: A Review. *Policy Research Working Papers*. Washington, DC: World Bank.

Brinkerhoff, D.W. 1994. "Institutional Development in World Bank Projects: Analytical Approaches and Intervention Designs". *Public Administration and Development* 12 (2): 135–151.

Broad, R. 2004. "The Washington Consensus Meets the Global Backlash: Shifting Debates and Policies". *Globalizations* 1 (2): 129–154.

Broad, R., Cavanagh, J. 1999. "The Death of the Washington Consensus?" *World Policy Journal* 16 (3): 79–88.

Bruno, M., Easterly, W. 1995. Inflation Crises and Long-Run Growth. *Policy Research Working Paper*. Washington, DC: World Bank.

Bruno, M. 1996a. Deep Crises and Reform: What Have We Learned? *Directions in Development*. Washington, DC: World Bank.

Bruno, M. 1996b. Why Crises Can Be Good for Growth. *DEC Notes*. Washington, DC: World Bank.

Bruno, M., Pleskovia, B. 1996. "Introduction". Annual World Bank Conference on Development Economics (ABCDE), Washington, DC.

Bugalski, N. 2016. "The Demise of Accountability at the World Bank?" *American University International Law Review* 31 (1): 1–56.

Burki, S.J. 2005. "World Bank Operations: Some Impressions and Lessons". In *At the Frontlines of Development: Reflections from the World Bank*, edited by Indermit S. Gill and Todd Pugatch, 121–150. Washington, DC: World Bank.

Burki, S.J., Haq, M.U. 1981. "Meeting Basic Needs: An Overview". *Development* 9 (2): 167–182.

Burki, S.J., Perry, G.E. 1997. *The Long March: A Reform Agenda for Latin America and the Caribbean in the Next Decade*. Washington, DC: World Bank.

Busch, P-O., Liese, A. 2017. "The Authority of International Public Administrations". In *International Bureaucracy: Challenges and Lessons for Public Adminstration Research*, edited by C. Knill, M.W Bauer, and S. Eckhard, 97–122. Palgrave Macmillan.

Caldwell, Dan. 1977. "Bureaucratic Foreign Policy-Making". *The American Behavioral Scientist* 21 (1): 87–110.

Capano, G., Howlett, M. 2009. "Introduction: The Determinants of Policy Change: Advancing the Debate". *Journal of Comparative Policy Analysis* 11 (1): 1–5.

Carey, P. 1985. "Indonesia in the 1980s: A Time of Transition". *Asian Affairs* 16 (2): 125–136.

Cassidy, J. 2007. "The Next Crusade: Paul Wolfowitz at the World Bank". *The New Yorker*, 36.

Chang, C.K. 2008. "The World Bank: Development Agency, Credit Union, or Institutional Dinosaur?" *International Journal of Political Economy* 37 (1): 24–50.

Chatterjee, B. 2011. *Resourcing Implementation of the World Bank's 2007 Governance and Anticorruption Strategy*. Washington, DC: World Bank.

Checkel, Jeffrey T. 1998. "The Constructivist Turn in International Relations Theory". *World Politics* 50 (2): 324–348.

Chen, Y. 2016. "International Organizations and Strategies of Self-Legitimization: The Example of the World Bank Anti-Corruption Sanctions Regime". *Manchester Journal of International Economic Law* 13 (3): 314–333.

Chenery, H.B. 1974. *Redistribution with Growth*. Oxford: Oxford University Press.

Chenery, H.B. 1980. "Poverty and Progress-Choices for the Developing World". *Finance and Development* 17 (2): 12.

Chenery, H.B. 1983. Interviewed by Robert Asher (January 27). Washington, DC: World Bank.

Chwieroth, J.M. 2008. "Organizational Change 'From Within': Exploring the World Bank's Early Lending Practices". *Review of International Political Economy* 15 (4): 481–505.

Chwieroth, J.M. 2015. "Professional Ties That Bind: How Normative Orientations Shape IMF Conditionality". *Review of International Political Economy* 22 (4): 757–787.

Cissé, H. 2012. "Should the Political Prohibition in Charters of International Financial Institutions Be Revisted?" *World Bank Legal Review* 3: 59–92.

Clague, C. 1997. "The New Institutional Economics and Economic Development". In *Institutions and Economic Development: Growth and Governance in Less-Developed and Post-Socialist Societies*, edited by Christopher Clague, 13–36. Baltimore, MD: Johns Hopkins Press.

Clark, D. 1999. *A Citizen's Guide to the World Bank Inspection Panel*. Washington, DC: Center for International Environmental Law.

Clark, R., Dolan, L.R. 2021. "Pleasing the Principal: US influence in World Bank Policymaking". *American Journal of Political Science* 6 (1): 36–51.

Clausen, A.W. 1986 [1981]. "Address to the Board of Governors (Washington DC, 29 Sep 1981)". *The Development Challenges of the Eighties: A.W. Clausen and The World Bank (Major Policy Addresses, 1981–1986)*, 1–20. Washington, DC.

Clausen, A.W. 1986 [1982]. "Address to the Board of Governors (Toronto Canada, 6 Sep 1982)". *The Development Challenges of the Eighties: A.W. Clausen and The World Bank (Major Policy Addresses, 1981–1986)*, International Bank for Reconstruction and Development, 97–123. Washington, DC: World Bank.

Clausen, A.W. 1988 [1983]. "Third World Debt and Global Recovery: The 1983 Jodidi Lecture at The Center for International Affairs, Harvard University: Boston MA, 24 Feb 1983)". In *The Development Challenges of the Eighties: A.W. Clausen and The World Bank (Major Policy Addresses, 1981–1986)*, International Bank for Reconstruction and Development, 133–156. Washington, DC: World Bank.

Clemons, M.A., Kremer, M. 2016. "The New Role for the World Bank". *Journal of Economic Perspectives* 30 (1): 53–76.

Coady, E.P. 1993. Interviewed by William Becker (George Washington University) and David Milobsky (World Bank History Office). Washington, DC: World Bank.

Conable, B.B. 1988. Advance Text of Remarks Prepared for Delivery by Barber B. Conable to the Board of the Governors of the World Bank Group. West Berlin, FDR: Federal News Service.

Coolidge, J., Rose-Ackerman, S. 1997. High-Level Rent-Seeking and Corruption in African Regimes: Theory and Cases. *Policy Research Working Paper*. Washington, DC: World Bank.

Cornia, G.A., Jolly, R., Stewart, F. (Eds.) 1987. *Adjustment with a Human Face: Volume I: Protecting the Vulnerable and Promoting Growth*. II vols. Vol. I. Oxford: Oxford University Press.

Coronel, L.V. 1986. "Interview with Yves Rovani, Director-General, Operations Evaluation, "All About OED"". *The Bank's World*, 2–5.

Cox, R.W., Jacobson, H.K. 1973. *The Anatomy of Influence: Decision Making in International Organizations*. New Haven, CT: Yale University Press.

Crawford, Gordon. 2006. "The World Bank and Good Governance? Rethinking the State or Consolidating Neo-Liberalism?" In *The IMF, World Bank and Policy Reform*, edited by Alberto Paloni and Maurizio Zanardi, 115–142. London: Routledge.

Creswell, J.W. 2009. *Research Design: Qualitative, Quantitative, and Mixed Methods Approaches*, 3rd edn. Los Angeles, CA: SAGE.

Dacin, M.T. 1997. "Isomorphism in Context: The Power and Prescription of Institutional Norms". *The Academy of Management Journal* 40 (1): 46–81.

Dawson, Thomas C. 1982. *Statement of Thomas C. Dawson, Deputy Assistant Secretary of the Treasury for Developing Nations*. US House of Representatives. June 22.

de Borchgrave, A. 2007. "More Brains Than Judgment". *The Washington Times*, 24 April, Commentary.

De Charzourne, L.B., Fromageau, E. 2012. "Balancing the Scales: The World Bank Sanctions Process and Access to Remedies". *The European Journal of International Law* 23 (4): 963–989.

De Janvry, A., Dethier, J-J. 2012. *The World Bank and Governance: The Bank's Efforts to Help Developing Countries Build State Capacity*. *Policy Research Working Paper*. Washington DC: World Bank.

De Neubourg, C., Castonguay, J., Roelen, K. 2007. *Social Safety Nets and Targeted Social Assistance: Lessons from the European Experience*. Washington, DC: World Bank.

De Wulf, L., Sokol, J.B. (Eds.) 2004. *Customs Modernization Initiatives: Case Studies*. Washington, DC: World Bank.

De Wulf, L., Sokol, J.B. (Eds.) 2005. *Customs Modernization Handbook*. Washington, DC: World Bank.

DeFrancesco, F., Guashino, E. 2020. "Reframing knowledge: A Comparison of OECD and World Bank Discourse on Public Governnace Reform". *Policy and Society* 39 (1): 113–128.

Dellmuth, L.M. 2020. "Interest Groups and the United Nations". In *The Palgrave Encyclopedia of Interest Groups, Lobbying and Public Affairs*, edited by P. Harris, A. Bitonti, C.S. Fleisher, and A.S Binderkrantz, 1–6. Camden: Springer Nature.

Dellmuth, L.M., Bloodgood, E.A. 2019. "Advocacy Group Effects in Global Governance: Populations, Strategies, and Political Opportunity Structures". *Interest Groups & Advocacy* 8: 255–269.

Delreux, T., Adriaensen, J. 2017. "Introduction. Use and Limitations of the Principal–Agent Model In Studying the European Union". In *Principal Agent Model and the European Union*, edited by Tom Delreux and Johan Adriaensen, 1–34. London: Palgrave Macmillan.

Demortain, D. 2017. "Experts and the Production of International Policy Knowledge". In *The Politics of Expertise in International Organizations*, edited by A. Littoz-Monnet, 76–92. London: Routledge.

Development Committee. 2002. Development Committee Communique. Washington, DC: Joint Ministerial Committee of the Boards of Governors of the World Bank and the International Monetary Fund on the Transfer of Real Resources to Developing Countries.

Development GAP. n.d. "The Development GAP's Programmatic History". DevelopmentGAP. Accessed Dec 3, 2021. https://www.developmentgap.org/program-history.html.

Dia, M. 1993. A Governance Approach to Civil Service Reform in Sub-Saharan Africa. *World Bank Technical Paper (No. 225) from the African Technical Department Series*. Washington, DC: World Bank.

Dijkstra, H. 2017. "Collusion in International Organizations: How States Benefit from the Authority of Secretariats". *Global Governance* 23 (4): 601–618.

Dillinger, W. 1994. Decentralization and its Implications for Service Delivery. *UNDP/UNCHS/World Bank: Urban Management Programme*. Washington, DC: World Bank.

Dolan, J., Rosenbloom, D.H. (Ed.) 2003. *Representative Bureaucracy: Classic Readings and Continuing Controversies*. Armonk, NY: M.E. Sharpe.

Doornbos, M. 2001. "'Good Governance': The Rise and Decline of a Policy Metaphor?" *Journal of Development studies* 37 (6): 93–108.

Drattell, A. 1985. "Jaycox Looks at a Changing Region: Q&A on Eastern and Southern Africa". *The Bank's World*, 2–5.

Drattell, A. 1986. "A.W. Clausen Talks About the World Bank". *The Bank's World*, 2–5.

Dubois, P.H., Fielder, J.D., Delonis, R., Fariello, F., Peters, K. 2019. "The World Bank's Sanction System: Using Debarment to Combat Fraud and Corruption in International Development". In *Good Governance and Modern International Financial Institutions*, edited by X. Gao and P. Quayle, 217–240. Leiden: Brill Nijhoff.

Easterly, W. 2003. "IMF and World Bank Structural Adjustment Programs and Poverty". In *Managing Currency Crises in Emerging Markets*, edited by Michael P. Dooley and Jeffrey A. Frankel, 361–392. Chicago, IL: University of Chicago Press.

Ebrahim, A., Herz, S. 2007. Accountability in Complex Organizations: World Bank Responses to Civil Society. *Faculty Research Working Papers Series*. Cambridge, MA: Harvard University.

Eckhard, S., Ege, J. 2016. "International Bureaucracies and Their Influence on Policy-Making: A Review of Empirical Evidence". *Journal of European Public Policy* 23 (7): 960–978.

Economist. 1986a. "Taking Up the Running: Dealing with Debt". *The Economist*, 27 September.

Economist. 1986b. "Taking up the Running: Promoting the Private Sector". *The Economist*.

Economist. 1997. "Who Will Listen to Mr. Clean?" *The Economist*, 2 August, 52.

Economist. 2000. "Angry and Effective". *The Economist*, 23 September.

Edwards, A.C. 2001. Social Security Reform and Women's Pensions. *Policy Research Report on Gender and Development, Working Paper Series*. Washington, DC: World Bank.

Edwards, B. 2009. "Reforming the World Bank: NGOs and the Wolfowitz Resignation". Montreal International Forum, Delhi.

Edwards, R.D. 1983. "The World Debt Problem Revisited; Short Term Looks Better—But What About the Future? Some World Bank Thoughts in a Major Report". *United States Banker*.

Edwards, S. 2018. World Bank launches highly anticipated human capital index. Accessed 2021. https://www.devex.com/news/world-bank-launches-highly-anticipated-human-capital-index-93623.

Edwards, S. 2019. As Jim Kim steps down, a tumultuous World Bank presidency comes to an end. Accessed 2021. https://www.devex.com/news/as-jim-kim-steps-down-a-tumultuous-world-bank-presidency-comes-to-an-end-94247#.XFhUXvgq9g8.twitter.

Ege, J. 2017. "Comparing the Autonomy of International Public Administrations: An Ideal-Type Approach". *Public Administration* 95 (3): 555–570.

Ege, J. 2020. "What International Bureaucrats (Really) Want: Administrative Preferences in International Organization Research". *Global Governance* 26: 577–600.

Ege, J., Bauer, M.W. 2017. "The Politics of International Organization's Budgeting" *Global Policy* 8 (Supplement 5): 75–84.

Ege, J., Bauer, M.W., Wagner, N. 2019. "Improving Generalizability in Transnational Bureaucratic Influence Research: A (Modest) Proposal". *International Studies Review* 22 (3): 551–575.

Elsig, M. 2011. "Principal–Agent Theory and the World Trade Organization: Complex Agency and 'Missing Delegation'". *European Journal of International Relations* 17 (3): 495–517.

Enkler, J., Schmidt, S., Eckhard, S., Knill, C., Grohs, S. 2017. "Administrative Styles in the OECD: Bureaucratic Policy-Making beyond Formal Rules". *International Journal of Public Administration* 40 (8): 637–648.

Enns, C. 2015. "Knowledges in Competition: Knowledge Discourse at the World Bank during the Knowledge for Development Era". *Global Social Policy* 15 (1): 61–80.

Erkkilä, T., Piironen, O. 2014. "(De) Politicizing Good Governance: The World Bank Institute, The OECD And the Politics of Governance Indicators". *The European Journal of Social Science Research* 27 (4): 344–360.

Esman, M.J., Montgomery, J.D. 1980. "The Administration of Human Development". In *Implementing Programs of Human Development*, edited by Peter T. Knight, 183–234. Washington, DC: World Bank.

Farnsworth, C.H. 1981. "Reagan Cautions Developing Lands on Economic Help". *New York Times*, September 30, A1, A.

Felix, D. 1983. "World Development Report, 1983". *Development and Cultural Change* 33 (2): 427–431.

Ferren, D., Montgomery, A. 1994. "World Bank, IMF: 50 Years is Enough!" *The Ottawa Citizen*, 29 July, A11, News/Opinions.

Ferroni, M., Kanbur, R. 1990. Poverty-Conscious Restructuring of Public Expenditure. *SDA Working Paper Series*. Washington, DC: World Bank.

Finer, H. 1941. "Administrative Responsibility in Democratic Government". *Public Administration Review* 1 (4): 335–350.

Fioretos, O., Heldt, E.C. 2019. "Legacies and Innovations in Global Economic Governance Since Bretton Woods". *Review of International Political Economy* 26 (6): 1089–1111.

Fischer, S. 1995. "Structural Adjustment: Lessons from the 1980s". In *Structural Adjustment: Retrospect and Prospect*, edited by Daniel M. Schydlowsky, 21–31. Westport, CT: Praeger.

Fischer, S. 2003. "Stanley Fischer". In *Economic and Financial Crises in Emerging Market Economies*, edited by M. Feldstein, 347–352. Chicago, IL: University of Chicago Press.

Fischer, S. 2005. *IMF Essays from a Time of Crisis: The International Financial System, Stabilization, and Development*. Boston, MA: MIT Press.

Fisman, R.J., Gatti, R. 2000. Decentralization and Corruption: Evidence Across Countries. Edited by World Bank Policy Research Working Paper. Washington, DC: World Bank.

Fleck, R.K., Kilby, C. 2006. "World Bank Independence: A Model and Statistical Analysis of US Influence". *Review of Development Economics* 10 (2): 224–249.

Fleischer, J., Reiners, N. 2021. "Connecting International Relations and Public Administration: Toward a Joint Research Agenda for the Study of International Bureaucracy". *International Studies Review*: 1–18. Doi: 10.1093/isr/viaa097.

Fox, J.A., Brown, J.D. (Eds.) 1998. *The Struggle for Accountability: The World Bank, NGOs, and Grassroots Movements*. Boston, MA: MIT Press.

Francis, D.R. 1985. "U.S. stepping up push for free enterprise via third-world aid". *Christian Science Monitor*, May 30, 19, Business.

Frederickson, H.G., Smith, K.B. 2003. *The Public Administration Theory Primer*. Boulder, CO: Westview Press.

Freedman, L. 1976. "Logic, Politics and Foreign Policy Processes: A Critique of the Bureaucratic Politics Model". *International Affairs* 52 (3): 434–449.

Friedrich, C.J. 1940. "Public Policy and the Nature of Administrative Responsibility". In *Public Policy: A Yearbook of the Graduate School of Public Administration*, edited by Carl J. Friedrich and Edward S. Mason, 3–24. Cambridge, MA: Harvard University Press.

Frumkin, P., Galaskiewicz, J. 2004. "Institutional Isomorphism and Public Sector Organizations". *Journal of Public Administration Research and Theory* 14 (3): 283–307.

FSB (Financial Stability Board). 2010. *FSB Framework for Strengthening Adherence to International Standards*. Basel: Switzerland: FSB.

Fukuyama, F. 1992. *The End of History and the Last Man*. New York: Free Press.

G7. 1980. Declaration. Venice, Italy.

G7. 1981. Declaration of the Ottawa Summit. Ottawa, Canada.

G7. 1982. Declaration of the Seven Heads of State and Government and Representatives of the European Communities. Versailles, France.

G7. 1983. Declaration on Economic Recovery. Williamsburg, VA.

G7. 1984. The London Economic Declaration. London.

G7. 1988. Toronto Economic Summit Economic Declaration. Toronto, Canada.

G7. 1990. Houston Economic Declaration. Houston, TX.

G7. 1991. Economic Declaration: Building World Partnership. London: G7.

G7. 1993. Economic Declaration: A Strengthened Commitment to Jobs and Growth. Tokyo: G7.

G7. 1995a. Halifax Summit Communiqué. Halifax, Canada: G7.

G7. 1995b. The Halifax Summit Review of the International Financial Institutions: Background Document. Halifax, Canada: G7.

G7. 1996. Summit Communiqué. Lyon, France: G7.

G7. 1998. Communiqué. Birmingham (UK): G7.

G8. 1999. Communiqué. Köln (Germany): G8.

GAP. 2007. "Wolfowitz Quits; Multiple GAP Documents Lead to Bank President's Resignation; New Whistleblower Policy Crucial Next Step". Government Accountability Project. Accessed Feb 10. http://www.whistleblower.org/content/press_detail.cfm?press_id=1016.

Gatti, R., Paternostro, S., Rigolini, J. 2003. Individual Attitudes Toward Corruption: Do Social Effects Matter? *Policy Research Working Paper*. Washington, DC: World Bank.

Gedda, G.L. 1981. "Reagan Dismisses Foreign Aid as Key to Global Prosperity". *Associated Press*, September 29, *Business News*.

Gelb, A., Honohan, P. 1989. Financial Sector Reforms in Adjustment Programs. *Policy, Planning, and Research Working Paper Series*. Washington, DC: World Bank.

George, A.L., Bennett, A. 2005. *Case Studies and Theory Development in the Social Sciences*. Cambridge, MA: MIT Press.

George, S., Sabelli, F. 1994. *Faith & Credit: The World Bank's Secular Empire*. Boulder, CO: Westview Press.

Gerard, K. 2019. "Rationalizing 'Gender-Wash': Empowerment, Efficiency and Knowledge Construction". *Review of International Political Economy* 26 (5): 1022–1042.

Gill, I.S. 1997. Reforming Social Security: Lessons from International Experience and Priorities for Brazil. *Economic Notes*. Washington, DC: World Bank.

Girishankar, N. 1999. Reforming Institutions for Service Delivery: A Framework for Development Assistance with an Application to the HINP Portfolio. *Policy Research Working Paper*. Washington, DC: World Bank.

Girishankar, N. 2013. *Why, What, and How of World Bank Group Strategy*. Washington, DC: World Bank.

Goldman, M. 2007. "Under New Management: Historical Context and Current Challenges at the World Bank". *The Brown Journal of International Affairs* 13 (2): 11–25.

Goldman, M. 2008. *Imperial Nature: The World Bank and Struggles for Social Justice in the Age of Globalization*. New Haven, CT: Yale University Press.

Gordon, D.L. 1983. Development Finance Corporations: State and Privately-Owned. *World Bank Staff Working Papers, No. 578; Management and Development Series, No. 5*. Washington, DC: World Bank.

Graham, E. 2014. "International Organizations as Collective Agents: Fragmentation and the Limits of Principal Control at the World Health Organization". *European Journal of International Relations* 20 (2): 366–390.

Graham, N.A., Jordan, R.S. (Eds.) 1980. *The International Civil Service: Changing Role and Concepts*. New York: Pergaman Press.

Gray, C.W. 1992. The Legal Framework for Private Sector Activity in the Czech and Slovak Federal Republic. *Policy Research Working Papers*. Washington, DC: World Bank.

Gray, C.W., Ianachkov, P. 1992. Bulgaria's Evolving Legal Framework for Private Sector Development. *Policy Research Working Papers*. Washington, DC: World Bank.

Gray, C.W., Stibla, F.D. 1992. The Evolving Legal Framework for Private Sector Activity in Slovenia. *Policy Research Working Papers*. Washington, DC: World Bank.

Gray, C.W., Hanson, R.J., Heller, M. 1992a. Legal Reform for Hungary's Private Sector. In *Policy Research Working Papers*. Washington, DC: World Bank.

Gray, C.W., Hanson, R.J., Ianachkov, P. 1992b. Romania's Evolving Legal Framework for Private Sector Development. *Policy Research Working Papers*. Washington, DC: World Bank.

Green, J.F. 2018. "Transnational Delegation in Global Environmental Governnace: When Do Non-State Actors Govern?" *Regulation & Governance* 12 (2): 263–276.

Grindle, M.S. 2004. "Good Enough Governance: Poverty Reduction and Reform in Developing Countries". *Governance* 17 (4): 525–548. doi: 10.1111/j.0952-1895.2004.00256.x.

Grindle, M.S. 2007. "Good Enough Governance Revisited". *Development Policy Review* 25 (5): 553–574.

Gros, J-G., Prokopovych, O. 2005. When Reality Contradicts Rhetoric: World Bank Lending Practices in Developing Countries in Historical, Theoretical and Empirical Perspectives. In CODESRIA Monograph Series, edited by Council for the Development of Social Sciences Research in Africa. Dakar (Senegal).

Guhan, S. 1998. "World Bank on Governance: A Critique". *Economic and Political Weekly* 33 (4): 185–190.

Guler, I., Guillen, M.F., Macpherson, J.M. 2002. "Global Competition, Institutions, and the Diffusion of Organizational Practices: The International Spread of ISO 9000 Quality Certificates". *Administrative Science Quarterly* 47: 207–232.

Gurgur, T., Shah, A. 2005. Localization and Corruption: Panacea or Pandora's Box? In *World Bank Policy Research Working Paper*. Washington, DC: World Bank.

Gutner, T. 2005. "Explaining the Gaps between Mandate and Performance: Agency Theory and World Bank Environmental Reform". *Global Environmental Politics* 5 (2): 10–37.

Güven, A.B. 2012. "The IMF, the World Bank, and the Global Economic Crisis: Exploring Paradigm Continuity". *Development and Change* 43 (4): 869–898.

Guyer, J.I. 1983. "The World Bank's Prescriptions for Rural Africa". *Review of African Political Economy* 3 (27/28): 186–191.

Gwin, C. 1994. U.S. Relations with the World Bank. *Brookings Occasional Papers*, edited by Brookings Institution. Washington, DC: Brookings Institution.

Haas, E.B. 1991. *When Knowledge is Power: Three Models of Change in International Organizations*. Oakland, CA: University of California Press.

Hammond, R., McGowan, L.A. 1992. *The Other Side of the Story: The Real Impact of World Bank and IMF Structural Adjustment Programs*. Washington, DC: Development Gap.

Hannan, M.T., & Freeman, J. (1977). The population ecology of organizations. *American Journal of Sociology*, 82 (5), 929–964.

Hanreider, T. 2014. "Gradual Change in International Organisations: Agency Theory and Historical Institutionalism". *Politics & Policy* 34 (4): 324–333.

Hanreider, T. 2015. "The Path-Dependent Design of International Organizations: Federalism in the World Health Organization". *European Journal of International Relations* 21 (1): 215–239.

Haq, M.U. 1980a. "Beyond the slogan of South-South Co-operation". *World Development* 8 (10): 743–751.

Haq, M.U. 1980b. "An International Perspective on Basic Needs". *Finance and Development* 17 (3): 11.

Hardt, H. 2014. *Time to React: The Efficiency of International Organizations in Crisis Response*. Oxford: Oxford University Press.

Harrigan, J., Mosley, P. 1991. "Evaluating the Impact of World Bank Structural Adjustment Lending: 1980–87". *The Journal of Development Studies* 27 (3): 63–94.

Harriss, J., Hunter, J., Lewis, C. (Eds.). 1995. *The New Institutional Economics and Third World Development*: London: Routledge.

Hartland-Thunberg, P. 1986. "Sources and Implications of the Global Debt Crisis". *Washington Quarterly*, 94.

Hassett, K.A. 2007. "Volcker Shows Us Why the World Bank Doesn't Work". *Foreign and Defense Policy*. Washington, DC: American Enterprise Institute.

Hay, J. 2021. MDBs' Extra-Cautious Capital Models Attract Scrutiny *Global Markets*. Accessed Jul 8, 2021. https://www.globalcapital.com/asia/article/28wqfgdlbyibw8lwyyubm/ssa/mdbs-extra-cautious-capital-models-attract-scrutiny.

Heaver, Richard, Israel, Arturo. 1986. Country Commitment to Development Projects. *World Bank Discussion Papers*. Washington, DC: World Bank.

Hedström, P., Bearman, P. (Eds.) 2009. *The Oxford Handbook of Analytical Sociology*. Oxford: Oxford University Press.

Helleiner, E. 2010. "A Bretton Woods Moment? The 2007-2008 and the Future of Global Finance". *International Affairs* 86 (3): 619–636.

Heltberg, R. 2019. Five Years Ago the World Bank Changed Its Operating Model. Where Do We Go from Here? Accessed Jun 30, 2021. https://ieg.worldbankgroup.org/blog/five-years-ago-world-bank-changed-its-operating-model-what-difference-did-it-make

Heynemann, S.P. 2003. "The History and Problems in the Making of Education Policy at the World Bank 1960–2000". *International Journal of Educational Development* 23: 315–337.

Hill, J.F. 1991. Rebirth of a Nation: The Difficulties of Transition in Eastern and Central Europe (Speech by J. French Hill, Deputy Assistance Secretary, U.S. Department of the Treasury before the Vanderbilt University School of Law in Nashville, Tennessee. Washington, DC: U.S. Treasury.

Hoogvelt, A., Phillips, D., Taylor, P. 1992. "The World Bank & Africa: A Case of Mistaken Identity". *Review of African Political Economy* 19 (54): 92–96.

Hout, Wil. 2007. *The Politics of Aid Selectivity: Good Governance Criteria in World Bank, U.S. and Dutch Development Assistance, Routledge Studies in Development Economics*. Oxford: Routledge.

Howlett, M., Cashore, B. 2009. "The Dependent Variable Problems in the Study of Policy Change: Understanding Policy Change as a Methodological Problem". *Journal of Comparative Policy Analysis* 11 (1): 33–46.

Huckel-Schneider, C. 2019. "Governance and Administration in Global Health Organizations: Considering the Legacies of the 'Golden Era' of Global Health Policy?" In *The Oxford Handbook of Global Policy and Transnational Administration*, edited by D. Stone and K. Moloney, 547–564. Oxford: Oxford University Press.

Humphrey, C., Miller, P., Scapens, R.W. 1993. "Accountability and Accountable Management in the UK Public Sector". *Accounting, Auditing & Accountability Journal* 6 (3): 7–29.

Huther, J., Shah, A. 2000. Anti-Corruption Policies and Programs: A Framework for Evaluation. *Policy Research Working Paper*. Washington, DC: World Bank.

IBRD (International Bank for Reconstruction and Development). 2021. "International Bank for Reconstruction and Development Voting Power of Executive Directors". World Bank. Accessed Jul 8. https://thedocs.worldbank.org/en/doc/1da86cb968275b94ab30b3d454882208-0330032021/original/IBRDEDsVotingTable.pdf.

IDA (International Development Association). 2009. "Ten Things to Know about IDA". World Bank. Accessed Feb 17. http://go.worldbank.org/BWQQ9YBGY0.

IDA (International Development Association). 2021a. "IDA Graduates". World Bank. Accessed Jul 8. https://ida.worldbank.org/about/ida-graduates.

IDA (International Development Association). 2021b. *IDA Terms*. Washington, DC: IDA.

IDA (International Development Association). 2021c. Interrnational Development Association Voting Power of Executive Directors.

IEG (Independent Evaluation Group). 2010a. *Cost-Benefit Analysis in World Bank Projects*. Washington DC: World Bank.

IEG (Independent Evaluation Group). 2010b. *Results and Performance of the World Bank Group*. Washington DC: World Bank.

IEG (Independent Evaluation Group). 2010c. *Safeguards and Sustainability Policies in a Changing World: An Independent Evaluation of World Bank Group Experience*. Washington, DC: World Bank.

IEG (Independent Evaluation Group). 2010d. *The World Bank's Country Policy and Institutional Assessment*. Washington, DC: World Bank.

IEG (Independent Evaluation Group). 2010e. *World Bank Group Cooperation: Evidence and Lessons from IEG Evaluations*. Washington, DC: World Bank.

IEG (Independent Evaluation Group). 2011a. *Self-Evaluation of the Independent Evaluation Group*. Washington, DC: World Bank.

IEG (Independent Evaluation Group). 2011b. *World Bank Country-Level Engagement on Governance and Anti-Corruption*. Washington, DC: World Bank.

IEG (Independent Evaluation Group). 2011c. *The World Bank Group's Response to the Global Financial Crisis – Phase I*. Washington, DC: World Bank.

IEG (Independent Evaluation Group). 2012. *Designing a Results Framework for Achieving Results: A How-To Guide*. Washington, DC: World Bank.

IEG (Independent Evaluation Group). 2013. *The Matrix System at Work: An Evaluation of the World Bank's Organizational Effectiveness*. Washington, DC: World Bank.

IEO (Independent Evaluation Office). 2020. *IMF Collaboration with the World Bank on Macro-Structural Issues.* Washington, DC: International Monetary Fund.

IMF (International Monetary Fund). 2009. "Public Financial Accountability Blog: Making Public Money Count". International Monetary Fund. Accessed 10 March. http://blog-pfm.imf.org/.

IMF-World Bank. 1989. "The IMF-World Bank Concordat". In SM/89/54, edited by the International Monetary Fund and the World Bank. Washington, DC: International Monetary Fund and World Bank.

INT (Integrity Vice Presidency). 2010. *Integrity Vice Presidency Annual Report.* Washington, DC: World Bank.

INT (Integrity Vice Presidency). 2011. *Integrity Vice Presidency Annual Report.* Washington, DC: World Bank.

Irwin, M.H.K. 1994. "Banking on Poverty: An Insider's Look at the World Bank". In *50 Years is Enough: The Case Against the World Bank and the International Monetary Fund,* edited by Kevin Danaher, 152–160. Boston, MA: South End Press.

Israel, A. 1983. "Management and Institutional Development: A Long, Hard Task, Especially in The Social Sectors" *Finance and Development* 20 (September): 15–19.

Israel, A. 1987. *Institutional Development: Incentives to Performance.* Washington, DC: World Bank.

Israel, A. 1989. *Institutional Development: Incentives to Performance.* Washington, DC: World Bank.

Israel, A. 1990. The Changing Role of the State: Institutional Dimensions. *Policy, Research, and External Affairs Working Papers.* Washington, DC: World Bank.

James, E., Ferrier, G., Smalhout, J., Vittas, D. 1999. Mutual Funds and Institutional Investments: What is the Most Efficient Way to Set Up Individual Accounts in A Social Security System? *Policy Research Working Paper.* Washington, DC: World Bank.

Johnson, T. 2014. *Organizational Progeny: Why Governments are Losing Control over the Proliferating Structures of Global Governance.* Oxford: Oxford University Press.

Johnston, M., Kpundeh, S.J. 2004. Building a Clean Machine: Anti-Corruption Coalitions and Sustainable Reform. *World Bank Policy Research Working Paper.* Washington, DC: World Bank.

Jones, L.P. 1991. Performance Evaluation for Public Enterprises. *World Bank Discussion Papers.* Washington, DC: World Bank.

Jones, M.D., Peterson, H.L., Pierce, J J., Herweg, N., Bernal, A., Lamberta Raney, H., Zahariadis, N. 2016. "A River Runs Through It: A Multiple Streams Meta-Review". *Policy Studies Journal* 44 (1): 13–36.

Jonker, J., Foster, D. 2002. "Stakeholder Excellence? Framing the Evolution and Complexity of a Stakeholder Perspective of the Firm". *Corporate Social Responsibility and Environmental Management* 9(4): 187–195.

Jönsson, C., Tallberg, J. (Eds.) 2010. *Transnational Actors in Global Governance: Patterns, Explanations, and Implications.* New York: Palgrave Macmillan.

Joshi, D., O'Dell, R.K. 2013. "Global Governance and Development Ideology: The United Nations and the World Bank on the Left-Right Spectrum". *Global Governance* 19(2): 249–275.

Kaletsky, A. 1982a. "Clausenomics: How the World Bank is Changing". *Financial Times,* 14, Section I.

Kaletsky, A. 1982b. "Top Two Lending Agencies Manoeuvre Closer Together". *Financial Times,* May 4, V.

Kamen, A. 2007. "The World Bank's Choice: Love Wolfowitz, or Hate Freedom". *The Washington Post*, 18 April, A Section.

Kanbur, R. 2016. "What is the World Bank Good For? Global Public Goods And Global Institutions". *Revue Deconomie Du Developpement* 24 (3): 9–24.

Katz, B., Kahn, R.L. 1966. The social psychology of organizations. New York: Wiley.

Kennard, A., Stanescu, D. 2019. "Do International Bureaucrats Matter? Evidence from the International Monetary Fund". Political Economy of International Organizations, Salzburg.

Kerler, M. 2007. "Triggering World Bank Reform: When Member States, NGOs and Learning Get Important". In *Management Reforms in International Organizations*, edited by Michael W.Knill and Christoph Bauer, 133–146. Auflage: Nomos.

Khalilzadeh-Shirazi, J., Shah, A. (Eds.) 1991. *Tax Policy in Developing Countries*. Washington, DC: World Bank.

Kiely, R. 1998. "Neo Liberalism Revised? A Critical Account of World Bank Concepts of Good Governance and Market Friendly Intervention". *Capital & Class* 22 (1): 63–88.

Kikeri, S. 1990. Bank Lending for Divestiture: A Review of Experience. *Policy, Research, and External Affairs Working Papers*. Washington, DC: World Bank.

Kikeri, S., Kolo, A. 2007. Privatization Trends: What's Been Done? *Public Policy for the Private Sector*. Washington, DC: World Bank.

Kim, J. 2013. "Time for Even Greater Ambition in Global Health". *The Lancet* 382 (9908): E33–E34.

Kim, J. 2018. "The Human Capital Gap: Getting Governments to Invest in People". *Foreign Affairs* 97 (4): 92–101.

King, B. 1986. Interviewed by Robert W. Oliver (July 24 and 25). Washington, DC: World Bank.

Kingdon, J.W. 2003. *Agendas, Alternatives, and Public Policies*, 2nd edn. New York: Longman.

Kingsley, J.D. 1944. *Representative Bureaucracy: An Interpretation of the British Civil Services*. Yellow Springs, OH: Antioch Press.

Klutznick, P.M. 1988. "A Boost for the World Bank: Congress Shouldn't Hesitate". *The Washington Post*, 29 September, Editorial Page.

Knack, S. 2006. Measuring Corruption in Eastern Europe and Central Asia: A Critique of the Cross-Country Indicators. *World Bank Policy Research Working Paper*. Washington, DC: World Bank.

Knill, C., Bauer, M.W. 2016. "Policy-Making by International Public Administrations: Concepts, Causes and Consequences". *Journal of European Public Policy* 23 (7): 949–959.

Knill, C., Eckhard, S., Grohs, S. 2016. "Administrative Styles in the European Commission and the OSCE Secretariat: Striking Similiaries Despite Different Organisational Settings". *Journal of European Public Policy* 23 (7): 1057–1076.

Knill, C., Bauer, M.W., Eckhard, S. (Eds.) 2017. *International Bureaucracy: Challenges and Lessons for Public Administration Research*. London: Palgrave Macmillan.

Knill, C., Bayerlin, L., Enkler, J., Grohs, S. 2019. "Bureaucratic Influence and Administrative Styles in International Organizations". *Review of International Organizations* 14 (1): 83–106.

Kohler, J.C., Bowra, A. 2020. "Exploring Anti-Corruption, Transparency, and Accountability in the World Health Organization, the United Nations Development Programme, the World Bank Group, and the Global Fund to Fight AIDS, Tuberculosis and Malaria". *Globalization and Health* 16: 1–10.

Komisar, L. 2011. Interview with Joseph Stiglitz. *Global Policy Forum.* Accessed 10 Jul 2021. https://archive.globalpolicy.org/social-and-economic-policy/the-three-sisters-and-other-institutions/internal-critics-of-the-world-bank-and-the-imf/50588-interview-with-joseph-stiglitz.html.

Kopiński, D., Wróblewski, M. 2021. "Reimagining the World Bank: Global Public Goods in an Age of Crisis". *World Affairs* 184 (2): 151–175.

Kramarz, T. 2016. "World Bank Partnerships and the Promise of Democratic Governance". *Environmental Policy and Governance* 26: 3–15.

Kranke, M. 2020. "IMF-World Bank Cooperation before and after the Global Financial Crisis". *Global Policy* 11 (1): 15–25.

Kraske, J., Becker, W.H., Diamond, W., Galambos, L. 1996. *Bankers with a Mission: The Presidents of the World Bank, 1946-91.* Washington, DC: World Bank and Oxford University Press.

Krueger, A.O. 1983. "The Role of the World Bank as an International Institution". *Carnegie-Rochester Conference Series on Public Policy* 18: 281–311.

Krueger, A.O. 1986. "Changing Perspectives on Development Economics and World Bank Research". *Development Policy Review* 4 (3): 195–210.

Krueger, A.O. 1990. "Government Failures in Development". *Journal of Economic Perspectives* 4 (3): 9–23.

Kubr, M., Wallace, J. 1983. Successes and Failures in Meeting the Management Challenge: Strategies and their Implementation. *World Bank Staff Working Paper, No. 585; Management and Development Series, No. 12.* Washington, DC: World Bank.

Kumari, K. 1995. *Proceedings of the World Bank Annual Conference on Development Economics* Washington, DC: World Bank.

Kuperman, R.D. 2006. "Making Research on Foreign Policy Decision Making More Dynamic". *International Studies Review* 8 (3): 537–554.

Lacey, R. 1989. Managing Public Expenditure: An Evolving World Bank Perspective. *World Bank Discussion Papers.* Washington, DC: World Bank.

Ladi, S. 2019. "European Studies as a Tributary of Global Policy and Transnational Administration". In *Oxford Handbook of Global Policy and Transnational Administration,* edited by Diane Stone and Kim Moloney, 293–310. Oxford: Oxford University Press.

Lafourcade, O. 2005. "Lessons of the 1990s: A Personal Account". In *At the Frontlines of Development: Reflections from the World Bank,* edited by Indermit S. Gill and Todd Pugatch, 163–196. Washington, DC: World Bank.

Larmour, P. 2011. Civilizing Techniques: Transparency International and the Spread of Anti-Corruption. *Asia Pacific School of Economics and Government Discussion Papers.* Canberra: Australian National University.

Le Prestre, P. 1989. *The World Bank and the Environmental Challenge.* Cranbury, NJ: Associated University Presses.

Lederman, D., Loayza, N., Reis Soares, R. 2001. Accountability and Corruption: Political Institutions Matters. *Policy Research Working Paper.* Washington, DC: World Bank.

Lee, B., Nellis, J. 1990. Enterprise Reform and Privatization in Socialist Economies. *World Baik Discussion Papers.* Washington, DC: World Bank.

Legrand, T. 2019. "Sovereignty Renewed: Transgovernmental Policy Networks and the Global-Local Dilemma". In *Oxford Press Handbook of Global Policy and Transnational Administration,* edited by Diane Stone and Kim Moloney, 200–222. Oxford: Oxford University Press.

Lemisch, J. 2000. A Movement Begins: The Washington Protests Against IMF/World Bank. *New Politics* VIII (1): 5.

Leroy, A-M., Fariello, F. 2012. *The World Bank Group Sanctions Process and Its Recent Reforms*. Washington DC: World Bank.

Lethem, F., Cooper, L. 1983. Managing Project-Related Technical Assistance. *World Bank Staff Working Paper, No. 586; Management and Development Series, No. 13*. Washington, DC: World Bank.

Littoz-Monnet, A. 2017. "Production and Uses of Expertise by International Bureaucracies". In *The Politics of Expertise in International Organizations*, edited by A. Littoz-Monnet, 1–18. London: Routledge.

Loewenberg, S. 2015. "The World Bank under Jim Kim". *The Lancet* 386 (9991): 324–327.

Loxley, J. 1983. "The Berg Report and the Model of Accumulation in Sub-Saharan Africa". Review of African Political Economy 27/28: 197–204.

Lyne, M.M., Nielson, D.L., Tierney, M.J. 2006. "Who Delegates? Alternative Models of Principals in Development Aid". In *Delegation and Agency in International Organizations*, edited by D.A. Lake, D.G. Hawkins, D.L. Nielson, and M.J. Tierney, 41–76. Cambridge: Cambridge University Press.

McCleary, W. 1991. "The Earmarking of Government Revenue: A Review of Some World Bank Experience". *The World Bank Research Observer* 6 (1): 81–104.

McIntyre, D. 1996. "Anti-Corruption Campaign Signals New Bank-Fund Activism". *Deutsche Presse-Agentur*, 2 October.

McKenna, B. 2007. "Washington Negotiating Wolfowitz's Exit: Controversy over Beleaguered President has Highlighted Tensions between U.S.; Europe". *The Global and Mail*, 17 May, International News.

McKeown, T.J. 2009. "How U.S. Decision-Makers Assessed Their Control of Multilateral Organizations, 1957–1982". *The Review of International Organizations* 4 (3): 269–291.

McNamar, R.T. 1982, January 7. Remarks of R.T. McNamar on the Future Role of the World Bank Group (Speech) before the Brookings Institution. Washington.

McNamar, R.T. 1984. Remarks by the Honorable R. T. McNamar, Deputy Secretary of the Treasury before the Davos Symposium (Speech). Davos, Switzerland.

McNamara, R.S. 1981. "Speech to the United Nations Conference on the Human Environment". In *The McNamara Years at the World Bank: Major Policy Addresses of Robert S. McNamara, 1968-1981*. Baltimore, MD: Johns Hopkins University Press.

Maehlum, J. 1994. Interviewed by William Becker of George Washington University (June 22). Washington, DC: World Bank.

Maertens, L., Louis, M. 2021. *Why International Organizations Hate Politics: Depoliticizing the World*. London: Routledge.

Major, J. 1990. Prime Minister's Statement on the Economic Declaration. Houston, TX: G7.

Makinder, S. 2020. "Ideas, Institutions and the World Bank: The Social Protection and Fragile States Agendas". *Global Policy* 11 (1): 26–35.

Malan, P. 2007. *Report of the External Review Committee on Bank-Fund Collaboration*. Washington, DC: International Monetary Fund and the World Bank.

Malena, C. 2000. "Beneficiaries, Mercenaries, Missionaries, and Revolutionaries: 'Unpacking' NGO Involvement in World Bank-Financed Projects". *IDS Bulletin* 31 (3): 19–34.

Mallaby, S. 2004. *The World's Banker: A Story of Failed States, Financial Crises, and the Wealth and Poverty of Nations*. New York: Penguin Press.

Mallaby, S. 2012. The Quiet Revolutionary Who Saved the World Bank. *Financial Times*. Accessed 2018, January 5. https://www.ft.com/content/dd59766a-57da-11e1-b089-00144feabdc0

Malpass, D. 2019a. Remarks by World Bank Group President David Malpass on Bretton Woods 75th Anniversary. Washington, DC: World Bank.

Malpass, D. 2019b. World Bank Group President David Malpass at the Center for Global Development. Washington, DC: World Bank.

March, J.G., Olsen, J.P. 1989. *Rediscovering Institutions*. New York: The Free Press.

Marcussen, M. 2006. "Institutional Transformation? The Scientization of Central Banking as a Case Study". In *Autonomy and Regulation: Coping with Agencies in the Modern State*, edited by P. Lægreid and T. Christensen, 81–109. London: Edward Elgar.

Marquette, H. 2004. "The Creeping Politicisation of the World Bank: The Case of Corruption". *Political Studies* 52 (3): 413–430.

Marquette, H. 2007. "The World Bank's Fight against Corruption". *The Brown Journal of International Affairs* 13 (2): 27–39.

Matthews, J. 1997. "Power Shift". *Foreign Affairs* 76 (1): 50–66.

Mearsheimer, J. 1995. "The False Promise of International Institutions". *International Security* 19 (3): 5–49.

Michaud, N. 2002. "Bureaucratic Politics and the Shaping of Policies: Can We Measure Pulling and Hauling Games?" *Canadian Journal of Political Science* 35 (2): 269–300.

Middleton, J., Rondinelli, D.A., Verspoor, A. 1987. Designing Management for Uncertainty and Innovation in Education Projects. *Education and Training Series*. Washington, DC: World Bank.

Migliorisi, S., Wescott, C. 2011. A Review of World Bank Support for Accountability Institutions in the Context of Governance and Anticorruption. *IEG Working Paper*. Washington, DC: World Bank.

Mintrom, M., Norman, P. 2009. "Policy Entrepreneurship and Policy Change". *Policy Studies Journal* 37 (4): 649–667.

Mitchell, R.K., Agle, B.R., Wood, D.J. 1997. "Toward a Theory of Stakeholder Identification and Salience: Defining the Principle of Who and What Really Counts". *The Academy of Management Review* 22 (4): 853–896.

Mitra, Pradeep; Stern, Nicholas. 2002. *Tax Systems in Transition*. Washington, DC: World Bank.

Mkandawire, T. 2007. "'Good Governance': The Itinerary of an Idea". In *Deconstructing Development Discourse: Buzzwords and Fuzzwords*, edited by D. Eade and A. Cronwall, 265–268. Warwick: Practical Action Publishing.

Moloney, K. 2009. "Public Administration and Governance: A Sector-Level Analysis of World Bank Aid". *International Review of Administrative Science* 75 (4): 609–627.

Moloney, K. 2014. "Review of Development Aid Confronts Politics: The Almost Revolution. Thomas Carothers and Diane de Gramont". *Governance* 27 (2): 361–364.

Moloney, K., Rosenbloom, D.H. 2020. "Creating Space for Public Administration in International Organization Studies" *American Review of Public Administration* 50 (3): 227–243.

Moloney, K., Stone, D. 2020. "Transnational Administration of Regional and Global Policies". *Oxford Research Encyclopedia of Politics*. Doi: 10.1093/acrefore/9780190228637.013.1734.

Moloney, K., Stoycheva, R. 2018. "Partial Two-Way Mirror: International Organization Budget Transparency". *Global Policy* 9 (1): 26–40.

Moloney, K., Bowman, J.S., West, J.P. 2019. "Challenges Confronting Whistleblowing and the International Civil Servant". *Review of Public Personnel Administration* 39 (4): 611–634.

Moore, D. 1998. "Many World Bank Projects Haunted by Grand Delusions". *Forum for Applied Research and Public Policy* 13 (1): 26–31.

Moran, D. 2000. "World Bank: 'Can We Talk?'". *Prague Post*, 7 June.

Moretti, F., Pestre, D. 2015. "Bankspeak: The Language of World Bank Reports". *New Left Review* 92 (2): 75–99.

Morrison, K.M. 2013. "Membership No Longer Has Its Privileges: The Declining Informal Influence of Board Members on IDA Lending". *The Review of International Organizations* 8: 291–312.

Mortisugu, K. 2000. "China Denied Loan by the World Bank". *The Philadelphia Inquirer*, 8 July, A4, National.

Moss, T. 2012. Dr. Kim and the Future of the World Bank. Washington, DC: Center for Global Development. Accessed 30 Jun 2021. https://www.cgdev.org/article/dr-kim-and-future-world-bank-new-yorker.

Muir, R., Saba, J.P. 1995. Improving State Enterprise Performance: The Role of Internal and External Incentives. *World Bank Technical Paper*. Washington, DC: World Bank.

Muis, J.W. 2000. Interviewed by William H. Becker and Marie T. Zenni. Washington, DC: World Bank.

Murray, D.J. 1983. "The World Bank's Perspective on How to Improve Administration". *Public Administration and Development* 3 (4): 291–297.

Nabli, M.K., Nugent, J.B. 1989. "The New Institutional Economics and Its Applicability to Development". *World Development* 17 (9): 1333–1347.

Naím, Moisés. 1995. "Agendas for the Bretton Woods Institutions". Fifty Years after Bretton Woods: The Future of the IMF and World Bank (Proceedings of a conference held in Madrid, Spain, September 29-30, 1994), Washington, DC.

Naím, Moisés. 2000. "Fads and Fashion in Economic Reforms: Washington Consensus or Washington Confusion?" *Third World Quarterly* 21 (3): 505–528.

Nanda, V.P. 2006. "The "Good Governance" Concept Revisited". *The Annals of the American Academy of Political and Social Science* 603 (1): 269–283.

Nay, O. 2012. "How Do Policy Ideas Spread Among International Administrations? Policy Entrepreneurs and Bureaucratic Influence in the UN Response to AIDS". *Journal of Public Policy* 32 (1): 53–76.

Nedergaard, P. 2008. "The Reform of the 2003 Common Agricultural Policy: An Advocacy Coalition Explanation". *Policy Studies* 29 (2): 179–195.

Nellis, J. 1986. Public Enterprises in sub-Saharan Africa. *World Bank Discussion Papers, No. 1*. Washington, DC: World Bank.

Nellis, J. 1991. Contract Plans and Public Enterprise Performance. *Working Paper Series*. Washington, DC: World Bank.

Nellis, J., Lieberman, I. 1994. Russian Privatization: An Impressive Record. *Viewpoint: FPD Note*. Washington, DC: World Bank.

Nelson, P. 2000. "Heroism and Ambiguity: NGO Advocacy in International Policy". *Development in Practice* 10 (3 & 4): 478–490.

NGO Working Group. 1995. Examining Structural Adjustment. Edited by NGO Working Group on the World Bank: NGO Working Group on the World Bank.

Niehuss, J.M. 1990. Statement of John M. Niehuss, Senior Deputy Assistant Secretary for International Economic Policy, U.S. Department of the Treasury in the Afternoon Session of the Development Committee of the World Bank and the International Monetary Fund. Washington, DC: U.S. Treasury.

Nielson, D.L., Tierney, M.J. 2003. "Delegation to International Organizations: Agency Theory and World Bank Environmental Reform". *International Organization* 57 (2): 241–276.

Nielson, D.L., Tierney, M.J. 2005. "Theory, Data and Hypothesis Testing: World Bank Environmental Reform Redux". *International Organization* 59 (3): 785–800.

Nielson, D.L., Tierney, M.J., Weaver, Catherine. 2006. "Bridging the Rationalist-Constructivist Divided: Re-engineering the Culture of the World Bank". *Journal of International Relations and Development* 9 (2): 107–139.

North, D.N. 1995. "The New Institutional Economics and Third World Development". In *The New Institutional Economics and Third World Development*, edited by John Harriss, Janet Hunter, and Colin M.Lewis, 17–26. London: Routledge.

Novosad, P., Werker, E. 2014. Who Runs the International System? Power and Staffing of the United Nations Secretariat. Washington, DC: Center for Global Development.

Nunberg, B. 1988. Public Sector Pay and Unemployment Reform. *Policy, Planning, and Research Working Paper Series*. Washington, DC: World Bank.

Nunberg, B. 1992. Managing the Civil Service: What LDCs Can Learn from Developed Country Reforms. *World Bank Policy Research Working Papers*. Washington, DC: DC.

Nunberg, B. 1995. Managing the Civil Service: Reform Lessons from Advanced In-dustrialized Countries. *World Bank Discussion Papers*. Washington, DC: World Bank.

Nunberg, B., Nellis, J. 1990. Civil Service Reform and the World Bank. *Policy, Research, and External Affairs Working Papers*. Washington, DC: World Bank.

Nunberg, B., Nellis, J. 1995. Civil Service Reform and the World Bank. *World Bank Discussion Paper*. Washington, DC: World Bank.

O'Leary, R. 1993. *Environmental Change: Federal Courts and the EPA*. Philadelphia, PA: Temple University Press.

OED (Operations Evaluation Department). 1999. *Civil Service Reform: A Review of World Bank Assistance*. Washington, DC: World Bank.

Oestreich, J.E., ed. 2012. *International Organizations as Self-Directed Actors*: London: Palgrave Macmillan.

Olsen, J.P. 1991. "Modernization Programs in Perspective: Institutional Analysis of Orga-nizational Change". *Governance* 4 (2): 125–149.

Olsen, J.P. 2006. "Maybe It Is Time to Rediscover Bureaucracy". *Journal of Public Adminis-tration Research and Theory* 16 (1): 1–24. Doi: 10.1093/jopart/mui027.

Olson, M. 1997. "The New Institutional Economics: The Collective Choice Approach to Economic Development". In *Institutions and Economic Development: Growth and Gover-nance in Less-Developed and Post-Socialist Societies*, edited by Christopher Clague, 37–66. Baltimore, MD: Johns Hopkins University Press.

Olsson, E-K., Verbeek, B. 2013. "International Organizations and Crisis Management". In *Routledge Handbook of International Organization*, edited by B. Reinalda, 350–362. London: Routledge.

Otani, I., Villanueva, D. 1989. "Major Determinants of Long-Term Growth in LDCs: A Quantitative Analysis of Long-Term Growth Performance". *Finance and Development* 26 (3): 41.

Ozgediz, S. 1983. Managing the Public Service in Developing Countries. *World Bank Staff Working Papers, No. 583; Management and Development Series, No. 10*. Washington, DC: World Bank.

Pace, E. 1994. "Hollis B. Chenery Dies at 77; Economist for the World Bank". *The New York Times*, 5 September, 1.

Packard, T.G. 2001. Is There A Positive Incentive Effect from Privatizing Social Security? Evidence from Latin America. *Policy Research Working Paper*. Washington, DC: World Bank.

Packard, T.G., Shinkai, N., Fuentes, R. 2004. *The Reach of Social Security Reform in Latin America and the Caribbean*. Washington, DC: World Bank.

Pal, L.A. 2012. *Frontiers of Governance: The OECD and Global Public Management Reform*. London: Palgrave Macmillan.

Pannier, D., ed. 1996. Corporate Governance of Public Enterprises in Transitional Economies. *World Bank Technical Paper, No. 323*. Washington, DC: World Bank.

Park, S. 2005. "Norm Diffusion Within International Organizations: A Case Study of the World Bank". *Journal of International Relations and Development* 8 (2): 111–141.

Park, S. 2009. "Ask the Experts? The World Bank International Development Lending In The Twenty-First Century". *Review of International Political Economy* 16 (2): 329–349.

Park, S. 2019. Electing the World's Banker. *Australian Institute of International Affairs* (18 February).

Park, S., Vetterlein, A. (Eds.) 2010. *Owning Development: Creating Policy Norms in the IMF and the World Bank*. Cambridge: Cambridge University Press.

Park, S., Weaver, C. 2012. "The Anatomy of Autonomy: The Case of the World Bank". In *International Organizations as Self-Directed Actors*, edited by J.E. Oestreich, 92–117. Palgrave Macmillan.

Parsons, T. 1947. "Introduction". In *The Theory of Social and Economic Organization*, edited by Talcott Parsons, 3–86. New York: The Free Press.

Patrinos, H.A., Ariasingam, D.L. 1997. Decentralization of Education: Demand-Side Financing. In *Directions in Development*. Washington, DC: World Bank.

Patz, R., Goetz, K.H. 2017. "Changing Budgeting Administration in International Organizations: Budgetary Pressures, Complex Principals and Administrative Leadership". In *International Bureaucracy: Challenges and Lessons for Public Administration Research*, edited by Michael W. Bauer, Christoph Knill, and Steffen Eckhard, 123–150. London: Palgrave MacMillan.

Paul, S., Israel, A. (Eds.) 1990. *Nongovernmental Organizations and the World Bank*. Washington DC: World Bank.

Paulson, Jr., H.M. 2007. Prepared Statement by Secretary Henry M. Paulson, Jr. at the Development Committee Meeting. Washington, DC: U.S. Treasury.

PEFA (Public Expenditure and Financial Accountability). 2009. "Public Expenditure & Financial Accountability". World Bank. Accessed Mar 10. http://www.pefa.org/index.php.

Pereira, A.E., Horochovski, R.R., Cruz, M.M.dA., Rodrigues, N. 2017. "Accountability in International Organizations: The Case of the World Bank Inspection Panel (1993–2015)". *Brazilian Political Science Review* 11 (1). https://www.ft.com/content/dd59766a-57da-11e1-b089-00144feabdc0.

Pevehouse, J.C., Nordstrom, T., McManus, R.W., Jamison, A.S. 2020. "Tracking Organizations in the World: The Correlates of War IGO Version 3.0 datasets". *Journal of Peace Research* 57 (3): 492–503.

Pfeffer, J., Salancik, G.R. 1978. *The External Control of Organizations: A Resource Dependence Perspective*. New York: Harper & Row.

Pfeffermann, G.P. 1987. "Public Expenditure in Latin America: Effects on Poverty". *WDP-5*. Washington, DC: World Bank.

Philipps, D. 2009. *Reforming the World Bank: Twenty Years of Trial—and Error*. Cambridge: Cambridge University Press.

Picciotto, R. 2000. Interview by William Becker and Marie Zenni (November 1). Washington, DC: World Bank.

Pincus, J.R., Winters, J.A. (Eds.) 2018. *Reinventing the World Bank*. Cornell, NY: Cornell University Press.

Please, S. 1986. Interviewed by Charles Ziegler (August 26). Washington, DC: World Bank (n.p.).

Polak, J.J. 1994. The World Bank and the International Monetary Fund: A Changing Relationship. *Brookings Occasional Papers*. Washington, DC: The Brookings Institution.

Pomerantz, P. 2005. "A Little Luck and a Lot of Trust: Aid Relationships and Reform in Southern Africa". In *At the Frontlines of Development: Reflections from the World Bank*, edited by Indermit S. Gill and Todd Pugatch, 49–63. Washington, DC: World Bank.

Poortman, C. 2005. "Leadership, Learning, and Luck: Reflections on the Balkan States". In *At the Frontlines of Development: Reflections from the World Bank*, edited by Indermit S. Gill and Todd Pugatch, 197–212. Washington, DC: World Bank.

Potter, N.F. 1993. Interview by William Becker and David Milobsky (July 19). Washington, DC: World Bank.

Pradhan, Sanjay. 1996a. *Evaluating Public Spending: A Framework for Public Expenditure Reviews*. Washington DC: World Bank.

Pradhan, Sanjay. 1996b. Evaluating Public Spending: A Framework for Public Expenditure Reviews. *World Bank Discussion Papers*. Washington, DC: World Bank.

PREM. 1999. "Rethinking Civil Service Reform". *PREM Notes*, October, 1-4.

PREM. 2000. "Reforming Tax Systems: Lessons from the 1990s". *PREM Notes*, April, 1-4.

PREM. 2001a. "Decentralization and Governance: Does Decentralization Improve Public Service Delivery?" *PREM Notes*, June, 1-4.

PREM. 2001b. Public Expenditure Management and Accountability: Evolution and Current Status of World Bank Work. Washington, DC: World Bank.

Price, L. 1991. "Governance: Experience in Latin America and the Caribbean". *LATPS Occasional Paper Series*. Washington, DC: World Bank.

Princen, S. 2007. "Advocacy Coalitions and the Internationalization of Public Health Policies". *Journal of Public Policy* 27 (1): 13–33.

Provan, Keith G. 1982. "Interorganizational Linkages and Influence over Decision Making". *The Academy of Management Journal* 25 (2): 443–451.

Provost, C. 2014. A World Bank of trouble? Accessed 30 Jun, 2021. https://www.theguardian.com/global-development-professionals-network/2014/dec/04/a-world-bank-of-trouble.

PSI (Public Sector International). 1993. *PSI Policy and Strategy on the Role of the Public Sector*. Ferney-Voltaire, France: Public Sector International.

PSI (Public Sector International). 1995. *A Public Sector Alternative Strategy: The PSI Vision*. Ferney-Voltaire, France: Public Sector International.

PSI (Public Sector International). 1997a. Privatisation in Transition Economics. *Briefing Notes for Current Debates on Public Sector Issues*, edited by Public Sector International. Ferney-Voltaire, France: Public Sector International.

PSI (Public Sector International). 1997b. Public Services in a Globalised Economy: The PSI Alternative Strategy Revisited. Ferney-Voltaire, France: Public Services International.

PSI (Public Sector International). 1997c. The Roots of Privatisation. *Briefing Notes for Current Debates on Public Sector Issues*. Ferney-Voltaire, France: Public Sector International.

QAG (Quality Assurance Group). 2006. *2006 Quality at Entry Annex.* Washington, DC: World Bank.

Qureshi, M.A. 1991. *Reflections on Development: Issues Facing Developing Countries.* Washington, DC: World Bank.

Radalet, S., Sachs, J.D. 1998. "The East Asian Financial Crisis: Diagnosis, Remedies, Prospects". *Brookings Papers on Economic Activity* 1998 (1): 1–74.

Rajagopalan, V. 1993. Interviewed by William Becker (George Washington University) and David Milobsky (World Bank Historian) (no date). Washington, DC: World Bank.

Rao, V., Woolcock, M. 2007. "The Disciplinary Monopoly in Development Research at the World Bank". *Global Governance* 13: 479–484.

Ravallion, M. 2015. *The World Bank: Why It Is Still Needed and Why It Still Disappoints.* Washington, DC: Center for Global Development.

Raynor, J. 2009. "Understanding Policy Change as a Historical Problem". *Journal of Comparative Policy Analysis* 11 (1): 83–96.

Regan, D.T. 1982. Statement of the Honorable Donald T. Regan, Secretary of the Treasury, Washington DC, April 1.

Regan, D.T. 1984a. Statement of the Honorable Donald T. Regan, Secretary of the Treasuring, April 10.

Regan, D.T. 1984b. Remarks by Donald T. Regan, Secretary of the Treasury before the Annual Meeting of the International Monetary Fund and the World Bank Group. Washington DC, September 24.

Reiling, D., Hammergren, L.A., Di Giovanni, A. 2007. *Justice Sector Assessments: A Handbook.* Washington, DC: World Bank.

Reuters. 1987. "Stable Rating Seen for World Bank". *The New York Times*, 7 August, D.

Rice, A. 2016. Is Jim Kim Destroying the World Bank—or Saving It from Itself? *Foreign Policy.* Accessed 30 Jun 2021. https://foreignpolicy.com/2016/04/27/is-jim-yong-kim-destroying-the-world-bank-development-finance/.

Rich, B. 1994. *Mortgaging the Earth: The World Bank, Environmental Impoverishment, and the Crisis of Development*: Beacon Press.

Ripberger, J.T., Gupta, K., Silva, C.L., Jenkins-Smith, H.C. 2014. "Cultural Theory and the Measurement of Deep Core Beliefs within the Advocacy Coalition Framework". *Policy Studies Journal* 42 (2): 509–527.

Risse-Kappen, T. (Ed.) 1995. *Bringing Transnational Relations Back In: Non-State Actors, Domestic Structures and International Institutions.* Cambridge: Cambridge University Press.

Rodrik, D. 1990. "How Should Structural Adjustment Programs Be Designed?" *World Development* 18 (7): 933–947.

Roger, C.B. 2020. *The Origins of Informality: Why the Legal Foundations of Global Governance Are Shifting, and Why It Matters.* Oxford: Oxford University Press.

Rondinelli, D.A., Nellis, J.R.; Cheema, G.S. 1983. Decentralization in Developing Countries: A Review of Recent Experience. *World Bank Staff Working Papers, No. 581; Management and Development Series, No. 8.* Washington, DC: World Bank.

Rose-Ackerman, S. 1998. "The Role of the World Bank in Controlling Corruption". *Law and Policy in International Business* 29: 93–114.

Rose-Ackerman, S. 2017. "What Does 'Governance' Mean?" *Governance* 30 (1): 23–27.

Rostow, Walter W. 1959. "The Stages of Economic Growth". *The Economic History Review* 12 (1): 1–16.

Rostow, Walter W. 1960. *The Stages of Economic Growth: A Non-Communist Manifesto.* Cambridge: University of Cambridge.

Rotberg, E.H. 1994. Interviewed by William Becker (George Washington University), Jochen Kraska (World Bank Historian), and David Milobsky (Assistant to the Historian) (April 22). Washington, DC: World Bank.

Rowen, Hobart. 1984. "'Underused' World Bank Rethinks Lending Role". *Washington Post*, July 1, Business & Finance.

Rowen, H. 1986. "Can the World Bank Move Fast Enough?" *Washington Post*, 21 March, Op-Ed.

Rowen, H. 1991. "Democrats Tie IMF Aid, World Bank Plan". *The Washington Post*, 22 June, D2, Financial.

Rubin, R.E. 1997. Treasury Secretary Robert E. Rubin, International Development Conference (Speech). Washington, DC: U.S. Treasury.

Rubin, R.E. 1998. Statement of Treasury Secretary Robert E. Rubin at the Development Committee. Washington, DC: World Bank.

Sabatier, P.A. 1987. "Knowledge, Policy-Oriented Learning, and Policy Change". *Knowledge: Creation, Diffusion, Utilization* 8 (4): 649–692.

Sabatier, P.A. 1988. "An Advocacy Coalition Framework of Policy Change and the Role of Policy-Oriented Learning Therein". *Policy Sciences* 21: 129–168.

Sabatier, P.A., Jenkins-Smith, H.C. 1999. "The Advocacy Coalition Framework: An Assessment". In *Theories of the Policy Process*, edited by Paul Sabatier, 117–166. Boulder, CO: Westview Press.

Sachs, J.D., Woo, W.T. 2000. "Understanding the Asian Financial Crisis". In *The Asian Financial Crisis: Lessons for a Resilient Asia*, edited by J. Sachs, W.T. Woo, and K. Schwab, 13–43. Boston, MA: MIT Press.

Sader, F. 1993. Privatization and Foreign Investment in the Developing World, 1988-92. In *Policy Research Working Papers*. Washington, DC: World Bank.

Salamon, L.M. 1994. "The Rise of the Nonprofit Sector". *Foreign Affairs* 73 (4): 109–122.

Salmon, F. 2005. "The End of the Wolfensohn Era". *Euromoney*.

Santiso, C. 2001. "Good Governance and Aid Effectiveness: The World Bank and Conditionality". *The Georgetown Public Policy Review* 7 (1): 1–22.

Sarfaty, G.A. 2005. "The World Bank and the Internalization of Indigenous Rights Norms". *The Yale Law Journal* 114 (7): 1791–1818.

Schäferhoff, M., Campe, S., Kaan, C. 2009. "Transnational Public-Private Partnerships in International Relations: Making Sense of Concepts, Research Frameworks, and Results". *International Studies Review* 11 (3): 451–474.

Sender, J., Smith, S. 1985. "What's Right with the Berg Report and What's Left of Its Critics?" *Capital & Class* 8 (3): 125–146.

Sending, O.J. 2017. *The Politics of Expertise: Competing for Authority in Global Governance*. Ann Arbor, MI: University of Michigan Press.

Shafer, J.R. 1994. Statement by the Honorable Jeffrey R. Shafer, Treasury Assistant Secretary for International Affairs to the Global Legislators Organization for a Balanced Environment (GLOBE) (Speech). Washington, DC: U.S. Treasury.

Shah, A. 2006. Corruption and Decentralized Public Governance. *World Bank Policy Research Working Paper*. Washington, DC: World Bank.

Shah, A. (Ed.) 2007. *Local Public Financial Management*. Washington, DC: World Bank.

Shah, A., Baffles, J. 1991. Do Tax Policies Stimulate Investment in Physical and Research and Development Capital? *Policy, Research, and External Affairs Discussion Papers*. Washington, DC: World Bank.

Sharma, P. 2013. "Bureaucratic Imperatives and Policy Outcomes: The Origins of World Bank Structural Adjustment Lending". *Review of International Political Economy* 20 (4): 667–686.

Shenav, Y. 2003. "The Historical and Epistemological Foundations of Organization Theory: Fusing Sociological Theory with Engineering Discourse". In *The Oxford Handbook of Organization Theory: Meta-Theoretical Perspectives*, edited by Hardimos Tsoukas and Christian Knudsen, 183–209. Oxford: Oxford University Press.

Shihata, I.F.I. 1995. "Legal Framework for Development: Role of the World Bank in Legal Technical Assistance". *International Business Law* 23: 360.

Shihata, I.F.I. 2000a. "The Dynamic Evolution of International Organizatoins: The Case of the World Bank". *Journal of History of International Law* 2: 217.

Shihata, I.F.I. 2000b. Interviewed by William Becker and Marie T. Zenni (May 23, 24). Washington, DC: World Bank.

Shihata, I.F.I. 1994. Interviewed by William Becker (George Washington University), Jochen Kraske (World Bank Historian), and David Milobsky (Assistant to the Historian) (May 11). Washington, DC: World Bank.

Shihata, I.F.I. 2000. Interviewed by William Becker and Marie T. Zenni (May 23, 24). Washington, DC: World Bank.

Shihata, I.F.I. 2001. *The World Bank Legal Papers*. Leiden: Martinus Nijhoff.

Shinohara, M. 1981. Japanese and Korean Experiences in Managing Development. *World Bank Staff Working Papers, No. 574 // Management and Development Subseries*. Washington, DC: World Bank.

Shirley, M. 1983. Managing State-Owned Enterprises. *World Bank Staff Working Papers, No. 577; Management and Development Series, No. 4*. Washington, DC: World Bank.

Shirley, M. 1986. *Improving Parastatal Performance in Zambia*. Washington, DC: World Bank.

Shirley, M. 1989. Evaluating the Performance of Public Enterprises in Pakistan. *Policy, Planning, and Research Working Paper Series*. Washington, DC: World Bank.

Shirley, M., Nellis, J. 1991. *Public Enterprise Reform: The Lessons of Experience, EDI Development Series*. Washington, DC: World Bank.

Simon, H.A. 1946. "Proverbs of Administration". *Public Administration Review* 6 (1): 53–67.

Simon, H.A. 1947. *Administrative Behavior*. New York: The Free Press.

Simon, H.A. 1956. *Models of Man: Social and Rational*. New York: John Wiley & Sons.

Sindzingre, A. 2004. "The Evolution of the Concept of Poverty in Multilateral Financial Institutions: The Case of the World Bank". In *Global Institutions & Development: Framing the World?*, edited by D. McNeill and M. Bøås, 164–177. Abingdon: Routledge.

Smith, J.L. 2002. "A Beautiful Mind at the Barricades". *Financial Times Weekend*.

Smyth, R. 1998. "New Institutional Economics in the Post-Socialist Transformation Debate". *Journal of Economic Surveys* 12 (4): 361–398.

Snow, J.W. 2004. Secretary Snow Development Committee Statement for the Record. Washington, DC: U.S. Treasury.

Soederberg, S. 2001. "The Emperor's New Suit: The New International Financial Architecture as a Reinvention of the Washington Consensus". *Global Governance* 7 (4): 453–467.

Solomon, R. 1981. ""The Elephant in the Boat?" The United States and the World Economy." *Foreign Affairs* 60 (3): 573–592.

Spahn, P.B. 1999. Decentralization, Local Government Capacity and Creditworthiness: Macroeconomic Aspects. *ECSIN Working Paper*. Washington, DC: World Bank.

Spiro, P.J. 1995. "New Global Communities: Nongovernmental Organizations in International Decision-Making Institutions." *The Washington Quarterly* 18 (1): 45–56.

Stackhouse, J. 1994. "Money Meeting Rich in Drama." *Globe and Mail*, 3 October.

Stanton, William J. 1986. Interviewed by Robert W. Olivier (July 16). Washington.

Stein, H. 2008. *Beyond the World Bank Agenda: An Institutional Approach to Development.* Chicago, IL: University of Chicago Press.

Stern, Robert N., Barley, Stephen R. 1996. "Organizations and Social Systems: Organization Theory's Neglected Mandate." *Administrative Science Quarterly* 41 (1): 146–192.

Stevens, M. 2004. *Institutional and Incentive Issues in Public Financial Management Reform in Poor Countries.* Washington, DC: World Bank.

Stiglitz, J.E. 2003. "Democratizing the International Monetary Fund and the World Bank: Governance and Accountability." *Governance* 16 (1): 111–139. Doi:10.1111/1468-0491.00207.

Stiglitz, J.E. 2000. "What I Learned at the World Economic Crisis." *New Republic* (17 April).

Stinchcombe, A.L. 1968. *Constructing Social Theories.* Chicago IL: University of Chicago Press.

Stokes, Bruce. 1991. "The World Bank at a Crossroad." *The National Journal*, 10 August.

Stone, D. 2001. "Think Tanks, Global Lesson-Drawing and Networking Social Policy Ideas." *Global Social Policy* 1 (3): 338–360.

Stone, D. 2008. "Global Public Policy, Transnational Policy Communities, and Their Networks." *The Policy Studies Journal* 36 (1): 19–38.

Stone, D. 2013. "'Shades of Grey': The World Bank, Knowledge Networks and Linked Ecologies of Academic Engagement." *Global Networks* 13 (2): 241–260.

Stone, D., Ladi, S. 2015. "Global Public Policy and Transnational Administration." *Public Administration* 93 (4): 839–855.

Stone, D., Moloney, K. (Eds.) 2019a. *Oxford Handbook of Global Policy and Transnational Administration.* Oxford: Oxford University Press.

Stone, D., Moloney, K. 2019b. "The Rise of Global Policy and Transnational Administration." In *Oxford Handbook of Global Policy and Transnational Administration*, edited by Diane Stone and Kim Moloney, 3–20. Oxford: Oxford University Press.

Storeng, K.T. 2014. "The GAVI Alliance and the 'Gates Approach' to Health System Strengthening." *Global Public Health* 9 (8): 865–879.

Summers, L.H. 1993. Opening Press Statement by Under Secretary Summers at the International Monetary Fund/World Bank Spring Meetings. Washington, DC: U.S. Treasury.

Summers, L.H. 1996. "No Short-Cuts to Development" (Remarks by Lawrence H. Summers, Deputy Secretary of the Treasury to the IDB Conference on Development Thinking and Practice). Washington, DC: U.S. Treasury.

Summers, L.H. 1998. "Opportunities Out of Crises: Lessons from Asia," Remarks by Deputy Treasury Secretary Lawrence H. Summers to the Overseas Development Council (Speech. Washington, DC: World Bank.

Summers, L.H., Pritchett, L.H. 1993. "The Structural-Adjustment Debate." *The American Economic Review* 83 (2): 383–389.

Sureda, A.R. 1999. "The World Bank and Institutional Innovation." Studies of Transnational Legal Policy 31: 11–20.

Syrquin, M., Chenery, H.B. 1989. *Patterns of Development, 1950–1983.* Washington, DC: World Bank.

T Hart, P., Rosenthal, U. 1998. "Reappraising Bureaucratic Politics". *Mershon International Studies Review* 42 (2):233–240.

Tallberg, J., Sommerer, T., Squatrito, T., Jonsson, Christer. 2013. *The Opening Up of International Organizations: Transnational Access in Global Governance*. Cambridge: Cambridge University Press.

Tao, J. 2019. "Transnational Administration from the Beginning: The Importance of Charisma in Shaping International Organization Norms." In *Oxford Handbook of Global Policy and Transnational Administration*, edited by Diane Stone and Kim Moloney, 419–436. Oxford: Oxford University Press.

Taylor, F. 1911. *The Principles of Scientific Management*: Dover Publications.

Tenney, S., Salda, A.C. 2013. *Historical Dictionary of the World Bank*. Lanham, MD: Scarecrow Press.

Theobald, C. 1999. "The World Bank: Good Governance and the New Institutional Economics." *Law and State* 59 (60): 17–39.

Thomas, M.A. 2004. "Can the World Bank Enforce Its Own Conditions?" *Development and Change* 35 (3): 485–497.

Thomas, M.A. 2007. "The Governance Bank." *International Affairs* 83 (4): 729–745.

Thomas, V., Chhibber, A. 1989. "Experience with Policy Reforms under Adjustment." *Finance and Development* 26 (1): 28–31.

Thomas, V., Luo, X. 2011. *Overlooked Links in the Results Chain*. Washington DC: World Bank.

Thomson, R. 1993. "Profile: Principal Lender to the Poor: Ernie Stern Gets Things Done at the World Bank." Accessed 28 Jan. http://www.independent.co.uk/news/business/profile-principal-lender-to-the-poor-ernie-stern-gets-things-done-at-the-world-bank-writes-richard-thomson-he-may-soon-be-muscling-in-on-jacques-attali-at-the-ebrd-1492802.html.

Thornburgh, D., Gainer, R.L., Walker, C.H. 2000. Report to Shengman Zhang, Managing Director and Chairman of the Oversight Committee on Fraud and Corruption, The World Bank: Concerning Mechanisms to Address Problems of Fraud and Corruption. Washington, DC: World Bank.

Thurow, L.C. 1997. *The World Bank: Its First Half Century*. Vols. I and II. Washington, DC: Brookings Institution.

Tillier, E. 1983. "1983 WDR's Special Theme." *The Bank's World*, 9–10.

Tillier, E. 1984. "Rotberg: A Talk on the Borrowing Side." *The Bank's World*, 2–5.

Tillier, E. 1985. "Husain Says Bank-Fund Collaboration High on Agenda of Both Organizations: Dialogue on 19th Street." *The Bank's World*, 2–5.

Toye, J., Jackson, C. 1996. "Public Expenditure Policy and Poverty Reduction: Has the World Bank Got It Right?" *IDS Bulletin* 27 (1): 56–66.

Trettin, F., Junk, J. 2014. "Spoilers from Within: Bureaucratic Spoiling in United Nations Peace Operations." *Journal of International Organization Studies* 5 (1): 13–27.

Tribunal, World Bank Administrative. 2009. Decisions 408–423 v. IBRD. Edited by World Bank Administrative Tribunal. Washington, DC: World Bank.

Trofimov, I.D. 2012. "The Failure of the International Trade Organization (ITO): A Policy Entrepreneurship Perspective." *Journal of Political and Law* 5 (1): 56–68.

Trondal, J. 2011. "Bureaucratic Structure and Administrative Behavior: Lessons from International Bureaucracies." *West European Politics* 34 (4): 795–818.

Trondal, J. 2016. "Advances to the Study of International Public Administration." *Journal of European Public Policy* 23 (7): 1097–1108.

UIA (Union des Associations Internationales). 2013. *The Yearbook of International Organizations*. Vol. 2013. Brussels: Union des Associations Internationales.

ul Haq, M. 1980. *The Treatment of Public Manufacturing Enterprises in Bank Reports: A Review* (Internal Office Memorandum). Washington, DC: World Bank.

ul Haq, M. 1982. Interviewed by Robert Asher (December 3). Washington, DC: World Bank.

Umaña, A. (Ed.) 1998. *The World Bank Inspection Panel: The First Four Years (1994–1998)*. Washington, DC: World Bank.

UNESA (United Nations Economic and Social Affairs). 2002. "Monterrey Consensus of the International Conference on Financing for Development." UNESA, Last Modified 21-22 March. Accessed Aug 28. http://www.un.org/esa/sustdev/documents/Monterrey_Consensus.htm.

U.S. House of Representatives. 1982a. Subcommittee on International Development, Institutions and Finance (Committee on Banking, Finance, and Urban Affairs). *Statement of Thomas C. Dawson, Deputy Assistant Secretary of the Treasury for Developing Nations.* June 22.

U.S. House of Representatives. 1982b. Subcommittee on Foreign Operations (Committee on Appropriations). *Statement of the Honorable Donald T. Regan, Secretary of the Treasury.* April 1.

U.S. House of Representatives. 1984. Subcommittee on Foreign Operations (Committee on Appropriations). *Statement of the Honorable Donald T. Regan, Secretary of the Treasury.* April 10.

U.S. House of Representatives. 1990. Subcommittee on International Development, Finance, Trade and Monetary Policy, Committee on Banking, Finance and Urban Affairs. *Statement of the Honorable David C. Mulford, Under Secretary of the Treasury for International Affairs.* 1 March.

U.S. House of Representatives. 1992. Subcommittee on International Development, Finance, Trade and Monetary Policy of the Committee on Banking, Finance and Urban Affairs. *Statement of the Honorable Olin L. Wethington, Assistant Secretary of the Treasury for International Affairs.* 29 January.

U.S. House of Representatives. 2005. House Committee on Financial Services, Subcommittee on Domestic and International Monetary Policy, Trade and Technology. *Statement of Under Secretary of the Treasury for International Affairs Timothy Adams.* 27 September.

U.S. House of Representatives. 2007. House Committee on Financial Services. *"State of the International Financial System," Testimony of Treasury Secretary Henry M. Paulson, Jr.* 20 June.

U.S. Senate. 2010. *The International Financial Institutions: A Call for Change.* A Report to the Committee on Foreign Relations. Washington DC: US Senate.

U.S. Treasury 1982. *United States Participation in the Multilateral Development Banks in the 1980s.* Washington, DC: U.S. Treasury.

Vabulas, F. 2019. "The Importance of Informal Intergovernmental Organizations: A Typology of Transnational Administration without Independent Secretariats." In *Oxford Handbook on Global Policy and Transnational Administration*, edited by D. Stone and K. Moloney, 401–418. Oxford: Oxford University Press.

Van Hecke, S., Fuhr, H., Wolfs, W. 2021. "The Politics of Crisis Management by Regional and International Organizations in Fighting Against a Global Pandemic: The Member States at a Crossroads." *International Review of Administrative Sciences* 87 (3): 672–690.

Vaubel, R. 2006. "Principal-Agent Problems in International Organizations." *The Review of International Organizations* 1 (2): 125–138.

Vaubel, R., Dreher, A., Soylu, U. 2007. "Staff Growth in International Organizations: A Principal-Agent Problem? An Empirical Analysis." *Public Choice* 133 (3–4): 275–295.

Vestergaard, J. 2011. *The World Bank and the Emerging World Order: Adjusting to Multipolarity at the Second Decimal Point.* Copenhagen: Danish Institute for International Studies.

Vestergaard, J., Wade, R.H. 2013. "Protecting Power: How Western States Retain the Dominant Voice in the World Bank's Governance." *World Development* 46: 153–164.

Vestergaard, J., Wade, R.H. 2015. "Still in the Woods: Gridlock in the IMF and the World Bank Puts Multilateralism at Risk." *Global Policy* 6 (1): 1–12.

Vetterlein, A. 2007. "Change in International Organizations: Innovation or Adaptation? A Comparison of the World Bank and the International Monetary Fund." In *The World Bank and Governance: A Decade of Reform and Reaction*, edited by Diane Stone and Christopher Wright, 125–144. London: Routledge.

Vodopivec, M. 2004a. *Income Support for the Unemployed: Issues and Options.* Washington, DC: World Bank.

Vodopivec, M. 2004b. Unemployment Insurance: Efficiency Effects and Lessons for Developing Countries. *World Bank Employment Policy Primer.* Washington, DC: World Bank.

Volcker, P., Gaviria, G., Githongo, J., Heineman, Jr. B.W., VanGerven, W., Vereker, J. 2007. *Independent Panel Review of the World Bank Group: Department of Institutional Integrity.* Washington, DC: World Bank.

Volkmer, I. 2019. "The Transnationalization of Public Sphere and Global Policy." In *Oxford Handbook of Global Policy and Transnational Administration*, edited by D. Stone and K. Moloney, 240–256. Oxford: Oxford University Press.

Wade, R.H. 2001. "Showdown at the World Bank." *New Left Review* 7 (Jan/Feb): 124–137.

Wade, R.H. 2010. "How Are We Doing? The State of the World Bank." *Challenge* 53 (4): 43–67.

Wade, R.H. 2011. "Emerging World Order? From Multipolarity to Multilateralism in the G20, the World Bank, and the IMF." *Politics & Society* 39 (3): 347–378.

Waldo, D. 1984 [1948]. *The Administrative State*, 2nd edn. New York: Ronald Press.

Wapenhans, W.A. 1993. Interviewed by William Becker (George Washington University). Washington, DC: World Bank.

Waterman, R.W., Meier, K.J. 1998. "Principal-Agent Models: An Expansion?" *Journal of Public Administration Research and Theory* 8 (2): 173–202.

Weaver, C. 2007. "The World Bank and the Bank's World." *Global Governance* 13: 493–512.

Weaver, C. 2008. *Hypocrisy Trap: The World Bank and the Poverty of Reform.* Princeton, NJ: Princeton University Press.

Weaver, C. 2010. "Reforming the World Bank." In *Global Governance, Poverty and Inequality*, edited by R. Wilkinson and J. Clapp, 144–164. New York: Routledge.

Weaver, C., Leiteritz, R.J. 2005. "'Our Poverty Is a World Full of Dreams:' Reforming the World Bank." *Global Governance* 11 (3): 369–388.

Weaver, C., Moschella, M. 2017. "Bounded Reform in Global Economic Governance at the International Monetary Fund and the World Bank." In *International Politics and Institutions in Time*, edited by O. Fioretos, 274–292. Oxford: Oxford University Press.

Weaver, C., Park, S. 2007. "The Role of the World Bank in Poverty Alleviation and Human Development in the Twenty-First Century: An Introduction." *Global Governance* 13: 461–468.

Webber, D. 2007. Good Budgeting, Better Justice: Modern Budget Practices for the Judicial Sector. *Law and Development Working Paper Series.* Washington, DC: World Bank.

Weber, M. 1947. *The Theory of Social and Economic Organization.* Trans. by Talcott Parsons, New York: The Free Press.

Weible, C.M., Sabatier, P., McQueen, K. 2009. "Themes and Variations: Taking Stock of the Advocacy Coalition Framework." *Policy Studies Journal* 37 (1): 121–140.

Welch, D.A. 1992. "The Organizational Process and Bureaucratic Politics Paradigm: Retrospect and Prospect." *International Security* 17 (2): 112–146.

Weldes, J. 1998. "Bureaucratic Politics: A Critical Constructivist Assessment." *Mershon International Studies Review* 42 (2): 216–225.

Weller, P., Xu, Y-C. 2010. "Agents of Influence: Country Directors at the World Bank." *Public Administration* 88 (1): 211–231.

Weller, P., Xu, Y-C. (Eds.) 2015. *The Politics of International Organizations: Views from Insiders.* London: Routledge.

Westerwinter, O. 2018. "Transnational Public-Private Governance Initiatives in World Politics: Introducing A New Dataset." *The Review of International Organizations*: 1–38. Doi:10.1007/s11558-019-09366-w.

Wilhelm, V., Fiestas, I. 2005. Exploring the Link between Public Spending and Poverty Reduction: Lessons from the 90s. *WBI Working Papers.* Washington, DC: World Bank.

Williams, A. 1990. "A Growing Role for NGOs in Development." *Finance and Development* 27 (4): 31–33.

Williams, D. 1999. "Constructing the Economic Space: The World Bank and the Making of Homo Oeconomicus." *Millennium: Journal of International Studies* 28 (1): 79–99.

Williams, D. 2008. *The World Bank and Social Transformation in International Politics.* London: Routledge.

Williams, G. 1983. "The World Bank and Nigeria's 'Green Revolution.'" *Review of African Political Economy* 10 (27/28): 192–196.

Williams, S. 2007. "The Debarment of Corrupt Contractors from World Bank-Financed Contracts." *Public Contract Law Journal* 36 (3): 277–306.

Williamson, J. 1990. "What Washington Means by Policy Reform." In *Latin American Adjustment: How Much Has Happened?*, edited by John Williamson, chap. 2. Washington, DC: Institute of International Economics.

Williamson, J. 2000. "What Should the World Bank Think about the Washington Consensus?" *The World Bank Research Observer* 15 (2): 251–264.

Williamson, J. 2004. "The Washington Consensus as a Policy Prescription for Development." Institute for International Economics. Accessed June 15. www.iie.com/publications/papers/williamson0204.pdf.

Williamson, O.E. 1975. *Markets and Hierarchies: Analysis and Antitrust Implications.* New York: Free Press.

Williamson, O.E. 1985. *The Economic Institutions of Capitalism.* New York: Free Press.

Williamson, O.E. 1995. "The Institutions and Governance of Economic Development and Reform." Proceedings of the World Bank Annual Conference on Development Economics (1994), World Bank.

Williamson, O.E. 2000. "The New Institutional Economics: Taking Stock, Looking Ahead." *Journal of Economic Literature* XXXVIII (September): 595–613.

Wilson, W. 1887. "The Study of Administration." *Political Science Quarterly* 2: 197–222.

Winkler, D.R., Gershberg, A.I. 2000. Education Decentralization in Latin America: The Effects on the Quality of Schooling. *LCSHD Paper Series.* Washington, DC: World Bank.

Winters, M.S. 2011. "The World Bank and the Global Financial Crisis: The Reemergence of Lending to Middle-Income Countries." *Whitehead Journal of Diplomacy and International Relations* 12 (2): 57–72.

Wolfensohn, J. 1996. Opening Address by the President of World Bank Group, James D. Wolfensohn. Fifty-First Annual Meeting of the Board of Governors. Washington, DC: World Bank and International Monetary Fund.

Wolfensohn, J. 2002. Social Equity, Social Justice and Poverty Reduction, Closing Remarks at the Joint United Nations (Office of the UN High Commissioner for Human Rights) and World Bank Staff Learning Seminar on Human Rights and Development. Washington, DC: World Bank.

Wolfowitz, P. 2006. Good Governance and Development: A Time for Action (Speech given in Jakarta, Indonesia). Washington, DC: World Bank.

Woods, N. 2003. "Making the IMF and the World Bank more Accountable." *International Affairs* 77 (1): 83–100.

World Bank. 1983. Management in Development. *World Development Report*. Washington, DC: World Bank.

World Bank. 1985. Indonesia Management Development. Edited by East Asia and Pacific Regional Office. Washington, DC: World Bank.

World Bank. 1988. Opportunities and Risks in Managing the Economy: Public Finance in Development. *World Development Report*. Washington, DC: World Bank.

World Bank. 1989. *From Crisis to Sustainable Growth: The Long-Term Perspective Study on sub-Saharan Africa*. Washington, DC: World Bank.

World Bank. 1990. Argentina: Tax Policy for Stabilization and Economic Recovery. *A World Bank Country Study*. Washington, DC: World Bank.

World Bank. 1991a. *Lessons of Tax Reform*. Washington, DC: World Bank.

World Bank. 1991b. *Managing Development: The Governance Dimension*. Washington, DC: World Bank.

World Bank. 1992a. *Effective Implementation: Key to Development Impact*. Washington, DC: World Bank.

World Bank. 1992b. Poland: Decentralization and Reform of the State. *A World Bank Country Study*. Washington, DC: World Bank.

World Bank. 1994a. "Building Capacity for Decentralization and Local Governance in sub-Saharan Africa: The Municipal Development Program." *Findings (Africa Region)*, 1–6.

World Bank. 1994b. *Governance: The World Bank's Experience*. Washington, DC: World Bank.

World Bank. 1995a. "Decentralization: A New Strategy for Rural Development." *Dissemination Notes (Agriculture & Natural Resources Department)*, 1–3.

World Bank. 1995b. *Financial Accounting, Reporting and Auditing Handbook*, 1st edn. Washington, DC: World Bank.

World Bank. 1995c. *Philippines: Public Expenditure Management for Sustained and Equitable Growth*. Washington, DC: World Bank.

World Bank. 1997a. Civil Service Reform in Francophone Africa: Proceedings of a Workshop, Abidjan, January 23-26, 1996. *Regional Workshop on Civil Service Reform in Francophone Africa*, edited by Lapido; de Lusignan Adamolekun, Guy; Atomate, Armand Abidjan. Cote d'Ivoire: World Bank.

World Bank. 1997b. The State in a Changing World. *World Development Report*. Washington, DC: World Bank.

World Bank. 1998a. *Beyond the Washington Consensus: Institutions Matter*. Washington, DC: World Bank.

World Bank. 1998b. *East Asia: Road to Recovery*. Washington, DC: World Bank.

World Bank. 1998c. Rethinking Decentralization in Developing Countries. *Sector Policy Series*. Washington, DC: World Bank.

World Bank. 2000. Reforming Public Institutions and Strengthening Governance: A World Bank Strategy. Edited by Public Sector Group. Washington, DC: World Bank.

World Bank. 2001. *Assessment of the Strategic Compact*. Washington, DC: World Bank.

World Bank (Ed.) 2002a. *2002 Annual Review of Development Effectiveness*. Washington, DC: World Bank.

World Bank. 2002b. Allocating IDA Funds Based on Performance. *Fourth Annual Report on IDA's Country Assessment and Allocation Process*. Washington, DC: World Bank.

World Bank. 2002c. *Better Measuring, Monitoring, and Managing for Development Results*. Washington, DC: World Bank.

World Bank. 2003a. *Reforming Public Institutions and Strengthening Governance: A World Bank Strategy Implementation Update*. Washington, DC: World Bank.

World Bank. 2003b. *World Bank Operations Evaluation Department: The First 30 Years*. Washington, DC: World Bank.

World Bank. 2003c. "World Bank Sector Codes, effective October 2003." Washington, DC: World Bank. Accessed Dec 3, 2021. https://www.google.com/url?sa=t&rct=j&q=&esrc=s&source=web&cd=&ved=2ahUKEwjSqq3Nhcf0AhWxxYUKHQBVACYQFnoECAIQAQ&url=http%3A%2F%2Fweb.worldbank.org%2Farchive%2Fwebsite00521%2FWEB%2FDOC%2FWBSECTOR.DOC&usg=AOvVaw2jB5KOJe6iCBsiKZqOgZBv.

World Bank. 2004. *Making Services Work for Poor People*. Washington, DC: World Bank.

World Bank. 2005a. 2004 *Annual Report on Operations Evaluation*. Edited by Operations Evaluation Department. Washington, DC: World Bank.

World Bank. 2005b. Minutes of Meeting of the Executive Directors of the Bank and IDA held in the Board Room on Thursday, June 2, 2005 at 10:06am. Washington, DC: World Bank.

World Bank. 2005c. Minutes of Meeting of the Executive Directors of the Bank and IDA held in the Board Room on Thursday, June 7, 2005 at 10:02am. Washington, DC: World Bank.

World Bank. 2005d. Minutes of Meeting of the Executive Directors of the Bank and IDA held in the Board Room on Thursday, June 23, 2005 at 12:43pm. Washington, DC: World Bank.

World Bank. 2006. *Public Sector Reform Evaluation: Approach Paper*. Washington, DC: World Bank.

World Bank. 2007a. Governance Reform under Real-World Conditions: A Dialogue on Communication Strategies. *Governance Reform under Real-World Conditions: A Dialogue on Communication Strategies*. Washington, DC: World Bank.

World Bank. 2007b. *Implementation Plan for Strengthening World Bank Group Engagement on Governance and Anti-Corruption*. Washington, DC: World Bank.

World Bank. 2007c. Minutes of Meeting of the Executive Directors of the Bank and IDA, held in the Board Room on Tuesday, March 20, 2007, at 10:08am. Washington, DC: World Bank.

World Bank. 2007d. *Strengthening World Bank Group Engagement on Governance and Anti-Corruption*. Washington, DC: World Bank.

World Bank. 2007e. The World Bank and the Social Dimension of Globalization: An Update to the Board on the Bank's Activities on Employment and Collaboration with the ILO.

World Bank. 2008a. "Country Policy and Institutional Assessment: Frequently Asked Questions." World Bank. Accessed Nov 20, 2009. http://go.worldbank.org/Y8XXHZVDN0CE.

World Bank. 2008b. "How IBRD is Financed." World Bank. Accessed Nov 24, 2009. http://go.worldbank.org/LAG4BZ1VD1.

World Bank. 2008c. "International Bank for Reconstruction and Development." World Bank. Accessed Nov 24, 2009. http://go.worldbank.org/SDUHVGE5S0CE.

World Bank. 2008d. *Projects Database*. World Bank.

World Bank. 2008e. "Trust Funds: At a Glance." World Bank. Accessed Nov 24, 2009. http://go.worldbank.org/GABMG2YEI0CE.

World Bank. 2009a. "Board Considers Sardar Sarovar Review Panel Recommendations." World Bank. Accessed Feb 12, 2010. http://go.worldbank.org/9SG07GA4V0.

World Bank. 2009b. "Lewis Thompson Preston." World Bank. Accessed Feb 27, 2010. http://go.worldbank.org/MY98DL7RU0.

World Bank. 2009c. "PEFA Framework." World Bank. Accessed Mar 10, 2010. http://go.worldbank.org/XS9RD1JSG0CE.

World Bank. 2009d. "This Week in World Bank History: September 15-28 (World Bank Press Release September 27, 1971)." World Bank. Accessed Feb 21, 2010. http://go.worldbank.org/XOW1XIB6U0.

World Bank. 2012. *Strengthening Governance: Tackling Corruption. The World Bank Group's Updated Strategy and Implementation Plan*. Washington, DC: World Bank.

World Bank. 2013. *World Bank Group 2013 Employee Engagement Survey: Summary of Results*. Washington, DC: World Bank.

World Bank. 2015. Project Database. edited by World Bank. Washington, DC.

World Bank. 2020. *How the World Bank Group is Helping Countries with COVID-19*. Washington, DC: World Bank.

World Bank. 2021a. Projects. Edited by World Bank. Washington, DC: World Bank.

World Bank. 2021b. Remarks to the Media by World Bank Group President David Malpass on World Bank Group Action on COVID-19 Vaccines for Developing Countries. Washington. DC: World Bank.

World Bank/IMF. 2002. *Civil Service Reform: Strengthening World Bank and IMF Collaboration. Directions in Development*. Washington, DC: World Bank and the International Monetary Fund.

World Bank Staff. 2007. A Message to the President and the Board of Executive Directors. Washington, DC.

Wouters, J., Odermatt, J. 2014. "Comparing the 'Four Pillars' of Global Economic Governance: A Critical Analysis of the Institutional Design of the FSB, IMF, World Bank, and WTO." *Journal of International Economic Law* 17: 49–76.

Wright, E.P. 1980. "World Bank Lending for Structural Adjustment." *Finance and Development* 17 (3): 20.

Xu, Y.C., Weller, P. 2008. "'To be, but not to be seen': Exploring the Impact of International Civil Servants." *Public Administration* 6 (1): 35–51.

Xu, Y.C., Weller, P. 2009. *Inside the World Bank: Exploding the Myth of the Monolithic Bank*. New York, NY: Palgrave MacMillan.

Xu, Y.C., Weller, P. 2015. "Understanding the Governance of International Organizations." In *The Politics of International Organizations: Views from Insiders*, edited by YC Xu and P. Weller, 1–16. London: Routledge.

Xu, Y.C., Weller, P. 2018. *The Working World of International Organizations: Authority, Capacity, Legitimacy*. Oxford: Oxford University Press.

Yagci, F., Kamin, S., Rosenbaum, V. 1985. Structural Adjustment Lending: An Evaluation of Program Design. *World Bank Staff Working Papers*. Washington, DC: World Bank.

Yanguas, P., Hulme, D. 2015. "Barriers to Political Analysis in Aid Bureaucracies: From Principle to Practice in DFID and the World Bank." *World Development* 74: 209–219.

Yin, R.K. 1981. "The Case Study Crisis: Some Answers." *Administrative Science Quarterly* 26 (1): 58–65.

Yin, R.K., Heald, K.A. 1975. "Using the Case Survey Method to Analyze Policy Studies." *Administrative Science Quarterly* 20:371–381.

Yousefzadeh, P. 2007. "Forces of Corruption at the World Bank." *Human Events Online*, In the News.

Zoellick, R.B. 2008a. Fragile States: Securing Development (Speech delivered to the International Institute for Strategic Studies, Geneva, Switzerland). Washington, DC: World Bank.

Zoellick, R.B. 2008b. Remarks of Robert B. Zoellick, President, World Bank Group to the Annual Meeting of the Board of Governors of the World Bank Group. Washington, DC: World Bank.

Zoellick, R.B. 2008c. World Bank Group President, Robert B. Zoellick at the International Labour Organization (Speech). Washington DC: World Bank.

Zoellick, R.B. 2012. "Why We Still Need the World Bank." *Foreign Affairs* 91 (2): 66–78.

Zviniene, A., Packard, T.G. 2004. *A Simulation of Social Security Reforms in Latin America: What has been Gained?* Washington, DC: World Bank.

Name Index

Subject Index